FROM SCYTHIA TO CAMELOT

GARLAND REFERENCE LIBRARY
OF THE HUMANITIES
(VOL. 1795)

The Golden Man of Issyk. Courtesy of the Institute of History, Archeology and Ethnography, Alma-ata, Kazakhstan.

FROM SCYTHIA TO CAMELOT

*A Radical Reassessment of
the Legends of King Arthur,
the Knights of the Round Table
and the Holy Grail*

C. Scott Littleton
Linda A. Malcor

Taylor & Francis Group

Published in 2000 by
Routledge
Taylor & Francis Group
270 Madison Avenue
New York, NY 10016

Published in Great Britain by
Routledge
Taylor & Francis Group
2 Park Square
Milton Park, Abingdon
Oxon OX14 4RN

© 2000, 1994 by C. Scott Littleton and Linda A.Malcor
Routledge is an imprint of Taylor & Francis Group

Printed in the United States of America on acid-free paper
10 9 8 7 6 5 4 3 2

International Standard Book Number-10: 0-8153-3566-0 (Softcover)
International Standard Book Number-13: 978-0-8153-3566-5 (Softcover)
Library of Congress Card Number 94-8776

No part of this book may be reprinted, reproduced, transmitted, or utilized in any form by any electronic, mechanical, or other means, now known or hereafter invented, including photocopying, microfilming, and recording, or in any information storage or retrieval system, without written permission from the publishers.

Trademark Notice: Product or corporate names may be trademarks or registered trademarks, and are used only for identification and explanation without intent to infringe.

Library of Congress Cataloging-in-Publication Data

Littleton, C.Scott.
    From Scythia to Camelot : a radical reassessment of the legends of King Arthur, the Knights of the Round Table, and the Holy Grail / C. Scott Littleton, Linda A. Malcor.
        p. cm. — (Garland reference library of the humanities ; vol. 1795)
    Includes bibliographical references and index.
    ISBN 0-8153-3566-0
    1. Arthur, King. 2. Britons—Kings and rulers—Legends—History and criticism.
3. Legends—Great Britain—History and criticism. 4. Grail—Legends History and criticism. 5. Great Britain—Antiquities, Celtic. 6. Arthurian romances—Sources.
7. Mythology, Iranian. 8. Mythology, Celtic. I. Malcor, Linda A.
II. Title. III. Series.
DA152.5.A7L58   1994
936.1—dc20   94-8776

Visit the Taylor & Francis Web site at
http://www.taylorandfrancis.com
and the Routledge Web site at
http://www.routledge-ny.com

Taylor & Francis Group
is the Academic Division of T&F Informa plc.

To the Memory
of Georges Dumézil

"Thus the Halani [the Alans] . . .
are divided between the two parts
of the earth [Europe and Asia]."

Ammianus Marcellinus 31.2,17
(Rolfe 1939:391)

Contents

Foreword		xiii
Acknowledgments		xxi
Preface		xxiii
Introduction		xxv

Part I: The Cultural and Historical Background

1.	The Northeast Iranians	3

Part II: Figures

2.	Arthur and the Sarmatian Connection	61
3.	Lancelot and the "Alan of Lot"	79
4.	The Knights and the Narts	125
5.	Women, Water, and Warriors	153

Part III: Themes and Images

6.	The Sword in the Stone	181
7.	The Serpent Image	195

Part IV: The Holy Grail

8.	The Holy Grail, the Cauldron of Annwfn, and the Nartamongæ	209
9.	The Alans and the Grail	233
10.	The Grail Keepers	255

Conclusions	281
Appendix 1. A Note on Sources	285
Appendix 2. Genealogies	293
Appendix 3. A Reinterpretation of Nennius's Battle List	327
References Cited	333
Index	369

Illustrations

Plates

Frontispiece: The Golden Man of Issyk ... ii
1. Sarmatians on Trajan's Column ... 9
2. The Animal Style
   (Gold plaque, Transbaikalarea) ... 12
3. Mounted Sarmatian
   (Chester) ... 14
4. Arthurian Knights with Banner
   (MS Paris, Bibliothèque Nationale fr. 95, fol. 173) ... 15
5. The Death of King Arthur
   (British Library MS Add. 10294, fol. 94) ... 67
6. The Perilous Cemetery
   (Pierpont Morgan Library MS 806, fol. 207) ... 93
7. The Cathedral of Modena, Archivolt of Porta della Pescherisa ... 127
8. Perceval Meets Knights in the Forest
   (Louvre OA 122) ... 129
9. Lancelot and the Sword Bridge/ Gawain and the Perilous Bed
   (Ivory casket. Metropolitan Museum of Art, Parisian, ca. 1325) ... 136
10. Mark Slays Tristan
    (MS Paris, Bibliothèque Nationale f.fr. 101, fol. 383v) ... 140
11. The Dame du Lac
    (MS Paris, Bibliothèque Nationale f.fr. 113, fol. 156v) ... 155

12. The Sword in the Stone
    (MS Paris, Bibliothèque Nationale f.fr. 95,
    fol. 159v) — 182
13. Mounted Horsemen from the Golden Psalter
    (St. Gallen, Stiftsbibliothek) — 196
14. Merlin with the Pendragon
    (MS Paris, Bibliothèque Nationale f.fr. 95,
    fol. 327v) — 198
15. Ecclesia with the Grail
    ("Book of Pericopes of Heinrich II," originally
    from Reichenau [ca. 850]; Munich, Bayerische
    Staatsbibliothek, clm 4452) — 212
16. The Procession of the Grail
    (MS Paris, Bibliothèque de l'Arsenal 5218,
    fol. 88) — 238
17. The Temple Treasure on the Arch of Titus — 241
18. King Alain with the Grail
    (MS Bonn, Prose *Lancelot* of 1286,
    Universitätbibliothek 526, fol. 57v) — 265

Figures

1. Proposed Development of the Legends of
   Arthur, Lancelot, and Batraz — xxix
2. Tamgas — 10
3. The Excavations at Ribchester — 20
4. Apollo Maponus Inscription — 22
5. The Welsh-Origin Hypothesis — 79
6. Ford's Hypothesis — 80
7. Proposed Etymology of Lancelot — 98
8. The Dame du Lac and Morgan Le Fay — 163

Maps

1. Ancient Scythia — 4
2. Major Migrations of Steppe Cultures — 6
3. Ancient Steppe Cultures — 7
4. The Iazyges, ca. 175 C.E. — 17

5.	Britain at the Time of the Sarmatian Settlement	21
6.	Arthurian Sites in Britain	24
7.	Alan Invasions of Gaul	29
8.	Roman Gaul	30
9.	Alano-Sarmatian Sites in Europe	31
10.	Medieval Alania	41
11.	Modern Ossetia	42
12.	Riothamus's Route	65
13.	The Geography of the Prose *Lancelot*	83
14.	Celtic Immigration to Armorica	87
15.	Arthurian Sites in Gaul	97
16.	Sites Associated with the Legend of Tristan	142
17.	The Travels of Joseph of Arimathea	211
18.	The Sack of Rome and the Invasion of Gaul	239
19.	Some Religious Sites in France	246

Foreword

Few people have not heard of King Arthur and his knights of the Round Table, and fewer still can read any of the multitude of forms that this myth has taken without some evocation of deep moral, historical, or dramatic sensibility. For the West, and by extension much of the world, the Arthurian cycle has had one of the greatest influences on modern culture of any epic or myth. No one writes plays or musicals based on the *Ṛg Veda*, on the *Iliad* or *Odyssey*, on *Beowulf*, or, with the exception of Wagner, on the Norse tales, and yet rewritings of Arthurian material are part of current literature, and popular literature at that, while the musical *Camelot* was enormously popular two decades ago and directors still produce films about Arthur. Not only are the trappings, manners, and fantasies of the Arthurian cycle familiar to most readers, but the values and mores depicted therein, specifically in the "canonical" form as first presented in the fifteenth century by Sir Thomas Malory as a romantic vision of the Middle Ages, need little explanation. There is little in Camelot and its citizens that seems alien or inexplicable, little that needs academic explication in order to understand what is transpiring and why, whereas a reader can often be baffled by the motives or actions of such heroes as Sigurd (Siegfried) or Beowulf, or even Achilles or Agamemnon, not to mention those of the yet more remote Indra or Vishnu of the *Ṛg Veda*, all of whom often require a learned insight to make them even tentatively comprehensible. Arthur and his knights, as the romantic embodiment of chivalry, are close to the modern West, so much so that we may read learned studies of their origins or development with some equanimity, but we are hardly prepared to entertain a remote and exotic origin for figures so familiar as these.

The present book does precisely that: it seeks Arthur's origins in an all but vanished civilization and in doing so resurrects intimate aspects of that lost world and forces us to examine a remote and neglected region of Europe, the Caucasus. This pioneering effort will engender controversy in academic circles concerned with the Arthurian cycle as well as challenge our own historical sense of the origins of much of Western culture. It will force, perhaps gradually because of the resistance of orthodoxy, a restructuring of the field of Arthurian scholarship and will force those concerned to come to terms not only with the lost Iranian civilization of the Scythians, Sarmatians, and Alans, but also with the vivid lore of their surviving descendants, the Ossetians of the Caucasus.

Littleton and Malcor have done three important things. First, they have attained a degree of detachment regarding the Arthurian cycle that has enabled them to suggest new origins for many of the important figures and themes of the tradition, if not for the whole tradition, and thus to offer new solutions to longstanding problems of Arthurian scholarship. Arthur and his knights can be traced back beyond Malory to such writers as Wace and Layamon, and beyond them still to anonymous fragments written in Old Welsh. Many figures are transparently Celtic, such as Uther Pendragon, Arthur's father, whose name means "Glorious Head of the Troops" in Welsh, or the Celtic Aphrodite figure, Queen Guinevere (Irish Finnabair, from Old Irish Findabair; Welsh Gwenhwyfar), whose name in Irish means "Born on the White," much as the Greek name Aphrodite means "Born on the Foam," and whose Welsh variant means "White Phantom." Other figures, however, such as that of Arthur himself or of Lancelot, have enigmatic origins and have been the objects of enormous scholarly effort, much of it inconclusive. This divergence in names is a symptom of one of the central problems of Arthurian scholarship—that the Arthurian cycle is seen to have arisen from the Celtic cultures of Britain and France (Armorica), indeed to have been the last great bequest of medieval Celtic culture to world civilization, but nevertheless to have an overall aspect and to contain numerous details none of which appear to be Celtic. Its origins, therefore, are a conundrum, with this apparently seamless tradition revealing itself upon closer scrutiny to be an amalgam of Celtic lore with something else.

Following the earlier work of such scholars as Georges Dumézil, Bernard S. Bachrach, and Helmut Nickel, Littleton and Malcor have sought this unknown "something else" in the culture of the Sarmatians, specifically of the Iazyges tribe, and of their kinsmen the Alans.

At this point the reader can be forgiven for asking, "Culture of who?" In this matter even the specialist must continually exercise imagination in order to keep in mind a realistic image of these vanished peoples. The Scythians of early Classical Antiquity, the Sarmatians, and the Alans of late classical times were nomads of the steppes of Central Asia, extending in their heyday from the plains of what is now Hungary to those of western China, perhaps as far as present-day Kansu, nearly in the center of China. As far as we can determine from contemporary accounts, archaeological findings, and consideration of scanty linguistic remains, these peoples were of European appearance (often blond and blue-eyed), left behind enormous hordes of animal-style art (much of it golden), entombed their chieftains in burial mounds (the ultimate origin of the pagoda by way of the Buddhist stupa), and spoke Iranian languages. While their culture was shaped by its underlying nomad economy, many of its aspects had parallels among the more familiar ones of European antiquity, thus setting them apart from the later nomads of Hunnish, Turkic, and Mongol origin and placing them closer to the Europeans of antiquity. Furthermore, they seem to have shown little similarity with the Iranians of present-day Iran. The latter appear to have undergone a cultural specialization early on, so that even in ancient times the Medes and Persians may have viewed the steppe Iranians as alien.

In a larger context all the Iranians are related to the Indo-Aryans that came to reside in India, bequeathing world civilization the Ṛg Veda among other things. In a still larger context these Indo-Iranians were in turn part of the Indo-European family of languages and cultures, encompassing the ancestors of the Celtic, Germanic, Italic, Baltic, Slavic, Greek, Armenian, Albanian, and other, more obscure, peoples and found from Ireland to China and from Scandinavia to India. This prehistoric people, the Proto–Indo-Europeans, retrieved from the obliteration of time by diligent linguistic comparison, has been the abused vehicle for racists from the early nineteenth century through the Nazis down to today. Nevertheless, a dispassionate assessment of them, as scholarship delineates their language and culture, cannot but rank them among the most fascinating intellectual discoveries of all time and see in their existence a deep, if remote, historical unity of many of the peoples of Eurasia.

One trend in modern scholarship is to locate the Indo-European homeland in the northwest Caucasus, among the "Kurgan" (burial mound) culture, at a time depth of three to five thousand years B.C.E. Clearly the vast spread of the Indo-Europeans through the millennia was aided by, if not solely due to, their conjectured nomadism. As they spread out from the steppes north of the Caucasus, they encountered non–Indo-European sedentary cultures and blended with them to create the peoples of attested European and western Asian history. What is most interesting about the steppe Iranians is that this was the one Indo-European people whose culture underwent an evolution that was primarily internal, in that it remained nomadic and did not blend with some major sedentary civilization. In this sense then, the steppe Iranians, as depicted during the classical period, continued ancient Indo-European civilization in a direct way. This fact in itself makes the steppe Iranians interesting for understanding the history of much of Eurasia. And, it makes their loss all the more regrettable.

By the close of the classical period these steppe Iranians had been pushed to the peripheries of their nomad homeland by the Altaic-speaking (non–Indo-European) Huns and their kinsmen the Turks. Some fled into what is now Tajikistan, Afghanistan, eastern Iran (Sistan), and western India. Others went into the Roman Empire, at times causing parts of it to dissolve while in other parts helping to maintain it against others by becoming mercenaries of the Caesars. They are known to have migrated to Britain (the Iazyge Sarmatians), Italy, France, Spain, and North Africa (the last three areas having largely Alanic contingents). Others fled into Poland, European Russia, and the Caucasus. The standing assumption is that, apart from tantalizing traces as laid out by Bachrach and Nickel, these peoples vanished without a trace. This assumption is difficult to challenge for two reasons. First, those undergoing the obliteration no longer have representatives to step forward and speak for themselves. Second, the civilization in question is so exotic and so far removed from our contemporary view of Eurasia, that it tends to have an insubstantial quality even in the mind of the most dedicated scholar and therefore lends itself to obscurity.

This assumption cannot be right, however, as a little thought shows: European armies enter the Middle Ages looking like those of the late Roman Empire and come out of this period wearing chain mail and jousting. One must turn to engraved scenes found in Iranian burial hordes that antedate the Middle Ages by a thousand years and are removed from Europe by several thousand kilometers in order to see warriors dressed this way and fighting this way. In other words, the Europeans enter the Middle Ages looking like Romans and emerge from them looking like Sarmatian or Alanic warriors. Clearly the steppe Iranians had an enormous influence on Europe. Clearly, they are much closer to us than we are accustomed to thinking, so close that they are hard to see.

The Iranians who fled into Poland and Russia survive only as a vague tradition among the aristocracies of those nations and perhaps in the names "Russia" and "Belarus" themselves, which may reflect earlier *rukhsh—(with the Middle Iranian shift of khsh to ss), as in Roxalani (an Alanic tribe) and Roxanne (the Alanic wife of Alexander the Great), meaning "white" or "northern." A sense reinforced by the bela—"white" part of "Belarus." There is one place, however, where the Alans persist down to the modern day (without an obscuring overlay of first Zoroastrianism and later Islam, as is the case in the Pamirs of Tajikistan and in Afghanistan), and that is in the Caucasus. This time the reader can be forgiven for asking, "Where?"

The Caucasus Mountains lie between the Black and Caspian seas, in what is now southern Russia, Georgia, Armenia, and Azerbaijan. They are the tallest mountains in Europe, with fifty-six ethnic groups in an area the size of Spain, fully thirty-six of which are indigenous to this remote and beautiful region. The center of the North Caucasus was the one place into which the Alans retreated and in which they retained their identity down to the time of Chingis Khan. Until the thirteenth century the North Caucasus had a region or nation called Alania, first part of the Khazar Empire and later a kingdom or empire in its own right. At first these Alans, like their neighbors the Circassians, Chechens, and Daghestanis (indigenous Caucasian peoples), successfully resisted the Mongol onslaught, saving eastern Europe in the process, but under subsequent attack they were pushed higher into the mountains and disappeared as a political entity. They shortly emerged again in the late thirteenth century as the "Ossetes" or "Ossetians," having at this time pulled up into the highlands of the center of the Caucasus chain and spilled down the southern slope of the Caucasian massif into what is now the Republic of Georgia. They were incorporated into the tsarist empire in 1774 as a protectorate. They were divided into North and South administrative units during the late nineteenth century, and this was continued under Communist rule by the creation of the South Ossetian Autonomous Region as part of the Georgian SSR in 1922 and the North Ossetian Autonomous Region as part of the Russian RSFSR in 1924 and upgraded to an Autonomous Republic in 1936.

Today this fascinating people, perhaps totaling half a million souls and still preserving its Iranian language, is split between the Russian Federation and the Georgian Republic. When Georgia left the USSR in late 1990, it took with it South Ossetia, which promptly declared its intention to unite with North Ossetia and thereby join the Russian Federation. This was seen by Georgia as a provocation and in early 1991 the Georgian-Ossetian war erupted in South Ossetia. This small but savage conflict continued into 1992, stopping only when a ceasefire was mediated and guaranteed by the Russians. Since 1992 the peace in South Ossetia has been maintained by Russian forces. South Ossetia has held a referendum and overwhelmingly chosen to join North Ossetia. North Ossetia has endorsed this intention to unite and thereby bring all of Ossetia into the Russian Federation. Russia, fearful both of offending Georgia and of alienating the Ossetians, has refrained from any political response. As if matters were not bad enough, in late 1992 North

Foreword xix

Ossetia and neighboring Ingushetia (a politically distinct unit of the indigenous Caucasian Chechen peoples) indulged in a brief but bitter bloodbath over a disputed region (Prigorodny), so that the present-day Alans face serious threats from two adversaries. This violence also resulted in Russian peacekeepers being brought in.

The position of the Ossetians in the Caucasus is strategically crucial; their capital, Dzaujikau, was renamed Vladikavkaz ("Ruler of the Caucasus") by the Russians. It is unlikely that Russia will let matters unfold there without further direct intervention. One can only hope that the Ossetians will survive the current turmoil that afflicts the Caucasus.

If the Ossetians are known at all in the West outside of linguistic circles, where they play a minor role in Indo-European studies, it is because they are the bearers of the so-called Nart sagas. These are a set of heroic tales, somewhere between myth and saga in tone, which the Ossetians share with their non–Indo-European neighbors to the west, the Circassians, Ubykhs, Abazas, and Abkhaz, and to some extent with those to the south, the Svans and Georgian highlanders, and to the east, the Chechen-Ingush and the Daghestanis, as well as with some of the small neighboring Turkic peoples, such as the Balkars and Karachays. No one can read these vivid, complex, chaotic tales without a sense of astonishment, for not only do they show numerous, striking, detailed parallels with the lore of ancient India and Greece, as one might expect from their intermediate position between these two great traditions, but they also show similar parallels with, of all things, the Arthurian cycle. One's first impulse, as was mine, is to dismiss these Arthurian parallels as due to mere chance. One's second impulse, as was mine too, is to set them aside as curious but enigmatic. What Littleton and Malcor did, however, was take the third inexorable step and examine these parallels critically and in detail. This is their second great achievement.

As their third achievement, regardless of which arguments or etymologies one might find compelling or otiose, Littleton and Malcor have added four new dimensions to the field of Arthurian studies. They have opened the doors to Eurasian steppe archaeology and the iconography of its artifacts; they have shown the worth of carefully examining the scanty European remains of the vanished Iranians of the steppes; they have shown at least the possibility, and most likely the plausibility, that the Arthurian cycle, however seamless and whole it may seem, is comprehensible only in terms of an Iranian core, much like the Nart sagas, with an overlay of Celtic material, which has been strongly influenced by Roman hegemony; and finally, they have brought long overdue attention to the Nart sagas of the Caucasus and to the cultures and languages of the Ossetians and their neighbors. Examining many of their claims and arguments will entail a vast amount of new study and hard work for the Arthurian scholar. Nevertheless, the parallels between the Iranian material and the Arthurian cycle are so numerous, and in many cases so exact, that this effort must be taken on by the scholarly establishment concerned with Arthur and his origins. The study of the Arthurian corpora will never be the same after this book, and our understanding of the origins of so much of our own civilization, I may safely say, will never look quite the same again.

John Colarusso
McMaster University
Hamilton, Ontario
16 August 1993

Acknowledgments

First we would like to thank Anne C. Thomas for her early collaboration with Littleton on the paper that eventually led to this book.

A special thanks to John Colarusso, Sigmund Eisner, Karlene Jones-Bley, J.P. Mallory, Felix Oinas, Edgar Polomé, and Jaan Puhvel for their tireless support, invaluable comments, and eager willingness to read drafts of all or part of the present manuscript in the final stages of preparation. Special thanks also go to Jim Ridge, Honorary Curator of the Ribchester Museum Trust, for his avid support of our research.

The authors also wish to thank Geoffrey Ashe, Elizabeth Barber, Paul Barber, Robert L. Benson, Henrik Birnbaum, Molly Blecha, Peter Brown, Jan Brunvand, Frances Cattermole-Tally, Norine Dresser, the late Georges Dumézil, the late Carol Edwards, Gunar Freibergs, Bernard D. Frischer, Robert A. Georges, J.L. Giller, Joël Grisward, the late Wayland D. Hand, Joseph Holman, Sarah Jack, Ioli Kalavrezou-Maxeiner, V.A Kolve, Kazuo Matsumura, Ronald J. Mellor, Elise Moore, Helmut Nickel, Taryo Obayashi, James W. Porter, Robert A. Segal, Udo Strutynski, Dian Teigler, Wolfgang von Chmielewski, Donald J. Ward, the late D.K. Wilgus, Joanna Woods-Marsden, Atsuhiko Yoshida, and the staff of the Princeton Index of Christian Art for their invaluable comments, suggestions, criticisms, and support over the years, both before and after our collaboration began. We offer our sincere apology to anyone whom we have inadvertently omitted.

Although they do not agree with the arguments presented in this book, we wish to thank Patrick K. Ford and Joseph F. Nagy for their helpful criticisms of various aspects of our work.

Many thanks to Sue Flaherty for her endless hours of proofreading. Thanks to Sherry Couchman, Carl Flaherty, Jocelyn Markey, Sharon Morgan, and Gloria Peterson for their proofreading efforts as well. Special thanks are owed to Gary Kuris for his insightful queries and attention to detail and to Tamara Park for her computerized maps and figures.

We also wish to express our thanks to Debbie Tegarden for her unwavering support and encouragement and to the Louis & Hermione Brown Humanities Support Fund for its generosity during the final preparation of the manuscript.

We wish to express our heartfelt thanks to our spouses, Mary Ann Littleton and Daniel Malcor, for their patience, understanding, and unstinting support during a long and sometimes difficult period. A special note of thanks to Daniel for his computer skills and talents that guided us expertly through the computer systems and programs used to compile this book.

Finally we wish to emphasize that the ideas and interpretations that are presented in this work are strictly our own, and we take full responsibility for them.

Preface

This edition of *From Scythia to Camelot* corrects some unfortunate errors that managed to find their way into the 1994 hardcover edition and incorporates some significant new discoveries and reinterpretations. The most important of these relate to the career of Lucius Artorius Castus, the second century C.E. Roman officer whose name and exploits provided the historical basis of the legends of King Arthur (see Chapter 2). We now know vastly more about him than we did five years ago. Indeed, it has recently become evident that the twelve victories attributed to "Arthur" by Nennius and others, including the famous one at Badon Hill, which are conventionally dated to the early sixth century C.E., may actually have been won by Lucius Artorius Castus between 183–185 C.E. in Northern Britain, and that the defeated enemy were not invaders from the so-called "Saxon Shore," but rather marauding Caledonians from what is now Scotland (see Appendix 3). We have also updated our discussion of the Iazyges role in, and impact on, the Roman military system in late second-century Britain to reflect some recent archaeological discoveries at Ribchester and other Roman sites associated with these Sarmatian *numeri* from north of the Danube, who brought with them a treasury of hero tales that eventually became the core of the Arthurian and Holy Grail legends (see Chapter 1). Moreover, we have taken to heart the legitimate criticisms of those scholars who have reviewed the hardcover edition and have modified and/or deleted several passages that can no longer be supported as originally written.

In addition to the people thanked in the Acknowledgments, many of whom also had input into the current edition, we would like to express our profound appreciation to Victor H. Mair, Robert A. Segal, and Elizabeth "Libby" Borden for their unwavering support and enthusiastic encouragement. Without that support and encouragement, which has been expressed both informally and in print, this new edition of *From Scythia to Camelot* would never have come to pass. We would also like to thank the people at Garland Publishing, Inc., and especially our editor, James Morgan, and our production editor, Nicole Ellis, for their invaluable assistance, as well as the Louis and Hermione Brown Humanities Support Fund for once again facilitating the final preparation of the manuscript. Finally, we would like to thank all those readers who have shared with us their reactions to our work, including those who have done so online. Indeed, we encourage a continued dialogue with our readers, and will be happy to respond to messages addressed to our respective e-mail addresses.

C. Scott Littleton
yokatta@oxy.edu

Linda Malcor
legend@malcor.com

September, 1999

Introduction

Some ideas develop slowly, as bits and pieces of a puzzle begin to assume a pattern. Other ideas leap into focus fully armed and ready for battle.

The initial discovery that led to this book, that the medieval Arthurian legends are rooted in an epic tradition that flourished in ancient Scythia (i.e., the south Russian and Ukrainian steppes; see map 1) in the first millennium Before the Common Era (B.C.E.), belongs to the latter category. This discovery was made with remarkable suddenness one morning in the fall of 1975 in the course of a casual conversation with J.P. Mallory, who at the time was a doctoral candidate in Indo-European Studies at UCLA.[1]

Mallory happened to observe that at the end of the Marcomannian War in the year 175 of the Common Era (C.E.), the Roman emperor Marcus Aurelius sent a contingent of 5,500 Sarmatian *cataphracti*, or heavily armed auxiliary cavalry, from Pannonia (modern Hungary) to Britain. He also pointed out that their descendants managed to survive as an identifiable ethnic enclave at least until the beginning of the fourth century, and perhaps longer. Mallory had just read an abbreviated account of these events in Tadeusz Sulimirski's *The Sarmatians* (1970) and simply wanted to share what at the time seemed to be nothing more than a curious bit of trivia.

However, C. Scott Littleton had recently read a pair of fascinating articles by the eminent French medievalist Joël Grisward (1969, 1973) that pointed out some remarkable parallels between the death of King Arthur, especially as described in the fifteenth century by Sir Thomas Malory in his celebrated *Le Morte Darthur*, and a saga told by the Ossetians, a contemporary Caucasian people, about the death of their most important hero, Batraz.

Batraz, the leader of a band of heroes known as the Narts, like Arthur possesses a magical sword.[2] After wreaking vengeance on the Narts for the death of his father, the repentant Batraz commands the surviving Narts to throw his sword into the sea. Dismayed at the size of the wondrous weapon, they hide it, telling their leader that they have carried out his last wish. But only Batraz knows what will happen when the sword is consigned to the water, and he implores the Narts to do as he has ordered. When they finally manage to throw the sword into the sea, a prodigious thing happens. The water suddenly becomes extremely turbulent and then turns blood-red. As soon as this is reported to Batraz, he dies and is buried by the Narts.[3]

The details are different: the Narts as a group hide the sword, whereas in Malory it is Bedivere alone who hides Excalibur, and the prodigious event in the Ossetic tale does not involve a hand rising from the water to grasp the sword. Otherwise the stories are so similar that the possibility of a chance parallelism is remote. Grisward could not explain this and other parallels between the tales and simply suggested that there may have been an ancient contact of one sort or another between the ancestors of the Ossetians and the ancestors of the Celts, who, he presumed, originally shaped the Arthurian romances.

As we shall see, that contact is clearly much more recent and specific. Linguistically the Ossetians are the last surviving descendants of the ancient Alans and related tribes, who in turn were almost indistinguishable from the Sarmatians. It was this fact that rang a bell in Littleton's head when he began to digest Mallory's comment. It was not long before Littleton located the *locus classicus*: a passage in Dio Cassius's *Roman History*,[4] written ca. 225 C.E., that describes how, at the end of the Marcomannian War, 8,000 *cataphracti* from a Sarmatian tribe known as the Iazyges (or Jazyges) were impressed into the Roman legions. Of these Iazyges 5,500 were sent to Britain.[5] Thus, thanks to Mallory's chance remark, Littleton had made the "Sarmatian Connection," that is, the historical connection that explains the parallels Grisward had discovered.

Littleton soon learned that the Iazygian auxiliaries were posted in groups of five hundred to the garrisons along Hadrian's Wall. When their period of service was over, the veterans were settled in a *vicus*, or veterans' colony, at Bremetennacum Veteranorum, an important Roman cavalry post near the modern village of Ribchester in southwest Lancashire.[6] He also learned that their first commander was a Roman officer named Lucius Artorius Castus, prefect of the VI Legion Victrix, which was headquartered at York (Eboracum) and charged with the defense of northern Britain.[7]

More pieces of the puzzle began to fall into place. The famous Sword in the Stone episode, wherein the young Arthur pulled a sword from a stone and thereby established his right to the throne of Britain, is mirrored in the ancient Alanic custom of thrusting swords into the earth as symbols of a warrior-deity.[8] Similarities have come to light between other Nart heroes and heroines, such as Soslan (or Sozryko), Syrdon, Xæmyc, and Satana, and Arthurian figures, such as Gawain, Kay, Uther Pendragon, and the Lady of the Lake, respectively (see chaps. 2, 3, 4, and 5).

Then the literature concerning the quest for the Holy Grail, an integral part of the Arthurian corpus,[9] began to come into clearer focus. It became apparent that these enigmatic tales are similar to a series of Nart sagas that describe a dispute over which Nart—or, more accurately, which clan of Narts—will have the honor of guarding a magical cup (or cauldron) called the Nartamongæ, or "Revealer of the Narts." Although unrelated to the Chalice of the Last Supper, the Nartamongæ, like the Grail, is a magical vessel that never runs dry and that appears at feasts before the bravest of heroes.

By 1978, when the first article on this subject by Littleton and an early collaborator, Anne C. Thomas, appeared in the *Journal of American Folklore*,[10] it was clear that both the origin and distribution of at least the core of the Arthurian and Holy Grail legends were not rooted in the ancient Celtic tradition, as many scholars had heretofore believed,[11] but rather were derived from the same Northeast Iranian epic tradition that gave rise to the Nart sagas.

To say that this hypothesis was (and is) controversial is an understatement. As time went on, however, Littleton began to receive support from several scholars in the field, including Helmut Nickel, currently Curator Emeritus of Arms and Armor at the Metropolitan Museum of Art in New York, whose own research into the origins of European chivalry had led him to similar conclusions.[12]

Nevertheless, there were some major lacunae. Lancelot, for example, the most distinguished, if morally flawed, of Arthur's knights, resisted interpretation in terms of the "Sarmatian Connection." It was at this point, in the spring of 1983, that Linda A. Malcor (née Peterson) came into the picture.

Malcor had long been interested in the origin and evolution of Lancelot and the Arthurian tradition in general, and when she learned of Littleton's hypothesis it seemed to make good sense. She set about attempting to apply the hypothesis in her ongoing attempts to understand the Lancelot materials. Littleton still considered the knight in question to be a major Celtic component of the tradition,[13] and he, like many contemporary Arthurian scholars,[14] implicitly accepted the assumption that the name Lancelot could be analyzed as "Lance à Lot," and that underlying this was a reference to the spear wielded by the widespread ancient Celtic divinity Lug.[15] Both Lug and Lancelot were identified with the lance or spear, and both were at or near the apexes of their respective traditions. It seemed extremely probable that this famous hero, who, after Arthur himself, is arguably the most important figure in the tradition, had no connection whatsoever with the Sarmatian or any other Northeast Iranian steppe culture.

But Malcor persisted in her efforts to tie this enigmatic figure into the same steppe tradition that Littleton believed had spawned Arthur. One afternoon, in the course of a discussion in which he was stoutly defending Lancelot's Celtic pedigree, she dropped the bombshell that ultimately led to this collaboration: might the name in question be derived from an as-yet-unattested sobriquet, "Alanus à Lot," that is, "the Alan of Lot?"

All at once a great many more pieces of the puzzle fell into place. The Alans, first cousins of the Iazyges, who in company with the Visigoths, Vandals, and other Germanic tribes had

Introduction

settled in small enclaves in Gaul and the Iberian Peninsula in the early years of the fifth century,[16] had brought with them an independent reflex of the common Northeast Iranian steppe epic tradition. In addition, as will shortly be demonstrated, the Lot region of southern Gaul (see map 8) was a center of Alan activity, as well as power, since almost from the start the Romans saw fit to entrust their Alan "allies" with local administrative duties.[17]

Evidence rapidly began to accumulate that this *(A)lan(u)s-à-Lot, whose name eventually came to be rendered as Lancelot,[18] was in all probability derived from the same prototype as Arthur and Batraz (see fig. 1). Indeed Lancelot has more in common with Batraz than does Arthur; and the Lancelot corpus, with its emphasis upon horsemanship and carts, is far more reminiscent of the steppes than is the "Celticized" British variant. In short, thanks to Malcor's insight, an important dimension of what was now clearly the "Alano-Sarmatian Connection" had come to light.

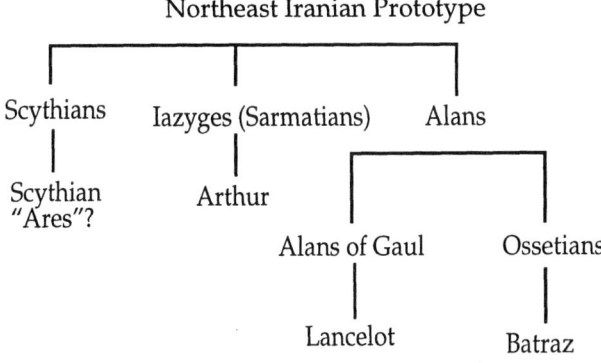

FIG. 1. Proposed Development of the Legends of Arthur, Lancelot, and Batraz

At the same time Malcor began to discover a strong Alan component in the Holy Grail legends. Here too the continental Alans appeared to have played a major role. One group of Alans, allied with Alaric's Visigoths, seems to have stolen some vessels from the Basilica of St. Peter's during the sack of Rome in 410 (see chaps. 9 and 10), and one of these objects was probably a sacred chalice of some sort, perhaps a holy relic associated by the early church with the Last Supper, which these still-pagan marauders came to associate with the prototype of the magical Nartamongæ. This treasure was eventually carried to southern Gaul, to the region traditionally associated with the Grail legends. Yet as a result of a sequence of events that will be traced in chapter 9 the sacred cup, as well as the rest of the treasure, disappeared from sight shortly thereafter. This disappearance fostered the ideas that the Holy Grail, like the Nartamongæ, was hidden from all but the bravest or purest warriors and that the cup was the object of a sacred quest.

All of these matters will be addressed in the chapters that follow. Before considering them, however, we should point out that we are not the first to suggest that the legends of the Round Table developed in the East and diffused to the West. For example, in 1170 a certain Alanus[19] commented that Arthur was perhaps "better known to the peoples of Asia Minor than to the *Britanni* [the Welsh and Cornish]," making what is perhaps the earliest allusion to the notion that the stories of the Round Table came from the East.[20] Several modern scholars have also suggested that many of the Arthurian legends, as well as other legends that arose in medieval France, had their roots in the Orient. Karl Pannier suggests that the core of the story of "Flore and Blanscheflur" came from the Orient but that the form that diffused throughout Western Europe was forged in the north of France.[21] Closs went so far as to suggest that the concept of the Grail originated on the "borders of Persia and Afghanistan."[22] Although Stein has argued that this "oriental" influence consists only of the most basic folkloric motifs, other scholars feel that this influence is more direct.[23] Some of them attribute this influence to the Crusades, with knights returning from the East with tales that were then recast in a European form.[24] This influence, however, can be attributed to a much earlier historical context.

It is also possible to suggest that the historical Arthur fought most of his battles in northern Britain and that his association with Wales, Glastonbury, and other southern locations came much later.[25] That some, if not all of the

Arthurian legends originated in northern Britain and later diffused southward is supported by Eisner, who also suggests that some "Mediterranean" themes may have diffused to this region, as well as to Ireland, via the early Christian monks.[26] Yet it is now clear that the themes in question originated in an area remote from the Mediterranean and arrived in northern Britain almost three centuries before the legendary Arthur rode over the British countryside with his knights. These legends were then imprinted by specific historical events that occurred in Late Antiquity, the major participants in which were the dramatically displaced tribes of Sarmatians and Alans who found themselves settled in Britain and Gaul.

Methodology and Plan of Research

Rather than starting from the assumption that the Arthurian tradition is of Celtic derivation and searching through the evidence to support our position we have chosen to examine the entire Arthurian tradition from scratch and see where that analysis leads us. The best means of securing a "comprehensive view of . . . [a] whole [narrative] tradition" is still to use the historic-geographic, or "Finnish," method of study.[27] Some scholars have previously conducted studies using a hybrid of the historic-geographic method, drawing on such media as sculpture, painting, architecture, manuscript illumination, metalwork, and glasswork in addition to narrative texts.[28] The mass of evidence available for folklore studies of this nature makes such studies enormously time-consuming, and they often produce unsatisfactory results.[29]

The first step in this research project, then, was to assemble a data base by means of an extensive search of the medieval visual arts, church ritual, liturgical and secular dramas, literature, and popular traditions.[30] The next step was to analyze the collected material and to break the examples of folklore into categories of variation (e.g., "Sword in the Stone" vs. "Sword Thrown into the Lake"). We examined each piece of evidence, as far as possible, in context and used almost every available analytic technique, from neo-euhemerism to traditional comparative mythology.[31]

We examined the results. We studied less popular variants for geographical or historical limits to their distribution. We noted frequency of occurrence for the specific stories, as well as the extent of the distribution of each variant. We examined each datum in light of similar data from the same medium (i.e., literary examples were compared with literary examples) and in light of similar data from different media (i.e., an illumination was compared with similar variants found in enamelwork and literature). We compared contextual information for each example in each group of variants to see if there was any correlation between specific combinations of contextual data and specific forms of the variant. The ultimate goal of this portion of the research was to identify sources for the legends of King Arthur, the Knights of the Round Table, and the Holy Grail.

The final step was to search for sources for these stories, based on our analysis of their content, amid historical, theological, artistic, and folkloric sources. This book is the summary of our results. Where necessary we have included "scenarios," that is, hypothetical sequences of events, based on our findings, that we believe took place in order to produce the Arthurian tales as we have them in their twelfth- and thirteenth-century forms.

Although there is a remote possibility that the legends of the Round Table and the Nart sagas are parallel only at the hypothetical Indo-European level, with the different strands of these legends developing independently of one another, evidence of more recent contact between the Northeast Iranian-speaking peoples and the peoples of Europe strongly suggests that these tales were transmitted from one of these cultures to the other. Our preliminary findings indicated that a non-Celtic source lay at the center of the Arthurian tradition, with Celtic, Christian, Germanic, and many other overlays, depending upon the geographical and cultural point of generation of each datum. Sometimes this non-Celtic source seemed to derive from the folklore of the "Scythian" (i.e., general Northeast Iranian) culture; at other times the source seemed more closely related to the documented history of various Alano-Sarmatian tribes of these peoples. Moreover contact between the Northeast Iranian-speaking peoples and the peoples of Europe during Late Antiquity occurred on a scale that could easily have affected the tales that were recorded in the manuscript evidence of the Middle Ages.[32]

In this book we show that there were numerous opportunities for the transmission of these legends, that there was information to be transmitted, that there is evidence that such transmission in fact took place, and that the direction of this diffusion was from the homeland of the Northeast Iranian-speaking peoples to Europe. We do not claim that we have discovered the final "truth" about the nature and origin of these legends. If what follows serves to stimulate new research that eventually disproves our conclusions, we will count ourselves successful. It is in this spirit that this book, which admittedly challenges a great many commonly held assumptions, ought to be read.

So now, before moving to the consideration of specific figures, themes, and images, let us review the cultural and historical evidence relative to "Scythia" and its denizens in the early years of the Common Era and the trail that led from there to Camelot.

NOTES

1. Mallory is currently senior lecturer in archaeology at the Queen's University in Belfast, Northern Ireland.

2. Cf. Dirr 1912; Dumézil 1930, 1965.

3. Dumézil 1930:69.

4. Cary 1927.

5. Dio 71.11; Cary 1927:37.

6. For a detailed study of this settlement see Richmond (1945).

7. Malone 1925. As Nickel (1975a:10–11) points out, Castus had served in Pannonia and would thus have been thoroughly familiar with

both the customs and the fighting ability of his new Sarmatian auxiliaries. According to Malone (1925:370–372) this Roman general also seems to have led the Iazyges in an expedition to Armorica (northern Gaul), where they helped put down a local rebellion. The year was probably 184 C.E. (Ashe 1985:116).

8. Cf. Ammianus Marcellinus 31.4.22; Rolfe 1939:395.

9. E.g., Weston 1957. Weston's reliance on the theories of Sir James Frazer strongly colored her interpretation of the Grail tradition. See Segal 1993:xix–xxxv.

10. Littleton and Thomas 1978:512–527.

11. E.g., Loomis 1991.

12. Cf. Nickel 1975a, 1975b.

13. Cf. Littleton and Thomas 1978:524.

14. E.g., Jenkins 1975:78–79.

15. Cf. Lugh, Ludd, Lleu, et al.

16. Sulimirski 1970:186–187; Bachrach 1973:136; see chaps. 3 and 9.

17. Bachrach 1973:33–37; Goffart 1980:111–114.

18. As Bachrach (1973:135–136) points out, it was not unusual for Alanic names to lose the initial vowel as they passed into French, Spanish, and Italian. There are numerous examples of the loss of the initial *A-* in Alanic place-names in both France and Italy, especially in toponyms in which an "of" element is present. The modern north Italian name Landriano derives from Alan d'Riano (*Dizionario Enciclopedico dei Comuni d'Italia*, 1950, 2:747); the French toponym Lanet (a town in the Aude, a region that played host to more than its share of Alan settlements) was originally called Villa de Alianto (ca. 951; Sabarthés 1912:195–196). We cannot offer any attested personal names that exhibit this characteristic, but its presence in several place-names lends powerful support to Malcor's reconstruction of **(A)lanus-à-Lot*. Colarusso (personal communication, MS comment, August 1992) has suggested that such a name, passing through a Celtic "filter," would tend to lose the initial *A-*, since this would have been seen as a definite article. The name would then be rendered **A-lanus-à-Lot*.

19. Given the hypothesis advanced in this book, it is curious to note that someone named Alanus would be credited with the earliest example of the notion that the Arthurian legends were of eastern origin.

20. Loomis 1963:13.

21. Stein 1988:44.

22. Matthews 1984:41–42.

23. Stein 1988:44; cf. Adolf 1947.
24. Faugère 1979:198–205.
25. Cf. Goodrich 1986.
26. Eisner 1969.
27. Thompson 1946:440. Cf. Woods 1955, 1959; Pentikäinen 1968. This method was pioneered by the eminent Finnish folklorists Kaarle Krohn (1926) and Antti Aarne (1961).
28. E.g., Mellinkoff 1970; Malcor 1991.
29. However, as Thompson (1946:430) points out:

> Though this scheme has . . . been subjected to some adverse criticism, it has been employed in a number of excellent studies, the general validity of which can hardly be doubted, and the method has been continually improved. No one who really knows about the behavior of oral tales can take exception to the careful analysis which is the foundation of the technique.

30. The results of all such studies should be treated with caution for the purpose of analysis, since some data will be inadvertently omitted by the researchers' own oversights as well as by the loss or destruction of evidence over the course of time.
31. E.g., Bolle 1970; Puhvel 1987.
32. E.g., Bachrach 1973.

PART I

The Cultural and Historical Background

CHAPTER 1

The Northeast Iranians
Scythians, Sarmatians, Alans, and Ossetians

This book argues that the core of the Arthurian and Holy Grail legends derives originally from a region known in antiquity as Scythia, that is, the western portion of the great "sea of grass" that stretches from the Altai Mountains to the Hungarian Plain (see map 1). We must therefore take a closer look at several of the ethnic groups that originated in this vast steppe region. Almost all of them spoke languages belonging to what linguists call the Northeast Iranian branch of the Indo-Iranian substock of the Indo-European language family;[1] most scholars now think that the linguistic differences among these several groups were minimal and that they not only shared a closely related set of dialects but also a common culture.[2]

Scythians

One of the earliest of these Northeast Iranian steppe peoples, or at least the earliest to have an impact on the ancient civilizations of the Mediterranean basin, was known to the Greeks as the Σκύθαι (i.e., Scythians). Here we encounter a major terminological paradox: "Scythian" can be used in two ways. In the narrow sense it is limited to the ancient Scythian tribes, as described by Herodotus and other Greco-Roman authorities. In the broad sense it applies to *all* of the groups we will survey in this chapter, including the modern Ossetians,[3] who can perhaps be considered "epi-Scythians." The region's ancient name,

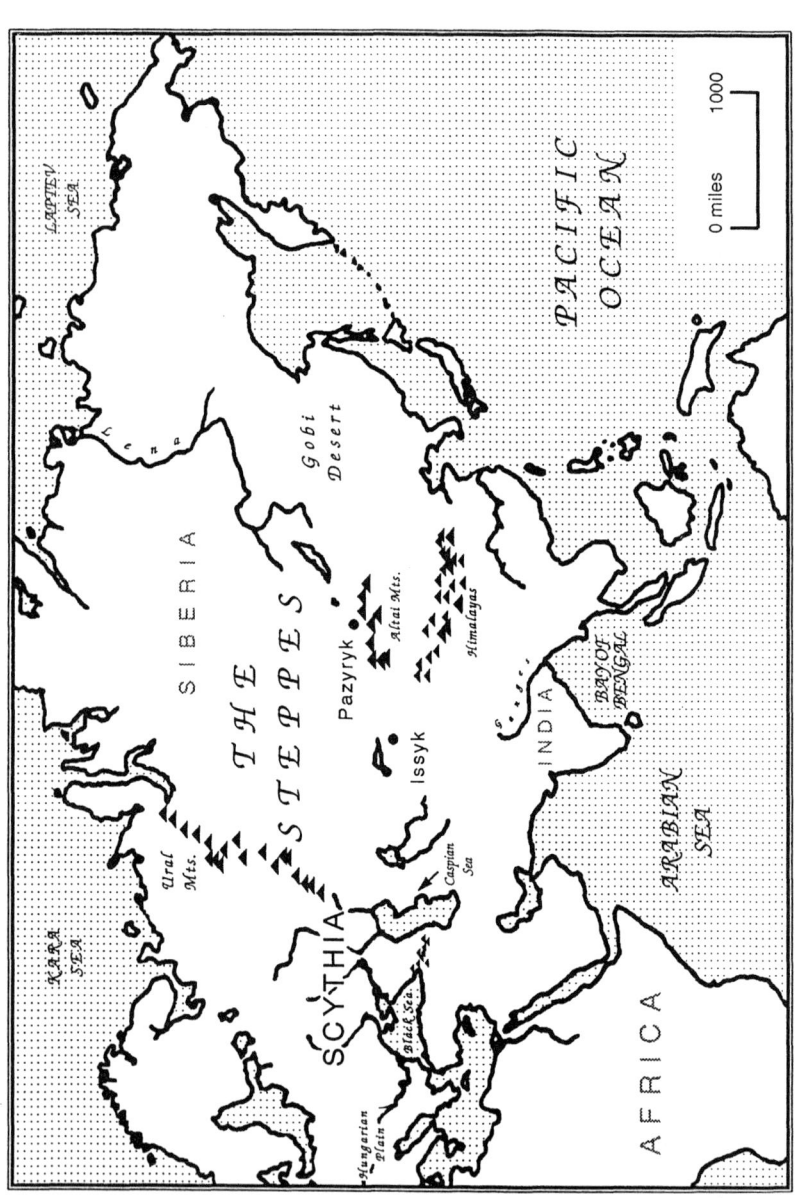

MAP 1. Ancient Scythia

Scythia, reflects this inclusive notion that anyone who called the "sea of grass" home was a "Scythian."

The Scythians expanded into the West in several major waves (see map 2). The first, which Gimbutas describes as "proto-Scythian," originated well east of the Urals.[4] Known archaeologically as the Timber-Grave Culture, this wave began expanding westward as early as 1800 B.C.E.[5] A second wave, this time of Scythian mounted nomads who buried their dead in timber-lined tumuli, swept across the more settled, agricultural communities of the north Pontic steppes and incorporated some of the indigenous cultivators, who became known as "Agricultural Scythians" (ca. 1100 B.C.E.).[6] Then, ca. 600–550 B.C.E., a third wave migrated westward out of southern Siberia.[7] These latecomers, who eventually pushed west along the north coast of the Black Sea as far as Bulgaria and who invaded northeast Iran as well, bore several ethnic labels (see map 3). Among them were the Massagetae (southeast of the Aral Sea), the Saka (northeastern Iran, western Afghanistan), the Thyssagetae (the central Urals), and a people Herodotus calls the "Sauromatae,"[8] who seem to have been the immediate ancestors (or earliest known example) of the Sarmatians.

Although all of these subtribes seem to have shared a similar way of life, the westernmost group, which roamed the Pontic steppes in the fifth century B.C.E. (ca. 450 B.C.E.), provided most of our nonarchaeological information about Scythian culture.[9] According to Herodotus[10] there were three major social strata (or tribes): "Royal Scythians," pastoral nomads who formed the ruling elite; "Warrior Scythians," also nomads, who maintained and extended the power of the former group; and "Agricultural Scythians," most likely comprising conquered, "Scythianized," indigenous peoples.

The Scythian economy was a mixture of pastoralism and settled cultivation, although the former seems to have taken precedence, as it still does among the Kazakhs and other modern inhabitants of the eastern portion of this region.[11] As among those Altaic peoples who came to the region in more recent times, the horse was the primary, or at least the most prestigious, animal herded. The Scythians were the first great cavalry nation. Unlike the ancient Celts, who still relied on horse-drawn chariots

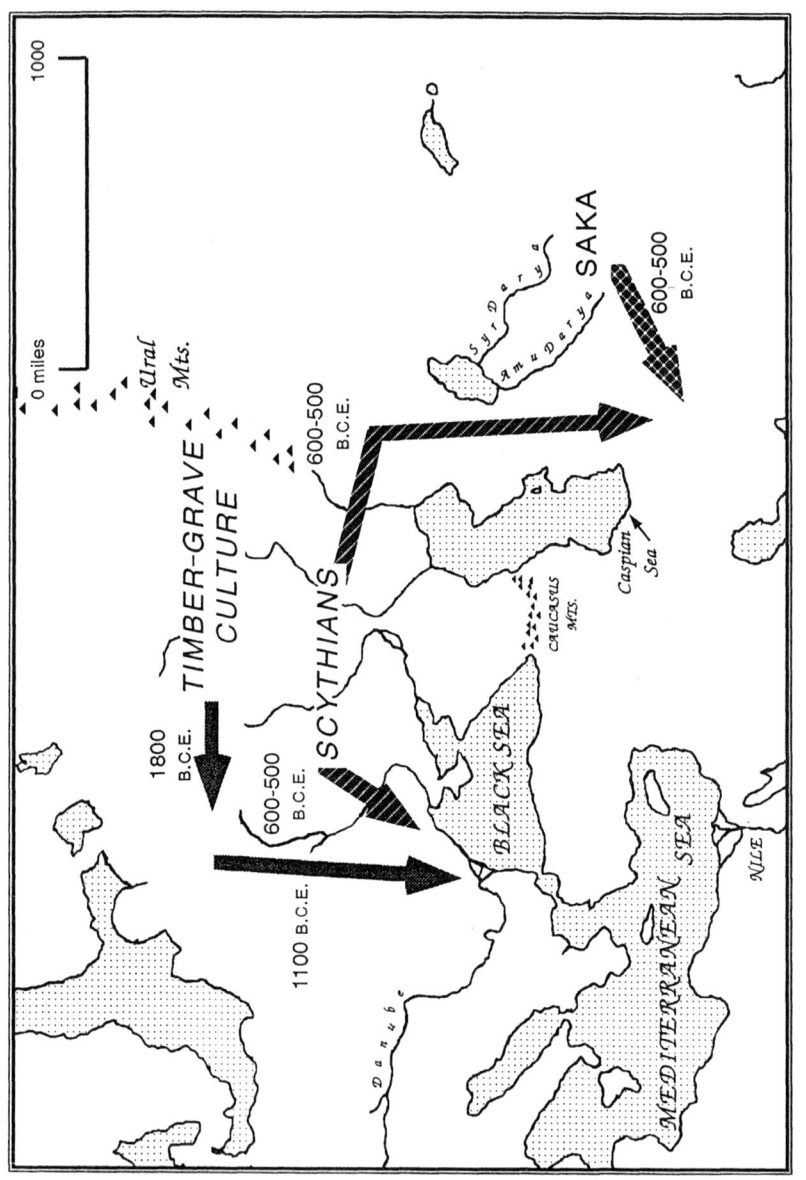

Map 2. Major Migrations of Steppe Cultures

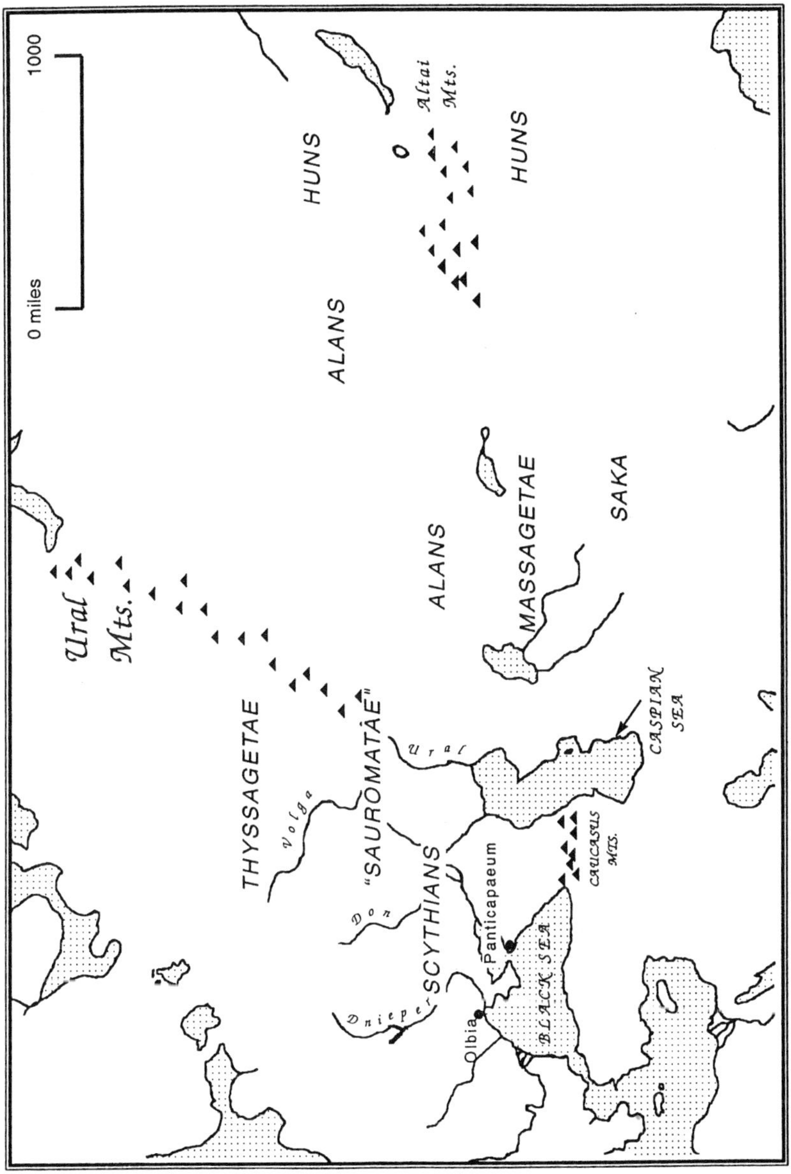

MAP 3. Ancient Steppe Cultures

as late as the first century C.E., the Scythians were mounted warriors who fought with both lances and bows, as well as long, slashing swords.[12] These steppe nomads also wore trousers, overlapping scale armor, and conical helmets. A millennium and a half later this warfare pattern, which was also characteristic of the Sarmatians and the Alans, was to have a fundamental impact on medieval European society; as Nickel points out, it was the basis upon which the concept of chivalry developed.[13]

Unlike the Romans and, for the most part, the Celts, Arthur's people, as they are depicted in the medieval chivalric romances, seem to have preferred to fight from horseback and to have relied primarily upon a long slashing sword[14] rather than upon a heavy thrusting spear and a javelin (or *pilum*) characteristic of the foot-slogging legionnaires. This, together with their relatively heavy body armor, which consisted of overlapping scales attached to a leather tunic, tallies well with what evidence we have of Sarmatian military technology, such as the images on Trajan's Column (see plate 1).[15] Even the custom of designating warriors by means of an emblem, which eventually evolved into the medieval concept of the heraldic device, may have its roots in the Sarmatian and Alanic practice of identifying clans and other kinship units by means of *tamgas* ("sacred symbols") emblazoned on helmets, shields, and other pieces of equipment (see fig. 2), many examples of which have been found in south Russian sites associated with the cultures in question.[16]

As with the Alans draft animals and carts also played an important part in the Scythian economy, and we have evidence that while on the move they lived in wagons: indeed Herodotus said that they had no other homes.[17] These carts were covered by felt tents that functioned like the yurts still to be found among the steppe nomads of central Asia.

The role of women in Scythian society, and in Northeast Iranian society as a whole, also needs to be noted, as it not only differed markedly from that played by women in the Greco-Roman world but also has implications for the role of women in the Arthurian tradition.[18] The Greek legends about the Amazons are almost certainly derived from their observations of this culture. Scythian wives were expected to fight alongside their

PLATE 1. Sarmatians on Trajan's Column. ALINARI/ART RESOURCE, NY.

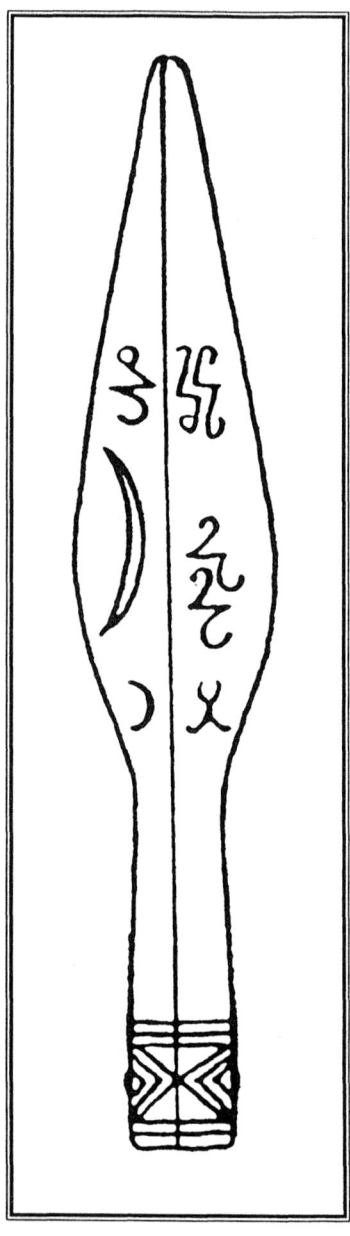

FIGURE 2. Tamgas

husbands when the occasion demanded, and Herodotus went so far as to assert that among their eastern cousins, the "Sauromatae, . . . [there is] a marriage law which forbids a girl to marry until she has killed an enemy in battle."[19]

According to Herodotus the Scythian religion centered on seven divinities, chief among them a goddess called Tabiti, whom he glosses as "Hestia."[20] Another was a war-god whom he refers to as the "Scythian Ares," who was symbolized by a sword thrust into a pile of wood. Yet another major divinity seems to have been called Don Bettyr,[21] who most likely was associated with the Don River (known to the Greeks as the Tanais) and who presided over plant and animal fertility.

The way the Scythians conceived of their own origins also has important implications for our thesis. According to Herodotus the primeval being, whose name he transliterates as "Targitaos," had three sons.[22] When three burning golden objects fell from the sky—a cup, a battle-ax,[23] and a yoked plow—each son in turn attempted to gather them. Only the youngest, whom Herodotus calls "Kolaxaïs," was successful. From him were descended the "Royal Scythians" (the Paralatai), who had sovereignty over all. From the second son, "Lipoxaïs," descended the "Warrior Scythians" (the Aukhatai), while from the eldest, "Arpoxaïs," sprang the "Agricultural Scythians" (the Katiaroi and the Traspies).[24] While there is still some argument as to whether these were separate tribes or social classes within a single tribe, one aspect of this myth is extremely important for our purposes: the emphasis placed on cups (see chaps. 8, 9, and 10).[25]

Golden objects figure prominently in Scythian expressive culture, that is, graphic art, particularly in the so-called "animal style": highly realistic depictions of both wild and domestic animals on buckles, harnesses, brooches, and other objects (see plate 2).[26] Often these pieces were made of the gold that is still to be found in the region, especially in the streams that issue from the northern foothills of the Caucasus Mountains.

Although the Scythians dominated the steppe region for several centuries, trading furs and gold for the manufactured products of the civilized world to the south and the west, by the beginning of the fourth century B.C.E. the western part of Scythia,

PLATE 2. The Animal Style (Gold plaque, Transbaikalarea). Courtesy of the Hermitage Museum.

or at least the territory controlled by the "Scythians proper," had been invaded by their eastern cousins, the Sarmatians.

The Sarmatians

The earliest mention of this branch of the Northeast Iranian community, which will loom large in what follows, can be found in Herodotus, who, as we have seen, called them the "Sauromatae."[27] Once again we are confronted with a labeling problem—actually several labeling problems. The first of these concerns the relationship between "Sauromatae" (cf. Greek Σαυρομάτης or "Sauromatian") and "Sarmatian" (cf. Greek Σαρμάτης). According to Herodotus the Sauromatae were the immediate eastern neighbors of the Scythians. But were these Sauromatae a subset of a more widespread group, or nation, called Sarmatians?[28] Or are the two labels synonymous?

"Sauromatae" probably can be interpreted as "Lizard People" (cf. Greek σαῦρος "lizard").[29] This is most likely a reflection of their principal totem, which seems to have been a windsock-like serpentine banner attached to a pole (see plate 3). Whether all of the tribes later lumped together as "Sarmatian" (Greek Σαρμάτης)—the Roxolani,[30] the Aorsi, the Iazyges, etc.— were actually "Lizard People" is still an open question. The prominent role played by lizards (or dragons) in the symbolism associated with the Arthurian legends, however, may indicate that the Sarmatian tribe that eventually found its way to Britain did indeed venerate this creature.[31] In contrast the prominence given to cups in the continental traditions surrounding the Holy Grail indicates that the Alans, whose concern with cups survives in the Ossetic accounts of the Nartamongæ, or "Revealer of the Narts," and who settled in various regions of Gaul and Spain in the fifth century,[32] had a slightly different emphasis within the mythological system and were therefore to some degree culturally distinct from their Sarmatian cousins.

Here we encounter a second, and more complex, terminological confusion: that between "Sarmatian" (or "Sauromatian") and "Alan."[33] The two nations, who almost certainly spoke closely related dialects, were frequently confused

PLATE 3. Mounted Sarmatian (Chester). Courtesy of the Chester City Council.

PLATE 4. Arthurian Knights with Banner (MS Paris, Bibliothèque Nationale fr. 95, fol. 173). Photograph courtesy of Bibliothèque Nationale, Paris.

by outside observers. The ethnic self-identification terms Sarmatian and Alan may have been applied synonymously by these "eastern Scythians" themselves.[34] In Britain, for example, we find the surnames Aleyn, Alan, and FitzAlan in particular abundance in the region most closely associated with Sarmatian settlement.[35] Yet Sulimirski refers to the Alans as simply a "late Sarmatian people."[36] The two labels are difficult to separate neatly. Although in this book we reserve the label Alan for the Northeast Iranians who settled in Gaul, Spain, and elsewhere, it is possible that the peoples in question did not make this distinction with any degree of consistency.

At this point we need to follow the fortunes of a particular Sarmatian tribe, the Iazyges. According to Sulimirski these steppe nomads were among the first of the Sarmatians to cross the Don River (ca. 200 B.C.E.), and by 20 or 30 C.E. they had reached the northern part of what is modern Hungary, that is, Upper Pannonia, north of the Danube on the periphery of the Roman Empire.[37] There they would remain an identifiable ethnic group for at least the next 450 years.[38] The history of this Sarmatian presence in Hungary is conventionally divided into three periods: Early (ca. 20–160 C.E.), Middle (160–260), and Late (260–430).

During most of the Early Period the Iazyges seem to have been on good terms with the Romans. They refrained from invading the nearest Roman province of Pannonia and occasionally served as auxiliaries in the legions (see map 4). In 50 C.E. an Iazygian cavalry detachment fought alongside the Suevian king Vannius, a Roman vassal, and in 85–88 they fought as allies of Rome in Trajan's Dacian Wars.[39] Thus long before the Romans actively engaged the Iazyges in combat they had come to respect their military capabilities.

The Iazyges' first confrontation with Rome did not come until 92 C.E., a few years after the Dacian Wars, when they ravaged Roman Moesia. In 105 C.E. they again moved south of the Danube and invaded Dacia (modern Transylvania), in concert with their fellow Sarmatians (or Alans), the Roxolani, who attacked it from the east. The emperor Hadrian,[40] however, eventually repulsed the Iazyges, and a peace treaty was concluded that was to last for fifty years.

The Northeast Iranians

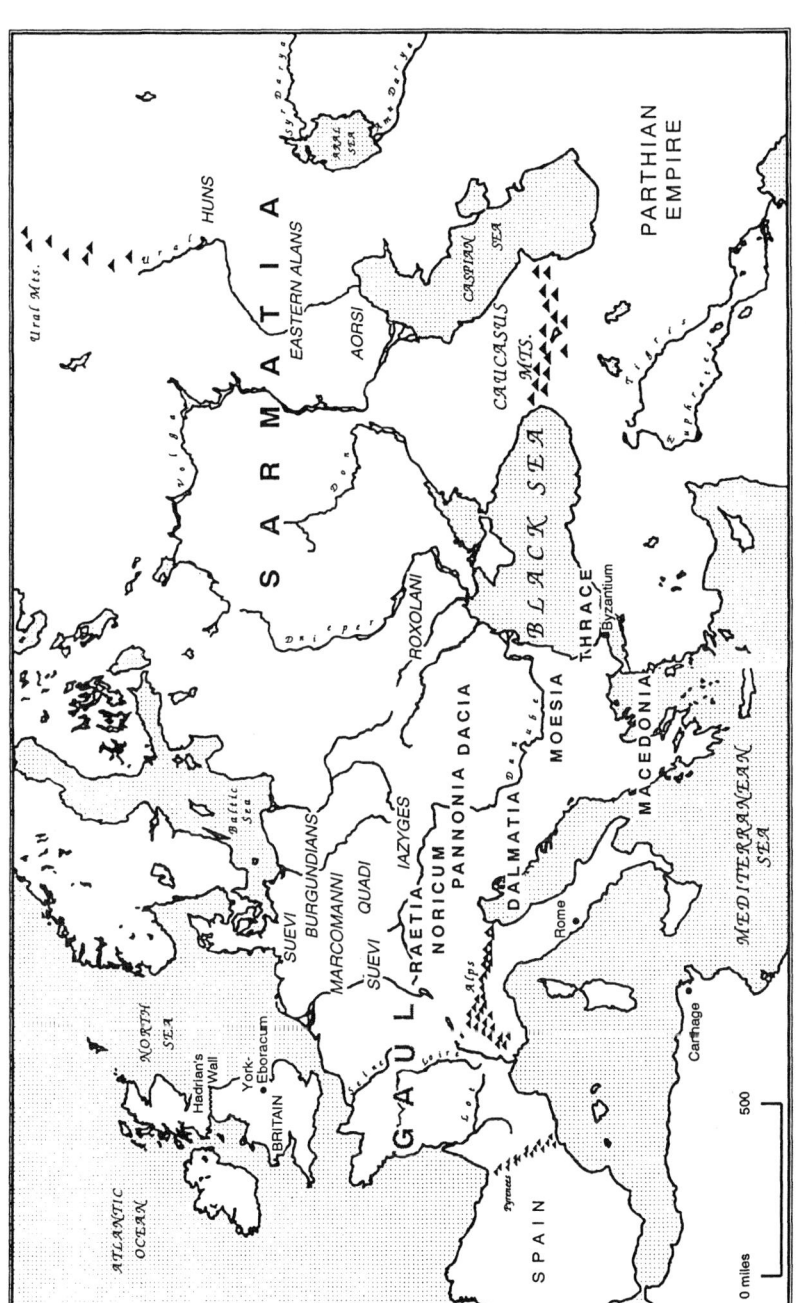

MAP 4. The Iazyges, ca. 175 C.E.

At the beginning of the Middle Sarmatian period, in 169 C.E., the Iazyges threw in their lot with two adjacent Germanic tribes, the Marcomanni and the Quadi, and invaded Pannonia. In 175 C.E., after a hard-fought campaign, they were decisively defeated by the emperor Marcus Aurelius, who as a result took the title Sarmaticus and used it on his coins.[41] The Iazyges' "king," whom Dio Cassius calls Zanticus,[42] came in person to Marcus's camp to sue for peace. Among the harsh terms the emperor imposed were that the Iazyges remove themselves from the immediate vicinity of the Danube and that they contribute 8,000 armored cavalry to the Roman army. Some 5,500 of these new recruits, as Dio Cassius pointed out, were sent to Britain.[43]

The Sarmatians in Britain

As the war was rapidly winding down in Pannonia, it was possible to divert troops to another hot spot: the north of Britain, where the Caledonian tribes, as well as the Picts, were making trouble. Like many a colonial power in more recent times—the British use of Sikhs and Gurkhas comes to mind—the Romans knew quality when they saw it and wasted no time recruiting their former foes into the legions. At the same time, of course, this reduced Zanticus's potential to make trouble, as his best warriors were now Roman soldiers. Most of the new recruits were sent to Bremetennacum, a major Roman cavalry post on the Ribble River near the modern Lancashire town of Ribchester.[44] It was responsible for the defense on the region and portions of Hadrian's Wall, which at the time marked the effective limits of Roman control (see map 4). Unlike the local Britons, most of whom had kinsmen north of the Wall, the Iazyges would be well over a thousand miles from home and therefore could be trusted not to open the gates to their relatives. This practice too has modern counterparts: the former East Germans typically recruited the guards along the Berlin Wall from Lower Saxony, about as far from Berlin as you could get and still be in East Germany.

From the available evidence it seems that few if any of the Iazygian auxiliaries ever managed to get back to their homeland in the steppes, and in accordance with Roman policy in these matters a colony of Sarmatian veterans was established

Bremetennacum Veteranorum, a major Roman cavalry post near the modern Lancashire town of Ribchester in or near the vicus,[45] or village, adjacent to the fort. Though we do not possess any specific description of the *vicus* at Bremetennacum, the *Ravenna Cosmography* refers to it as "Bresnetenaci veteranorum," which clearly designates it as a veterans' settlement.[46] This particular *vicus*, together with the nearby fort, seems to have been strategically located, as several Roman roads passed through it from north to south, and there was an excellent highway leading eastward to the legionary headquarters at York (Eboracum).

Archaeological investigations at Ribchester and in an area just to the northwest, called the Fylde, have yielded a considerable amount of evidence that a Sarmatian community existed there for several centuries.[47] An inscription dedicated to the Romano-British god Apollo Maponus asking for the continued well-being of the emperor Gordian was sponsored ca. 238–244 by the "N(umerus) eq(uitum) Sarmat(arum) Bremetenn(acensium) Gordian(orum)."[48] Another artifact, now lost, seems to have included not only an image of a Sarmatian cavalryman but also an inscription mentioning "Sarmatae."[49] From the account of this image given by Thomas Braithwaite in 1604 it closely resembled the relief found at Chester of a mounted warrior holding a dragon banner.[50] The lost piece was described as a "naked horseman," which Richmond explains as most likely due to weathering.[51] If the scaled armor depicted in relief were to have worn down, the mounted figure could easily have been mistaken for a nude man.

A fair number of Sarmatian-type artifacts—pots, tools, and so forth—have been found at Ribchester, and the whole impression is that of a stable ethnic enclave, one that endured long after the original veterans were dead and buried.[52] Many of these Sarmatian emigres probably brought along their wives and children. But others may have married local British women; as Leslie Alcock puts it in discussing the *vicus* as a social institution in Roman Britain, "here was the meeting place of auxiliary soldiers, whether provincial or barbarian in origin, and native women, which was to breed the future garrison of the fort."[53] However, the community's close association with the Roman military establishment—as in other veterans' communities sons of soldiers were strongly motivated to follow their fathers'

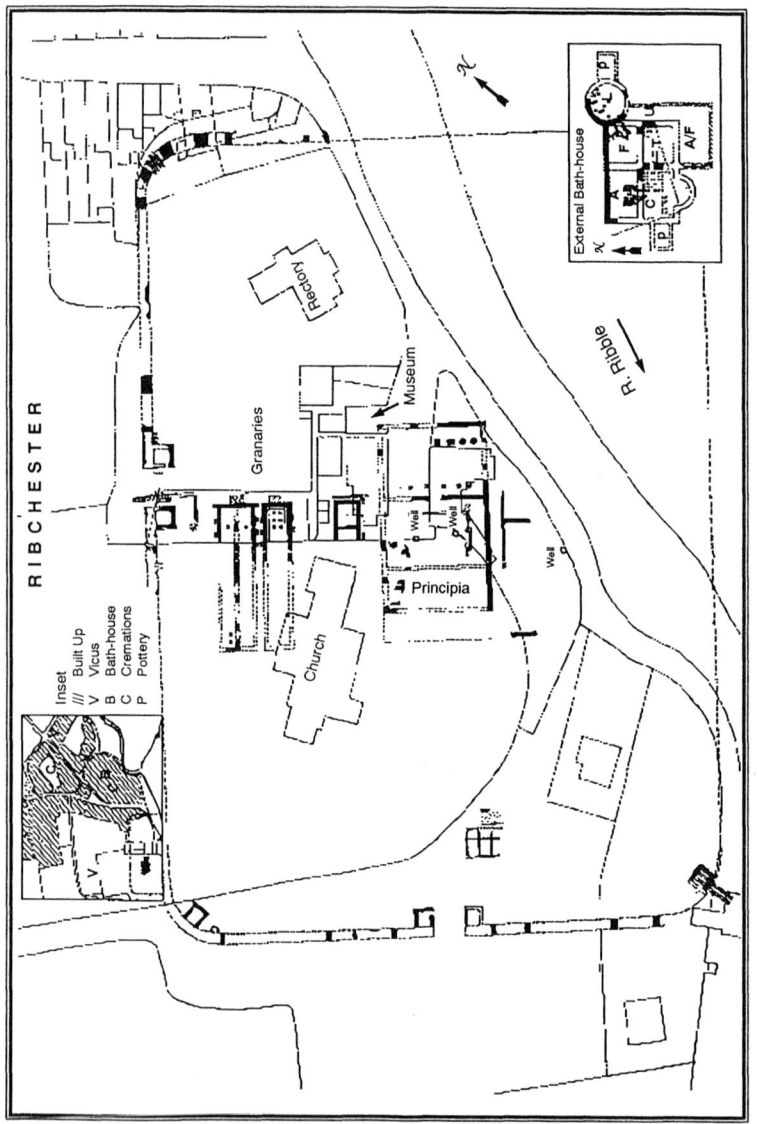

FIGURE 3. The Excavations at Ribchester. Courtesy of the Ribchester Museum Trust.

MAP 5. Britain at the Time of the Sarmatian Settlement

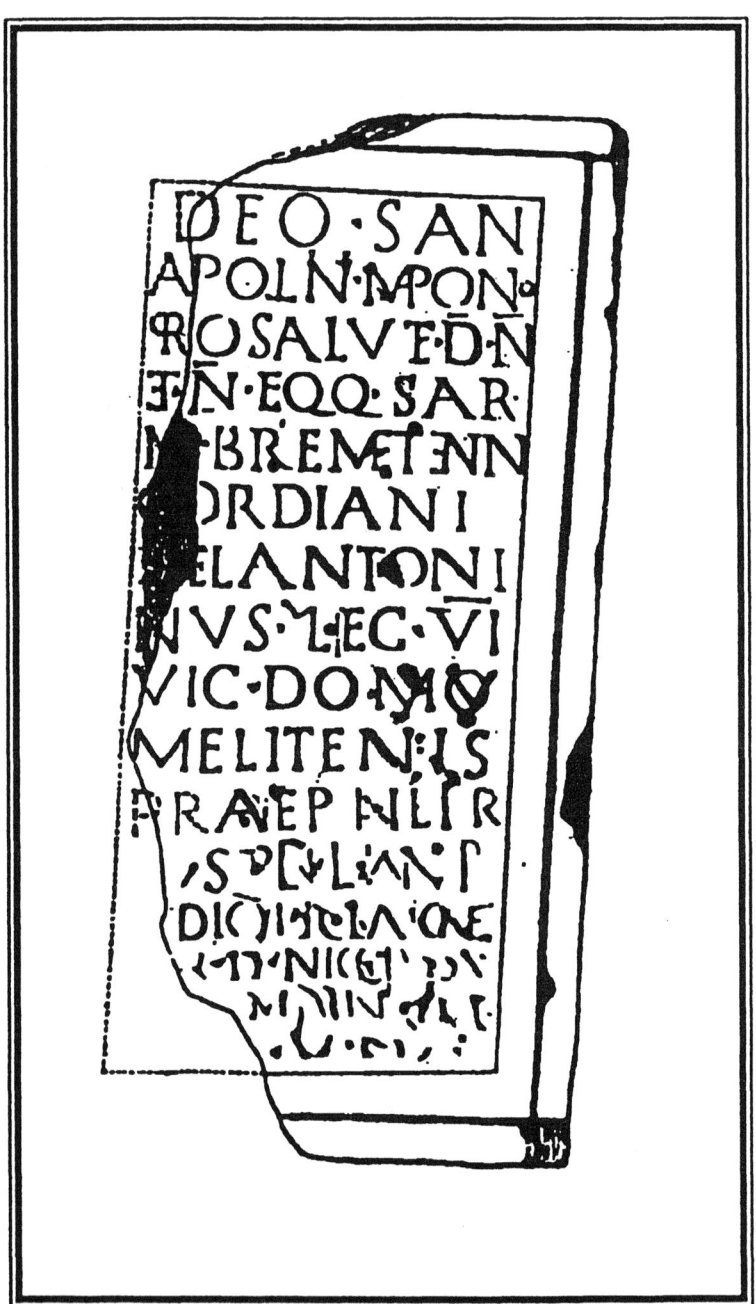

FIGURE 4. Apollo Maponus Inscription. Courtesy of the Ribchester Museum Trust.

footsteps, as by doing so they could become citizens[54]—probably helped it to maintain its ethnic identity and to resist total assimilation into the indigenous Celtic population.

In any event, as Sulimirski points out, the Sarmatian veterans' settlement at Bremetennacum was still in existence "in the early fifth century."[55] In light of the Ossetic evidence (which will be discussed shortly) it is now possible to suggest that the quasihistorical Arthur, the *dux bellorum* ("war leader") who, according to Nennius and the *Annales Cambriae* (*Welsh Annals*), defeated the Saxons at the Battle of Badon,[56] may well have been a member of this community. A leader who successfully led the descendants of the Iazygian veterans and a fair number of Celts in a temporarily successful campaign against the Saxon invaders would have inspired his own cycle of legends that may have eventually become identified with the epic tradition shared by the community he led.[57]

Many Arthurian sites (see map 6) have been identified with Scottish locales around the region where the Iazyges were stationed on Hadrian's Wall.[58] For example, the twelve battles of Arthur against the Saxons are said to have taken place at: (1) the "mouth of the river called Glein," (2–5) "on another river, ... called Dubglas ... in the region of Linnuis," (6) "on a river ... called Bassas," (7) "in the wood of Celidon" (Cat Coit Celidon), (8) at "Castle Guinnion," (9) at "the city of the Legion" (probably Chester or York), (10) on "the shore of the river ... called Tribruit," (11) "on the mountain ... called Agned," and (12) at "Mount Badon."[59] The *Annales Cambriae* (960–980) give the date for the Battle of Badon as 518; however, this conflicts with testimony from Gildas, who lived at a time when witnesses to the battle were still living and who gives the date for this battle as ca. 495.[60]

A reference to the ninth battle of Arthur against the Saxons may occur in the *Gododdin*, a poem in which Aneirin of central Scotland tells of a disastrous expedition, supposedly by Celts, into Yorkshire near Catterick. Only one thirteenth-century manuscript of this poem survives. The language suggests a date of composition of ca. 600 C.E.; however, the original poem may have been composed much earlier and the language updated during oral transmission. In this tale all but one of the three hundred warriors are slain. The leader of this expedition was

MAP 6. Arthurian Sites in Britain

said to be "no Arthur."[61] We believe that those responsible for this transmission were descendants of the Iazyges who were in charge of defending Yorkshire and the border regions.

As we discussed earlier, there is some confusion about the use of "Sarmatian" and "Alan." Although the name Alan (both as a first name and as a last name) was extremely popular on the Continent, the name is barely attested in Britain before the Norman Conquest (1066). Some scholars derive the name Alan in the Arthurian tradition from the Celtic-Breton name Alan, which is attested only after the settlement of the Sarmatians and the Alans in Britain and Gaul.[62] Charvet argues that Alein is a Celtic name and that the two saints named Alain from the north of Britain, one of whom founded the Abbey of Lavaur (600s) in Brittany, were descended from the Celts.[63] As Bachrach points out, however, it is far more probable that the name Alain (and variants like Ailan and Ellaini) came from the Alans who invaded Gaul in the fifth century, while it is possible that, given the confusion over the use of the term Alan, these saints Alain came by their unusual name from a Sarmatian, rather than Celtic or Alanic, source.[64] For example, inscriptions in northern Britain read "Elainus" ("Alan") as well as *Ala Sarmatarum* ("wing of Sarmatians").[65] Moreover, such names as Aspianis, which look more Alanic than Sarmatian, also appear.[66]

Given the number of historical figures named Alan who appear in southern Scotland[67] and northern Britain, it is probable that Ribchester was not the only settlement of Sarmatians in Britain and that some of the Iazyges served closer to the Wall. Weston notes that the Verdam edition of the Dutch *Fergus* (*Fergus et Galienne*)[68] lists a "great Alan of Gallowy [i.e., Gallway]" ("*groote Alanus de Galweia*"). Weston firmly believed that this Alan of "Gallowy" in Scotland had a definite influence on the Arthurian tradition.[69] In northern Britain Brian FitzAlan de Bedale, grandson of Brian FitzAlan, sheriff of Northumberland and Yorkshire (who came from a succession of Bryan FitzAlans and Alan FitzBryans), held lands on both sides of the Scottish border, and his genealogy was traditionally derived from Alain Fergant, duke of Brittany.[70] He owned a copy of the *Perlesvaus*, which was copied especially for him on a visit to the Continent.[71] The *Perlesvaus* is probably the most Alanic of all the Grail texts, and, of all the manuscripts of the Grail available to the continental monks who copied this manuscript for FitzAlan, it is curious that the abbot thought that this particular version was somehow so appropriate a gift for the British noble that thirteen monks were set to copy the story in a mad rush so that FitzAlan could take the manuscript back with him to England without suffering any delay in his mission.[72]

The Alans

We now turn to the other major contributors to the contact between East and West. The Alans were said to be "tall and handsome, [and] their hair inclines to be blond."[73] Like the other Northeast Iranians we have considered they moved frequently, practiced polygamy, and lived much of their lives in their carts and wagons. Ammianus Marcellinus, the fourth-century Roman historian who provides the most vivid picture of these nomads, was moved to observe that "in the wagons the males have intercourse with the women, and in the wagons their babies are born and reared; wagons form their permanent dwellings, and wherever they come, that place they look upon as their natural home."[74]

They were also consummate horsemen—"the young men grow up in the habit of riding from their earliest boyhood and regard it as contemptible to go on foot"—and loved fighting.[75] Indeed, they considered war their primary profession and typically sided with whoever offered them the most in exchange for their skills.[76] The Romans took advantage of this cultural trait and used the Alans as *laeti*, or military colonists, who were designated to control other "barbarian" tribes (cf. the Iazyges). In Italy the Romans forced the Alans to remain stationary. As a result these Alans assimilated rapidly into Roman culture, losing their fighting ability and value as *laeti* within two generations. In Gaul the Romans allowed the Alans to maintain their nomadic way of life, and these warriors, as they journeyed across the Continent, through the Pyrenees and into northern Spain, had a significant impact on the cultures that surrounded them. In some ways these Alans still assimilated readily into the territories they occupied.⁷⁷ They intermarried both with Romans and indigenous peoples,⁷⁸ often settling in villages and learning to speak the local language.⁷⁹ But their Alanic heritage was important to them. An example of this can be seen in the tendency of Christian Alans to name their sons Goar after the famous, pagan, Alanic war leader of the fifth century.⁸⁰ They also preserved other elements of their way of life that would have a great effect on the regions in which they settled.

Markale argues that the religion of fifth-century Gaul was a synthesis of "oriental" cults, druidism, and Roman traditions.⁸¹ One of these "oriental" religions was that of the non-Christian Alans.⁸² He sees the arrival of all of the "barbarians" in Gaul as a boon to Christianity, which he views as more compatible with the "barbarian spirit" than with the rationally and historically oriented spirit of Rome. About this time Cassian came from "Scythia Minor (known today as Dobruja, a region in Rumania and Bulgaria between the Danube and the Black Sea)."⁸³ He landed at Marseilles and founded a monastery near the Church of St. Victor, bringing more eastern influence of a particularly Scythian nature into the region.⁸⁴ Monks from the resulting orientalized church in Gaul (rather than from the Celticized church in Ireland), who were led by St. Augustine,⁸⁵ converted Britain to Christianity in 597.⁸⁶ Given the number of Alans who were in the church of Gaul by this time, there may well have been Alans among these monks. Alan mercenaries may have accompanied these monks as well. Perhaps this missionary activity was responsible for the legends of Joseph of Arimathea's arrival in Europe via Marseilles, of his missionary work in Britain, and of his carrying the Grail to that country, in the company of a bodyguard of soldiers from the East.

According to Goffart the Romans thought of the Goths as "Scythians" because they inhabited the lands the ancient Scythians had inhabited and used "Goth" as a new term for the same people instead of thinking of a new people on the old land.⁸⁷ In actuality the Romans may have known what they were talking about, given the number of Sarmatian and Alan tribes that were allied with the various tribes of Goths. Two Alan tribes who boasted such alliances were primarily responsible for the Alan settlements of Gaul, with one group invading from the north by crossing the Rhine in 406 (the northern contingent) and the other group sacking Gaul by crossing the Alps from the south ca. 411 (the southern contingent; see map 7).

The Northern Contingent. Honorius was emperor of the Western Roman Empire when the Alans of Pannonia, with the Asding and Siling Vandals and the Suevi, crossed the Rhine on December 31, 406.[88] There the Alans split into two groups under the kings Goar and Respendial when Goar offered his services to Rome.[89] Respendial's Alans and the Asding Vandals,[90] after defeating the Franks, sacked Trier, Reims, Amiens, and Arras (406–407).

Constantine III, who usurped the imperial throne in Britain in 407,[91] forced Respendial's anti-Roman Alans across the Pyrenees into Spain,[92] but he allowed Goar's pro-Roman Alans to settle in Gaul near the Loire (see map 8). These Alans remained a major influence in Gaul throughout the Middle Ages (see map 9).[93] The name Goar has many variations, and may be reflected in the name of Lancelot's half-brother "Ector" (for all the connections to "Hector"), since "Goar" appears as Goar, Goeric, and, notably, Eothar (the name that is used for Arthur in some continental legends)[94] in France and Iaeukhar in modern Ossetic. King Euric (r. ca. 467), whose name may be derived from yet another form of Goar, held power on both sides of the Pyrenees.[95] Although he is said by many historians to be Visigothic, his name would indicate that he at the very least had Alanic ties, if not Alanic blood.[96]

In 443 the Roman general Aëtius moved the Burgundians from the Rhine to Sapaudia (Savoy) to protect "the Alpine passes to Italy," instead of employing his usual tactic of using Alans.[97] His reasoning seems to have been that these tribes were less frightening to the local settlers than were the Alans, the only non-Teutonic people who ever settled permanently in Gaul.[98] This use of Burgundians, however, is unusual. Aëtius's preference for using Alans in strategic positions in Gaul is well documented. He frequently employed the Alans as a buffer against the Visigoths and the *bacaudae*, or rebellious peasants, of Armorica. He also placed the Alans under Sambida "around Valence [i.e., Valencia] along the Rhône in 440,"[99] and he settled Goar's Alans near Orléans, which became the Alan capital in

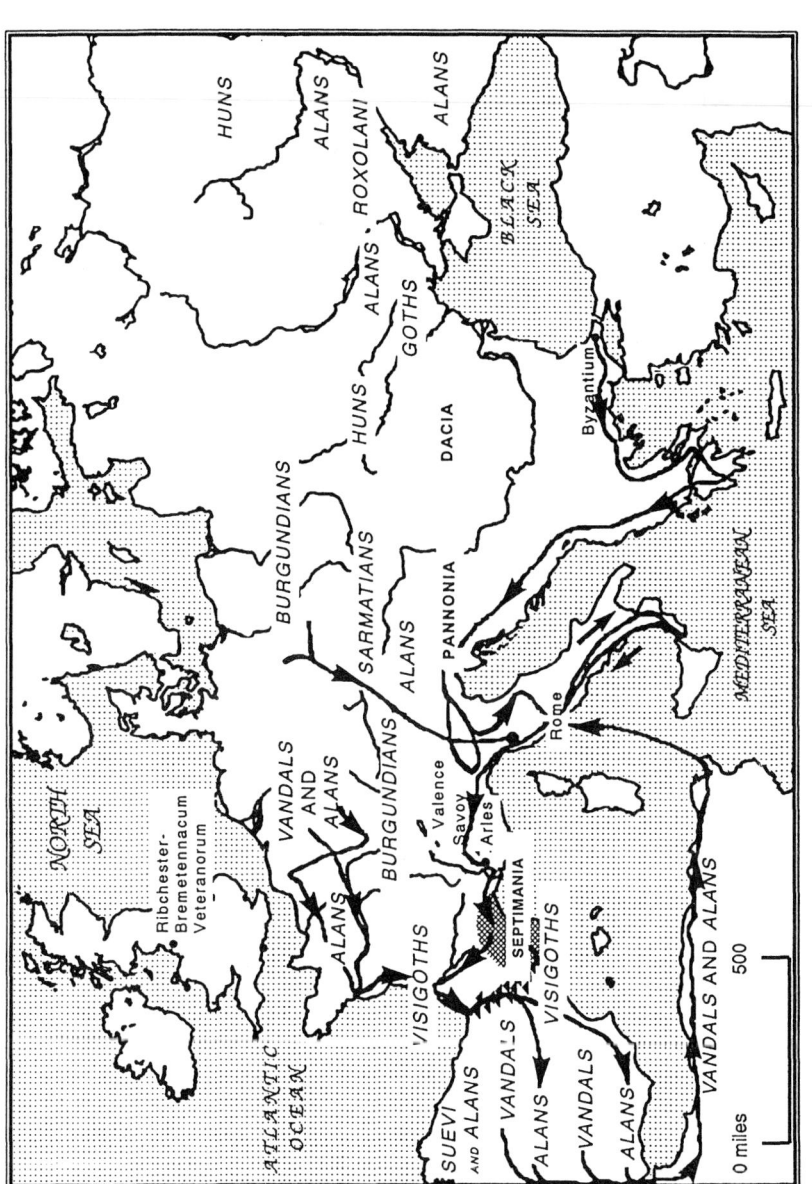

Map 7. Alan Invasions of Gaul

MAP 8. Roman Gaul

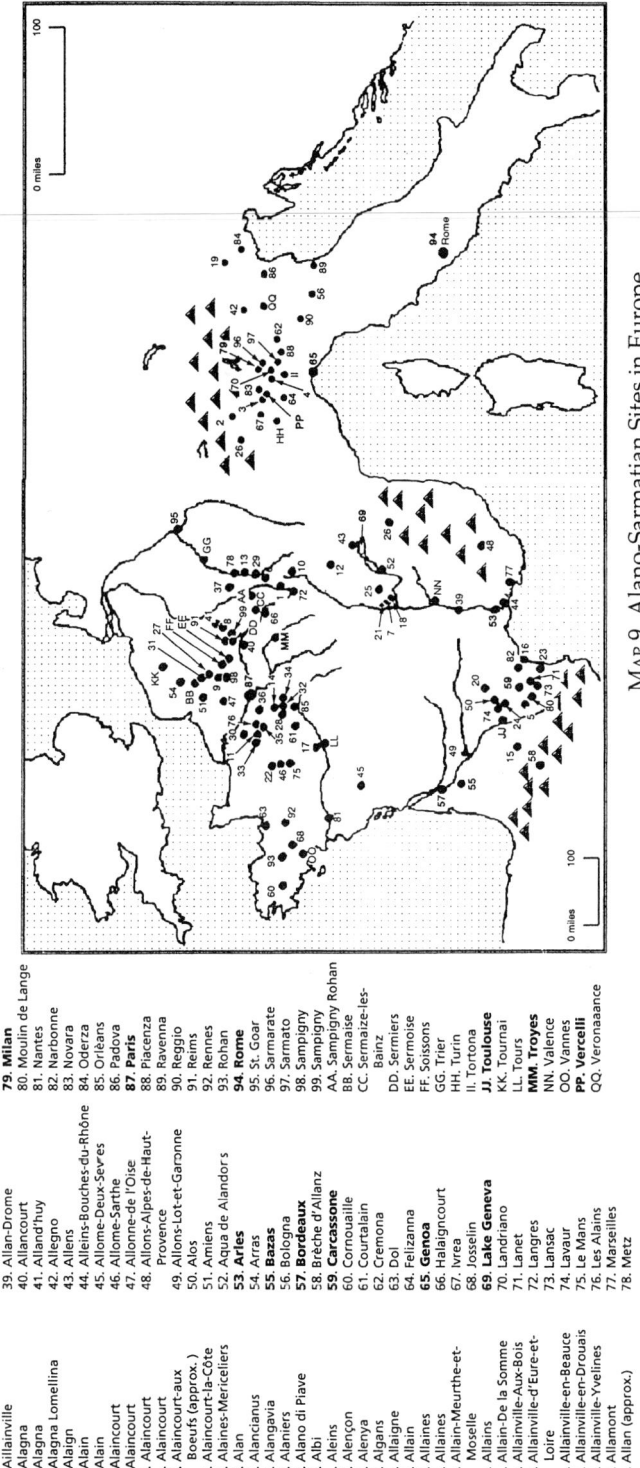

MAP 9. Alano-Sarmatian Sites in Europe

Sites numbered in bold-faced type are for location reference

1. Aillainville
2. Alagna
3. Alagna
4. Alagna Lomellina
5. Alaign
6. Alain
7. Alain
8. Alaincourt
9. Alaincourt
10. Alaincourt
11. Alaincourt
12. Alaincourt-aux-Boeufs (approx.)
13. Alaincourt-la-Côte
14. Alaines-Mericeliers
15. Alan
16. Alancianus
17. Alangavia
18. Alaniers
19. Alano di Piave
20. Albi
21. Aleins
22. Alençon
23. Alenya
24. Algans
25. Allaigne
26. Allain
27. Allaines
28. Allaines
29. Allain-Meurthe-et-Moselle
30. Allains
31. Allain-De la Somme
32. Allainville-Aux-Bois
33. Allainville-d'Eure-et-Loire
34. Allainville-en-Beauce
35. Allainville-en-Drouais
36. Allainville-Yvelines
37. Allamont
38. Allan (approx.)
39. Allan-Drome
40. Allancourt
41. Alland'huy
42. Allegno
43. Allens
44. Alleins-Bouches-du-Rhône
45. Allome-Deux-Sevres
46. Allome-Sarthe
47. Allome-de l'Oise
48. Allons-Alpes-de-Haut-Provence
49. Allons-Lot-et-Garonne
50. Alos
51. Amiens
52. Aqua de Alandors
53. **Arles**
54. Arras
55. **Bazas**
56. Bologna
57. **Bordeaux**
58. Brèche d'Allanz
59. **Carcassone**
60. Cornouaille
61. Courtalain
62. Cremona
63. Dol
64. Felizanna
65. **Genoa**
66. Halaigncourt
67. Ivrea
68. Josselin
69. **Lake Geneva**
70. Landriano
71. Lanet
72. Langres
73. Lansac
74. Lavaur
75. Le Mans
76. Les Alains
77. Marseilles
78. Metz
79. **Milan**
80. Moulin de Lange
81. Nantes
82. Narbonne
83. Novara
84. Oderza
85. Orléans
86. Padova
87. **Paris**
88. Piacenza
89. Ravenna
90. Reggio
91. Reims
92. Rennes
93. Rohan
94. **Rome**
95. St. Goar
96. Sarmarate
97. Sarmato
98. Sampigny
99. Sampigny
AA. Sampigny Rohan
BB. Sermaise
CC. Sermaize-les-Bainz
DD. Sermiers
EE. Sermoise
FF. Soissons
GG. Trier
HH. Turin
II. Tortona
JJ. **Toulouse**
KK. Tournai
LL. Tours
MM. **Troyes**
NN. Valence
OO. Vannes
PP. **Vercelli**
QQ. Veronaaance

Gaul, where the Alans remained as a documentable, influential force throughout the early Middle Ages.[100] Aëtius gave these Alans *agri deserti*, "property entered in the public assessment registers that, for whatever cause, was not paying its tax."[101] In a sense these Alans became the Roman tax collectors in Gaul.[102] Along with the Germanic invaders they "took only portions of the old Roman estates while establishing new ones on much the same pattern."[103] The colonists who refused to divide their estates with the Alans were ejected by the nomads.[104] We know so much about the details of these settlements because, as Goffart noted, "for some reason, the chroniclers entered into greater detail when relating Alan settlement than when concerned with Visigoths or Burgundians."[105] This interest among chroniclers may stem in part from the fact that the Alans were so distinct from their neighbors in the region that they were noticed more readily, and in part from the possibility that, given the number of Alans in the region,[106] the chroniclers themselves may have been part-Alan and hence fascinated with the history and culture of their own people.

Soon after the settlement at Orléans Aëtius allowed Goar's Alans to sack and settle in Armorica.[107] In 445–446 Germanus, Bishop of Auxerre, forced Goar and his Alans to stop their advances on Armorica, but the old bishop died on his way to Ravenna to ask Galla Placidia, the half-sister of Emperor Honorius, who was serving as regent for Emperor Valentinian III and who had had extensive contact with the Alans of southern Gaul, for aid in the matter.[108] The Alan settlements were concentrated around the areas where the author (or authors) of the Vulgate Cycle and Chrétien de Troyes composed their works, as well as in Brittany (formerly Armorica), where the first references to Lancelot appear in written texts.[109] It is conceivable that any one of the descendants of these Alans or of the people whose traditions they influenced carried an oral version of the legends of Lancelot with them to Switzerland, where Ulrich von Zatzikhoven heard the tale and composed the *Lanzelet* (ca. 1194–1205).

Alans, *bacaudae*, Burgundians, and Franks made up the force that in 451 sent Attila into retreat from Châlons-sur-Marne toward Troyes.[110] These Alans were led by Sangiban, who was by then in command of the Alans at Orléans (remember that Goar and his Alans were now settled in Armorica).[111]

Aëtius's successor, Aegidius,[112] used the Alans, Sarmatians, and Armoricans against the Franks (450s). He armed his troops from the weapons factories at Soissons.[113] At Orléans in 463 he added Franks from Tournai, under Childeric, to his forces to defeat the Visigoths.[114] (The Tournai treasure in Childeric's tomb included "a cloak ornamented in Sarmatian style with a swarm of golden cicadas."[115]) Childeric's successor, Clovis, used these same Franks to defeat Syagrius,[116] Aegidius's son, and to take Soissons.[117] The Frankish chroniclers rewrote the history of their battles, claiming that the Franks repeatedly defeated the Alans of Armorica.[118] The Merovingian attitude toward the Alanic and Sarmatian settlers in Gaul, however, was to remain ambiguous. Clovis himself (ca. 490–491) commanded some units of colonial Sarmatians.[119] Although the Merovingians later exhibited great animosity toward the Alans of the region that by this time was called Brittany,[120] there is every reason to suspect that the Alans who took part in the Battle of Orléans maintained a good relationship with the Merovingian kings (see chap. 9). The Merovingian kings favored Alanic advisers, particularly from the families of Aquitaine,[121] and the Carolingians were descended from the Alans (through Goeric's relative St. Arnulf).[122]

Geoffrey Ashe points out that "there is some evidence for a British presence in Armorica [prior to the fifth century] . . . but serious colonization took place in the late 450s."[123] Although Gildas describes this settlement as flight from the Saxons, most of the emigrants came from southwestern Britain probably by arrangement with Aegidius, the Roman military commander of northern Gaul, for the purpose of bolstering defenses, particularly in the Loire Valley.[124] Moreover several late fifth-century "saints," mostly Welsh, are said to have crossed to Armorica and to have been active in organizing Breton communities. In any case the population of Europe went into a steep decline in the sixth century, in part due to the "violence and depopulation following Rome's collapse in the West, aggravated by the great plague cycle that commenced in the 540s."[125] Thus, when a fresh wave of emigration occurred on a larger scale in the first half of the sixth century, the settlement was largely peaceful because of the abundance of vacant land. The aristocratic landholders of the Roman colonial period, several of whom were Alans, generally maintained control of their estates.[126] These landholders and not their serfs were the patrons of the medieval Arthurian manuscripts. The local Armorican people were absorbed, with the Celts and the free Germanic farmers of the region usually slotting into the political structure at the level of the "semi-servile ... villagers (or villains)."[127] About this time the name Brittany started to be used. As a result of this settlement some rulers seem to have reigned on both sides of the Channel.[128]

In the mid-seventh century the well-known, historical Judikaël (Jézéquel or Gicquel) was king of the Dumnonii (see map 7). Judikaël sided with the counts of Rennes and Nantes under the Gallo-Franks.[129] He founded the Abbey of Paimpont, and Markale believes that the nearby Camp des Rouets was the location from which the stories of the Round Table were spread on Armorican soil.[130] Judikaël was the son of the daughter of King Rispoé and Alain, the brother of Paskweten,[131] which suggests that Judikaël may well have been of Alanic heritage. Upon reaching old age Judikaël entered a monastery.[132] Note that the Alans considered only death in battle to be honorable.[133] Old men were held in great scorn.[134] The original Alanic method of handling this problem was for the son to kill his parents.[135] Once the Alans became Christians, this practice would no longer have been accepted. Given the number of Alans who entered the church upon reaching "old age"[136] at a time when it was fashionable for most people to enter the church in their teens (e.g., St. Patrick), this custom among the descendants of the Alans may have been an adaptation of the earlier ritual killings, with the entry into the monastery or nunnery serving as something akin to "death" as far as the world was concerned.

Later a certain Alain the Great (le Grand) became governor of Brittany. He defeated the Normans and installed Bretons as rulers of this "colony."[137] This Alain was the brother of Paskweten and the ultimate ancestor of many Alains of Brittany, including Alain the Red, who fought at the Battle of Hastings.

Markale argues that the courts of the kings of Vannes and of the Dumnonii constituted for a time in Armorica a political and religious center between the lands of the Gallo-Romans and the Gallo-Franks.[138] Although Markale does not see Vannes as becoming definitively Breton until the seventh century, remaining largely Gallo-Roman until that time, he still proposes this capital as the main source for the distribution of Celtic culture on the Continent.[139] In particular Markale sees Vannes as being in the lands of the Rohans.[140] The Rohans supposedly settled Armorica from Britain in the time of the Romans.[141] Although Markale assumes that this family is Celtic, it is more likely that the family is descended from the Alans of Vannes. Several of the Rohans bore the name Alain. For example, Viscount Alain IX de Rohan (1431) constructed a church on the site of the Battle of Trente following the Hundred Years War (1337–1453).[142] In the seventeenth century the Rohan family of the village of Josselin claimed that their lineage was more ancient than that of the kings of France, tracing their roots to the legendary Conan Meriadoc, who appears in the writings of Geoffrey of Monmouth.[143] According to Bachrach this illustrious ancestor reputedly cut out the tongues of the Alanic women and children (the men were executed) whom he captured "so that the strange barbarian speech from the steppes would not corrupt the purity of the conquerors' language."[144] Some scholars, however, argue that Meriadoc's barbaric treatment of the Alans is an onomastic legend rather than historical fact.[145] Historical evidence indicates that a number of Alans survived this violent conflict with the Celts, with the Celts slotting into the existing social system in Brittany below the level of the nobility.[146] Since at least some of these Alans appear to be ruling in the vicinity of Vannes throughout much of the Middle Ages, Meriadoc's people probably intermarried eventually with these powerful local Alans, if for no other reason than political expediency. Given the number of Alains in the Rohan line alone, this family at the very least seems to have adopted this practice.

Vannes was a center of continental rather than of insular Christianity.[147] The church at Vannes, dating from the seventh century, is older than those at Rennes and Nantes. It was founded by a Gallo-Frankish enclave in Breton territory. These

Gallo-Franks are said to be not Breton but from the "Pays de Galles."[148] Although this phrase is traditionally taken to mean "Wales," there is a strong possibility in this case, given the number of rulers of Vannes who bore the name Alan (see chaps. 3, 4, and 9), that this ruling family came from a much greater distance than Wales, namely the steppes. Their dialect is more Gallo-Roman than the other dialects derived from the insular British dialects, bearing similarity to the "occitan" dialect.[149] This odd fact indicates that the rulers of this region were not native Celtic speakers. Markale argues that Vannes was ruled by Celts, albeit under Roman influence from 56 B.C.E. onward. However, this was not the case.[150]

Alan, count of Vannes, a descendant of Goar's Alans and Alan Judual (see chap. 4), united these and other major cities of Brittany under his control before his death in 907. Alain Barbetorte defended these newly unified cities against raiders from the north, and his kinsman, Conan, founded a line of nobles in Brittany, many of whom bore the name Alan. One of the most famous of these descendants was Count[151] Alan the Red of Brittany, who in the eleventh century was one of the closest allies of William of Normandy.[152] Early in the Battle of Hastings he used the Alanic battle tactic of the feigned retreat.[153] Later in the encounter William copied the maneuver and won the battle. For his role Count Alan was singled out after the battle.[154]

Constance, daughter of William the Conqueror and wife of Alan IV (Fergant), count of Brittany, was buried in the cathedral of Rennes. In her sepulcher was found a cross that was inscribed:

> Here lies Constance, daughter of William, duke of Normandy, and wife of Alan, duke of Brittany, who departed from the living A.D. 1073.[155]

This line of Alan nobles survived until the marriage of Conan IV's heir, Constance, to Geoffrey, son of Henry II and Eleanor of Aquitaine, in 1181, well into the period when the Grail romances were written.[156]

Aside from being members of the nobility of the region, the Alans had a great impact on what would eventually become Norman and Breton chivalry. They introduced the highly praised steppe pony and the Alan hunting dog to the region.[157] The Alans' horses gave them great mobility and unpredictability in movement. Boys were trained to ride at a very early age, and the warrior spent most of his life on his horse.[158] The Alans were mounted spearmen who also fought with bows and arrows at a distance and lasso and sword at close range. Their war cry was a well-practiced battle tactic, as was their "feigned retreat," which was feared by the Roman generals. The "feigned-retreat" tactic occasionally was recorded as an actual retreat by chroniclers unfamiliar with this method of fighting (cf. the "cowardly" behavior of the Alans at the Battle of Châlons). The Alan dislike for fighting on foot also appears in Breton cavalry units at the Battle of Hastings, where the Breton units refused to dismount even though this was an accepted practice in medieval warfare.[159] Similarly Chrétien de Troyes has the knights remain mounted to fight with swords, a practice that the German author Hartmann von Aue (b. ca. 1155) finds "boorish."[160]

The connection between Arthur and Brittany was still strong in the twelfth century when Eleanor (Aliénor) of Aquitaine (with her Alan-style name) was championing the legends through her courts of love (see chap. 5).[161] In the Latin chronicle *Draco Normannicus*, by Étienne de Rouen (1169), Arthur is still alive in the twelfth century. He exchanges letters with Henry II in which the monarchs discuss the sovereignty of Brittany. Arthur eventually reserves final authority over Brittany, but he allows Henry to claim the feudal rights to the land as his vassal.[162] This seems to reflect the Alanic attitude toward other rulers on the Continent from Gallo-Roman times on: allowing Roman, Merovingian, Carolingian, French, and even British kings to rule over them while seeing themselves as having ultimate control over the land. This attitude can be seen in such figures as Lancelot, who shares the rule of his kingdom with Arthur.

The Southern Contingent. The history of the Alans of southern Gaul begins in the East, where they fought sometimes for and sometimes against the Romans. As scholars are beginning to point out, the very concept of distinguishing between "Romans" and "barbarians" in Late Antiquity is a bit absurd.[163] For example, the famous Visigothic Roman general Stilicho (d. 408) used a force of Huns, Alans, and Goths under the command of Sarus[164] to defeat Radagaisus (ca. 402).[165]

In the late fourth century Stilicho settled several tribes of Alans in Raetia and Noricum (the western portion of modern Switzerland near the sources of the Rhine and the Danube). These Alans were still practicing their native religion, and their descendants still spoke their own language as late as the sixth century. But by far Stilicho's most enduring alliance was with the Visigothic commander Alaric, who had under his command an important contingent of Alans. According to Stilicho's plan Alaric was supposed to take his troops to Gaul, defeat Constantine III of Britain, and drive out the Vandals and Respendial's Alans. He was then supposed to establish military bases at Mainz and Strasbourg.[166] Stilicho and Alaric both died before the plan could be put into effect. The usurper Constantine III of Britain chased the Vandals and Respendial's Alans into Spain. He pursued the barbarians, only to be defeated by the future emperor Constantius and beheaded (408). Athaulf,[167] Alaric's brother-in-law and successor, apparently tried to carry out the remainder of Stilicho's plan. An eyewitness, Paulinus Pellaeus (see chaps. 9 and 10), records that these Alans were among the barbarians who held him hostage at Bordeaux and that he later made a deal with them to support him against their Visigothic allies at Bazas. It was here, at Bazas in 414, that Athaulf ran afoul of this same Constantius. The Visigoths headed for Spain, where Constantius gave chase and ransomed Galla Placidia, shortly after the murder of Athaulf.

In 454 Valentinian III murdered Aëtius in Rome. The following year the Vandals under Gaiseric, with their Alan allies, used their sea power to sack Rome, and two of Aëtius's retainers, Optila and Thraustila, who are identified simply as "barbarians," assassinated Valentinian. Valerin, who captures Guinevere in an attempt to rape her in the *Lanzelet*, might be a representation of this emperor.[168]

Many of the Alan families in the region begin to rule bishoprics as early as the sixth century. With the collapse of the imperial government in Gaul bishops usually filled the political vacuum.[169] These bishops were generally drawn from the "office-holding families of the old Roman aristocracy,"[170] which by the mid-fifth century included the Alans of Gaul. There is an unbroken line of Alan rulers in both northern and southern

Gaul, in both the church and in the nobility, well into the period in which the Arthurian legends were composed.

It is thus probable that people descended from the Alans of Gaul, who preserved the name, armor, horse, dog, and fighting techniques of their ancestors, might have preserved a few ancient Alanic stories as well.[171]

The Alans in the East

The Alans were also influential in the eastern Roman Empire from the late fourth century. In 378 one tribe of Alans fought alongside the Goths in the assault against Emperor Valens.[172]

Several important figures in the eastern empire were related to Alans. Emperor Maximinus the Thracian (r. 235–238) had an Alan mother and a Gothic father.[173] The famous sixth-century eastern general Vitalian (died ca. 518) was a "Scythian," whose relative, a "Scythian" monk, bore the name Leontius.[174] The "Scythian" monks, who traveled to Constantinople in 519 under Leontius, were noted for their adherence to the "Scythian formula," which attempted to reconcile the differences between the Chalcedonians and the Monophysites by proclaiming that "*Unus ex trinitate passus carne*" ("One of the Trinity became flesh").[175]

In addition to physical relationships the Alanic culture influenced the eastern empire's traditions as well. Randers-Pehrson points out that "even Theodosius's heavenly supporters were hardly Roman. The apostles John and Philip came to him in a vision, on horseback like Gothic cavalrymen. Mounted saints were usually eastern, . . . but they were also enormously popular among the Copts."[176]

Perhaps the most important eastern Roman who figures in the Arthurian traditions is the emperor Leo I. With the death of Valentinian III and the series of short-lived emperors who followed him, Leo I, emperor of eastern Rome and his Alan general, Aspar, become the major obstacles to the "barbarian" invasions in history and to Arthur's claiming the crown of western Rome in legend.[177] Note that these traditions of eastern Romans in the Arthurian legends are known only in the West.

With the death of Aspar the Alanic influence in the East diminished. The result was that a buffer zone of sorts was raised between any western versions of Alanic stories, in their Arthurian or other forms, and the lands of Alania and its environs in the Caucasus (see map 10) where the legends of the Narts would flourish.

Ossetians

It remains for us to discuss the last remnants of the Alans in the East. Among the several small ethnic enclaves that have managed to survive in the northern foothills of the Caucasus Mountains is a curious people known as the Ossetians (see map 11). Although sharing in the Caucasic culture developed over the centuries by such immediate neighbors as the Kabardians, the Circassians, and the Georgians, the roughly half-million Ossetians[178] possess a unique culture and linguistic heritage, for they are the last living descendants of the Alano-Sarmatians to speak a Northeast Iranian dialect.[179] As we have seen, these people tell a cycle of legends, known as the Nart sagas, that bear a strong resemblance to Europe's Arthurian tradition. Although it is conceivable that the European Arthurian tradition diffused to the Caucasus Mountains, there is no evidence to justify this assumption.

We do know that certain Celtic tribes had penetrated the Danube area as early as the fifth century B.C.E.,[180] and another far-flung Celtic tribe, the Cotini, seems to have had some contact with the Germanic Quadi and possibly with the Sarmatians in the same general region at the end of the first century C.E.[181] Campbell argued that the legends claiming that the Celts descended from a people from the East Mediterranean were true.[182] It appears extremely doubtful, however, whether these eastern Celts could have transmitted the raw material from which the Ossetians later fashioned their heroic sagas, for the available evidence suggests that whatever their prototypes, the British legends about Arthur are not attested until at least the

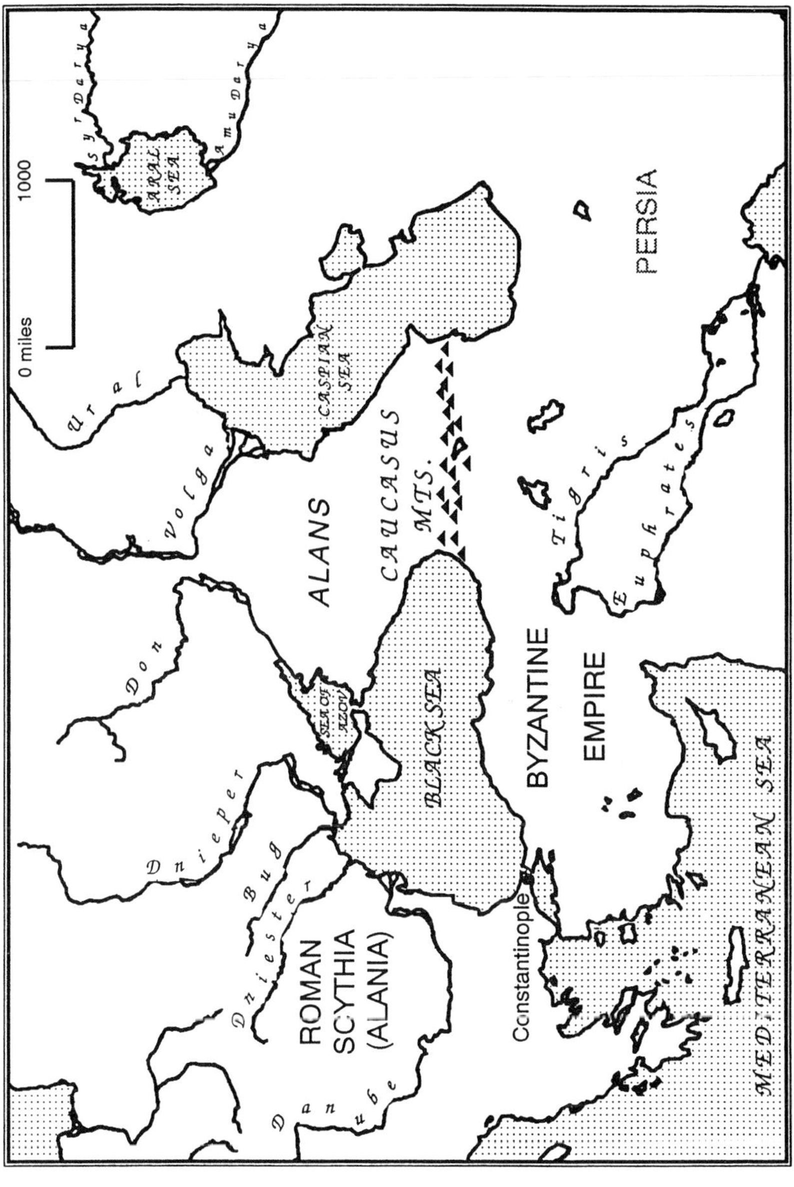

The Northeast Iranians

Map 10. Medieval Alania

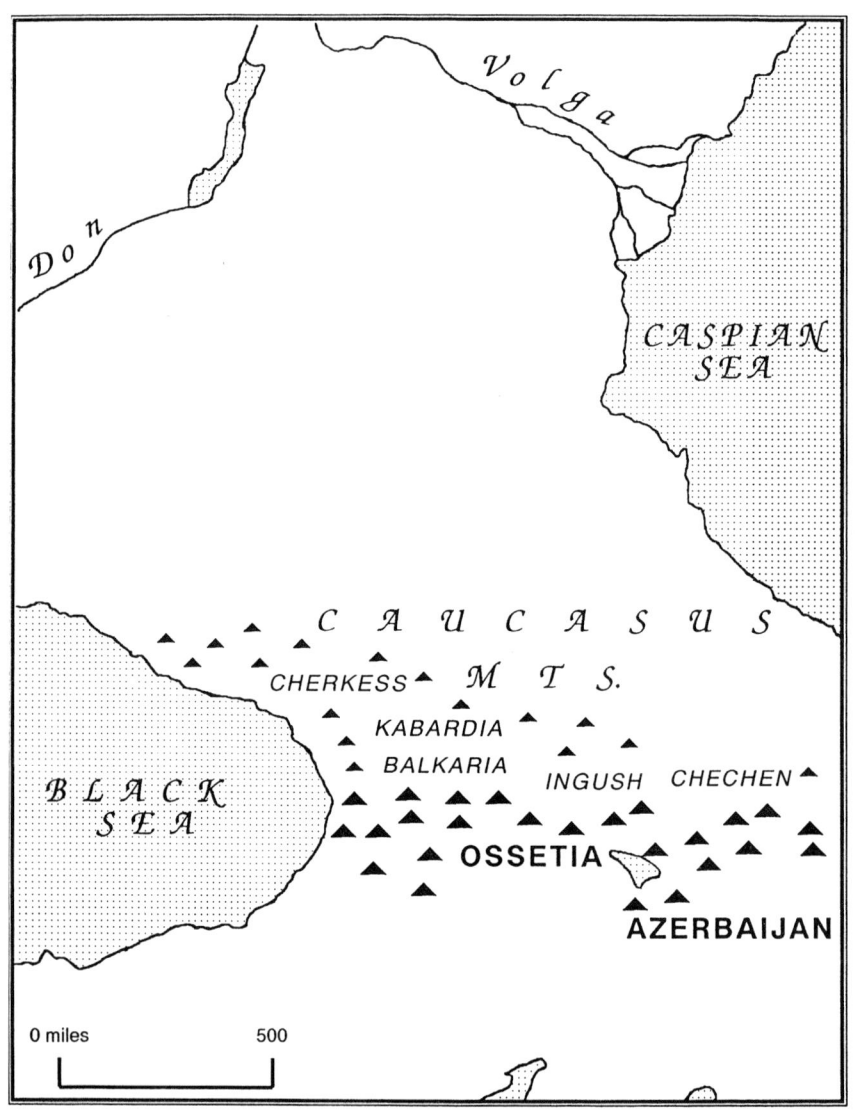

MAP 11. Modern Ossetia

fifth century. Such details as the story of Arthur's death, which so remarkably parallels the Ossetic account of the death of Batraz, had probably not yet evolved in Europe—let alone diffused to what was then the other end of the Celtic-speaking world—at the time the Cotini and other eastern Celts might have been in contact with some Sarmatians.[183]

There is also the remote possibility that some elements of the fully developed Arthurian tradition may have diffused to the Caucasus in the early Middle Ages, for we do know that these stories penetrated the German-speaking regions of central Europe at least by the beginning of the twelfth century, and there is an image of Arthur in the Cathedral of Otranto in southern Italy that can be dated to ca. 1050.[184] In the late 1200s the Dominicans sent missionaries into Armenia, Azerbaijan, Turkestan, India, and China.[185] Yet it is unlikely that these missionaries got up into the northern Caucasus region, and thus they almost certainly did not transmit the Arthurian legends to that territory.

But Ossetia is still a long way from central Europe, to say nothing of southern Italy, and if these stories did eventually reach the Caucasus one would expect to find evidence that they were known also to the medieval Slavs, Romanians, Georgians, and other Eastern European peoples who lived between the Germans and the Ossetians ca. 1000. To the best of our knowledge there is no such evidence. The immediate neighbors of the Ossetians all know some of the Nart sagas,[186] but the pattern of diffusion here clearly centers on Ossetia; just as the stories of King Arthur diffused from western to central and southern Europe in the early Middle Ages, so the stories of Batraz, Satana, Uryzmæg, and the rest seem to have diffused in fairly recent times throughout the Caucasus.

Having surveyed the background of the Northeast Iranian cultures, we are now in a position to examine several of the important parallels between the Arthurian and Ossetic traditions, beginning with the figures of Arthur and Batraz.

NOTES

1. Abaev 1960:1; Dumézil 1978:8; Comrie 1987:514. There is evidence that the Tokharians of Sinkiang, who also spoke an Indo-European language, were nomadic conquerors in Afghanistan and northwest India, but they do not seem to have traveled farther west (Mallory 1989:56–63, 263).

2. Sulimirski 1970:27–38.

3. This name derives from the name of the ancient Alans, the "Oss" or "Ass." Cf. *As-* (or *Az-*; cf. the Sea of Azov) and *Os-* (cf. modern Ossetian).

4. Gimbutas 1965:576–577.

5. Gimbutas 1965:576–577; Phillips 1965:45. The remains of timber-lining in graves date to as early as Yamnaya times (Jones-Bley, personal communication). The practice of building timber-lined graves persisted among the Scythians, Sarmatians, and Alans who follow the Timber-Grave Culture (Rolle 1980:19–37). The Hallstatt Celts also used this same method of timber-lining in their graves (Ross 1967:10).

6. Cf. Herodotus 4.21; de Sélincourt 1972:277.

7. Phillips 1965:54–55.

8. We are following the transliteration of this word as it appears in de Sélincourt (1972).

9. Herodotus 4; de Sélincourt 1972:271–340.

10. Herodotus did what amounted to "ethnographic fieldwork" among one or more Scythian communities located near the mouth of the Bug River, on the outskirts of the Greek colony of Olbia (see map 2).

11. Hudson 1964; Olcott 1987.

12. Chadwick 1970:38.

13. Nickel 1983:19–21.

14. E.g., Geoffrey of Monmouth's description of the arming of Arthur; Thorpe 1966:217.

15. Sulimirski 1970:151–152. The use of *tamgas* persists into the Middle Ages in Poland as heraldic devices (Sulimirski 1970:167). Nickel suggests that this type of equipment, which later became universal in Western Europe, was introduced not only by the Sarmatians settled in Britain (and presumably elsewhere in the Roman Empire, although we cannot yet account for the balance of the Iazygian auxiliaries recruited by Marcus Aurelius) but also by the several communities of Alans, close

relatives of the Sarmatians, that sprang up in Gaul and Spain in the fifth and sixth centuries (cf. the arming of Arthur [Thorpe 1966:217] and the arming of Lancelot [Webster 1951:29–30, ll. 302–388]). The toponyms Alençon and Catalunia (the latter of which derives from "Goth-Alania") both reflect the presence of these displaced steppe nomads (Nickel 1975b:152). Cf. the arming of Ferdia (Kinsella 1969:193), who, like Cūchulainn, fights either from a chariot or on foot.

16. Sulimirski 1970:176. For a discussion of the origin and evolution of *tamgas*, see Sulimirski 1970:151–154. For their influence on medieval Polish heraldry, see Nickel 1973, 1975a:12.

17. Herodotus 4.46; de Sélincourt 1972:286; Sulimirski 1970:26. The Franciscan friar William of Rubruk's description (quoted by Lamb 1943:42-43) of the Mongols (ca. 1250) provides a vivid picture of what life in a cart-dwelling, pastoral nomadic steppe culture, such as that of the ancient Sarmatians and the Alans, must have been like:

> The houses in which they [the Mongols] sleep are covered with white felt, over a framework of wattle rods. Sometimes the felt is brightened with paintings of vines and beasts. They are mounted upon wagon frames, and I measured the distance between the wheels of one to be twenty feet. I have counted twenty-two bullocks dragging one wagon house.
>
> ... The married women get the more beautiful carts made for them. One rich Mongol or Tartar will have from a hundred to two hundred such carts with chests.... When I met such a camp, on the move, I thought that a great city was traveling toward us. I was astonished at the immense droves of oxen and horse and flocks of sheep, though I saw very few men to herd them.

18. Newark 1989:9–30.

19. Herodotus 7.119; de Sélincourt 1972:480; cf. Sulimirski 1970:34.

20. Herodotus 4.59–62; de Sélincourt 1972:289–290.

21. This god's name is closely connected with that of the Ossetian hero Batraz (Dumézil 1978:214–216).

22. Herodotus 4.4–6; de Sélincourt 1972:272.

23. Some versions of this story list the second object as a bow (Lamberg-Karlovsky 1991:14). This second version survives in several of the Nart sagas (e.g., Dumézil 1930:67).

24. Herodotus 4.3–9; de Sélincourt 1972:272–273; Littleton 1982a:137–138.

25. Littleton 1982a:138.

26. The Alans continued to favor this style of art, and the Alanic invaders of Europe are credited with introducing such motifs into Gothic art (Wenskus in Beck et al. 1881:122).

27. Herodotus 4, passim; de Sélincourt 1972:271–340.

28. Cf. Harmatta 1950:38–40.

29. Colarusso (personal communication) has suggested that this may also be a reference to the Sarmatians' scaly armor. He has also suggested that the original name of these people meant "the free ones" (cf. Ossetic *særmae læg,* "free man," plural form *-tae*). Herodotus may have misheard an ethnic self-identification term similar to the hypothetical **særmatae* as the Greek Σαρμάτης ("Sauromatians"). Ethnic self-identification terms are nearly universal. The great majority include a form that translates to "the people" or something similar (e.g., Hopi, Navajo). Often there is an adjectival element that is almost always positive or boastful (e.g., Indo-European *Árya*, or "the Free People" [whence Ossetic *Iron*, etc.]; Puhvel 1987:45; Pokorny 1959, 1:24). In South America we have the Yanomamö, whose name Chagnon (1983) translates as "the Fierce People." Thus Colarusso's speculation regarding the indigenous term that spawned Herodotus's "Sauromatae" makes perfect sense.

30. Colarusso (personal communication) has suggested that this name derives from *Ruxš-ālānī,* White Alans."

31. E.g., the famous medieval illumination depicting Arthur and his knights riding to battle under a dragon banner; see plate 4. For a discussion of the Sarmatian *draconarius,* i.e., the bearer of the dragon banner, see Dixon and Southern 1992:60-61.

32. Vernadsky 1963:401–434.

33. E.g., Wenskus in Beck et al. 1881:122; Ozols in Beck et al. 1881:124.

34. Colarusso (personal communication) has suggested that "Alan" is simply the Northeast Iranian reflex of "Aryan." As such he sees "Alan" as late in its appearance, with "Sarmatian" and similar names as early tribal designations.

35. Such names do not appear in abundance in Britain until after the Norman Conquest. Two saints named Alan are noted in Northumbria, and one St. Alun was known in Wales. To our knowledge ancient and medieval Celtic languages contain no nouns that could have

given rise to such names. The verb *allan* ("I may be able") appears in Old Cornish and is a mutation from *gallan* (Williams 1865:5). The Old Cornish adverb *alena* ("from that place") is a compound form (*a*—"from"; *le*—"place"; *na*—"there"; Williams 1865:5), but this could hardly account for the inscription by "Elainus" ("Alan"; Collingwood and Wright 1965:#2321) on Hadrian's Wall. St. Alun's name derives from the Celtic *alun* ("harmony"; Withycombe 1947:6) and has nothing to do with the name Alan. So "Alan" appears only in the northern portions of Britain, those regions that were impacted by the Iazyges, and in the family lines of Cornwall that intermarried with the Alans of Brittany, until after the Norman Conquest, when the name became popular in Britain because of the appointment of Breton nobles named Alan to estates throughout Britain. From this and other evidence we suggest that the name Alan as it appears in Britain derives from Alano-Sarmatian sources rather than from a Celtic source.

36. Sulimirski 1970:26.

37. Sulimirski 1970:171; see also Phillips 1965:98.

38. Pekkanen (1973:60) documents the persistence of a Iazygian community in Hungary until the fifteenth century, although by that time it seems to have merged with the dominant Magyar society.

39. Sulimirski 1970:173–174; see plate 1.

40. In another possible example of the interchangeability of "Sarmatian," "Alan," "Roxolani," and so on, Hadrian named his horse "Borysthenes Alanus" (i.e., "Borysthenes the Alan"; Colafrancesco and Massaro 1986:69; Bachrach 1973:10) even though he was fighting Sarmatians and Roxolani.

41. Sulimirski 1970:175, pl. 45.

42. Dio 72.22.16; Cary 1927:35. A "second king," whom Zanticus had apparently deposed, was called Banadaspes, or "Leader of Horses" (cf. chap. 3).

43. Dio 72.22.16; Cary 1927:35.

44. Richmond 1945; see fig. 3 and map 5; cf. Edwards and Webster 1985–1987.

45. Alcock 1971:174; Blair 1963:63; see chap. 2; cf. chap. 3.

46. That is, a variant form of "Bremetennacum veteranorum." The *Notitia Dignitatum* (300s) refers to the garrison at Bremetennacum as "cuneus Sarmatarum," which seem to have replaced the earlier designation "numerus Sarmatarum," as found in a third-century inscription. See Richmond 1945:21.

47. Richmond 1945:16, 29.

48. Hübner 1873:58, no. 218; cf. Seeck 1876:212 n. 31; Collingwood and Wright 1965, 1:194–195; see map 5 and fig. 4; i.e., "[Dedicated to] Gordian by the troop of Sarmatian cavalrymen [stationed at] Bremetennacum" (translation ours).

49. Richmond 1945:17.

50. See plate 3; Richmond 1945:17; Sulimirski 1970:175–176. The passage as it appears in *Corpus Inscriptionum Latinarum* 7, no. 230 (Hübner 1873:61) reads:

> Ribchester. Their is of it the picture of an naked man ridinge on horsebacke withoute sadle and bridle, houldinge a speare in bothe his handes, the lefte hande before. Under the horse feets lyeth a naked man, his face upward, the horse havinge his nar forefoote upon the mans heade and the man houldeth his right hand up towards the man on horsebacke and in his lefte hand houldeth a square like unto a booke shutt. Betweene the horsebelly and the naked man are these twoe lettres viz:
>
> D   M
>
> and under the naked mans bodie, which lyethe from his feete towardes his lefte hand, which houldethe the square like unto a booke, are these lettres, as the seemed unto us, viz:
>
> GAL: SARMATA
>
> and under those lettres lower on the stone it semeth their have been more lettres, which nowe cannot be knowen.
>
> Thom. Braithwaite, 'Lancaster 18 of Ianuarie 1604' in cod. mas. Brit. Cotton Iulius FVI f.287 (inde Camden ed. VI [1607] p. 615 qui titulum et anaglyphum similiter prorsus, sed brevius, describit; ex Camdeno Just *assoc. journ.* 6, 1851, p. 233). Apparet titulum fuisse anaglypho solio ornatum positumque
>
> d(is) M(anibus) hominis alicuius, qui fuit [eq(ues)] al(ae) Sarmata[rum].

51. Richmond 1945:17.

52. Sulimirski (1970:176) suggests that Bremetennacum survived into the fifth century, the time of the historical King Arthur; see chap. 2.

53. Alcock 1971:174.

54. See Malcor 1999.
55. Sulimirski 1970:176.
56. This battle is referred to by various authors as taking place at Badon Hill, Mount Badon, and other variations on the name Badon. We will refer to it simply as the Battle of Badon.
57. Littleton and Thomas 1978:522–523.
58. E.g., Goodrich 1986.
59. Nennius 4.56; Brengle 1964:5–6.
60. Alcock 1971:22; Morris 1980:39.
61. Jackson 1969:112.
62. E.g., Meyer 1956:36.
63. Charvet 1967:25.
64. Bachrach 1973:136.
65. Collingwood and Wright 1965; nos. 2321 and 594–595.
66. Ibid., no. 1603.
67. The Scottish surname Allan could have derived from the Gaelic name Ailín (Edgar Polomé, personal communication); however, for the specific families that we are discussing in this book, the name was introduced into Scotland by nobles from the Continent who received land grants from William the Conqueror following the Norman invasion.
68. Weston 1906–1909, 2:333–334. *Fergus et Galienne* was written ca. 1200–1233 by Guillaume le Clerc [Romatus and de Haan 1976; Frescoln 1983], who is not to be confused with the author of the *Bestiaire*.
69. Weston 1906–1909, 2:333–334, n. 2.
70. Nitze and Jenkins 1932–1937:3. This would make him a descendant of the younger brother of Count Conan, father of Constance, who was the wife of Geoffrey of Anjou and mother of Prince Arthur. He may actually be the descendant of Scolland of Richmond, *dapifer*, or steward, of Alain the Black (Alan II), earl of Richmond, who received Bedale in 1190 from Alain Fergant (Markale 1989:113; Nitze and Jenkins 1932–1937, 2:4–5; Clay 1921:281–290). Alan Fergant was best known for defending Dol, a city long protected by Alan families, against William the Conqueror. He was married to Constance as part of the peace settlement (Douglas 1964:402).
71. Robinson 1935:22; Nitze and Jenkins 1932–1937, 2:4–5, 7; Clay 1921:281–290.

72. Examples of the name are found in other families at later periods as well. Bogdanow (Loomis 1959:541–542) has noted that Vinaver (1959:541–542) believed a certain John Aleyn of Essex to be a "friend and accomplice" of Sir Thomas Malory.

73. Ammianus Marcellinus 31.2.2; Rolfe 1939, 3:391. For a recent overview of Alan history and culture, see Kouznetsov and Lebedynsky 1997.

74. Ammianus Marcellinus 31.2.18; Rolfe 1939:391.

75. Ammianus Marcellinus 31.2.20; Rolfe 1939:393.

76 Cf. Ammianus Marcellinus 31.2.20; Rolfe 1939:393.

77. Bachrach 1973:36; cf. Hollister 1982:55.

78. Intermarriage between Arthur's people and the Roman soldiers is acknowledged in the legends as well. Cador, whose son Constantine succeeds Arthur, appears as the cousin of Guinevere through his mother (who was of Roman blood; see Rhys 1928:54).

79. In the seventh century some Alans of Brittany were still speaking their mother tongue (Bachrach 1973:80; Chadwick 1965:270–273; Fleuriot 1958:164 ff.; Jackson 1953:27–30; cf. Plaine 1882, 1:222). By the tenth century Cartulaire de Llandaff wrote of the Bretons of Gaul and Armorica as "*unis nationis et unius linguae*" (Marx 1965:78–79), but families still tended to name their sons Alan and to call some locations by their Alanic names.

80. Wallace-Hadrill 1962:30; Bachrach 1973:79.

81. Markale 1983a:11, 58–59.

82. Claudius Marius Victor, *Alethia*, ll. 189–200; Schenkl 1888:335–498; Bachrach 1973:31–32.

83. Randers-Pehrson 1983:245.

84. Randers-Pehrson 1983:245.

85. Not to be confused with Augustine of Hippo.

86. Hollister 1982:63. St. Patrick's mission to Ireland took place in 463 (Charvet 1967:29). Some newly converted Alans may have been among these missionaries. Ireland's mission to the Continent, and hence the influx of Celtic influence on the continental church, did not take place until the 600s (Hollister 1982:58). Anglo-Saxon Benedictine missionaries from Northumbria journeyed back to the Continent in the 740s (Hollister 1982:66), carrying with them the learning of the Northumbrian Renaissance, and possibly some Iazygian-influenced legends as well (e.g., the two saints Alan who journeyed to southern Gaul).

St. Patrick himself was born in Britain near a Romano-British village called Bannaventa Burniae or Bannavem Taburniae (cf. the discussion of *ban* in chap. 3). Some scholars have argued that this village was in the north of Britain on the Irish Sea (e.g., Thompson 1985:9–10) or on a river that flowed into the Irish Sea (e.g., Hanson 1968:113; cf. the Iazygian veterans' settlement on the Ribble River). Thompson (1985:25–31) also argues that after Patrick escaped from the pirates who captured him as a boy and took him to Ireland, the future saint trained at the monasteries in Gaul. These monasteries would have had extensive contact with the Alan invaders of Gaul, and several Alans entered monastic orders as they converted to Christianity (e.g., St. Goar; see chaps. 9 and 10). Whether or not Patrick acquired Alans among his missionaries, he almost certainly had contact with the Alans of Gaul during his training, just as he may have had contact with the Iazyges of northern Britain during his youth.

87. Goffart 1980:6, 7 n. 5; cf. Maenchen-Helfen 1973:5–9.

88. Gregory of Tours in Krusch and Levison 1951, 1/1:55; Zosimus 6.3.1 in Mendelssohn 1887:284; Orosius in Raymond 1936:387; Bachrach 1973:52. These Alans are not to be confused with the Iazyges of that region.

89. Wenskus in Beck et al. 1881:123.

90. The Vandals, who invaded Gaul with the Alans, were granted land in Aquitaine by the emperor Honorius. By 428 these Vandals were a maritime power, especially after 422, when Valentinian III recognized the Vandal king as an independent ruler. In 455 the Vandals used their sea power to sack Rome. Perhaps the Alanic contact with this horseriding-turned-seafaring people accounts in part for the associations of Lancelot with the Lady of the Sea (see chaps. 3 and 5).

91. Constantine, who was murdered in 411, figures as Arthur's grandfather in many legends; see Cavendish 1978:27. He is said to have had three sons: Constans, Ambrosius, and Uther. Constans was said to be a monk who was called out of a monastery to lead Constantine's troops on the Continent. The historical Constans was killed shortly after the death of Constantine of Britain (although the legend assigns his death to the hands of Vortigern). Ambrosius and Uther, according to the legend, were raised by King Ban on the Continent then sent back to Britain to reclaim the lands Vortigern had taken from Constantine. A Roman general, Ambrosius Aurelianus, does emerge in a position of power in Britain several years after the death of Constantine of Britain and just prior to the appearance of Riothamus, the best candidate for the historical King Arthur (Ashe 1985:33–34; see chap. 2).

92. Alans under the command of Gerontius allowed Respendial's Alans to escape through the passes in the Pyrenees into Spain. The Alans of Spain remained a vital force for at least the next century and perhaps longer. Isidore of Seville (Donini and Ford 1966:30) saw the Goths of Spain and Gaul as descendants of the Scythians. There is some evidence for his position, given the extensive contact and frequent alliances between the Gothic and the Alano-Sarmatian tribes. Isidore (Donini and Ford 1966:32) also said that "by the strength of the Goths the Alani were annihilated," but the truth seems to be that the Alans simply moved on or settled among and blended with the other peoples of Gaul and Spain. Some of the Alans joined Gaiseric's forces and invaded Africa. The majority of the Alans who invaded Gaul and Spain, however, eventually became part of the nobility of those regions.

The Alans traveling with the Vandals continued to have a pronounced impact on the history of Rome. But in 421 the emperor Constantius III, who should not be confused with the usurper Constantine III of Britain (d. 411), died and the western Roman Empire passed to the regency of Honorius's sister (Constantius's widow), Galla Placidia, until Constantius's son, Valentinian III, could be crowned. It was under this regency that the Vandals acquired their maritime power. At the same time Aëtius emerged as the leader of the Roman troops in Gaul, including the Alan *laeti*.

93. The Romans granted the Alans land and the right to levy taxes. Because of this policy the Alans of Gaul found their way into Roman politics, and when the feudal system developed the Alans became members of the French nobility (Bachrach 1973:117; Goffart 1980:111–114).

94. E.g., Levison 1920:271, chapter 28 passim. See also Borius 1965. According to Colarusso (personal communication) Goar was probably spelled **Gahwar* or **Gaxwar*. The *h* would then shift to *th* in a Celtic dialect, rendering something like **Gathwar*, which through usage could become Eothar. Eothar has also been rendered as Eochar, an Alan king of Armorica at the time of Aëtius (Wenskus in Beck et al. 1881:123), who may or may not be indentical with Goar.

95. Ashe 1985:52–54.

96. Lacy et al. 1986:453–455. Bromwich (1960:464–466) has argued that the name Erec and its variants (such as Euric) derive ultimately from the Alanic name Goeric. Names ending in "-ric" probably reflect the Old Germanic *ric* ("king"; cf. Latin *rex*, Sanskrit *raja*, Celtic *rix*); hence "Goeric" may have meant "King Goar."

97. Cf. Lacy et al. 1986:453–455.

98. The tribes probably came from the vicinity of Denmark; Randers-Pehrson 1983:190.

99. Wolfram 1988:238; Wenskus in Beck et al. 1881:123.

100. Randers-Pehrson 1983:190; Bachrach 1973:32, 84; Goffart 1980:112. The Latin reads "Deserta Valentinae urbis rura Alanis, quibus Sambiba praeerat, partienda traduntur" (*Chronica Gallica* of 452, Mommsen 1892, 9:660, sec. a. 440).

101. Goffart 1980:112–113. The antagonist in *Sir Gawain and the Green Knight* is Bercilak de Haut Desert. Lancelot's best friend in many of the texts is Galehaut le Haut Desert (also called "le Haut Prince," "the High Prince").

102. Goffart 1980:111–114.

103. Hollister 1982:54.

104. Bachrach 1973:62–64; Goffart 1980:111–114.

105. Goffart 1980:112.

106. The Vandals and their Alan allies are said to have numbered about 50,000, later numbering at least 80,000 in Africa alone (Procopius 3.3.5.80-125; Dewing 1916, 2:53).

107. The Latin reads: "Alani, quibus terrae Galliae ulterioris cum incolis dividendae a patricio Aetio traditae fuerant, resistentes armis subigunt et expulsis dominis terrae possessionem vi adipiscutur" (*Chronica Gallica* of 452, Mommsen 1892, 9:660, sec. a. 442). The region of Armorica did not receive the name Brittany until after the sixth-century Celtic settlements of natives of Britain who were fleeing from the invading Saxons.

108. Randers-Pehrson 1983:126–127; Bachrach 1973:64.

109. E.g., Loomis 1963b:14.

110. Randers-Pehrson 1983:163; Wenskus in Beck et al. 1881:123.

111. Cf. Sambiba and cf. the discussion of *ban* in chap. 3.

112. Aegidius was the Roman military commander of northern Gaul 457–461.

113. These were among a series of factories that included Mâcon, Autun, Trier, Reims, and Amiens; Randers-Pehrson 1983:255.

114. Randers-Pehrson 1983:255.

115. These cicadas were "the ancestors of Napoleon's bees"; Randers-Pehrson 1983:260.

116. One fictional genealogy (late 500s-early 600s) lists Syagrius as a descendant of "Primus rex Romanorum Allanius" (Kurth 1893:87, 96,

517–523; Bachrach 1973:85). While the presence of Alans in Syagrius's family tree can not be proven (though, given the Alanic practice of intermarriage with their allies, this is not improbable), Syagrius inherited the command of the Amorici, who included descendants of Goar's Alans, from his father (Kurth 1893:521; Bachrach 1973:77; Junghans 1879:12–15; Lair 1898:3–29).

117. Randers-Pehrson 1983:255.

118. The truth was quite the opposite; Krusch 1888:242–243; Bachrach 1973:84–85.

119. Bachrach 1973:5; Randers-Pehrson 1983:261–262.

120. E.g., Alan Judual.

121. E.g., Goeric aka Bishop Abbo; Krusch 1888:440, 442–443; Bachrach 1973:96; see chaps. 9 and 10. The Franks and the Alans of Armorica were hostile toward each other (e.g., Alan Judual's imprisonment by Childebert I; Bachrach 1973:84).

122. See pertinent articles in Delaney 1980.

123. Lacy et al. 1986:64.

124. The whole case for this depends on the assumption that a large British force that operated in Gaul ca. 468–470, was recruited in Armorica, implying a large British population there; but records indicate that most if not all of this army came directly from Britain.

125. Hollister 1982:55. A great famine struck Europe in 791 as well, driving many peasants to cannibalism and further depopulating the countryside (Hollister 1982:82–83). Thus finding land for people to settle on was not a problem in the Middle Ages. Finding living, breathing people to settle on the land was.

126. Hollister 1982:33.

127. Hollister 1982:55.

128. E.g., Mark Conomor.

129. Markale 1989:56.

130. Markale 1989:64.

131. Markale 1989:110. This Alain is identified as "the brother of Paskweten" simply to distinguish him from the other Alains in Brittany at this time. Paskweten is simply a Breton noble.

132. Markale 1989:95–96.

133. Curiously, Nascien, in the manuscripts of the *Estoire del Saint Graal* that were derived from Robert de Boron's *Joseph*, believed that if his warriors died in battle, they would go to heaven (Lovelich 1874–

1905, 2:161). Cf. the Germanic tradition in which only warriors who died in battle were eligible to be brought by the Valkyries to Valhalla.

134. Ammianus Marcellinus 31.2.5; Rolfe 1939:383; Bachrach 1973:21.

135. Dumézil 1978:262–272.

136. E.g., Bishop Abbo.

137. Markale 1989:110.

138. Markale 1989:89.

139. Markale 1983:53–62. Keep in mind that just because a region may have been converted to a Celtic form of Christianity does not mean that all of the Christians in that area were Celts.

140. Markale 1989:89–90.

141. Markale 1989:62.

142. Alain IX also built the Château of Josselin; Saintsbury 1922, 4:100–101; Markale 1989:62.

143. "Cynan Merdiawg au Pays de Galles"; Geoffrey of Monmouth 5.9–16; Thorpe 1966:134–144.

144. Bachrach 1973:112. Cf. Geoffrey of Monmouth, chaps. 81–88, 92, 115, 194, in Faral 1929: 154–164, 168–169, 194–195, 290–291; Le Moyne de la Borderie 1883: preface, 2–3.

145. E.g., Lacy 1980:64.

146. Hollister 1982:55.

147. Markale 1989:90.

148. Markale 1989:90.

149. I.e., Langue d'Oc, or Provençal; Markale 1989:63, 90–91.

150. Markale 1989:91–92.

151. There is endless confusion in the records of Brittany as to the appropriate title for the Alans in this family. Roughly half of the records call them "counts," while the rest (including the gravestone of William of Normandy's daughter) call them "dukes." "Duke" was most likely still being used in the military sense of a leader of battles (cf. Latin *dux*, as in *dux bellorum*, the title given to Arthur by Nennius), while "count" was the correct political designation for these figures. In most cases we have chosen "count" over "duke" because of this confusion.

152. William of Normandy himself had been tutored in battle tactics by Count Alan III of Brittany (Douglas 1964:37). In addition to Alan III three other Alans from this family were contemporaries of William the

Conqueror: Alan I (the Red), earl of Richmond; Alan II (the Black), earl of Richmond; and Alan IV (Fergant) of Brittany.

153. William of Poitiers in Foreville 1952:195, 2.21; Lemmon (1966:94) argues that Count Brian led this retreat. However, most scholars (e.g., Wright 1986 and Douglas 1964:199) agree that Alan the Red was the count who led the contingent of Bretons in the battle. Furneaux (1966:209) points out that Brian (Brient de Brettagne), according to the Falaise Roll, was the count of Vannes, which had been ruled by Alan families since Gallo-Roman times.

154. Geffrei Gaimar in Bell 1860:168–169, ll. 5309–5312; Bachrach 1973:92. Alan the Red became one of the two non-Norman lords to receive a heavy settlement of land from William following the invasion. Alan was granted at least four hundred manors (positioned in eleven different shires in England). He also received Yorkshire, Lincolnshire, East Anglia, and lands in the southwest (probably Cornwall). His most significant possession was Richmond, where he reigned as earl until his death in 1093.

155. Le Roux de Lincy 1840:253–254. The Latin reads:

> Hîc jacet Constantia filia Guillelmi/Ducis
> Normanniae et conjux Alani/Ducis Britanniae,
> quaer è vivis/Discessit anno Domini millesimo
> septuagesimo tertio.

156. Warren 1973:563.

157. For pictorial representations of the Alan hunting dog see Woods-Marsden 1988:pl. 60, 62, and 127.

158. Ammianus Marcellinus 31.2.20; Rolfe 1939:393.

159. Some leaders eventually gave up trying to get the Bretons to conform and ordered them to remain mounted—saving face for both parties.

160. Sparnaay in Loomis 1959:430–442.

161. Markale 1982:43, 102; Frappier 1977:230. This also appears as a male name. In *Les Sept Sages de Rome* Laurin travels under the name Alyenor to rescue Baudemagus.

162. Howlett 1855, 2:589 ff.

163. E.g., Randers-Pehrson 1983:3–4.

164. Sarus was a sworn enemy of Alaric; given his reptilian name, he may have been Sarmatian; cf. the discussion of "Sauromatae."

165. Randers-Pehrson 1983:100.

The Northeast Iranians 57

166. Randers-Pehrson 1983:109.

167. This commander of the Alans and Goths that sacked Rome later killed Sarus because of the Goth's feud with Alaric (Randers-Pehrson 1983:117).

168. Paton 1929:13.

169. Hollister 1982:26.

170. Hollister 1982:26.

171. Bachrach 1973:74ff.

172. Randers-Pehrson 1983:49.

173. "Maximini Duo," ll. 1.5, 2.1, 2.5, 4.4–5, 9.3–6 in Hohl 1927:3–5; Bachrach 1973:13–17, 44; Grant 1985:137–139.

174. Randers-Pehrson 1983:205–206. Note the similarity between this name and that of Guinevere's father, Leodegrance, both of which seem to contain the root for "lion."

175. Randers-Pehrson 1983:205–206; cf. The Gospel of St. John 1:14. Unless otherwise specified all Biblical references are to the 1899 Douay version.

176. Randers-Pehrson 1983:78. As, for example, St. George of Merrie England; cf. Uastyrdži ("Saint George") in the Nart sagas; (Dumézil 1930:24–25) and the mounted image of St. George on the recently restored Russian national crest.

177. Malory 5.12 in Cowen 1969, 1:190–193; Wenskus in Beck et al. 1881:123.

178. Comrie (1981:164) states that in 1970 there were 488,038 Ossetians in what was then the U.S.S.R. Wixman (1984:152) sets the population at 541,893 in 1979. These people currently live in North Ossetia, which is part of the Russian Republic, and South Ossetia, which is part of Georgia (Rothstein 1954; see map 11).

179. For a discussion of the Ossetian language (i.e., "Ossete") see Comrie (1981:164), Benveniste (1959), and Abaev (1960). For a discussion of the history of the Alans in the Caucasus, from the Kingdom of the Alans (tenth and eleventh centuries), through the Mongol period(thirteen and fourteenth centuries), to modern times and the emergence of the Ossetians as an ethnic group, see Kouznetsov and Lebedynsky 1997, especially pp. 79-154.

180. Chadwick 1970:52–53.

181. Hubert 1974:164.

182. Campbell 1860–1862:298–299.

183. For a discussion of the Celtic penetration of western Romania (fourth to second centuries B.C.E.) see Zirra 1976:1–42.

184. Gianfreda 1965.

185. Cf. Loenertz 1932:1–83.

186. E.g., the Kabardians, Armenians, Georgians, and especially the Circassians. Cf. Abaev 1949.

PART II

Figures

CHAPTER 2

Arthur and the Sarmatian Connection

Early traditions of King Arthur were mainly oral and were probably built on a historical foundation. The pieces of scattered evidence, however, do not add up to much. From the outset there has been an assumption that at least part of the Arthurian legends reflect some historical truth. Paton notes that Wace (1152), who claims to have heard the story of the Round Table from the Bretons, thought that the legends of Arthur were "not all lies, nor all true, all foolishness, nor all sense; so much have the storytellers told, and so much have the makers of fables fabled to embellish their stories that they have made all seem fable."[1]

Camelot is first mentioned in the *Conte de la charrette* (1179),[2] by Chrétien de Troyes, who places Arthur's court in Brittany.[3] Yet it has long been recognized that the historical Arthur dates to an earlier period, with his court supposedly located somewhere in Britain. The *Annales Cambriae* (*Welsh Annals*) dates the Battle of Camlann twenty-one years after Arthur's most famous battle, which took place near somewhere called Badon (518 C.E.).[4] Albericus Trium Fontium (1227–1251) makes an allusion to a possible historical Arthur called Riothamus and sets the dates for the legendary British king at 454–470, as do the thirteenth-century *Salzburg Annals*, Martinus Polonus (ca. 1275), Jacques de Guise (late 1300s), and Philippe de Vigneulles (1525).[5]

By far the most famous source for the Arthurian tradition is Geoffrey of Monmouth's *Historia Regum Britanniae* (*History of the Kings of Britain*; completed ca. 1136), which survives in Cambridge University Library MS 1706.[6] Geoffrey (d. 1154–1155) was from southeast Wales, but he exhibits interest in Brittany and a pro-Breton bias, which suggests that his family came from across the Channel, as numerous Bretons did in the wake of the Norman Conquest. His sources include Gildas, Nennius, Bede, probably the *Annales Cambriae*, and "a certain very ancient book written in the British language," which he claims to be translating and which was given to him by Archdeacon Walter.[7] Perhaps Geoffrey's most important contribution to the legends is the portrait of Arthur as a Gallic conqueror, which has no Welsh antecedents.[8] Geoffrey places the British king as contemporary with the eastern Roman emperor Leo I (r. 457–474), and he sets Arthur's death at 542.[9] Geoffrey could have meant 470 if his primary source for his chronology used Victorius of Aquitaine (who counts years from Christ's Passion).[10] Dates in other sources are similarly confused. The Breton *Legend of St. Goeznovius* and some chronicle references reckon the dates for Arthur's period from the Passion. Henry of Huntingdon's *Historia Anglorum* (ca. 1129)[11] includes a vague account of Arthur, which is placed between 527 and 530.[12] The Breton *Chronicon Montis Sancti Michaelis in Periculo Maris* (*Chronicle of Mont-Saint-Michel*)[13] dates Arthur to 421.

With these dates in mind we see several candidates for a historical King Arthur emerge from the shadows of late antiquity—strangely enough, in the company of Alans and Sarmatians.

The Historical King Arthur

The Welsh name Arthyr is derived from the Roman Artorius. While no Artorius is attested at the time in which Arthur is said to have lived (ca. 500), there is some reason to suspect that the name Arthur itself, which has always posed problems from the standpoint of Celtic etymology,[14] derived from the name of the Roman commander to whom the Iazgyes were initially assigned: Lucius Artorius Castus, prefect of the VI Legion Victrix, which was charged with defending the northern frontier against the depredations of the Picts and other Caledonian tribes living beyond Hadrian's Wall.[15] A career soldier of the equestrian class who hailed from Campania,[16] Castus had served in Upper Pannonia and was intimately acquainted with the fighting abilities of his new Izaygian recruits.[17] The evidence both from Ribchester, Chester, and several camps along the Wall where these *numeri* served in detachments from the main unit stationed at Bremetennacum,[18] indicates that they were well treated and most likely formed a special unit within the local military system. When Castus was appointed prefect of Bremetennacum the Iazyges came to idolize him, with several of them choosing either "Lucius" or "Castus" as a cognomen when they obtained their citizenship.[19]

As we noted in the Introduction, in 185 or 186, Lucius Artorius Castus led elements of the VI Legion Victrix and the XX Legion Valeria Victrix to Armorica, where he put down a local rebellion.[20] For this expedition Castus was appointed to the office of *dux*,[21] just as the Arthur who led British troops to the Continent in some accounts is said to have been a *dux bellorum*.[22] This continental expedition, which almost certainly included several troops of Iazyges armored cavalry, seems to have conflated with the more extensive overseas adventures of Riothamus (see below). In other words, the fifth century British leader may have been hailed as a "second Artorius."[23] Some years later, after Castus had been posted to Dalmatia as *procurator centenarius* of Liburnia,[24] he probably accompanied Emperor Septimius Severus to Gaul in 196-197 to fight against British cavalry, who included some of his former Iazygan troops.[25] These events may have given rise to tales of Arthur's two invasions of Gaul, the second of which was a civil war. [26]

While all this is largely speculative, the fact that the Sarmatians first Roman commander bore a name identical with the "Latinized" form of the name Arthur would not seem to be fortuitous. Military forces of the late Roman period were sometimes known by the names of their leaders.[27] There is evidence that a group called "Arthur's Men may have continued as a war band after the historical Arthur's death in the chronicles and other sources.[28] In any case, the name Arthur is probably a "Celticization" of Artorius, [29] and not vice versa.

Another historical figure who contributed to the legendary portrait of Arthur was Maximus, who was proclaimed emperor in Britain in 383. He captured Rome in 388 and granted land on the Continent to Britons in his army.[30] In the *Mabinogi*[31] Maximus marries the British princess Elen and gives Armorica to her brother Cynan (i.e., Conan Meriadoc, according to the *Legend of St. Goeznovius*).[32] It is interesting, however, that here we have an Elen associated with Brittany, which was famous for its dukes and counts named Alan.[33]

One promising candidate for the historical King Arthur is a shadowy figure known only as Riothamus, or "High King."[34] Letters from Sidonius to this Riothamus still survive.[35] A monk of Uriscampum (i.e., Orcamp; ca. 1175) was the first to suggest that Arthur was Riothamus.[36] Other sources, which do not always mention Riothamus by name, that are used to support this hypothesis are Geoffrey of Monmouth,[37] Jordanes,[38] and Gregory of Tours.[39] Some scholars, including Fleuriot, have identified Ambrosius Aurelius (Uther Pendragon's brother in some Arthurian texts and an actual Roman general in history) as Riothamus, but there is no real evidence for this.[40]

According to Geoffrey of Monmouth, Arthur's antagonist during the continental invasion was "Leo, emperor of Rome."[41] This is odd, since the eastern Roman emperor at the time of Riothamus was in fact Leo I, who was supported by the famous Alanic general Aspar.[42] In 467 Leo I appointed Anthemius, a Byzantine noble, as his western colleague, and Anthemius negotiated a British alliance, as a result of which the "king of the Britons," Riothamus, came to Gaul in 468 "by the way of Ocean" with 12,000 ship-borne troops.[43] This "king" led his troops in a series of battles on the Continent that penetrated into the heart of the region that serves as the setting for the legends of Lancelot (see map 12).[44] Temporarily stationed north of the Loire, he possibly led his troops against the Saxons near Angers. Riothamus next led his troops to Berry and occupied Bourges. Sidonius wrote to the Briton king on behalf of a landowner whose slaves the Britons were enticing away.[45] In response Riothamus moved his troops to Déols near Châteauroux. Arvandus, Gaul's imperial prefect, wrote to Euric (King of the Visigoths, r. 466–484),[46] inciting him to crush Riothamus's troops and to divide Gaul with the Burgundians. The *Chronicles of Anjou* give Arthur's betrayer as Morvandus. This form of the name may be a conflation between the name of the traditional betrayer of Arthur (i.e., Mordred), and the name of this imperial prefect (i.e., Arvandus), who betrayed Riothamus.[47] Euric called up, among other troops, the Alans of southern Gaul.[48] Because Riothamus's troops were fighting Alans, who had served for

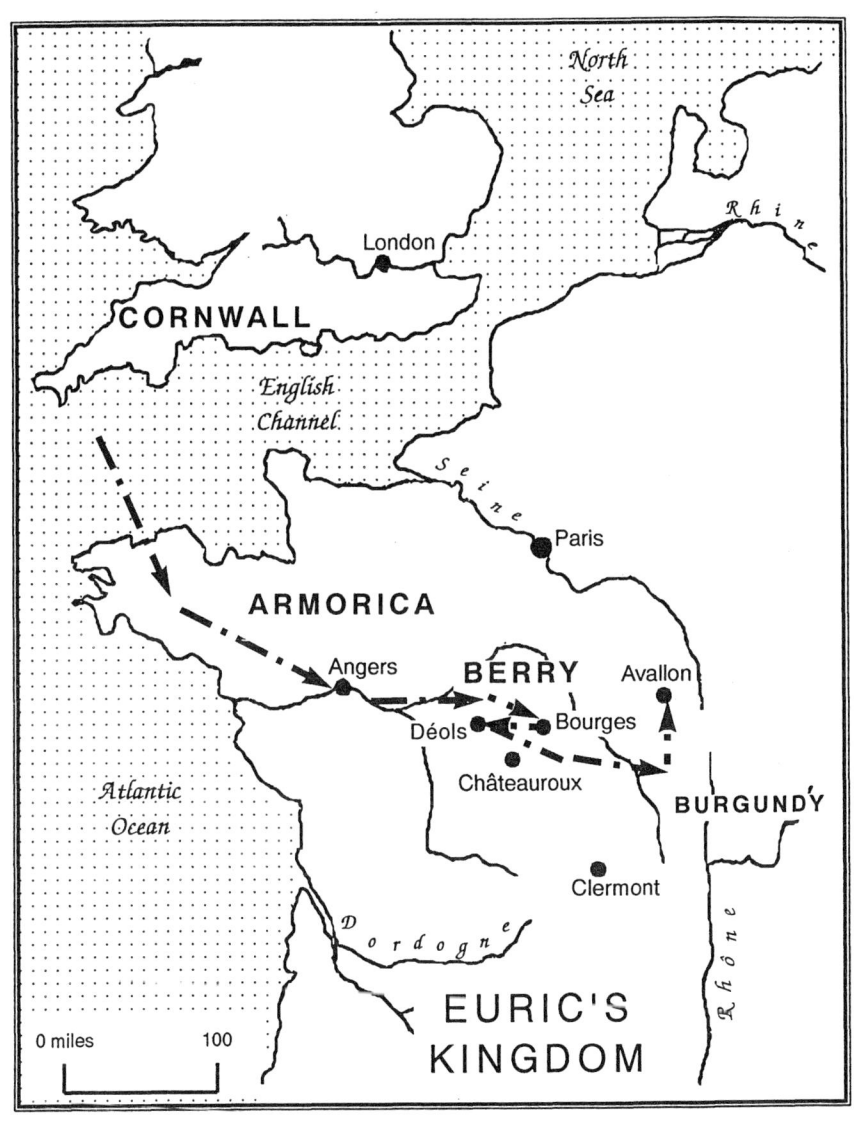

Map 12. Riothamus's Route

decades as elite Roman troops in the region, and because Leo was seen as the puppet emperor of the Alan general Aspar, Riothamus was probably viewed by the locals as fighting against Rome rather than fighting for Rome, and thus, by association, as fighting Leo.

As the Britons marched toward Burgundy, Euric attacked Riothamus with an overwhelming force "before the Romans (probably led by Syagrius) could come to the British king's aid."[49] This situation may have provided the seeds for the legend that Lancelot was unable to join Arthur in time for the Battle of Camlann, where the legendary British king received his mortal wound. Following this battle Riothamus, who had, like Arthur at Camlann, received a serious wound, retreated from Bourges, escaping with his army into the nearby territory of the friendly Burgundians in late 469 or 470. There is no record of Riothamus's death, but the last reference to him places him moving in the direction of a town called Avallon, just as the last reference to Arthur states that the wounded king was being carried to an island called Avalon. From this and other evidence Ashe proposes that Riothamus was the historical King Arthur.[50]

This battle between Riothamus and the Alans of Gaul echoes loudly in the Arthurian legends. In addition to supplying the historical seed for the legends of Arthur's invasion of the Continent it may also have supplied the basis for the legends of the wars between Lancelot and Arthur in the final days of the Round Table. Descendants of the Iazyges in Britain may well have been among Riothamus's troops.[51] With the loss of their leader many of these troops probably never returned to Britain. After three hundred years of separation the Iazyges and the Alans were reunited, and for the first time each group's derivative of the legends from the steppes had an opportunity to meet on a large scale.[52] The result of this meeting may well have been the birth of the Arthurian tradition.

The Death of Arthur

Perhaps the best-known story about Arthur is that of his death (see plate 5), and it is precisely this legend that finds such

PLATE 5. The Death of King Arthur (British Library MS Add. 10294, fol. 94). By permission of the British Library.

a striking parallel in the Ossetic tales of Batraz. Systematically collected and analyzed in the course of the last century or so by V. Miller, Adolf Dirr, and, most extensively, the late French mythologist Georges Dumézil,[53] the Ossetic tradition concerning the death of Batraz can be summarized as follows: After slaughtering a vast number of his fellow Narts in revenge for their complicity in his father's death and after resisting all the afflictions that God could throw at him, Batraz takes pity on the handful of survivors.[54] He tells them that he has satisfied his need for vengeance and that he himself is ready for death, adding that "I cannot die until my sword has been thrown into the sea."[55] This latter stipulation causes great concern among the Narts, as the sword is so heavy that only Batraz can wield it with ease. In desperation they decide to deceive him. Hiding the sword, they report back that it has been disposed of in accordance with his instructions. But when Batraz asks, "What prodigious things did you see when my sword fell into the sea?," they reply, "Nothing"—an answer that Batraz recognizes as a lie, since he alone knows what will happen when his sword enters the water.[56] When the Narts finally manage to drag the wondrous weapon to the coast and consign it to the water, the sea becomes turbulent, boils, and turns blood-red. As soon as this is reported to Batraz, he dies, secure in the knowledge that his last wish has been fulfilled.[57]

One need not be a specialist in the Arthurian romances to see the striking parallels between the foregoing account and that of the death of King Arthur:

> ... "Sir Bedivere, ..." said King Arthur, "... I would ask you to take my sword Excalibur to the shore of the lake and throw it in the water. Then return to me and tell me what you have seen."
>
> "My Lord, as you command, it shall be done."
>
> Sir Bedivere took the sword, but when he came to the water's edge, it appeared so beautiful that he could not bring himself to throw it in, so instead he hid it by a tree, and then returned to the king.
>
> "Sir Bedivere, what did you see?"
>
> "My lord, I saw nothing but the wind upon the waves."
>
> "Then you did not obey me; I pray you, go swiftly again, and this time fulfill my command."

> Sir Bedivere went and returned again, but this time too he had failed to fulfill the king's command.
> "Sir Bedivere, what did you see?"
> "My lord, nothing but the lapping of the waves."
> "Sir Bedivere, twice you have betrayed me! And for the sake only of my sword: it is unworthy of you! Now I pray you, do as I command, for I have not long to live."
> This time Sir Bedivere wrapped the girdle around the sheath and hurled it as far as he could into the water. A hand appeared from below the surface, took the sword, waved it thrice, and disappeared again. Sir Bedivere returned to the king and told him what he had seen. [58]

The need to throw Excalibur into the lake, the attempts on the part of the grieving Bedivere to deceive the dying king, and even the magical events that occur when the sword is finally hurled into the water recall the central elements of the Ossetic story; Grisward has suggested that they are reflexes (i.e., independent reflections) of a common "motif," which he calls "l'épée jetée au lac" ("the sword thrown into the lake").[59] In some variants of Arthur's death scene the body of water involved is even a sea instead of a lake. For example, in some stories Gifflet throws Caliburnus (rather than Excalibur) into the sea.[60]

The source for Malory's account of Arthur's last battle is said to be the fourteenth-century stanzaic *Le Morte Arthur*.[61] Although the two scribes of this fifteenth-century manuscript were from the East Midlands, their tale is generally considered to be from a northern tradition.[62] By the time of the composition of the stanzaic *Morte* these regions had long been influenced by the powerful FitzAlan family of northern Britain. The traditions expressed in the stanzaic *Morte* and in Malory's work could have been supplied by either the descendants of the Iazyges in northern Britain or by the Alans of Brittany, who after the Norman Conquest also had strong ties with the nobles of northern Britain.

While the events that lead up to this death scene in the Arthurian legends vary, it is usually preceded by a battle between Arthur and Mordred. In some cases this battle has particularly "Scythian" overtones. For example, in the *Chronicle* *of Elis Gruffydd*⁶³ an adder-like creature sits on Arthur's helm.⁶⁴ Mordred knocks the creature off. The creature then sits on Mordred's helm, and Arthur knocks it off. This creature is described as a "preve," a word that may be akin to either the Middle English *prive*, "magic,"⁶⁵ or *preve*, "to prove."⁶⁶ The two warriors fight under these emblems in much the same manner as the Sarmatian leaders fought under the serpent banner (see plate 3).

The events after the death scene also vary. Unlike Batraz, who is eventually entombed,⁶⁷ Arthur is usually said to have been carried to a place called Avalon. Nickel, in an unpublished paper on "The Last Days of Rome in Britain and the Origin of the Arthurian Legends," suggests that the twenty-mile distance between Camboglanna and Avallana,⁶⁸ two Roman forts near the west end of Hadrian's Wall, is just about as far as a seriously wounded man could be carried, at least in a single day. Thus Camboglanna may very well have been the site of the Battle of Camlann, in which Arthur was mortally wounded.⁶⁹ And the fact that Avallana was located on the water at the mouth of the Solway River may have given rise to what Nickel calls "the transport-to-Avalon story," as the last leg of the trip would probably have been more easily accomplished by boat.⁷⁰ Elsewhere the tale is told of the "Once and Future King." Gervais of Tilbury (ca. 1211) says that Arthur lives on in a Sicilian palace with wounds reopening annually. In similar stories Arthur is said to live in a hollow mountain (Etna), asleep, surrounded by knights. It is interesting to note that the Nart Sozryko, after he is mortally wounded, lives in a cave at the base of a mountain (Colarusso [personal communication]).

Not all branches of the Arthurian tradition employ this death scene. The *Annales Cambriae* in the Harley manuscript does not contain the motif of "l'épée jetée au lac."⁷¹

The absence of this scene of the sword thrown into the lake in the Lancelot corpus delayed the discovery of the Lancelot/Batraz connection. By the time the extant manuscripts of the Vulgate *Mort le roi Artu* were completed in the early thirteenth century, this death scene was firmly attached to the character of Arthur, and another scene had to be invented for Lancelot. Perhaps Lancelot does not have a death scene in most tales because his original death scene was the same as Arthur's and could not be used when both heroes appeared in the same story.[72] Many other parallels between the legends of Lancelot and the Nart sagas do exist, however, as we shall see in the next chapter.

NOTES

1. *Roman de Brut*, l. 10,038; Paton in Rhys 1928:x–xi, cf. 56; Lacy et al. 1986:616; Cavendish 1978; Chadwick 1965, 1969; Fleuriot 1980; Loomis 1959.

2. This work also goes by the titles *Le chevalier de la charrette* and *Lancelot*. We have chosen to use *Conte de la charrette* because this is the form preferred by Webster, Paton, and other Arthurian scholars and because the title *Lancelot* is easily confused with the prose *Lancelot* and other works about this particular knight.

3. Cavendish 1978:9; Micha 1957. Camulodunum (modern Colchester) is just one of the many places that have been advanced as the possible site for Arthur's legendary court (see map 5).

4. Cavendish 1978:9. However, Gildas, who lived at a time when witnesses to the Battle of Badon could still be found, makes no mention of Arthur and dates this battle to ca. 500, rather than 518; see Alcock 1971 and Morris 1980, vol. 8.

5. Ashe 1985; Chambers 1927; Fletcher 1906; Loomis and Loomis 1938; Fleuriot 1980.

6. This is the best of many copies. In all probability no extant copy reproduces Geoffrey's work in the original—all surviving manuscripts probably trace to a revision completed ca. 1140. A "Variant Version," which is extremely different, also exists. A twelfth-century copy of the *Historia* (Paris, Douai 880 fol. 66) was copied and illuminated in Flanders. For more information on Geoffrey of Monmouth see Thorpe 1966; Parry 1925; Ashe 1981:301–323; Chambers 1927; Hoffman 1984:1–10; Kendrick 1950; Parry and Caldwell in Loomis 1959:72–93; Piggott 1941; and Tatlock 1950. As an interesting sidenote, Geoffrey's father's name is said to have been Arthur (Lacy et al. 1986:209; Thorpe 1966:13).

7. No trace of this book exists today. Walter brought the book *ex Britannia*, i.e., probably from Brittany. It may well have been a Breton redaction of a truly ancient Latin original.

8. This suggests that Geoffrey's Arthur came from a non-Welsh source.

9. This date varies so greatly from other sources that it is probably a mistake or a corruption.

10. The system of dating the years from the Passion was employed during the late fifth century, but on the Continent it was superseded by the method of counting from the time of Jesus's birth during the sixth century. The Venerable Bede's *Ecclesiastical History* was "the first major work to employ the modern chronological framework based on the Christian era (A.D.—Anno Domini—the year of the Lord)" (Hollister 1982:65).

11. This is a Latin chronicle that draws mainly on Anglo-Saxon matter but uses material from Nennius as well.

12. Ashe 1985; Chambers 1927; Fletcher 1906; Loomis and Loomis 1938; Fleuriot 1980.

13. This is a Latin chronicle found in the Avranches MS 213 (Migne 1855, 202:col. 1323) from the library of Mont-Saint-Michel. It may predate Geoffrey.

14. As a thirteenth-century manuscript of Nennius (Morris 1980) contains a gloss explaining the name Arthur as *ursus horribilus*, or "horrible bear," and as the Ursus referred to by Gildas (chap. 32; Winterbottom 1978) can perhaps be identified with the historical Arthur, some earlier Arthurian scholars attempted to derive the name in question from the Celtic *artos*, "bear" (e.g., Chambers 1927:210 f.). It has also been suggested that Arthur is in some way connected with an ancient Gallic bear-goddess called Artio (MacCulloch 1918, 3:186–187). Other Celtic possibilities are that the name derives from the Irish *art*, "stone" (suggested many years ago by Holder [1891:226]), or even Welsh *arth*, "hammer" (which can also mean "bear"; for a critical assessment of the former etymology, see Malone [1924:463–465]). At a more general linguistic level Rhŷs (1891:39) sought to demonstrate the presence of the Indo-European **ar-*, "plow," in the name and that its bearer was originally an agricultural divinity—perhaps the Gallic god Artaios, whom the Romans identified with Mercury and who seems to have had some association with plows and plowing (MacCulloch 1918, 3:186).

Most contemporary scholars, however, see the name as intrinsically Latin and assume that it is in one way or another connected with the Roman *nomen*, or gentilic name, Artorius (e.g., Withycombe 1950:31; Jackson in Loomis 1959:2; Ashe 1985:97). As Lindsay (1958:220) points out, Artorius would normally undergo aspiration in passing into Welsh. A few scholars, like Alcock (1971:358), avoid the issue and simply label the name as "foreign." In short the bulk of the evidence does not support the possibility of a Celtic etymology here. On this point see also Nickel (1975a:9, 26).

15. On Lucius Artorius Castus see Malone (1925:367–377); see also Oman (1910:211), Nickel (1975a:9–11), Jackson (in Loomis 1959:2), Ashe 1885:116; and Malcor 1999.

16. Malone (1925:370) suggests that Castus was originally from Dalmatia. However, from all indications he was a native of central Italy, despite the fact that the. two inscriptions in Mommsen's *Corpus Inscriptionum Latinarum* that mention Lucius Artorius Castus, #1919 (1873, vol. 3, Part 1:303) and #12791 (1873, vol. 3, Supplement:2131), were discovered near Split, on the Adriatic coast of what is now Croatia (i.e., ancient Dalmatia/Illyria; see map 4; see also Oman 1910:211). Together, these stelae provide what amounts to a résumé of Castus's long and distinguished military career: His first post was as a centurion in the III legion Gallica in Syria. He held the same post in the VI legion Ferrata in Judea, the II legion Adiutrix on the Danube, and the V legion Macedonia in Potaissa in Dacia (modern Turda in Transylvania), where he was promoted to *primus pilus* (the highest ranking centurion). After serving at this rank he reenlisted in the traditional "equestrian *cursus.*" The first rank of the *cursus, praefectus cohortis,* is missing from Castus's résumé. He probably served this tour as a *praefectus* of *numeri* (an alternative rank to *praefectus cohortis*) by leading the Iazyges to Bremetennacum and settling them into the Roman military system. Castus subsequently was promoted to *praepositus* (a naval rank equivalent to *tribunus*) of the *classis Misenatium*, that is, co-commander, with five other *praepositae*, of the fleet based at Misentia, near Naples. His next post took him back to Britain as *praefectus* of the VI legion Victrix. But instead of serving as a simple *praefectus alae* (cavalry commander), he was given command of Bremetennacum. His stellar performance in that capacity earned him the unique post of *procurator centenarius iure gladii* for Liburnia (see note 24), a rank that put him into direct competition with Cassius Dio's father, who was the governor of Dalmatia at that time. This conflict may account for why Dio does not mention Castus by name in his history. The circumstances of Castus's death are not recorded, but it is likely that he died or was mortally wounded in the battle Septimius Severus fought against Albinus at Lyon in 196 and that the classis Misenatium shipped his body back to

Liburnia for burial. For an additional discussion of this Roman officer and how he may have influenced the Arthurian legends, see Nitze (1949:585-589) and Malcor (1999; n.d.).

17. As we have indicated (see the previous note), Castus was most likely the officer assigned to escort the Iazyges from Pannonia to Bremetennacum; see Malcor 1999.

18. Cf. Sulimirski 1970:176–177. The *Notitia Dignitatum* (Seeck 1876:209–210) also mentions that a Sarmatian unit was stationed at the fort of Morbium—a place that has never been located, and, as we have seen, there is evidence for the presence of Sarmatian units (if not veterans) at Chester and elsewhere in addition to the frontier posts (see map 4).

19. Malcor 1999.

20. Malone 1925:372.

21. Ashe 1985:116. See also Oman 1910: 211; Malone 1925:372, Malcor 1999.

22. E.g., Nennius, *Historia Brittonum*, chap. 56, in Brengle 1964:5.

23. Ashe 1985:116.

24. More completely, *procurator centenarius iure gladii*, a unique office that gave him the power of life or death in the region. See Pflaum 1960, 1:185, 535-537.

25. The territory controlled by the Iazyges *numeri* significantly decreased in size following this campaign, indicating that roughly half of the cavalry unit died in the battles at Tinurtium and Lyon. Cassius Dio 76.6-7; Cary 1932:207-211. See also Malcor 1999; n.d.

26. Some additional thematic parallels between Lucius Artorius Castus and Arthur can be summarized as follows: (1) To enter the army, Castus had to resign his hereditary rank as an equestrian, something that he recovered only after earning the legionary rank of *primus pilus* (see note 16) through military prowess. By the same token, Arthur was given to Merlin, losing his rank as Uther's heir, something he recovered only after he pulled the sword from the stone and consolidated the kingdom through military prowess. (2) Castus was a Roman soldier, and Arthur is described in early texts as a soldier rather than as a king (e.g., Nennius, *Historia Brittonum*, chap. 76; in Brengle 1964:6). (3) Camboglanna, proposed as the prototype of Camlann (cf. Ashe 1983:61, 65-99; and Lacy et al. 1986:69; see also Bruce 1978:228-229 1986:69) and Avalanna, proposed as the prototype of Avalon (cf. Helmut Nickel [personal communication]; see also Frère et al. 1987:13), were among the sites on the Wall defended by the Sarmatians under Castus's leadership.

(4) Just as Castus kept the region under his command at peace during a barbarian invasion (that of the Picts) and a civil war (the rebellion of the Victrix), so, too, did Arthur keep his kingdom at peace against the invasion of the Saxons and a civil war (i.e., the rebellions of the kings–Lot, et al.–that he put down and whose kingdoms he consolidated to form his own).

27. Ashe in Lacy, et al. 1986:6-7. The commander at Bremetennacum eventually came to hold the title of *praepositus numeri et regionari* (Collingwood and Wright 1965, 1:194-195, no. 583, and 196-199, no. 587; see also Wacher 1978:127). Bremetennacum was the only post in Britain where a *praepositus regionari* commanded *numeri* as well (Burnham and Wacher 1990:34), a combined rank that has puzzled classicists and archaeologists alike (Salway 1965:29; Richmond 1945:15ff.). The perpetuation of the Sarmatians as an ethnic cavalry unit that controlled the region is the most plausible explanation for the unusual title of the unit's commander.

28. Ashe 1985:124.

29. Nitze (1949b:585) recaps arguments by Zimmer and Rhŷs on this same point. Cavendish (1978:8) noted the name Arthur among the sons of British kings in the sixth century. Nitze (1949b:585) also mentions an Arturius, a prince from southwest Scotland, who died at the Battle of Tigernach in 596. This prince is thought to be Irish, but, given his proximity to Hadrian's Wall, it would not be impossible for him to have a Iazygian warrior or two in his genealogy.

30. Geoffrey of Monmouth 5.12; Thorpe 1966:139–140; Ashe 1985:48.

31. This is a mid-eleventh-century collection of tales found in the White Book of Rhydderch (ca. 1325) and the Red Book of Hergest (ca. 1400).

32. I.e., Macsen in the story *The Dream of Macsen Wledig*; Gantz 1976:118–127. While Markale (1975a:14, 21) argues for a date of ca. 392 for these events, Maximus (d. 411) and Conan Meriadoc (whom Geoffrey of Monmouth [Thorpe 1966:135–141] places as a contemporary of Constantine I [r. 306–337]) may have actually lived several generations apart.

33. This name may be a feminine form of "Alan."

34. See Lacy et al. 1986:453–455.

35. Dalton 1915.

36. Ashe 1985; cf. Chambers 1927; Fletcher 1906; Loomis and Loomis 1938; Fleuriot 1980.

37. Thorpe 1966.

38. Mierow 1915.

39. Thorpe 1974. Randers-Pehrson (1983:272) makes the curious observation that

> Gregory of Tours was born in 538. . . . He took an old Roman's pride in his descent from a long line of distinguished bishops, but even so he was barbarized. His language was strange, with Hunnic words in it, and his mind had absorbed a kind of crude superstition. . . . Amulets had awful power; every event had its signs and portents.

This sounds startlingly like the description of a colonial Alan.

40. Lacy et al. 1986:7; Coghlan 1991:190.

41. Thorpe 1966:246. Another Leo who lived at this time was Pope Leo I of Rome, who in 452, like the Alans of Gaul in 451, was credited with stopping Attila's advance into the Roman Empire (Hollister 1982:31).

42. This name derives from the Iranian root *asp* ("horse"). Cf. Sanskrit *áśva-* (cf. *ashvah*; Buck 1949:167). Aspar and his two oldest sons, Ardiburius (an Alanic name) and Patricus (a Roman name), were assassinated by Leo's command after Aspar refused to lead his eastern Roman troops against Gaiseric, the king of the Alans and Vandals in North Africa. Hermaneric (a Germanic name), Aspar's youngest son, was in Germany at the time and survived the attempt on his life.

43. Gregory of Tours 2.18 (Thorpe 1974:132); Jordanes 45 (Mierow 1915:117–119); Sidonius Apollinaris 1.7 (Anderson 1936, 1:367–379), 3.9 (Anderson 1936, 2:33–35; cf. Anderson 1936, 2:35–37); Ashe 1981:301–323; 1985; Campbell 1982; Fleuriot 1980; Jackson 1953.

44. Carman 1973.

45. Sidonius was formerly city prefect of Rome. He became bishop of Clermont ca. 468.

46. Coghlan 1991:87.

47. Ashe 1985; Chambers 1927; Fletcher 1906; Loomis and Loomis 1938; Fleuriot 1980.

48. This name may derive from the Alanic "Gueric" (i.e., Goeric). The name Gueric may derive from an attempt by the Alans' Germanic allies to pronounce the name Goar.

49. Ashe 1985:56–57.

50. Ashe 1985:96.

51. Littleton and Thomas 1978.

52. The second opportunity arose when Celticized Iazyges fleeing from the Saxons settled in Armorica and other regions of heavy Alanic settlement. Trade between Armorica and Cornwall could have allowed for some small-scale transmission even before this date.

53. Miller 1881; Hübschmann 1887:539–567; Dirr 1925; Dumézil 1930:69; 1946:249–255; 1960:141–154; 1965; 1968:441–456, 485–575.

54. Dumézil 1930:69.

55. Dumézil 1930:69.

56. Dumézil 1930:69.

57. The French reads

> ... Il [Batraz] leur [the Narts] dit qu'il était satisfait de sa vengeance et consentait à mourir lui-même; «mais, ajouta-t-il, je ne pourrai mourir tant que mon épée n'aura pas été jetée à la mer: ainsi en a décidé le destin.» Les Nartes tombèrent dans une nouvelle désolation: comment jeter à la mer l'épée de Batraz? Ils résolurent de tromper le héros, de lui persuader que son épée était jetée à la mer et que c'était pour lui l'heure de mourir. Ils s'approachèrent donc du malade et lui jurèrent que la condition du destin était remplie. «Quels prodiges avez-vous vus quand mon épée est tombée dans la mer?» leur demanda-t-il.— «Aucun,» répondirent les Nartes, tout penauds.— «C'est donc que mon épée n'est pas jetée à la mer; auterment vous auriez vu des prodiges.» Les Nartes durent se résigner: ils déployèrent toutes leurs forces, attelèrent plusieurs milliers d'animaux; à la fin, ils réussirent à traîner l'épée de Batraz jusqu'à la côte et la jetèrent dans la mer. Aussitôt s'élevèrent vagues et ouragans, la mer bouillonna, puis devint couleur de sang. Les Nartes étaient dans un étonnement et dans une joie sans bornes. Ils coururent raconter à Batraz ce qu'ils avaient vu; convaincu, il rendit le dernier soupir. (Dumézil 1930:69)

58. Baines 1962:500.

59. Grisward 1969:289–340; 1973:80–89. In *The Parlement of the Thre Ages*, from the North Midlands of England (ca. 1350–1390; Offord 1959;

Gardner 1971), Gawain, rather than Bedivere, throws Excalibur into a lake.

60. Gifflet was eventually replaced in this tale by Bedivere. Colarusso has suggested that this change took place because the name Bedivere (from proto-Celtic *bod(o)-wid-r, "grave-knower") meant "one who knows [Arthur's] grave." Thus Bedivere, if the old sense of his name was still known, was destined to supplant Gifflet in Arthur's death scene.

Another possible etymology for Bedivere (or Bedwyr) is that it derived from the Iranian *bahadur* ("god's servant"; Colarusso [personal communication]), a name often found attached to military commanders and the variants of which can be found in a number of Eastern European dialects (cf. the Russian noun *bogatyr* [mjufnßhm, "warrior"], and the Hungarian adjective *bátor* ["courageous"]). See Nickel 1975a:12.

61. British Library [B.L.] Harley 2252, fol. 86–133.

62. Bruce 1903; Hissiger 1975; Knopp 1978:563–582; Schmidt and Jacobs 1980; Wertime 1972:1075–1082.

63. In *Chronicle of the History of the World*; National Library of Wales MS 5276D and Mostyn MS 158. Gruffydd preferred Geoffrey of Monmouth to continental sources (Lloyd-Morgan [personal communication]), as well as preferring the idea that Arthur conquered extensively on the Continent. Most of Gruffydd's material cannot be pinpointed to Welsh native tradition, and Gruffydd himself claims that he took his story from an "English" source (Lloyd-Morgan [personal communication]). See also Ford 1976:379–390.

64. Lloyd-Morgan (personal communication): Lecture, "The Medieval Welsh *Y Seint Greal*: The Translation of Words and Traditions." Sponsored by the Department of English and the Celtic Colloquium, University of California, Los Angeles, April 18, 1986.

65. Kuhn and Kurath 1983:1334.

66. Therefore the creatures prove the worthiness of the combatants through their own prowess; see Kuhn and Kurath 1983:1281.

67. As is Lancelot.

68. Or Avallava; see map 6; cf. the French Avallon; see map 12.

69. Cf. the Welsh *Annales*, etc.

70. Cf. the town of Avallon that is associated with the campaign of Riothamus (see above).

71. Ca. 1316, B.L. Add. 10294, a composite text derived from older (and occasionally Irish) sources; Morris 1980:vol. 8; Alcock 1971.

72. Cf. Markale 1985:126.

CHAPTER 3

Lancelot and the "Alan of Lot"

Littleton and Thomas avoided discussion of the Lancelot corpus in their study of the Sarmatian influence on the Arthurian legends, since they accepted the widespread scholarly assumption that Lancelot was a heroic reflection of the Celtic figure Lug.[1] According to this hypothesis the Arthurian legends, including the stories of Lancelot, originated in Wales and were then, in the sixth century, carried to Armorica by Celts fleeing from the Saxons. The written records supposedly developed out of the tales told in what became Brittany by these Welsh immigrants (see fig. 5).

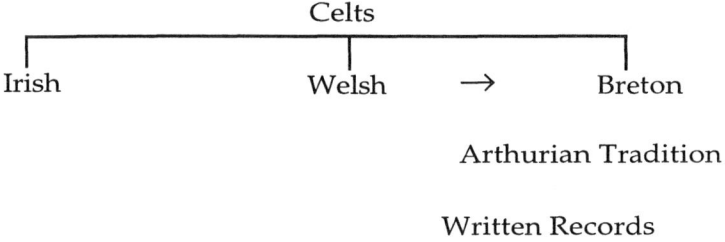

FIG. 5. The Welsh-Origin Hypothesis

Patrick K. Ford (personal communication) has revised this model so that the tales of the continental Arthur are parallel to the tales of the insular Arthur at the hypothetical Indo-European level (see fig. 6), rather than at the Celtic level, with both cycles of legends recorded in Brittany.

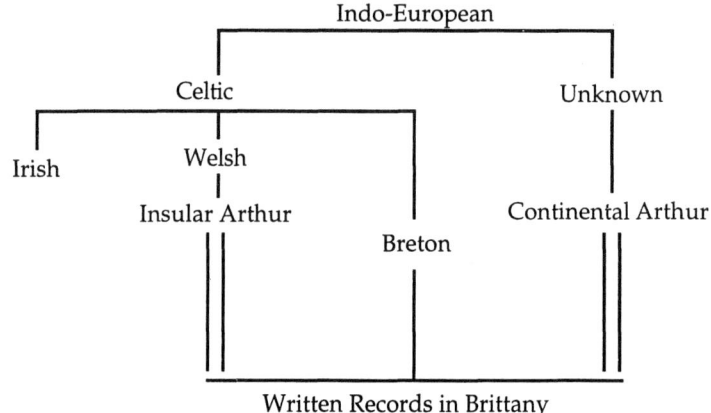

FIG. 6. Ford's Hypothesis

However, as early as 1901, when Jessie L. Weston attempted to trace the legends of Lancelot du Lac to their origin, she wrote in her introduction:

> I doubt if any scholar of standing would now argue that Lancelot and his relation to the queen [Guinevere] formed an integral portion of the early [Arthurian] tradition; if any, conversant with the literature of the cycle, would reckon Lancelot among the original band of heroes who gathered round the British King. (Weston 1901a:2)

We concur with Weston's findings, and we would like to go one step farther and suggest that the tradition that introduced the figure of Lancelot into the Arthurian legends was originally developed by the Alans of Gaul. Etymological and onomastic examination of the Lancelot legends reveals a prominent connection between the characters in the legends and Alanic names, as well as geographic designations within areas of heavy Alanic settlement. Some of the stories appear to reflect Alanic victories in battle that can be located historically in the fifth century, the century in which the Arthurian legends are set.[2] And structural analysis of the tales of Lancelot show that striking parallels exist not only between Lancelot and Batraz but also between Lancelot and Arthur.

We suggest that Lancelot, as well as Arthur, developed from the same prototype as the Ossetic hero Batraz (i.e., that Lancelot is the continental version of the figure represented by Arthur in the insular legends and by Batraz in the Nart sagas; see fig. 1) and that the core of the Lancelot corpus was formed by legends carried by Alans who settled in Gaul in the early fifth century. With this in mind let us examine the possibility that the original Lancelot might have been the "Alan of Lot."

The Legends of Lancelot

Lancelot's biography is well known.[3] His father is King Ban of Benoich (Benwick); his mother is Elaine. When Ban dies in a war against Claudas, the Dame du Lac (Lady of the Lake) kidnaps the infant Lancelot from the grieving Elaine. This mysterious woman raises the boy as her own son,[4] then supplies him with a magical ring, a mirror, a horse, and arms.[5] In the course of his adventures he visits a cemetery, where, after talking to a hermit, he finds a tomb, and a lady tells him that the name on the tomb is his true name.[6] He then is imprisoned by a woman who wants to marry him. While in jail he has an encounter with an antagonistic dwarf. He next meets the King of the Hundred Knights and fights incognito in a three-day long tournament bearing three-colored arms.[7] He also wins the right through combat to marry Guinevere.[8]

The first part of this biographical material has a clear parallel in the history of the Alans of southern Gaul. As already noted, the first group of Alans settled in Gaul in the early fifth century. In 414 a second group of Alans, along with the Visigoths, besieged Count Paulinus of Pella at Bazas. The count was a friend of the Alan leader, and midway through the siege they reached an agreement: the Alan leader would send his own wife and favorite son into the besieged city of Bazas and the count would give the Alans land after the Visigoths were defeated. The Alans drew their wagons into a circle around Bazas and turned against the Visigoths. The Roman military commander in the region, Constantius of Rome, chased the Visigoths into Spain, but he convinced Honorius to grant the

Alans the land between Toulouse and the Mediterranean Sea on the condition that the Alans would control the coastal roads (see maps 7 and 9).[9] These events recall the legend of Ban under siege with his wife and son endangered and a delay in the reclaiming of the land—an event that occurs through the agency of outside/foreign sources.

The name Lancelot du Lac first appears in Breton stories and legends.[10] Here the future preeminent knight of the Round Table is merely designated as belonging to Arthur's court, with none of his adventures recorded. Prior to these lays of the midtwelfth century Lancelot, as a name, simply does not exist in surviving texts. Then, in 1179, Lancelot emerges as the protagonist of Chrétien de Troyes's *Conte de la charrette*, where he is the lover of Guinevere,[11] willing to undertake any perilous task, endure any shame, and confront any opponent for the sake of Arthur's queen. The hero's past is contained in a single comment that a water-fay had nursed him and had given him a ring that enables him to detect enchantments.[12]

Between 1194 and 1205 Ulrich von Zatzikhoven, a Swiss poet, elaborated this story in his *Lanzelet*. Ulrich traces the adventures of Lancelot from the time of the hero's abduction by a *merfeine* ("sea-fairy"[13]) until the hero's death of old age. In the course of the poem the hero acquires at least three, but probably four, wives and wins the right to marry two others.[14] One of the last two women was Guinevere, whom Lancelot turns over to Arthur. The love affair between Lancelot and Guinevere was apparently unknown to Ulrich.[15]

Shortly after the composition of Ulrich's poem the prose *Lancelot* was written.[16] This collection of narratives is the subject of much controversy. Formerly attributed to the Welsh cleric Walter Map,[17] the prose *Lancelot* was written in French by someone who had detailed knowledge of the geography of Poitou, scanty knowledge of the geography of southeast Britain, and almost no knowledge of the geography of Wales.[18] The consensus among recent scholars of the Pseudo-Map Cycle is that the work was written near Poitou sometime during the early 1200s. The prose *Lancelot* combines elements found in both Chrétien and Ulrich's works, presenting Lancelot as the well-

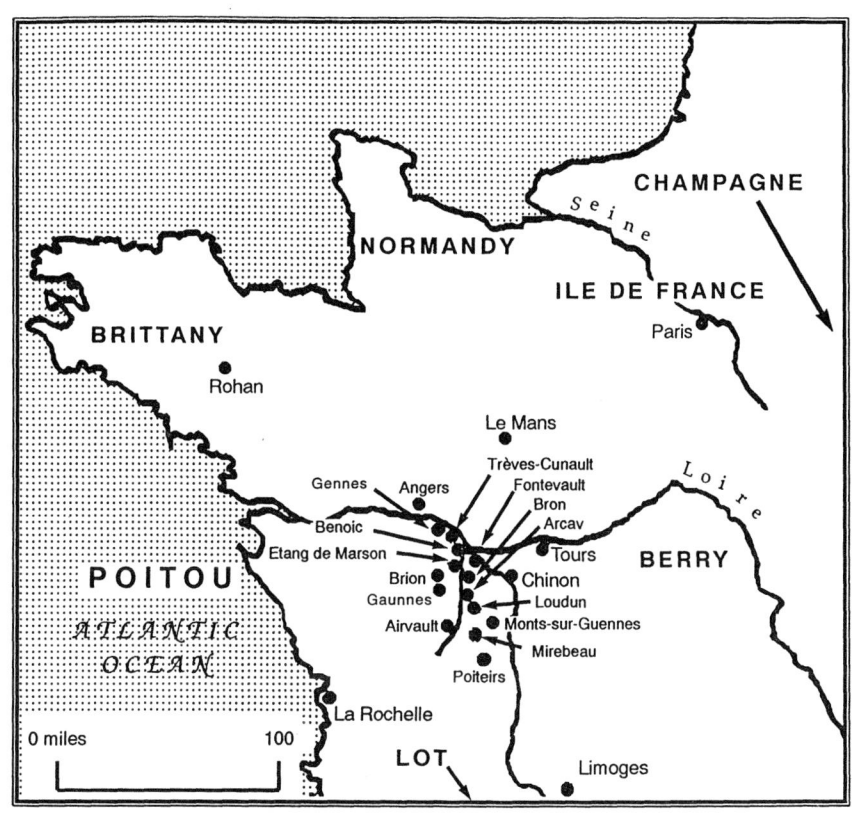

Map 13. The Geography of the Prose *Lancelot*

guarded protégé of the Dame du Lac and as the insane lover of Guinevere.[19]

The *Perlesvaus*, which was composed by an anonymous author sometime between 1203 and 1213, is written in Old French prose. The work is subtitled *The High Book of the Grail*, and better than half of the romance is spent following Lancelot's unsuccessful attempts to catch more than a glimpse of the Holy Grail. The problems caused by Lancelot's love for Guinevere are solved when she dies from grief for her murdered son, freeing Lancelot from anything that might hinder his conversion from his pagan ways to Christianity.[20]

The rest of the legends about Lancelot from the thirteenth century are all continental, with the majority claiming to be translations of the Old French prose *Lancelot*, or at least admitting a heavy debt to the prose *Lancelot*. The author of the thirteenth-century *Suite du Merlin* mentions that he knew the story that the Dame du Lac gave Lancelot a ring even though he did not include it in his work; he also notes that the tale was recorded in the Latin version from which he was working.[21]

In the fourteenth century Lancelot finally appears in the written records in Britain, and there his character follows the same pattern it did on the Continent: appearing first as a name on a list of Arthur's knights, then as the lover of Guinevere, and finally as the protagonist of other adventures.

So even though the legends of Lancelot are first recorded on the Continent as late additions to the Arthurian tradition and then are transmitted at an even later date to Britain, the proponents of the Welsh-origin hypothesis argue for a prior transmission of the legends of Lancelot from Wales to the Anglo-Normans to the French either through oral tradition or by way of a lost manuscript. Let us consider their evidence.

Lancelot and Lug

The case for the derivation of Lancelot from the god Lug begins with Loomis's suggestion that the name Lancelot derives from "the Welsh ... Llwch, alias Llenlleawc the Irishman, [whose] ... ultimate ancestor was the Irish god Lug [i.e.,

Lugh]."[22] Loomis's evidence is based on parallels between the legends of Lancelot and other Arthurian heroes. Lot (of Orkney), Lucius (of Rome), and Lancelot (of Benoich) are all presented by Loomis as representations of Lug who fight Arthur in a major battle. Lot and Lancelot both abduct Guinevere; Lot and Lancelot both have bastard sons (Gawain[23] and Galahad, respectively); Loomis believes that both of the women involved in these affairs (Morgawse of Orkney and Elaine of Corbenic, respectively) might be traced back to Morgan[24] and also suggests that the names of the sons, Gawain and Galahad, are related.[25]

We agree that the parallels between the legends exist, but these particular parallels can be found in a wide variety of legends, many of which bear no relation to Lancelot. For example, most Indo-European peoples have a legend about a warrior who fights in battle against his king. The abduction of Guinevere is attributed to Meleagant, Mordred, and several other warriors.[26] A hero who gets himself a bastard son does not automatically become a candidate for a parallel to Lancelot; other factors must enter into the story of the bastard's birth and life.

There are, however, some parallels between the legends of Lancelot and the legends of the Celtic Lug (as represented by the Welsh Lleu and the Irish Lugh) that bear pointing out.[27] Like Lleu, Lancelot initially has trouble acquiring the name by which others will call him. Lancelot, who originally carries a golden eagle on his shield as his device,[28] is often found stuck in a tree, just as Gwydyon finds Lleu when the latter is in eagle form after his "murder." Lancelot appears at Arthur's court, causes a disturbance, and is eventually accepted because of his skills, like Lugh in Irish tradition.[29]

Yet the differences between the legends of Lug and Lancelot are far more numerous than the similarities. Lancelot's mother is almost invisible in his life; Lleu's mother is one of his primary antagonists. Ban dies while Lancelot is an infant; Lleu's "father" is his constant companion and helper. Lancelot marries Elaine, the daughter of Pelles, the Fisher King of the Wasteland (a tale in which Spring is lost and then found); Lleu marries a girl made of flowers (a tale in which Spring is created and then lost).[30] Lancelot is connected to a sword, but Lleu's symbol is a spear. Lancelot is one of the three "Lions of Britain"; Lleu takes the shape of an eagle. Lancelot's wife is loyal (once she is married to him); Lleu's wife betrays him. Lancelot survives the Battle of Camlann; the Irish Lugh is killed at the Second Battle of Mag Tuired. In short the connection between Lancelot and the Celtic Lug appears to be superficial. Story parallels aside, however, there are three major points to the Welsh-origin hypothesis.

The first is that Celtic fairies exhibit a peculiar attachment to water,[31] and that Lancelot, in most of the legends, is intimately connected with a water-fairy. There are two basic problems with this point. First, the Bretons may have carried the same Celtic water-fairy traditions as the Welsh rather than as a result of Welsh transmission. The Celts who fled from Britain in the sixth century and who settled in Armorica certainly brought their traditions with them to the Continent (see map 14), and it is more likely that any insular Celtic influence on the traditions of the Bretons came from this source rather than from transmission of folktales from Wales to Brittany during the twelfth century. Yet remnants of the continental Celtic traditions may also account for the presence of water-fairies in the Breton lays. In this case the water-fairy tradition would be parallel at the Celtic level. The second problem is Ulrich's *Lanzelet*. The Teutonic peoples had as much of an affinity for water-fairies as the Celts.[32] Ulrich may have taken his sea-fairy from Teutonic rather than from Celtic tradition. Or he may have taken her from a legend of Alanic origin, since the Ossetic legends of the Narts also tell of women who live under the sea and who raise their sons and other heroes in this fairy kingdom.[33] In any case the tradition of the water-fairy of the Lancelot story may be parallel with the Welsh fairies at the hypothetical Indo-European level rather than at the Celtic level. Direct transmission from Wales is not required.[34]

The second point in the argument for a Welsh origin of the legends is that the Arthurian material of the Continent exhibits a knowledge of Welsh geography. While this is true for some works, such as Hartmann von Aue's *Erec*, the legends of Lancelot, if anything, show a lack of geographical knowledge in relation to Wales. Chrétien's *Conte de la charrette* takes place in a

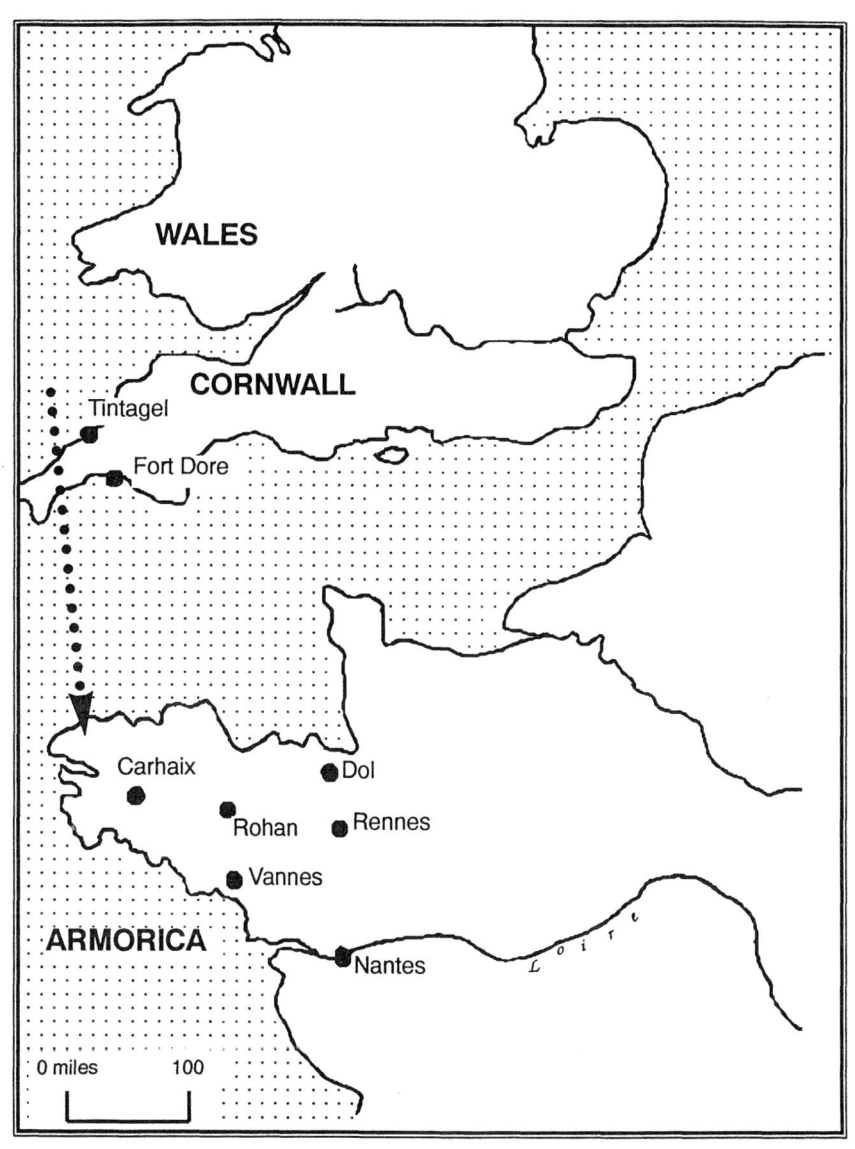

MAP 14. Celtic Immigration to Armorica

world akin to that of Ulrich's *Lanzelet*, where place-names are mentioned but cannot in most instances be located geographically. And the prose *Lancelot*'s detailed knowledge of the geography of Poitou actually argues against Walter Map's authorship of the work.

The third point is a series of fanciful etymologies that various scholars propose as a means of tracing the name Lancelot back to a Welsh name, such as Peredur.[35] As Weston pointed out, the majority of these etymologies fail to take into account that the only consistent factor among the legends of Lancelot is that Lancelot is always Lancelot *du Lac*.[36] Loomis considered this problem, and on several occasions he proposed the Welsh name Llwch Llawynnawc as the original form of Lancelot's name.[37] The problem with Loomis's hypothesis is that it relies solely on written transmission of the legends of Lancelot, because the pronunciation of the Welsh "Llwch" is not consistent with the pronunciation of the French "Lac." In response to this criticism Loomis proposed a missing text, a manuscript written in Old French and carried by Hugh de Morville from Britain to Germany when, according to Loomis, Morville was delivered as a hostage in February 1194 (along with several other nobles) in return for the release of the captured Richard the Lionheart. This manuscript was supposedly translated into Middle High German by Ulrich and given the title *Lanzelet*. This hypothetical manuscript raises several interesting questions.

Webster has convincingly shown that Chrétien, the pseudo-Map, and Ulrich all drew in part upon the same source for their works.[38] If that source was Morville's manuscript, how did Chrétien consult it before composing the *Conte de la charrette* in 1179 when Morville did not bring the manuscript to the Continent until 1194? And how did the manuscript get from Ulrich to the authors of the prose *Lancelot*? It is possible that all of these medieval authors were friends and that Chrétien borrowed the manuscript from Morville, who carried it to Ulrich,[39] who sent it to whoever composed the prose *Lancelot*. If this was the case, then we also have to believe that Chrétien just happened to select those adventures from the manuscript that were not used by the author(s) of the prose *Lancelot*[40] and that Ulrich simply translated the original work. It produces far less strain on the imagination to suppose that Chrétien, Ulrich, and the author(s) of the prose *Lancelot* took the seeds of their tale from a continental oral tradition. Consider too the improbability of Morville's manuscript being the only recorded instance of a British, not to mention Welsh, legend about Lancelot before the appearance of Lancelot in the insular Arthurian tradition more than a century after the *Lanzelet*.

Five of the thirteen parallels Webster finds among these works are actually commonplaces of medieval literature: (1) the knight wins a fight at a ford, (2) the knight suffers imprisonment, (3) the etiquette between a knight and a lady is discussed, (4) a tourney is held to gain news of a missing knight, and (5) the knight is attended by youths who are his protégés. Two of the other parallels are adventures that might easily happen to any number of knights: (1) the knight is obliged to take lodging in a castle where a damsel contrives to sleep with him, a circumstance that involves the knight in a bizarre fight (e.g., the story of Gawain and the Green Knight), and (2) the knight spends the night in a hall with three beds where he is subjected to a dangerous test (e.g., Sir Gareth in Malory's *Le Morte Darthur*). The remaining six elements are directly connected to Lancelot: (1) Lancelot was raised by a water-fairy, (2) Lancelot possesses a magic ring that enables him to detect enchantments, (3) Lancelot begins his career without a name, which is finally revealed in the presence of a lady in a cemetery near a monastery where Lancelot has had a conversation about tombs with the old monk in charge, (4) Lancelot plays the coward, (5) Lancelot has a special friendship with Gawain that leads to the heroes' searching for and rescuing each other on several occasions, and (6) Lancelot appears at the last moment to protect Guinevere from a would-be rapist, but the rapist kidnaps Guinevere; Lancelot follows and rescues her (with Gawain's help) after a series of adventures that involve an underwater bridge. These last six elements supposedly appeared in Morville's missing manuscript.[41]

But consider this: the *Lanzelet* contains fifty-three citations to a prior manuscript, yet only the last citation, 107 lines from the end of the 9,445-line poem, mentions Hugh de Morville. And, as Webster pointed out, each of the citations occurs in material that has come to be part of the traditional "biography" of Lancelot rather than in material that appears in the stories about other Arthurian knights. Hence it is at least probable that an oral tradition served as this source.[42]

Of all the authors who retell the legend of Lancelot only Chrétien does not claim a prior written source. He is also as unconcerned with tying his own work to history as he is in presenting his audience with the history of his hero. The other authors, however, seem to have felt a need to tie the legend of Lancelot to history.[43] They did so by tracing it to a prior written source, when the actual source has proven in part, at least in the case of the *Perlesvaus*, to be the result of oral transmission.[44] If the written source that supposedly stood behind the *Perlesvaus* did not exist, then those elements of the *Perlesvaus* that concern Lancelot had to come from some other source. The Grail material probably derived from the works of Robert de Boron,[45] but Robert covers only the early history of the Grail and the Round Table material in his *Joseph* and *Merlin*. The Lancelot material had to come from another source. This source was probably not the *Conte de la charrette*, the prose *Lancelot*, or the *Lanzelet*, because the author of the *Perlesvaus* is ignorant of Lancelot's connection with the Dame du Lac. The maidens who bring news of the Grail to Arthur's court still wear white and ride in carts[46] or use white mules for mounts, as do the female messengers of the Dame du Lac in the *Lanzelet* and the prose *Lancelot*. But the women do not have a special connection with water, let alone with a lake.

Whoever wrote the *Perlesvaus* also chose to emphasize the portion of the Lancelot cycle that involves Claudas, the knight who shared a claim to Lancelot's lands. Claudas is usually the enemy of the Dame du Lac, but he appears as the enemy of Lancelot in the *Perlesvaus*.[47] The *Agravain* (ca. 1230–1240) claims that Lancelot's lands fell to Claudas in 426.[48] There is confusion concerning whether Claudas or Clovis killed Ban and took Lancelot's patrimony from him. It is entirely possible that "Claudas" and "Clovis" are both "Romanizations" of the name Clodwig, and that the knight in question was originally the Merovingian king Clovis I (r. 481–511), who was certainly an enemy of the Alans of Armorica, where the *Perlesvaus* takes place.[49] Clovis I was also the final conqueror of the Alans of Gaul during the period in which the legends of Lancelot were formed. Perhaps his memory survived in the role of Lancelot's lifelong antagonist and the ruler of the Continent after Lancelot and the Round Table are destroyed.

Thus Lancelot was introduced into the Arthurian tradition by a continental source. Ulrich's phrase "welsches buoch" refers to a volume written in the French language, and Morville could have acquired such a book anywhere between the English Channel and Switzerland; and just because a book was *welsches* ("foreign") does not confirm that the hypothetical text was from Wales.[50] It is more likely that the source shared by Chrétien, Ulrich, the author(s) of the prose *Lancelot* and the authors of other tales about Lancelot was an oral tradition from the Continent that traveled to the British Isles only in the fourteenth century, when Lancelot finally takes his place alongside the Arthur of the British tradition.

Several stories in the Lancelot corpus seem to have specific Alanic parallels as well. For example, in one illumination from a fourteenth-century manuscript of the prose *Lancelot* Lancelot and Ector are seen walking through the Perilous Cemetery.[51] This cemetery is filled with the graves of the twelve brothers of Chanaan (Canaan), an evil follower of Joseph of Arimathea who killed his siblings because he felt that he was being punished for their sins. The marble tombs are all on fire, and each knight has a sword planted hilt-first (with the point up) into the marble of each tomb in place of a gravestone. Joseph of Arimathea declares that no man shall be able to remove the swords, but Lancelot shall successfully meet the challenge of the Perilous Cemetery and deliver Chanaan from his torment.[52] In this story we seem to see a survival of the Scythian practice of building hearths on graves combined with the Alanic practice of placing embedded swords in tombs.[53] The result of the successful completion of this adventure is that Lancelot learns his true name and royal heritage; hence this story seems to be Lancelot's version of Arthur's Sword in the Stone sequence.[54] The parallels with Alanic sources, however, run deeper in Lancelot's variant of the tale than in Arthur's. For example, in Alanic religion the father of Fire was the sun-god, but the goddess of the hearth, represented by Satana in the Nart sagas, seems to be the deity evoked in the Scythian custom of building hearths on graves.[55] Satana herself was intimately connected with graveyards, having been born in a tomb as the result of the rape of her mother's corpse by St. George.[56] In the Ossetian tales St. George has replaced the god of war, whose symbol was the sword planted in the ground.[57] We can cautiously deduce, then, that the goddess of the hearth was the daughter of the god of war in the Alanic religion.[58] Yet it is a fourteenth-century Arthurian illumination in which we find these images joined. In addition the son (or stepson or protégé) of the goddess of the hearth appears to have been the god of water in Alanic tradition.[59] This figure, represented in the Nart sagas by Satana's nephew, Batraz, most likely supplied the prototype for Lancelot du Lac, with his foster-mother, the Dame du Lac, and his primary adventure, which involves a graveyard and his ancestor's tomb.

Lancelot's excessive generosity is one of his most endearing characteristics. Batraz also is known for his generosity, although in his case it stems from simple steppe hospitality. Lancelot has the interesting epithet of the "Twice Dead Man." Batraz has no fear of death, being immortal, until God decides to punish him with death for massacring the Narts.[60] The reasoning behind Lancelot's epithet seems to be that death holds no fear for a man raised in the Land of the Dead.

The story of Lancelot's grandfather[61] as told in Lovelich's translation of the *Queste del Saint Graal* tells how the elder Lancelot was beheaded during a romantic assignation with the wife of an Irish duke.[62] Grandfather Lancelot's head fell into a well upon being severed from his body. The unlucky duke who performed the deed was unable to retrieve the head because the water burned like fire.[63] He had his followers place the body in a tomb to conceal the murder, but the tomb bled three drops of health-giving blood each day and as a result soon became guarded by two lions. The duke, upon returning home, was crushed by a stone that fell from his castle as he entered the gate.[64] Years later Lancelot du Lac happens upon the site and slays the lions—at which point the story unfortunately ends. This story also appears in the Portuguese *Liuro de Josep Abaramatia*.[65] In a slightly different tale Batraz avenges his

Lancelot and the "Alan of Lot" 93

PLATE 6. The Perilous Cemetery (Pierpont Morgan Library MS 806, fol. 207). The Pierpont Morgan Library, New York. MS. 806, f. 207.

grandfather, who is being forced to tend cattle in a foreign land.[66] The noble who rules the land is killed, and two women of his household are taken by Batraz and given to his father and grandfather as wives.

Parallels between the action in the legends of Lancelot and Alanic history seem to be present as well. In the *Lanzelet*, when Guinevere is stolen by Valerin the second time, Lancelot relies on bargaining rather than force of arms to get her back. Valerin keeps Guinevere in a castle surrounded by snakes, a barrier that Lancelot cannot pass. Therefore Lancelot surrenders Gawain and Erec, son of Lac, to Malduc, an enchanter who forces an opening in the barrier, allowing Lancelot to enter, kill Valerin, and rescue Guinevere. Lancelot later recovers Erec by enabling his army to cross an underwater bridge.[67] Now substitute the name Valentinian for Valerin. Between the first rescue of Guinevere and the second Lancelot gave an oath of loyalty to Arthur and his family. Constantius of Rome (benefactor of the Alans in Gaul) was Arthur's grandfather in legend and Valentinian's father in real life. "Lancelot" could not attack Valentinian without violating his oath to the family of Constantius. However, "Lancelot" could induce an old acquaintance to remove the problem for him. The story follows the same pattern as the historical events: the general in charge of the Alans, Aëtius, was murdered by the son of the man the Alans vowed to support. The Vandals, aided by another tribe of Alans, sacked Rome. Valentinian was killed, and the Alans of Gaul had their revenge without breaking their oath.

With these parallels in mind, then, let us take a closer look at the etymological arguments for the Welsh-origin hypothesis.

The Etymology

Loomis makes this case for the origin of the name Lancelot:

> Llwch, we know, could be and was translated into French as Lac, since the Welsh noun llwch means lake. It was natural for Bretons or Frenchmen to assume that Lac was

not the hero's name but rather referred to the place of his birth or upbringing. Llawwynnawc [Llawynnawc] or Llenlleawc would then be taken for the true name, and by assimilation to the name Lancelin, recorded in Brittany as early as 1034 and 1069, it became Lancelot. (Loomis 1952:190)

Based on this hypothesis of the origin of Lancelot's name, the generally accepted meaning of the name "Lancelot" is "Spear of Lug." This is arrived at by making the following division: "Lance-Lot," with "Lance" meaning "Spear" and "Lot" reflecting the possessor of the "Spear," in this case "Lot" or "Lug."

There are two basic problems with this etymology. The first is that Loomis makes the assumption that Lancelot was originally an insular figure, such as Llwch, while all of the texts agree that Lancelot originated on the Continent. The second problem is that *lot* in the Old French of the original texts does not mean either "lake" or "Lug." According to the *Nouveau dictionnaire étymologique* the word *lot* is (1) one's heritage or (2) one's destiny.[68] Maps from the period indicate that Lot was also the name of a river in southern France (see map 15). Some scholars have argued that Lancelot was, in effect, the surname of Ban's son Galahad, and surnames in the early Middle Ages were almost always the names of places.[69]

Working from the premise that the name Lancelot indicates a location, several place-names that resemble "Lancelot" become important. The *lan-* sequence appears in the names of Alanic settlements throughout Europe (see map 15). These place-names have undergone curious phonological shifts to reach their present form. For example, names that were originally phrases have been shortened to one word with the initial *A-* dropped: e.g., Alan d'Riano became Landriano.[70] Markale attributes all occurrences of the *lann-* sequence in Armorica to a Celtic word meaning "land."[71] Bachrach, however, has argued that some of these should be accounted for by the presence of Alans in the region. If Lancelot was a place-name, then it might have been Alancelot in the original. The possibility that Lancelot was actually a place-name is not an outlandish proposition, considering that the Old Spanish *Lançarote*[72] is also understood to designate a place as well as the hero's name.[73]

Gunar Freibergs (personal communication) has suggested that the *lanc-* sequence might be a derivative of the Latin "Alanus," which was "Gallicized" into "Alanus à Lot," that is, from "Alan" plus the Latin nomnitive singular ending "-us." In place-names that exhibit the *lance-* sequence the *ce* has been used to preserve the soft quality of the *c* after the cedilla was dropped.[74] The ç appears in the northern place-names and appeared in names that originally contained a z: e.g., Alenzon[75] becomes Alençon.[76] The z indicated the plural s, best illustrated by Alan place-names from the Pyrenees region: e.g., Brèche d'Allanz for "Gap [of the] Alans." If these same shifts are applied to the name Lancelot, then "(A)lanz(e)lot" results. One of the earliest texts that records the stories of Lancelot spells the hero's name "Lanzelet."[77]The form "Lanselos" is found in Chrétien's *Le Conte del Graal* (or *Perceval*),[78] the Huth *Merlin*,[79]and Guillaume le Clerc's *Fergus* (1200–1233),[80] and the form "Lawnslot" is attested in Welsh.[81]

If the *lanz-* sequence in Lancelot's name really stood for "Alans," then a new etymology begins to emerge. Perhaps due to the prolonged contact between the Alans and Teutonic tribes (e.g., the Visigoths) Alan place-names tend to use the Germanic possessive *s* (e.g., Alenzon means "Alans' town"[82]) in the north, while Alan place-names in the south tend to use the Germanic plural with a Latinate possessive in the form of "à" or "de" (e.g., Brèche d'Allanz). In the first case Lancelot would then read "(A)lanz-lot" and mean "the Alans' parcel of land." In the second instance the *a* (either dropped in the modern spelling or preserved by the *e* that gives "Lancelot" its second syllable when pronounced) would be inserted between "(A)lanz" and "lot," rendering the meaning "Alans of Lot" (see fig. 7).

This raises the question of where this place called Lot was located.[83] Since one of the heaviest regions of Alanic settlement was in the region surrounding the Lot River,[84] the notion that "Lancelot" might originally have been **(A)lans-à-Lot* or **Alanus-à-Lot* begins to make sense, especially if the legends of Lancelot originated in southern Gaul and were later developed in the vicinity of the Ile de France and Normandy (e.g., Marie de France and Chrétien de Troyes). "Lancelot" would then mean "Alan of the Lot [River]."

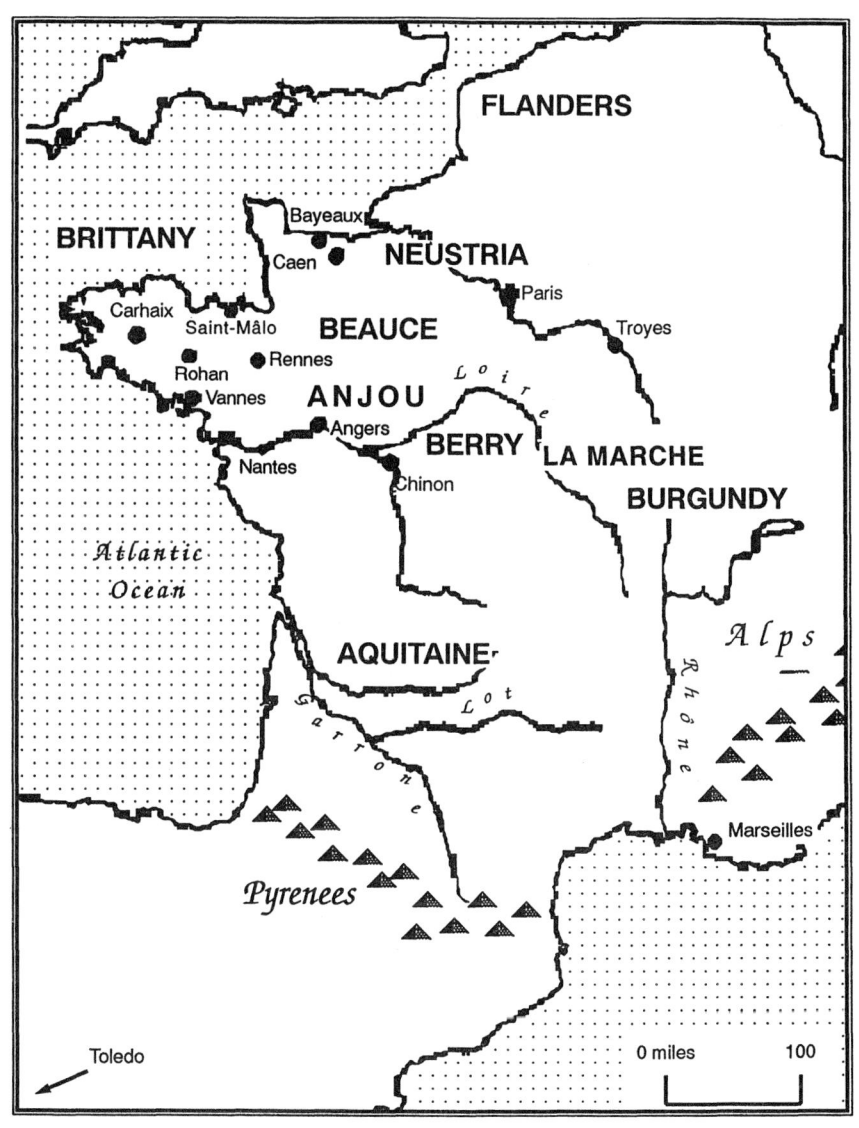

MAP 15. Arthurian Sites in Gaul

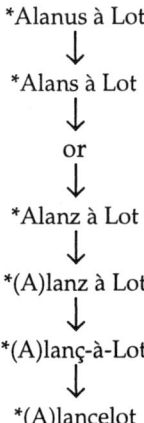

FIG. 7. Proposed Etymology of Lancelot

The genealogies given for the Grail knights, Perceval, Galahad, and Bors, are the most extensive among Arthurian heroes. These knights are all kin of Lancelot, and the name Alain appears several times in their lineage. Perceval's father in the *Perlesvaus* is Alain le Gros de la Vales.[85] There are many Elaines on both sides of the family as well.[86] The name Elaine, for all its connections to Helen, may be a survival of a feminine form of the name Alain,[87] since Helen is used as both a masculine and feminine name in some texts and as the name of figures identified as Alain in other texts.[88] In the Huth *Merlin* the author promises to tell of "Helain the White, who became Emperor of Constantinople," but this legend does not appear in the surviving version of this work.[89] Some scholars derive the name Alain in the Arthurian tradition from the Celtic-Breton name Alein.[90] Charvet argues that Alein is a Celtic name, and he sees the two saints Alain, one of whom founded the abbey of Lavaur (600s), as originating in the north of Britain.[91] Nelli argued that these names derived from the Breton name Alein in the Grail romances, which, he claimed, came from the East to the West and was then attached to the Breton legend of the magical cup.[92] As Bachrach has pointed out, however, it is far more probable that in this case the name Alein (Alain) came from the Alans who invaded Gaul in the fifth century.[93]

Perhaps the name that yields the most convincing evidence of Alanic influence on the Arthurian legends is that of Lancelot's father, King Ban de Benoich.[94] Bogdanow points out that in the *Suite du Merlin* the audience was already expected to know the story of Ban and his wife, Elaine (Helaine).[95] Merlin is heavily involved in this version of the story, prophesying that Lancelot will eventually defeat Claudas, urging Ban to ally with Arthur to solidify Britain under the young king, and otherwise meddling in the affairs of the continental monarch. Claudas's complaint against Ban involves a strip of land that both kings claim on which Ban builds a castle. This argument eventually leads to the death of Ban and the kidnapping of Lancelot by the Dame du Lac.

The sequence *Ban/Pant* appears in such forms as Pant,[96] Ban, Benoich, and possibly Pantdragon.[97] Because of the prolonged contact between the Alans and the Altaic-speaking Huns, who eventually intruded into the Alanic territories, it is conceivable that both steppe cultures might share similar words. The word *ban* seems to have meant "ruler" in both Alanic and Old Turkish.[98] We suggest that *ban* is a title found in the original Alanic and carried to Britain by the Iazyges and to Gaul by the Alans. Panticapaeum, a city east of the Kerch Peninsula, dominated trade (i.e., was the "ruling" or "chief" city for trade in the fourth century B.C.E.) with the Scythians in the Ukraine.[99] Alan leaders bear such names as Sangiban and Respendial, and the leaders of the Sarmatians who were defeated at the end of the Pannonian War are Zanticus and Banadaspes.[100] Thus the full name of Lancelot's father, Ban de Lancelot,[101] would translate as "Leader of the Alans of Lot."

Micha calls attention to the Ernée or Ernier who was the protector of Banvou, an ancient French fortress that could have been that of King Ban, or, more likely in Micha's opinion, in the care of an administrator of the *bannum* (the government of the *marche*, or borderland) that was Banvou in Arthurian times.[102] A *bannum benvoîcum* or *banvoïcum*, according to Micha, transferred its name from the place to the person, giving rise to the form Ban de Benoïc.[103] But, Micha wonders, on what map does this *bannum* appear? He is also troubled by the phonetic shift from *bannum benvoïcum* to Banvo/Banvou. *Bannum*, however, is probably related to an Altaic word that gave rise to the suffix *-ban* ("keeper of")[104] and to the word *bâni* ("founder, builder")[105] in modern Turkish and *ban* ("governor/viceroy [of Croatia]; warden of the southern marches of Hungary") in modern Hungarian and modern French.[106] The idea of "builder" is particularly interesting, since Ban's building of a castle on disputed land serves as the cause of the war with Claudas in the legends.

In any case the semantic field of the ancient word appears to include the notion of "ruler" (cf. *Zanticus*). The second half of Ban's name, Benoich (Benwick),[107] almost certainly divides Ben-oich, with the *a* shifting to *e* in the compound form and *oich* deriving from the Old High German *wîch* ("settlement"), which was apparently adapted from the Latin *vicus*.[108] Thus Benoich would mean either "The Ruler's Settlement" or "The Chief/Primary Settlement." So in essence Ban of Benoich's name simply tells us that this figure was the ruler of the capital city or military settlement in the region.[109] It is also interesting to note that a story similar to that of Ban and Bors is told about two Sarmatian kings of Hungary, Buka and Bani, who fell in battle against Theodoric of the Visigoths in 472.[110]

Micha traces the lands that belong to Ban and Bors (Bohort) to the part of Normandy that was given to Rollon à Saint-Clair "sur Epte" in 911, but he finds a difficulty with this hypothesis in that Lower Normandy was not adjacent to Berry, the traditional setting for the prose *Lancelot*.[111] Micha also discusses Ferdinand Lot's notion that Benoich is a fictional name for Saumur, a city on the Loire in France, but he identifies Gaunnes,[112] rather than Benoich, with Saumur (cf. map 13).

Another figure who possesses a name with the *ban*-sequence is Bandemagus.[113] Variants of this name include Bandemagu,[114] Bandemagús,[115] Baudemagus,[116] and Bandimagus.[117] The *-magus* element derives from Latin *magus* ("a learned man among the Persians, magician"). Given this proposed etymology for Ban, Bandemagus's name probably meant something like "Ruler of Learned Men" or "Magician King."

In another case where the *Pant-* sequence appears, Arthur's father, Uther Pendragon (Pantdragon), appears to be structurally equivalent to Batraz's father, Xæmyc. Although there is no onomastic connection between their names, Nickel has suggested that the name Pendragon is itself of Eastern European, and perhaps even Anatolian, origin and that Geoffrey of Monmouth's interpretation of it as a bastardized construction from Welsh *pen* ("head") plus Latin *draco* ("dragon") is an incorrect folk etymology.[118] Nickel sees the first element, *pen*, as more likely deriving from a widespread Eastern European word for "ruler," *pan/panje*, which would yield "Dragon Ruler"—a name consonant with several Roman images of Sarmatian warriors (e.g., on Trajan's Column in Rome; see plate 1) bearing banners with dragons emblazoned on them.

Another sequence of names involves the names of Lancelot's uncle and cousin Bors.[119] Bors, Boort, Boortz, Bohort, Boerte, and Bort may all be variations of the Ossetic Boratæ, the family of Batraz.[120] Also note that Bort is the name of a town in the region north of the county of Lot. Ferdinand Lot traced the name Bohort to the names of the kings of Ethiopia, which possibly could have been transmitted via contact with the Alans of Africa.[121]

The White Animal

Other Scythian elements appear in the Lancelot corpus as well. One of the most prominent is the motif of the hunt for the white animal. In Ulrich von Zatzikhoven's *Lanzelet* Guinevere is abducted by Valerin as Lanzelet (Lancelot) and Walewein (Gawain) join Arthur on the hunt for a white stag.[122] The custom that the successful hunter of the white stag would receive a kiss from the most beautiful woman was initiated, according to the text, by Uther Pendragon. The Middle Dutch verse romance *Lanceloet en het hert met de witte voet* (*Lancelot and the Deer with the White Foot*; 1200–1250;[123] transmitted exclusively in the *Lancelot-Compilatie*), the Second Continuation of Chrétien's *Perceval*, the Didot-*Perceval*, the Welsh *Peredur*, and the late twelfth-century Old French *Tyolet* all use the white-footed animal.[124] In *Tyolet* the hero cuts off the white foot of a stag, but a false knight claims to have accomplished the feat after Tyolet is attacked by lions who leave him for dead.[125] In related tales a hound (of unspecified color) leads Gawain over a bridge to the Waste Manor, where he finds a woman with a dead knight.[126] In Malory's *Le Morte Darthur* Lancelot follows a black brachet, or female hound, which had been tracking a deer, over a bridge and eventually to a castle, where he finds a woman, who sends him to the Chapel Perilous where he finds a dead knight.[127] At least on the surface these stories, combined with the Arthurian tales of the hunt for the white stag, resemble the Ossetic narrative in which a white stag leads Uryzmæg to an enchanted house where he meets a woman who involves him in an adventure.[128]

Loomis felt that the hunt for the white stag was of Celtic origin, since a similar hunt for a white animal is found in the *Mabinogi* as well as in the Breton lays of *Tyolet*, *Guingamor*, and *Guigemar*.[129] Note, however, that many of the Arthurian variants tell of the animal leading the hero across a stream, particularly in the legends of Lancelot. The "kiss" as the reward of this adventure has been thought to be an invention of Chrétien de Troyes;[130] but the notion of a woman waiting at the end of the hunt is well known in the Ossetic tradition as well. When Xæmyc, Batraz's father, goes on a similar hunt, he receives Batraz's mother in marriage.[131] The animal at the ford is a typical steppe motif and could have come from the Alans or Huns.[132]

Nitze and Jenkins also decide that the white beast of the Arthurian tradition is of Celtic origin, such as Henwen, the pig/boar.[133] However, they go on to say that

> William [of Malmesbury]'s account [from a dream of Edgar] of the "barking whelps" doubtless came (ultimately) from the Orient. Wesselofsky had pointed out an obvious parallel to it in the Twelve Dreams of Sehachi, a South Slavic and Rumanian vision with an Arabic variant. . . . The vision is rather widely known in the Balkan Peninsula and southern Russia, and has found acceptance as oral tradition by groups without a written literature. So that the possibility is not precluded that the author of P (or G) [of this manuscript]—like William of Malmesbury—knew the story from oral tradition.[134]

Yet, though admitting that one manuscript of the *Perlesvaus* drew on an oriental tale for its white animals, Nitze and Jenkins still favored the Celtic origin of the white beasts in the Arthurian sagas.[135]

As in the case of other Scythian elements in Celtic culture it is probable that this oriental tale with the white-animal motif as it appears in the Arthurian tradition was brought into western Europe by the Sarmatians and by the Alans.[136] With this hypothesis in mind let us take a closer look at the parallels between the tales of Lancelot and those of Batraz.

Lancelot and Batraz

Structural analysis[137] shows that the Lancelot legends exhibit parallels to those about Arthur; however, the greater number of parallels appear to be between Lancelot and Batraz. Batraz is a member of the Boratæ family; Lancelot's uncle and cousin are both named Boort. Batraz and Lancelot are both associated from birth with a fairylike female guardian; Arthur is not.[138] Batraz is born near the Black Sea, soon after which his father, Xæmyc, is murdered; in the prose *Lancelot* Lancelot is first seen as an infant near the shores of a lake, while his father, Ban, is dying after witnessing the fall of his last castle to his archenemy, Claudas. Batraz is associated with water and the Black Sea, and he is commonly given the epithet "of the Sea"; in the Grail texts Lancelot's family restores water to the Wasteland, and Lancelot's most common appellation is *dou Lac* ("of the Lake").[139] Both Batraz and Lancelot avenge their fathers' deaths; Arthur does not. Batraz and Lancelot get their swords from kinswomen associated with water; Arthur receives a sword from the Lady of the Lake only in Malory, and she is of no relation to him. All three heroes lead war bands. Batraz and Lancelot are not good kings; Arthur is. Batraz and Sozryko of the Nart sagas are "defined by their virtual war with the other Narts";[140] Lancelot is constantly attacking and being attacked by the other knights of the Round Table. Batraz massacres the Narts; Lancelot kills many of his fellow knights during his rescue of Guinevere from the stake and in the subsequent war against Arthur; Arthur never massacres his knights.[141] Batraz is not the traditional guardian of the Nartamongæ (the Ossetic counterpart of the Holy Grail),[142] although he briefly obtains the cup; Lancelot and Arthur do not become guardians of the Holy Grail, although Lancelot repeatedly sees the cup. Batraz is described thus: "Alone of the Narts . . . you are without flaw . . . or at most you have but one flaw";[143] Lancelot is traditionally "the best of all worldly knights," placing fourth behind the three Grail Knights, Galahad, Perceval, and Bors, who were without flaw (Bors transgressed only once) but who were of heaven, not earth. In addition the events in the tale "How Batraz Avenged His Father" bear a striking similarity to the closing sequence of the *Perlesvaus*.[144] In both tales a woman tells the hero about a castle; the hero enters by creatively crossing a moat by means of a weapon and then slaughters the occupants.

Just as Littleton and Thomas suggested that the Sarmatians provided the Batraz-prototype influence on the legends of Arthur, Peterson suggested that the Alans had a similar influence on the legends of Lancelot.[145] The Iazyges' stories about "Artorius" were able to develop freely between ca. 175 and 465 C.E. But after 465 there seems to be an overriding sense that Arthur was a historical figure, while other characters were perceived as existing only in the stories. Some authors, such as Jacob van Maerlant in the late thirteenth century, edited out references to Arthurian "fiction," especially Lancelot and Perceval.[146] The "real" Arthur, probably in the person of Riothamus, had a real history that many people knew.[147] So the memory of the Batraz-prototype was submerged beneath the historical overlay. A historical Arthur may be seen in Riothamus, a historical Ban in the Alan leader at Bazas, and a historical Tristan in the son of King Mark Conomar. Lancelot has no such historical counterpart—with the possible exception of the Alan who served as a hostage at Bazas and from whom the hero's name may be ultimately derived. This lack of a clearcut man-behind-the-legend may have worked in our favor in trying to discover the roots of the Lancelot legends. The stories told by the Alans would have developed freely until they were recorded in writing during the twelfth century. Arthur and Lancelot thus become reflections of the same hero.

When the descendants of the Iazyges invaded with Riothamus or fled from the Saxons to settle on the Continent, they almost certainly had contact with the Alans in Gaul. The two groups, telling stories of their greatest heroes, might have noticed that those about Arthur contained few if any references to Lancelot. Yet the storytellers sensed that the characters of these heroes belonged together, and the stories were adapted accordingly. In such texts as Malory's *Le Morte Darthur* Guinevere marries Arthur but Lancelot acts as her husband. Lancelot and Arthur carry twin swords that they draw from stones,[148] and Lancelot is the only knight of the Round Table who has the right to wield Excalibur. There is confusion over who is king of Lancelot's patrimony, because the continental hero defeats Claudas with troops that Arthur provided from the Round Table.[149] Both are military leaders of the same war band who are betrayed by each other: Lancelot betrays Arthur in Malory, and Arthur betrays Lancelot in the *Perlesvaus*. Neither hero achieves the Holy Grail. Both men, in addition, are tricked into begetting a son on a relative,[150] and the child somehow leads to their downfall.[151]

Since the Alans did not reach Gaul until the beginning of the fifth century, if they were carrying the legends of a prototype of Batraz and if Lancelot is the heroic reflection of that prototype, then a stronger parallel would be expected between the legends of Lancelot and the Northeast Iranian warrior than between Arthur and the same figure, because the Iazyges had more time to acculturate to surrounding Celts than did the Alans. This is precisely the case. It is our contention that Lancelot has more parallels with the Ossetic figure of Batraz than with the Celtic Lug. Arthur is in all probability a reflection of the same Alano-Sarmatian hero as Lancelot, but the Arthurian legends were skewed by the presence of the historical Arthur.

Geography

Throughout all the legends about Lancelot one fact remains the same: Lancelot, whoever or whatever he was, was born on the Continent. Even in the *Lanzelet*,[152] the action of which is set in Wales, many of the place-names and the character names appear to designate French locales. For example, "Dodone" may sound like Dodona of Greek myth, yet note the similarity of spelling between this "Germanization" of a French word and the name of the French river and county Dordogne (see map 15). Dodone is the dwelling place of the Lady of the Sea's antagonist and the land in which Lancelot eventually establishes his household.[153] Carman used the prose *Lancelot*'s careful attention to geography to reconstruct a map of the setting for this legend (see map 13).[154] The center of action is south of the Loire River in Berry. The Alans had many settlements throughout this region and played an important part in its history during the fifth century.[155]

There are four major regions of importance in the stories of Lancelot: the lake, the forest, the mountains, and the desert. The Grail legends in particular emphasize these four divisions. The lake initially seems to have the most influence on Lancelot's life. The forest is a means of getting from one place to another. The mountains are where castles, especially holy castles associated with the Grail, are found. And the desert pervades the narratives as a unifying element. Claudas, Lancelot's archrival, is described as "of the Desert." The legends of the Grail, in which Lancelot's family plays such a dominant role, deal with the return of water (the lake) to the Wasteland (the land that has been turned into a desert). Lancelot's best friend is Galahaut, who once appears under the name Galehaut de Haut Desert in Malory. The *Perlesvaus* contains a scene in which Lancelot is almost slain by a knight in a "Beheading Game" that shows remarkable parallels to the later poem *Sir Gawain and the Green Knight*, in which the nominal antagonist is Bercilak de Haut Desert. "Desert" in the Middle Ages referred to uncultivated land.[156] Recall that the original grant by the Romans to the Alans of Gaul was *agri deserti*, which could easily have corrupted into these "desert" references in the Arthurian tradition.

The country of Lot is dotted with lakes, and certainly the epithet *du Lac* as well as the story of his childhood at the Lake are central to the legends about Lancelot.[157] The major feature of the country is the Cevennes Mountains, the source of the Garonne. The landscape is sculpted with limestone plateaus and riddled with fertile valleys and vineyards. All this, and the fact that the Alans had many settlements throughout this Roman province,[158] suggests that a short history of Gaul would shed light on the possibility that the French tales about Lancelot were ultimately derived from legends preserved by the Alans of the region.

Evidence of Alanic Culture in the Tradition

For all the Alan prowess on horseback[159] it seems odd to find that Perceval, Galahad, and Lancelot have little or no knowledge of horsemanship when they begin their careers as warriors. During the Middle Ages it was common practice to make fun of the Breton inability to ride, even though the Bretons were in fact exceptional horsemen because of Alanic influence.[160] Perhaps the Alans originally told humorous stories about the Bretons only to have the same stories applied to themselves after they became part of the Breton nobility. It should be noted that, although Galahad, Perceval, and Lancelot have great difficulty when they first try to ride a horse, none of the heroes thereafter is easily separated from his horse's back. Perhaps the most charming example of Lancelot's reliance upon his horse is found in the *Perlesvaus*: the hero, tricked into fighting three horsemen while he is on foot, hesitates because "in combat he was not so sure of himself on foot as on horseback."[161]

In Chrétien's *Conte de la charrette* Lancelot rides in a cart to rescue Guinevere. Later interpretations of this episode claim that riding in a cart was humiliating and that Lancelot loved Guinevere so much that he was willing to endure this shame for her sake. If Lancelot had been an Alan, however, riding in a cart would be necessary for him if his wife, the usual driver, had been stolen. The Alans were a nomadic people who carried their households and belongings in carts. The men rode horses while the women drove the carts. If something happened to an Alan's wife, he would have to drive the cart himself until he could replace her unless he wished to abandon his goods.[162] In this light the title commonly given to translations of Chrétien's *Conte de la charrette*, "The Knight of the Cart," makes eminent sense.[163]

At least one of Lancelot's early magic items, the mirror, seems to have Sarmatian, if not Alanic, connections as well. The Sarmatian practice of carrying mirrors is discussed by Maenchen-Helfen.[164] Many Sarmatians, especially the warrior women, were buried with mirrors, and Sulimirski argues for the Sarmatian rather than for the Visigothic ethnicity of an occupant of a grave simply on the evidence of a mirror found within the grave.[165] One such grave was found in Strasbourg. Sulimirski felt that many brooches found from Troyes to Carthage, including the Saône Valley, the Department of Aube, and Albacin (in Spain near Granada), that are currently identified as Gothic may actually be Alanic.

Thus Arthur and Lancelot both exhibit marked parallels to figures in the Northeast Iranian traditions. These parallels, however, extend to yet other knights of the Round Table, as we shall see in the next chapter.

Notes

1. Littleton and Thomas 1978. Lug appears under such names as Lugh, Lleu, and Lludd. For the derivation of Lancelot from Lug see Loomis 1963b:161.

2. Note that the *Pi5reks saga*, the *Waltharius*, and even the *Nibelungenlied* are all set in the fifth century and deal with Goths and Huns.

3. Webster 1934:203–214; Zenker 1926:102. Achilles, Prometheus, and Zeus share several biographical elements with Lancelot. Each hero is the rightful heir to a conquered kingdom. As a child he is exposed on a hill beside a lake. He is rescued by a powerful woman (i.e., queen) who comes from the water, and he is raised among women. The warrior is given arms, a horse, and magic protection and is sent into the world. These are, however, all elements of the traditional biography of a hero (e.g., Raglan 1936).

4. The Ossetic Satana (Dumézil 1930:75–78) raises the hero Sozryko, whom she takes from a stone beside a river, in an otherworld. Sozryko is trained by supernatural beings by day and brought to Satana

every night, just as Lancelot is trained by the People of the Lake and brought to the Dame du Lac every night.

5. These items, especially the mirror, are all found in the graves of Sarmatian warrior women (Newark 1989:18–19; cf. Megaw and Megaw 1986:28). Bronze mirrors have been found in the graves of Alans as well (Ozols in Beck et al. 1881:125). Although mirrors are also found in British Celtic graves (Dent 1985:85–92), such graves usually included chariots as well. Note that the equipment supplied by the Lady of the Lake to Lancelot is that of a horseback-riding warrior, not of a chariot warrior, which is what would be expected if this story had come from a Celtic source. Celtic mirrors are thought to be primarily British, rather than pan-Celtic (Jones-Bley, personal communication). Other ancient cultures, such as the Etruscans (de Grummond 1982:166ff.), also included mirrors in men's graves. For a full discussion of Celtic mirrors, see Kilbride-Jones 1980:109–116.

6. Lancelot spends most of his early adventures refusing to give his name, simply because he does not know it himself. Cf. Dumézil (1930:32–34), where Don Bettyr raises the "nameless" son of Uryzmæg in an otherworld beneath the sea, which is accessed by a rock.

7. As de Vries (1942) pointed out, the colors white, red, and black (or dark green/dark blue) typically reflect the three Indo-European ideological functions (respectively, sovereignty, physical prowess, and fertility) as delineated by Dumézil; see, for example, Littleton (1991:89). Thus a three-colored shield is most likely a symbol of sovereignty, as an Indo-European king, even incognito, is a repository of all three functions (see Dumézil 1971).

8. Cf. Welsh Gwenhwyfar, Irish Finnabair (from Findabair; see Lewis and Pedersen 1961:174). Ford (1983:273) translates Guinevere's name as "white phantom." Colarusso (personal communication) thinks that a more likely source is *windo-br̥-yā ("white born"; possibly "born of the foam"; cf. Greek Aphrodite "foam born").

9. Constantius asked only that the Alans control the coastal roads, preventing Athaulf and the Visigoths from returning from Spain to Gaul. The Alans accepted.

10. Soudek 1972.v; App 1929:4. The earliest mentions of Lancelot in connection with King Arthur are in the third position of importance on a list of names that appears in Chrétien's *Erec* and *Cligés* (App 1929:4; Weston 1901a:4–5). Soudek (1972:v) and App (1929:3) argue that Lancelot's name is of Germanic origin even though his character takes on the role of a Breton knight.

11. Many knights fill the role of Guinevere's lover before the tradition settles on Lancelot. In Wace's version Mordred was Guinevere's lover before he abducted her in the final days of the Round Table (Rhys 1928:109), and Guinevere tries to engage Launfal as her lover in Marie de France's lay *Lanval* and Thomas à Chestre's lay *Sir Launfal*.

12. In some cases, as in the Old French *Balain*, this ring is able to break enchantments as well; Campbell 1972:119. The *Balain* is a fragment of the Post-Vulgate *Suite du Merlin*. Best known from Malory's *Morte Darthur*, Book II, the French fragments can be found in the Huth *Merlin* (B.L. Add. 38117) and in Cambridge University Library Add. 7071. The text also exists in Castilian (as part of *El Baladro del Sabio Merlin*, Burgos, 1498; Seville 1535) and in Gallician-Portuguese (Lacy et al. 1986:430).

13. This translation was provided by Donald Ward (personal communication). Note that the Ossetic stories also employ sea-fairies as the foster-parents of young heroes (e.g., Dumézil 1930:20–24).

14. The trait of Alan leaders having multiple wives was well known. Perhaps the most famous case was that of Aspar, a general of Eastern Rome, who had three wives, a Roman, an Alan, and a German, each of whom gave him a son (Bury 1889, 1:320; Bachrach 1973:50–51).

15. Or if he did know it, he did not feel his audience would be upset by his not presenting that variant of the legend.

16. The prose *Lancelot* is a portion of the early thirteenth-century Vulgate Cycle, which includes the *Estoire del Saint Graal*, the *Merlin* (and its sequel; Wheatley 1865–1899), the *Lancelot* proper, the *Queste del Saint Graal*, and the *Mort le Roi Artu*.

17. Although the text claims that Map wrote this work for Henry III of England, most scholars believe that this attribution is false (e.g. Lacy et al. 1986:374).

18. Carman 1973:65–84; see map 13. Carman includes a map of his findings that graphically illustrates the evidence discussed in this section.

19. Paton 1903. Paton identifies three functions of the Dame du Lac: the guardian of Lancelot, the opponent of Morgan, and the lover of Merlin. She determines that the most ancient of these is the function as the guardian.

Lancelot's insanity is a little-discussed aspect of his character. Most scholars ignore the problem altogether. Others attempt to link the hero's madness to the dictates of courtly love. Some scholars have compared it with the rage of Cūchulainn in the Irish *Táin Bó Cuailgne* and argued that this insanity demonstrates a connection between Lancelot and the Celtic tradition (Owen, diss., 16–21). However, most heroes like Lancelot and Achilles (who are destructive as well as beneficial to their culture) exhibit this madness, and, as Markale (1985:152–154) points out, the characters are more likely parallel at the hypothetical Indo-European level than at the strictly Celtic level.

20. This detail is interesting, since the pagans in the region of Berry at the time that Lancelot's conversion is supposedly taking place included many Alans.

21. Bogdanow in Loomis 1959:331. This prose redaction of Robert de Boron's *Merlin* (1191–1202) is also known as the Huth *Merlin*.

22. Loomis 1952:187–192. This is an extremely strange notion to begin with, since Lancelot's family is said to marry Irish women (e.g., his grandfather Lancelot marries the King of Ireland's daughter) and to have adventures in Ireland (e.g., Lancelot in *Rigomer*), but they are never said to be Irish.

23. Lot and Morgawse were not married at the time of Gawain's birth (West 1969:118).

24. Often said to be the Morr£gan of Celtic tradition (e.g., Moorman and Moorman 1978:92).

25. In Heinrich von dem Türlin's German romance *Diu Crône* (ca. 1230) Gawain also appears as the Grail hero. Weston (1906–1909, 1:316) argued on the basis of this and other evidence that he was the original Grail hero. However, we have difficulty identifying the lecherous Gawain with Galahad, the chaste seeker of the Holy Grail. Wauchier de Denain's Continuation of the *Perceval* presents an early version of the Grail legend with Gawain as hero. This rendition is credited to Bleheris, whom Wauchier believed was a native of Wales (Weston 1913:31–32). A character named Bleheri appears as the father of the hero in the French romance *Mériadeuc* (or *Le Chevalier aux deux épées*; ca. 1225–1259; Foerster 1877). Weston (1913:31–32) identified Wauchier's Bleheris with Blishis of the *Elucidation*, with Bréri of Thomas's *Tristan*, and with Bledhericus, a storyteller mentioned by Giraldus Cambrensis (Gerald of Wales).

The major problem with most of the Gawain/Galahad parallels is that Galahad was not a part of the original Arthurian tradition. Most scholars see this son of Lancelot as a creation of Cistercians attempting to supplant the popular, bloodthirsty, and immoral father with a character more to their own liking in the place of Gawain and Perceval in the Grail legends (e.g., Loomis 1963b:178–182).

26. This theme is a favorite in the Arthurian tradition. The name of Guinevere's abductor, from the earliest recorded legends, usually begins with *M*: Mardoc, Mordred/Modred/Medraut, Meleagant/

Meligraunt/Meliagrance/Mellyagaunce, Melwas. This element is significant, but we have found no satisfactory explanation for it.

27. See Ford (1977) and Gantz (1976) for Lleu, and MacCana (1970) and MacCulloch (1918) for Lugh.

28. The Roman eagle (Cirlot 1983:91–93), the symbol of the legions, bore crossed thunderbolts, representing the god of war. The Sarmatian eagle also bore crossed thunderbolts and represented a god of war. This eastern deity had a connection with water as well, much as we find the ideas of war and water melded in the character of Lancelot. The Christian eagle represented a messenger from heaven (remember that we are dealing with the Grail family when we speak of Lancelot). The Celtic eagle symbolized the god Lug, the multitalented deity represented in Irish literature by Lugh and in Welsh literature by Lleu. Perhaps this surplus of imagery surrounding Lancelot's heraldic device is why all devices disappear from his shield in later works (just as Atchity [1978] proposed happened with the shield of Achilles when it was represented in later Greek art).

29. Rees and Rees 1961:34–35.

30. We also find Loomis's identification of Elaine Sans Pere with Morgan Le Fay tenuous, inasmuch as it is based on his interpretation of Morgan as the possessor of a horn of healing and Pelles (Elaine's father) as the Grail Keeper (cf. chaps. 5 and 10).

31. Rhŷs 1901. This reference is found in the "Preface" of Rhŷs's work, paragraph five. The pages are not numbered at this point in the 1983 edition.

32. Consider, for example, the numerous references to water-nixies in *The German Legends of the Brothers Grimm* (Ward 1981).

33. E.g., Dumézil 1930:20–24.

34. The connection between Lancelot and water may have more to do with his family having Third Function characteristics (e.g., the connection of members of his family with the fertility of the land in the Grail tradition) than with any tradition of women associated with water training the young warrior.

35. For Peredur/Lancelot the argument is that both *pâr* and *lance* meant spear, therefore the names were connected (Weston 1901a:8–9).

36. Weston 1901a:8–10. It is remotely possible that the word that appears in the Arthurian legends as *lac* was originally related to the word that appears in the Eastern Caucasian languages as *lak* (Ossetic *læg*; *läg*, "man"; Benveniste 1959:118).

37. This hypothesis is still accepted by some scholars; see Jenkins 1975:78–79.

38. Webster 1934:203–214.

39. Aside from those characteristics that the *Conte* shares with the *Lanzelet*, as identified by Webster, Chrétien's poem is usually thought to be his own invention. See Loomis 1949.

40. Although the *Lanzelet* is dated over a decade after Chrétien's *Conte de la charrette*, the material in Ulrich's poem is generally considered to antedate the material in Chrétien's work (Webster 1934 and 1951).

41. Webster 1934:203–214.

42. Webster 1934.

43. A legend, by definition, is tied to history, since it "purports to be an extraordinary happening believed to have actually occurred" (Thompson 1977:8–9).

44. Nitze and Jenkins 1932–1937, 1:104.

45. Chrétien's romance the *Conte del Graal* is unfinished, and most of the later authors are believed to have relied on Robert's works for their source of the tradition.

46. The Franciscan friar William of Rubruk's description (quoted by Lamb 1943:42–43) of the Mongols (ca. 1250)

> One girl is able to drive twenty or thirty carts. The ground [in the steppes] is quite level, so they fasten the carts and wagons together, and the girl sits on the front of the leading cart, guiding the cattle, while all the rest follow. They travel slowly—only as fast as an ox or [a] lamb can walk.

47. The *Perlesvaus* does not mention the Dame du Lac.

48. Baumgartner 1981:65–66. Note that this date would place the action of the legends of Lancelot contemporary with the Alan invasions of Gaul rather than with the reign of Clovis.

The *Agravain* is the only surviving material from the Vulgate *Lancelot* that appears in the Post-Vulgate Cycle. The text of the French fragments can be found in B.N. 112 and the late thirteenth-century codex B.N. fr. 12599 (Lacy et al. 1986:430–431).

49. Nitze 1937:101.

50. "Welsh" and "Wales" derive from this word *welsches* ("foreign"). Thus the people of Wales are called "foreigners" when they

are actually Celtic people who call themselves the Cymri. Cf. Alain of the Foraign Lands and Galafer, King of Foraign (see appendix 2).

The French form of *welsches* is *galles*. The Old Cornish adjective *galec* (cf. Welsh *galeg*, Armorican *gallek*) meant "French, Gaulish" and seems to have carried with it this notion of "foreigner" (cf. *gales*, "hard, difficult," and *gallos/galloys/gallus*, Welsh *gallu*, Armorican *galloud*, "power, might, authority"; Williams 1865:159).

Several of the names in the Lancelot corpus begin with the sequence *Gala-*: Galahad (Galaad), Galatia, Gallacum, Galahodin, and Galahaut. The French *galles* has usually been assumed to have supplied these names to the Arthurian legend. We would argue that the significant idea behind these names is not "Welsh" but rather "foreign," as discussed above.

51. Pierpont Morgan Library 806 ex. MS Yates-Thompson, fol. 207; Loomis and Loomis 1938:99, fig. 253. Loomis and Loomis identify the figures in this illumination as Gawain and Ector. Since the devices on the shields are unreliable for such an identification (Gawain and Lancelot both carry the same shield in different manuscripts), we can only assume that Loomis and Loomis based their identification of the figures on the text of the manuscript that accompanied the illumination. However, since the illumination also depicts Lancelot/Gawain as battling the swords, which are wielded by the spirits of the dead knights, and since versions of the story outside of the prose *Lancelot* (e.g., Lovelich's version and Malory's *Le Morte Darthur*) assign this fight to Lancelot rather than to Gawain, we suspect that what we have here is an instance of the illumination and the text of the manuscript following different traditions (like illuminations that depict Joseph of Arimathea with the Chalice at the Cross while the text makes no mention of Joseph with the Chalice; Malcor 1991:261) and hence prefer the identification of the knight as Lancelot.

52. He was buried alive; Lovelich 1874–1905, 2:267–270; see plate 6.

53. Abaev 1980:12. For the distribution of Alan burial sites in Europe see Sulimirski (1970:190, fig. 70) and Bachrach (1973:69, map 5, and 70, map 6). For details of burials in which Indo-Iranian-speaking peoples thrust knives into piles of horse, sheep, or cattle bones see Sulimirski 1970:105, cf. 64.

54. It appears from this and other evidence that Arthur and Lancelot are carrying twin swords (see chap. 5).

55. Abaev 1980:12.

56. Dumézil 1930:24–25.

57. Cf. also Espor, god of sacrifices, from an Ingush variant of "The Death of Batraz" (Dumézil 1930:72-73). In this tale Pataraz (Batraz) seeks out Espor to request permission to die in order to restore the abundance to the world that was removed upon his birth (cf. the function of the Wasteland in the Grail tradition). Espor agrees to restore fertility to the women and the mares if Pataraz can return to earth and then return to Espor before the last rays of the sun leave the mountaintops. Pataraz accomplishes the feat and is allowed to die. Cf. Lancelot's connection with mares and fertility.

58. E.g., Satana in the Nart sagas; Abaev 1980:13.

59. Dumézil 1978:24.

60. Even then the folktale of the reluctant corpse has attached to his corpus; Dumézil 1930:71 ff.

61. This grandfather, who was also called Lancelot, was the son of the King of "Galles" and husband of the daughter of the King of Ireland. Given the lineage of Lancelot from Joseph of Arimathea through the male line, this "Roi de Galles" must have meant "King of Foreigners" (cf. Alain of the Foraign Lands and Galafer, King of Foraign and in Perceval's genealogy) in the original, since Joseph of Arimathea can hardly be considered Welsh, as in Lovelich's translation (1874-1905, 2:348-356).

62. Cf. Lovelich 1874-1905, 2:348-356. The story is almost identical to Uther Pendragon's assignation with Igraine, wife of Duke Gorlois of Cornwall, except that Uther survives his tryst, during which he sires Arthur. The same confusion as to whether the correct title for a figure is "Count" or "Duke" occurs in both the historical and the legendary families of Cornwall and Brittany.

63. Cf. Ford (1974), who discusses the "fire" that lurked in Nechtan's Well and that burned his wife, Bóand. See also Dumézil (1963).

64. So he ultimately fared no better than Gorlois, who died the night Uther slept with Igraine.

65. Carter 1967:50-51.

66. Dumézil 1930:59 61.

67. Chrétien de Troyes assigns this adventure to Gawain.

68. Dauzat, Dubois, and Mitterand 1964:429.

69. E.g., Kennedy 1986:148-149. The adventuring knight finds this name inscribed on a tombstone at Dolorous Guard, earning the right to be called by it.

70. *Dizionario Enciclopedico dei Comuni d'Italia* 1950, 2:747; Sabarthés 1912:195–196; Bachrach 1969:354–358; 1973:135–136.

71. Markale 1983:57; cf. Holder 1891:140–141.

72. Pietsch 1924–1925, 1:85, fol. 298v: "el rrey de Lançarote."

73. Similar sequences occur in the names of other heroes. The name Lantfrido is found in eighth- to twelfth-century German poetry (Müllenhoff and Scherer 1964, 1:48, 2:121). The name Lanto appears in at least one German text (Müllenhoff and Scherer 1964, 1:224, l. 18).

74. Cf. Alancianus in Aude; Bachrach 1973:30; cf. Sabarthés 1912:195–196.

75. The Alans settled in the region of Metz, in Normandy, in Armorica, on the Loire River, and near the Pyrenees, leaving placenames like this all over the European landscape.

76. Bachrach 1967:476–489. The counts of Alençon were still intimately connected with the kings of France during the time that the Arthurian romances were produced. Peter, count of Alençon, was the second son of St. Louis and uncle of Philip III (Bertoni 1922:84). Charles, duke of Alençon, made an unsuccessful attempt to use the feigned-retreat tactic at Pavia on February 14, 1525, following the surrender of his king. He was branded a coward and reputedly died of shame (actually pleurisy killed him) on April 11, 1525, after returning to Margaret of Navarre at Lyons with the news (Saintsbury 1922, 1:xxxvii–xxxviii).

77. Paton 1929:5. Ulrich von Zatzikhoven's *Lanzelet* (ca. 1194–1205) appears to have been based on a lost French original *Lanzelet* to which most scholars turn for early stories of Lancelot (Barber 1961:86–87; Lacy et al. 1986:588). The *Lanzelet* is a collection of five stories, all of which follow the same basic pattern: Lancelot fights an antagonist, wins, receives his enemy's daughter in marriage, and becomes king of the conquered warrior's lands. The main story line follows Lancelot from his birth through his childhood under the care of the Lady of the Sea and his training to meet the Lady's enemy in battle. When Lancelot finally achieves the goal the Lady has set for him, he receives Iblis as his bride (the only woman of the four he marries and the only love interest who appears in more than one section). Lancelot wins an unnamed woman, then Ade, then the Queen of Pluris, and then Guinevere in battle (although he allows Arthur to marry her—this is Arthur's only appearance in the tale). Lancelot wins Iblis when he defeats the Lady of the Sea's nemesis, and he wins Elidia by agreeing to kiss her while she is in serpent form. (Elidia seems to be the wife who becomes the cunning and deceiving Elaine in later tales.) Iblis passes a test of chastity, and

Lancelot conquers his homeland by defeating Claudas. Lancelot and Iblis have three sons and one daughter and live happily ever after.

78. Potvin 1865–1873, 1:14.
79. Hucher 1875–1878, 3:117.
80. Martin 1872:177, l. 6509.
81. Parry 1933:1.
82. Such place-names occur for fictional towns in the Arthurian legends as well as in actual continental geography. For example, Alantine was a castle/town in the cycle of Lancelot (Micha 1987:253).
83. Although Camelot and Lancelot seem to share this -*lot* ending, the traditional derivation of Camelot is from the Latin Camulodunum (modern Colchester) in Britain (Moorman and Moorman 1978:28). Other suggestions for the origin of Camelot include Cadbury (near the village of Camel; Ashe 1985:80–83) and Camboglanna (a fort on Hadrian's Wall, which may have been one of the posts for the Iazyges in 175 C.E.; Barber 1961:105; cf. chaps. 1 and 2). Camelot as the name of Arthur's primary residence is first used by Chrétien in his *Conte de la charrette* (Moorman and Moorman 1978:28; Rogers 1984), so a continental origin for or French influence upon the word cannot be completely discounted.
84. Sabarthés 1912, 5:195–196, 7:263; cf. 1907, 9:302, 312 for Lanet as a Roman place name that was originally rendered "Alanetum," which Sabarthés derives from Alnetum, "le lieu planté d'aulnes" ("stand of alders"); Dauzat and Rostaing 1963:8; de Vic and Vaissete 1879, 7:279; Longnon 1920:158; Bachrach 1969:354–358; Meyrat 1959:12. Towns with such names as Espalion can be found along this river.
85. Bryant 1978:20.
86. In the *Manuscrit du Petit Saint Graal et du Merlin* (the Huth Merlin) a woman named Aleine appears as Gauvin's niece (i.e., Gawain; Hucher 1875–78, 1:379).
87. Colarusso suggests that this name was *"*l#ny£* ("woman Alan"). Cf. the town of Alanya in southern Gaul (see map 9).
88. Bors's son in Malory is Helyn le Blank. Lovelich (1874–1905, 2:91) glosses Elyen as "Alains le gros." The spelling of the names Elaine and Hélène is interchangeable in Wace (e.g., Le Roux de Lincy 1838, 1:2, 265, 267, 270–271, 275; 2:125, 144, 148–152, 159). The form Elene appears in the *Hildebrandslied*, sec. 258 (Müllenhoff and Scherer 1964, 2:11). The adjective *elyn*- in ancient Cornish meant "clean, fair" (cf. Welsh *ellain*, Irish *aluin*, Gaelic *aluinn*, and Manx *aalin*; Williams 1865:134), forms that also exhibit the *e*/*a* shift and that could have influenced the variant spellings of Alan and Elaine in the Arthurian legends.

The color white seems to have been associated with several groups of Alans, especially those closely associated with the Huns in southern Poland (e.g., the Roxolani; cf. the White Huns) and elsewhere in Eastern Europe in the fifth century (Phillips 1965:120–124). Sulimirski (1970:189–190) suggests that the ethnic names Serb and Croat are not Slavic and originally referred to tribes of "White" Alans, i.e., the so-called White Serbs and White Croats. Colarusso (personal communication) has suggested that "white" was interpreted as "east" and "black" as "west," possibly as a result of influence from "the old Chinese system of color coding the compass."

89. Waite 1933:199. Nitze and Jenkins (1932–1937, 1:x) felt that the name Alain was also responsible for such names as Julain, Julien, Ulain, and Huilain, which appear in Arthurian tradition.

90. E.g., Meyer 1956:36.

91. Charvet 1967.

92. Nelli 1951:150.

93. Junk (1912:59–60), citing Plinius (770.16) and Solin, has suggested that the name Alanus can also be seen in "Alamîs" (Solin lists "Alamîs" among the Scythian peoples but not the Alani).

94. The only mention of a King Ban other than Lancelot's father appears in Chrétien's *Conte del Graal*, as Ban de Gomeret (Hilka 1932:20, ll. 459–467). The Old French reads:

> Quant grant furent vostre dui frere,
> Au los et au consoil lor pere
> Alerent a deus corz reaus
> Por avoir d'Escavalon ala
> Li ainznez et tant servi l'a
> Que chevaliers fu adobez;
> Et li autres, qui puis fu nez,
> Fu au roi Ban de Gomeret.
> (Cf. Potvin 1865–1873, 1:56, l. 1661.)

West (1969:76) agrees with Brugger (1927:227–229, 463–464 n. 3) that the name Gomeret probably refers to Vannes. So here we have a legend of a Ban ruling over Vannes, which was historically ruled by Alans.

In Welsh legend we find: "The Lake, that is, of Lén Limfiaclach, son of Ban Bolgach, son of Bannach . . ." (Stokes 1892:485). In Irish legend Ban is one of the ten husbands of one of Partholōn's ten daughters (Macalister 1940, 39:11, 27, 59). These examples are unusual, since *ban* in Celtic languages means "woman," a fact that renders a Celtic etymology of King Ban's name absurd. Brugger's (1927:465, 481) suggestion of the Gaelic *bán* ("white") as the source of this name is slightly more convincing, but, given the absence of the legends of King Ban in Ireland prior to transmission of the *Queste* from the Continent, an Irish origin for his name is a remote possibility at best. Williams (1865:17) renders the Old Cornish *ban* as "that which is high, a height, mountain, summit" (cf. Welsh *ban*, Irish *beann*, Gaelic *beann*, Manx *beinn*, Greek βουνός, Sanskrit *pinda*, German *bann*, *pinn*, Latin *pinnae*, *pinnacula*), which may have something to do with why Ban's death takes place on a hill.

95. Bogdanow 1966:35.

96. Loomis (1959:297) identifies Ban de Benoich with Pant von Genewis (Pant de Gaunnes).

97. Colarusso and other scholars argue that this last name is exclusively Celtic.

98. Vernadsky 1963:401–434; Hony 1957; Országh 1953. Colarusso (personal communication) suggests that *ban* in Old Turkish is probably a borrowing from Iranian.

99. Sulimirski 1970:93.

100. Dio Cassius 72.22.16; Cary 1927:35.

101. Lancelot du Lac was named after his paternal grandfather.

102. Payen 1984:142. The Latin *banvo* is attested in 1199 and may have derived, according to Payen (1983:10–11; 1984:142), from the Gallic *banvo** with the Gallic suffix *-avum*. Micha proposes that Mont Brûlé, a hill near Banvou, is the hill from which King Ban witnesses the destruction of his castle before he dies (cf. Payen 1983:216).

103. Cf. Ban de Benoich; cf. Payen 1983:10–11; 214, 216.

104. Hony 1957.

105. Hony 1957.

106. Országh 1953; Dauzat, Dubois, and Mitterand 1964. It is interesting to note that, as Le Roux de Lincy (1986:70) pointed out, the Hungarians claim that the name Pannonia came from Bannon, the name of their first king (i.e., Sarmatians in Hungary; Cuvier 1835, 1:244 ff.).

107. Nitze and Jenkins (1932–1937, 1:101) identify Benwick with Vannes. West (1969:72) and Brugger (1905:53–55; 1927: 459, 463–464 n. 3) agree with this identification, translating Gavoni (the site that the French verse romances give as the birthplace of Lancelot) as Vannes. Thus we seem to have a parallel development between two strands of

legends: one in which the hero is called Perceval and the other in which he is called Lancelot, with the father of the hero in both cases being a Ban who is the ruler of the Alan-controlled city of Vannes.

108. Cf. Greek οικος and Gothic *weihs*.

109. Cf. "Artorius" as a similar title.

110. Sulimirski 1970:188. There seems to be a dual-kingship pattern in Sarmatian tribes that is reflected by Ban and Bors in the Lancelot legends. (Cf. the two kings Banadaspes and Zanticus; Dio Cassius 72.22.16; Cary 1927:35.)

111. Micha 1987:270–271; cf. Carman 1973:5–7, 118. Examples from the Old French of the prose *Lancelot* include: "Benoïc marchit au Berry" and "Benoïc serait sur la Loire, le royaume de Ban est donc sur le territoire angevin."

112. Micha 1987:270–271, 273. Gaunnes eventually becomes the land of Ban's brother, Bors, in the legends. These two kings have sisters for wives (Elaine and Evaine, respectively). Ban fosters his bastard son, Bannyn, at Bors's court, and Bors's sons, Lionel and Bors, are fostered with Lancelot by the Dame du Lac. Given the overlap between the two families, either the legends of Ban and Bors may represent an Alanic example of the Divine Twins legend (Ward 1968) or Ban might have been Bors as well as the Ban (i.e., "ruler") of Benoich (i.e., one figure who split into two brothers in retellings of his legend).

113. Alvar 1980:50.

114. Old French; Potvin 1865–1873, 6:105, l. 43847.

115. Old Spanish; Bohigas 1957–1962, 2:67.

116. Middle English; Lovelich 1904–1932, ll. 16,174–16,256.

117. Welsh; Parry 1933:43. For more on this figure see Keller 1836; Alton 1889; Thorpe 1950; Palermo 1963–1964; Niedzielski 1966; Brodtkorb 1965; McMunn 1978; Runte, Wikeley, and Farrell 1984.

118. Nickel 1975a:1–18; 1975b:150–152.

119. Aspyol is the name of Lancelot's uncle in the *Lanzelet*. Cf. Such Alan names such as Aspar and Respendial.

120. See Bruce 1903, l. 230, for "Boerte."

121. Marx 1965:244–245.

122. Webster and Loomis 1951:117, 215–216. Although Loomis (Webster and Loomis 1951:215) saw this hunt as a "direct borrowing ... from Hartmann's *Erek*," tracing back ultimately to Chrétien's *Erec et Enide*, we are inclined to see both Chrétien's story and Ulrich's as different reflections of the same tradition. Perceval's shield, before he

acquired the shield of Joseph of Arimathea on the Grail Quest, bore the device of a white stag (Nitze and Jenkins 1932, 2:98).

123. This poem is related to, but not based on, the French lay *Tyolet* (Draak 1979).

124. Lacy et al. 1986:586; Tobin 1976.

125. Gawain reveals the deception; cf. Kay's claim to have killed a dragon after murdering Arthur's son, the real dragonslayer in the *Perlesvaus*; Bryant 1978:178.

126. E.g., Bryant 1978:57.

127. Cowen 1969, 1:220–221. This motif appears in non-Arthurian legends as well. Gregory of Tours (2.37; Thorpe 1974:152) records that on one occasion Clovis was miraculously shown a ford across a river by a deer. The Huns follow a hind through the Maeotian swamp on their way to Europe (Priscus, frag. 1; Blockley 1981, 2:222–225; Jordanes, *Getica*, 24.123–126; Gordon 1960:57–58).

128. Dumézil 1930:27.

129. Webster and Loomis 1951:215–216.

130. Webster and Loomis 1951:215.

131. Dumézil 1930:50–53.

132. Thorpe 1974:152.

133. Nitze and Jenkins 1932–1937, 2:139–143.

134. Nitze and Jenkins 1932–1937, 2:140. Cf. the Arthurian figure of the Questing Beast, with its stomach baying like "thirty coupyl hounds" (Lacy et al. 1986:445).

135. MS P in Nitze and Jenkins 1932–1937. Cf. Nitze and Jenkins 1932–1937, 2:144.

136. The traditional explanation for Scythian elements in Celtic culture is a hypothetical contact between the Celts and the Scythians (usually dated to ca. 500 B.C.E. or earlier; e.g., Powell 1980:67, 115–116). However, given the number of Sarmatians and Alans who settled in Europe from Late Antiquity onward, at least some of these elements may have been introduced (or reinforced) at this later date.

137. The structural analysis is our own.

138. Markale (1985:127) argues that this parallel is once again at the hypothetical Indo-European level, by pointing out that Cūchulainn is raised and trained in the otherworld and that the Irish hero's father was an otherworldly member of the Fomoire. It is Batraz's mother, however, who comes from the otherworld and who is associated with water (nothing is said about Lancelot's mother, Elaine, other than that she has

a sister, Evaine, and that she becomes a nun after Ban dies and Lancelot is stolen), and the protectiveness of Satana over Batraz and the Dame du Lac over Lancelot goes far beyond the involvement of otherworldly water-women in Cūchulainn's life.

139. Markale (1985:131) points out that the association between water and the hero is seen in many traditions (e.g., Moses and Taliesin; cf. Malcor, "First Bath," unpublished). The association with water follows Batraz and Lancelot throughout their lives and is an integral part of who they are.

140. Colarusso (personal communication).

141. Although Arthur fights several of the knights of the Round Table at Camlann, he never kills them indiscriminately the way Batraz and Lancelot slaughter their fellow warriors. Markale (1985:124–125) also sees the war between Arthur and Lancelot, in which Lancelot slays most of the knights of the Round Table while rescuing Guinevere from the stake, as a parallel at the hypothetical Indo-European level to Batraz's massacre of the Narts in retaliation for his father's death. He points out that the fear of the warriors in the *Táin* that Cūchulainn will massacre them, which inspires them to send naked women out to greet the returning warrior (which stuns him long enough so that they can dump him in several cauldrons of water to cool him off; cf. the birth of Batraz, Dumézil 1930:50–53; Hübschmann 1887:539–542) is another reflex of this same story. The difference between the story of Cūchulainn and those of Lancelot and Batraz is that Cūchulainn's warrior rage blinds him to the identity of the people he is attacking while Lancelot and Batraz both undertake their mass slaughters to protect/avenge a loved one.

142. Littleton 1979:326–333.

143. Dumézil 1930:60. The translation is our own. The French reads: "Seul des Nartes . . . tu es sans tare, ou du moins tu n'as qu'une tare." Note that "the knight with only one flaw" in the Arthurian tradition is Bors, Lancelot's cousin.

144. The *Perlesvaus* appeared in written form between 1203 and 1213. This epic, translated into English under the title *The High Book of the Grail*, deals with the adventures of Lancelot, Gawain, and Perceval as they search for the Holy Grail. The work is particularly notable for the reduction of the role of the affair between Guinevere and Lancelot, the placing of Lancelot in stories usually associated with Gawain or Mordred, Arthur's betrayal of Lancelot, and the concluding prophecy of Lancelot's death at the hands of Claudas (whereas Lancelot is victorious over Claudas in the *Lanzelet*).

145. Littleton and Thomas 1978; Peterson 1985:35.

146. Sodmann 1980; Hogenhout and Hogenhout 1978; de Vries and Verwijs 1863; Gerritsen 1981:368–388; Knuvelder 1970–1976, 1:207–218.

147. Ashe 1985.

148. Lancelot actually picks up his sword from a stone altar.

149. Similarly Ban and Bors supplied the troops that Arthur used to consolidate his own kingdom.

150. Morgawse tricks Arthur into begetting Mordred; Elaine tricks Lancelot into begetting Galahad; see appendix 2.

151. Mordred usurps Arthur's throne, while Galahad's introduction of the Grail Quest to the Round Table destroys Lancelot's military career, reputation, and sanity.

152. Paton 1929:5–19.

153. Dordogne is adjacent to the modern county of Lot.

154. Carman 1973.

155. Bachrach 1973:26–73; Sulimirski 1970:186–188.

156. Markale 1983:55–56.

157. The only other knight to bear this epithet is Aalardin du Lac of the *Book of Caradoc* (Weston 1906–1909:309–311). Erec, son of Lac, also appears in the legends of Lancelot. If the *lac-* element is related to Ossetic *læg* (see above), Erec's epithet would be "Son of Man."

158. The greatest number of these settlements are located in the southeast.

159. Ammianus Marcellinus 31.2.9; Rolfe 1936, 3:384–385; Wenskus in Beck et al. 1881:122; Bachrach 1973:86–92.

160. Bachrach 1973:86.

161. Bryant 1978:135.

162. Other Arthurian legends also tell of women driving carts (e.g., Bryant 1978:237, 259). Although there are some depictions of what may be Celtic women driving carts (on pottery from Sopron, Hungary; e.g., Piggot 1983:109; cf. Barber 1991:206, 379), the driving of carts by women was not nearly as ingrained in Celtic cultures as it was in the culture of the Alans. However, Sarmatians, whose women also wore large skirts, had also settled extensively in Hungary, so this depiction of a woman on a piece of pottery does not necessarily identify her as a Celt.

163. Rogers 1984:1. See Paton (1929:xi), who translates the title literally as *The Story of the Cart*. Cf. Rogers 1984.

164. Maenchen-Helfen 1973:340–342, 353; Loubo-Lesnitchenko 1973:28–29; Randers-Pehrson 1983:45.

165. Maenchen-Helfen 1973:341; Newark 1989:18; Sulimirski 1970:120, 188. However, see Dent 1985:85–92; de Grummond 1982:166ff.; Megaw and Megaw 1986:212–213; Kilbride-Jones 1980:109–116.

CHAPTER 4

The Knights and the Narts

In addition to Arthur and Lancelot other Arthurian figures, such as Kay, Perceval, and Gawain, exhibit strong parallels with characters in the Ossetic material. Still others, such as Erec and Tristan, are reflections of historical and documentable Alanic counts[1] or merely retain, like Bedivere, only a linguistic connection to the Alanic language. With this in mind let us take a closer look at the legends of some of these Arthurian heroes.

Kay and Bedivere

Arthur, Kay, and Bedivere have often been cited as the earliest figures in the legends of the Round Table.[2] Kay (Cai, Cei) and Bedivere (Bedwyr) appear among other Arthurian heroes in the *Stanzas of the Graves* (800s–900s)[3] of the early Welsh tradition. By 1100 the Arthurian legends had spread to Italy, as evidenced by the carving on the northern doorway of Modena Cathedral (ca. 1120), which depicts the abduction of Guinevere (see plate 7). Among the identified figures is "Che" (Kay).[4] Like Lancelot, however, Kay and Bedivere have a strong connection to the Continent from their earliest appearance. In Wace (1155) Arthur makes Kay earl of Angers (see map 15).[5] Kay is buried at Chinon, whose name Arthur changes to Kain (i.e., Caen; see map 15) in Kay's honor.[6] This story is simply an etiological legend that contains a medieval etymology for the name Caen. Yet Wace also calls Bedivere "Bedievere of Neustria"[7] and "Bedevere the Frenchman of Beauce,"[8] names that do not hint of medieval etymology, suggesting that this early Arthurian hero was indeed of continental origin. The continental connection with Bedivere also appears in the early story of his death. Wace and Layamon both give Bedivere's own burial site as Bayeux (Baeios in Layamon) in Normandy.[9] In some early stories Bedivere appears as the son of the Earl of Cornwall, but in the Welsh *Y Seint Greal* Constans (Constantine of Britain) replaces him in this role.[10] By the time of Malory, Constantine Cadorson had become this earl's offspring, and Bedivere's earlier relationship to this territory was forgotten. Perhaps Bedivere's Cornish ties reflect such historical figures as Drustan.[11]

Although there is no clear and immediate onomastic connection between the Alano-Sarmatian and Celtic traditions here, the name Kay cannot be decisively traced back to Celtic roots, and it is perhaps possible to derive these traditions from steppe-related sources. Although Nickel derives the name Kay from Latin *cajus* ("commander"), the name more likely is a variant of the ancient Iranian warrior name Kai.[12] Given the location of the ancestral homeland of the ancient Sarmatians, it is reasonable to assume that they, too, might have borrowed a variant of this and other ancient Turkish words. That at least some of the Iranian-speaking Sarmatian clans might have preserved this name in their hero tales seems possible.[13]

As Miller has pointed out, the Kay of Welsh tradition drastically differs from the sharp-tongued Sir Kay of the Arthurian legends.[14] Especially in *Culhwch and Olwen*, one of the Arthurian tales attached to the *Mabinogi*, Kay appears as a magician/trickster rather than as a hero/warrior.[15] This observation raises the possibility of a parallel between Sir Kay and the Ossetic trickster Syrdon.[16] The satiric tirades of both Sir Kay and Syrdon are the bane of their respective war bands.[17]

We can say even less about the other early companion of Arthur, Bedivere. The continental origin of Bedivere is interesting in light of the fact that he originally figured prominently in the tales in his role as Arthur's "cupbearer" (butler),[18] only to be replaced in popularity by the extremely Alanic Sir Lancelot.[19] This role virtually disappears from later texts. If Bedivere were originally a warrior associated with the Third Function, this "cupbearing" description is one of the few remnants left of the original character. Bedivere, however, does

PLATE 7. The Cathedral of Modena, Archivolt of Porta della Pescherisa. Courtesy of Norris J. Lacy.

still have ties to water in the later Arthurian tradition: early on he replaced Gifflet in the *Morte Darthur* scene, in which Excalibur is thrown into a lake.[20] This scene, as discussed above, has close parallels with the Ossetic tradition, and that Bedivere should be the sword-throwing companion in the Arthurian variant is intriguing.

Perceval

Although Perceval[21] was one of the best known of the Grail heroes in the Middle Ages, he "was not the original Grail hero."[22] Dozens of manuscripts from the twelfth to the fifteenth century tell non-Grail (as well as Grail) stories about him, and several of the more famous manuscripts bear one of the forms of his name.[23] Depictions of scenes featuring the Grail hero on everything from frescoes on dining room walls to carvings on ivory boxes were rivaled in popularity in fourteenth-century France only by those that featured Tristan. Perceval tapestries were owned by such notables as the duke of Burgundy, Philip the Bold, Margaret of Flanders, and Philip the Good.[24] In the fifteenth century King Charles VI of France owned a Grail Quest tapestry, and his wife, Queen Isabelle of Bavaria, owned a Perceval and a Grail tapestry.[25] The English also preferred stories of Lancelot and Perceval in tapestries to those of other knights.[26]

The notion that stories about Perceval were derived from an Iranian source was a recurrent theme in Arthurian scholarship in the early decades of the twentieth century. Coyajee saw marked parallels between the childhood tales of Perceval and those of Kai Khosraw (as told by Firdausi).[27] For example, Kai Khosraw's father is killed, and the hero, who is thought to be an idiot, travels to the king's court because "a knight passed me traversing hill and forest."[28] Similarly Perceval, who is thought to be an idiot, travels to Arthur's court years after the death of his father because he sees knights riding in the forest (see plate 8). Duval saw the legends of Perceval as a biography of Philippe d'Alsace, embellished with stories from Iran that had traveled to the Valois region of France via Spain.[29] Friedrich von Suhtschek "maintained the Arthurian cycle to be

PLATE 8. Perceval Meets Knights in the Forest (Louvre OA 122). Paris, first half of the fourteenth century, ivory casket: From the *Roman de Perceval*, Louvre, Photo © R.M.N.

of Iranian origin and Wolfram's *Parzival* and Gawain romance a free translation from the Persian."[30]

However, with the popularity of the Celtic-origin hypothesis originally advanced by Loomis, much of this scholarship has been ignored in recent years. There is some disagreement among scholars of the Grail tradition, particularly in its Perceval form, as to whether all of the Grail manuscripts ultimately drew upon Robert de Boron's *Joseph* as their source. Although Perceval was well known in the continental Grail tradition, the British *Sir Perceval of Galles*[31] (ca. 1300–1340) makes no mention of the Grail, even though images that employed the motif of the Chalice at the Cross were already known in Britain at this time.[32] This makes it unlikely that the Perceval branch of the Grail tradition developed out of the Welsh Pryderi or Peredur tales, as Loomis has suggested.[33] At base, though, Coyajee and his colleagues seem to have been on the right track—with only their proposed method of diffusion[34] and its accompanying late date, the eleventh and twelfth centuries, posing serious difficulty with this hypothesis as to the origin of the legends. The presence of large numbers of Sarmatians and Alans in Britain and Gaul during the period in which the Arthurian tradition was formed has once again made the eastern-origin hypothesis attractive.

The tradition of "Peronnik l'idiot" ("Peronnik the Fool") is found in the region of Vannes.[35] These folktales about a hero who fights the Devil bear some resemblance to the stories of Perceval.[36] Peronnik is associated with a lance and a golden basin, just as Perceval is associated with a lance and the Grail.[37] Some scholars have suggested a Celtic origin for these stories, seeing them as the lost Celtic source for the Grail tradition that Nutt had been unable to find.[38] Hertz argued that Peronnik is a modern Breton *Märchen* from the region of Vannes that can be traced back to Wolfram's *Parzival*.[39] However, given the connection of Arthurian figures like Tristan and Erec with the Alanic counts of Vannes, it is equally possible that the legends of Peronnik, a Perceval figure, are the modern survivals of legends of a Batraz-prototype that were carried to the region by Alans in the fifth century.

The name Perceval also seems to have eastern rather than Celtic ties. According to Ringbom, the Iranian words *gohr*, *gohar*, and *djauhar* (which probably formed the root of the Alanic name Goar) translate to German as *Perle*, with a semantic field that includes the notions of jewel and gem.[40] Consider the following etymology for Perlesvaux.[41] *Vaux* is well established as meaning "valley." Divide the name thus: Perles-vaux. Taking the *s* for the Germanic possessive, we now have: "Perle's Valley" or "Gohar's Valley," which makes sense, since this form of the name comes from the region of Brittany that is rich in valleys and that Goar and his Alans sacked and settled in the early fifth century.

The Perchevaux form of the name also makes wonderful sense if we assume that a syllable has been dropped—as happens so frequently in French—rendering the original as the hypothetical form Per[les]chevaux. This form would translate as "Perle's Horsemen" or "Gohar's Horsemen." With the notion of jewel included in the first part of the name Perlesvaus for speakers of Germanic languages, it is also understandable how Parzival,[42] the Germanic Perceval, became associated with a Grail that was in the form of a gem or stone. In the fifteenth-century German poem *Lorengel* the Grail appears as a "stone of victory" with which Parsifal drives back Attila and his troops at the moment when they were going to overthrow Christianity.[43] It was the Alans of Orléans in 451, however, who actually held the center line against Attila, and it was their feigned-retreat battle tactic that defeated the Hun and forced him to retreat to Troyes.[44] The Burgundians who had cooperated with the Alans against Attila (437) had been moved by Aëtius (443) from the Rhine to Spaudia (Savoy) to guard the passes through the Alps, a region that would eventually produce several images of the Chalice at the Cross.[45] These Alans were originally commanded by the fifth-century leader Goar, and the conjunction of the Perceval/stone story with these Alans yet again raises the possibility that Perceval was "Goar's Knight."

Perceval is often described as "li Gallois." Most scholars have taken this to mean that the knight was Welsh. Marx accepted this notion when he pointed out that there were reputedly "Welsh" (*gallois*) scribes attached to the dynasty of Poitou in his attempt to locate some means by which the Welsh could have influenced the development of Perceval's legends.[46] We submit that *gallois*, like "Welsh," simply meant "foreign," and that Perceval was originally known as "The Foreign Knight."[47] The legend of the knight from a foreign land is told primarily of Lancelot, but the story seems to have been attached to Perceval as well.

Perceval's genealogy, like that of Lancelot, is extensive and features several men named Alan. Perceval's father in the *Perlesvaus* is called Alain le Gros de la Vales.[48] Perceval's father is either an anonymous figure or one of a variety of characters: Alain, Alain le Gros, Guellans Guenelaus, Gales li Caus, and even Pellinore, a name derived from Pelles, which first appears as the name of the Maimed King of the Vulgate Cycle.[49] Robert de Boron's verse and prose *Joseph*,[50] the Didot-*Perceval*,[51] the *Perlesvaus*, the Berne conclusion to the Second Continuation of Chrétien's *Conte del Graal*, *Le Chevalier aux deux épées* (or *Mériadeuc*),[52] and one manuscript of the prose *Tristan*[53] all give Alain or Alain le Gros as the name of Perceval's father, tracing the hero's genealogy from Joseph of Arimathea through Perceval's mother and from Nicodemus through his father.[54] In an attempt to explain this proliferation of the name Alan, Evans identified Alain li [le] Gros, Perceval's father, as Alanus ab Insulis, who wrote against the Albigensians and died at Cîteaux ca. 1201.[55] Yet, aside from his first name, the Alain of the Grail legends has little in common with the famous cleric. Taken in conjunction with Bliocadran, yet another name given to Perceval's father, an alternative explanation for the appearance of the name Alan in this genealogy becomes likely. Wolfgang gives Perceval's father's name as Alain de Gomeret[56] and argues that Bliocadran, the name given to this character in the Prologue to Chrétien's *Conte del Graal*,[57] means simply "fair-haired" or "handsome." As we have seen, the Alans were consistently referred to as "bright-haired" or "fair-haired" by the Romans. If Perceval was "Goar's Knight," a "bright-haired Alan" might well have been his father.

Perceval shares several basic traits with the knights of Lancelot's clan. Like Galahad and Lancelot he has no knowledge of horsemanship when he first journeys to Camelot; however, like his distant kinsmen, he rapidly becomes one of the preeminent horsemen of the Round Table.[58] Almost without exception they are the only ones who can knock each other out of the saddle. Batraz of the Nart sagas also exhibits this initial lack of horsemanship: the detail of his inability to be unhorsed after learning to ride is also preserved in the Ossetic version.[59]

The story of Perceval was extensively Christianized by the monkish scribes who composed and copied it. A.C.L. Brown observed that "no story . . . close to folklore would regard Perceval's leaving his mother to become a warrior as a sin."[60] The main motif of the story of Perceval's childhood—that of the mother who raises her son in seclusion (with the son leaving her and going on to become a famous hero)—was well known in Celtic fairy lore, where no such stigma was attached to it.[61] The motif can be found in the Ossetic legends of Sozryko, which affirm the hero's warrior nature that will lead him to seek adventure away from his mother rather than condemn his behavior.[62] The medieval scribes, however, almost without exception frown on Perceval's action.[63] Hermit after hermit in the Perceval corpus gives one sermon after another about the proper way for a knight to lead a Christian life. The modern reader can almost hear the medieval warrior snoring through these moralizing passages, only to be awakened for the next exciting battle scene.[64] Yet the tendency to Christianize the tales appears mainly in the Grail material and may account in part for why, when the story of Perceval was adapted into English in *Sir Perceval of Galles*, the Grail theme was eliminated, even though the work otherwise follows Chrétien's *Conte del Graal*.[65]

Like Arthur and Lancelot, Perceval exhibits parallels with the Ossetic hero Batraz. All four heroes are the son of a widow[66] who (with the exception of Arthur) avenges his father's death. Each hero is belatedly given a horse, armor, and sword by his mother (or step-/foster-mother). All of these heroes (again with the exception of Arthur) travel incognito. Perceval even shares a few parallels with Batraz that Arthur and Lancelot do not: the Breton and the Ossetic heroes both successfully complete the adventure of obtaining a magical cup, and they are both renowned for their poor attire at the start of their career.[67]

Embedded in the First Continuation of Chrétien's *Conte del Graal*, the *Book of Caradoc*, which tells of Caradoc of Vannes, a city long ruled by Alanic counts, contains several interesting elements.[68] Caradoc is the son of Arthur's niece Ysave and the sorcerer Elïavrés, her adulterous lover. As heir to King Caradoc of Nantes, Caradoc of Vannes is sent to Arthur's court, where he is dubbed a knight of the Round Table. Caradoc shares the adventure of the "Beheading Game" with Lancelot and Gawain, although in his case the game is between father and son, with the father recognizing his son and relenting at the last moment.[69] Caradoc returns to Nantes, where he imprisons his mother in a tower.[70] After several adventures he returns to Nantes and embarrasses the sorcerer, who has had the audacity to visit Caradoc's mother in the tower. Caradoc's mother and the sorcerer try to kill the hero with a serpent, which tortures him—a trap from which he is freed by his lady, Guimier, and her brother.[71] Caradoc has also attracted the drinking-horn test[72] to his cycle, after which the story returns to the adventures of Perceval.[73]

Several elements in Caradoc's story closely parallel the story of Xæmyc and Batraz's mother. In the Nart saga the mother is forced to remain in the tower out of fear that someone will ridicule her. The sorcerer Syrdon pays an unauthorized visit to her and embarrasses her, after which she is forced to return to her own people. She implants the embryonic Batraz between Xæmyc's shoulders, then leaves. Nine months later the infant Batraz is released by his aunt, Satana (also his lover in the Circassian Nart sagas), who also relieves the torment of the heat that accompanies this "birth" by cooling the hero in water. What we have, then, in the *Book of Caradoc* seems to be a medieval French variant of the same story that eventually produced the Ossetic version of the birth of Batraz.

Gawain

Although Gawain's tomb was supposedly discovered during the reign of William the Conqueror,[74] it is impossible to trace him back to historical origins.[75] A late addition to the legends of the Round Table, Gawain appears in Arthurian manuscripts well after the appearance of Arthur, Kay, and

Bedivere.[76] Geoffrey of Monmouth is the first author to translate the Welsh name Gwalchmai as Gawain,[77] and several contemporary scholars have identified Gwalchmai as the original Gawain as a result.[78] Coyajee was perhaps on a better track when he pointed out that the Grail, as it is found in the legends of Gawain, is analogous to the Iranian *Xvarlnah* ("halo, nimbus, glory").[79] He noted that the "hero of the Quest for the Glory—according to the Iranian epic—is the warrior Giw (*Gevān* in Pahlavi, and *Gaevani* in the Avesta)."[80] He proposes that it is far easier to derive the French name Gauvain from these Iranian names than it is to derive Gauvain from the Welsh name Gwalchmai.[81] On surer ground Loomis argued that "the epithet Gwallt-advwyn, meaning 'Bright-Hair,' became first Galvagin and eventually Gawain."[82] As in the case of the name Bliocadran, this is a peculiarly Alanic epithet in Latin writings that may have been translated into Welsh.[83]

Markale sees the Nart hero Soslan as the Indo-European parallel of Gawain, just as he sees parallels among Cūchulainn, Lancelot, and Batraz.[84] As Markale has noted, Soslan's rivalry with Batraz strongly resembles the rivalry between Gawain and Lancelot (see plate 9).[85] Yet most of the parallels between Gawain and an Ossetic hero are with Batraz. Gawain (Walewein) was popular in the Low Countries; and he is portrayed in a positive light in Middle English.[86] However, just as Batraz is an antihero in many of the Nart sagas, German and French portrayals of Gawain of Orkney[87] are critical of the warrior.[88]

There appear to be historical parallels between the Iazyges and Gawain as well. In *De Ortu Waluuanii Nepotis Arturi* ("On the Rise of Gawain, Arthur's Nephew;" attributed to Robert of Torigni),[89] Gawain is trained by the Emperor of Rome as a cavalry officer. His first task is to defeat the Persian champion so as to raise the siege of Jerusalem; his second task is to defend Hadrian's Wall.[90] This sounds strangely like the tale of the Iazyges, who were conquered by a Roman emperor, trained to be cavalry officers, and then sent to guard the Wall.

There also seems to be a strong sense in the stories that Lancelot and Gawain (like Lancelot and Arthur) somehow go together. Lancelot has a special friendship with Gawain, and these heroes alternately search for and rescue each other in a

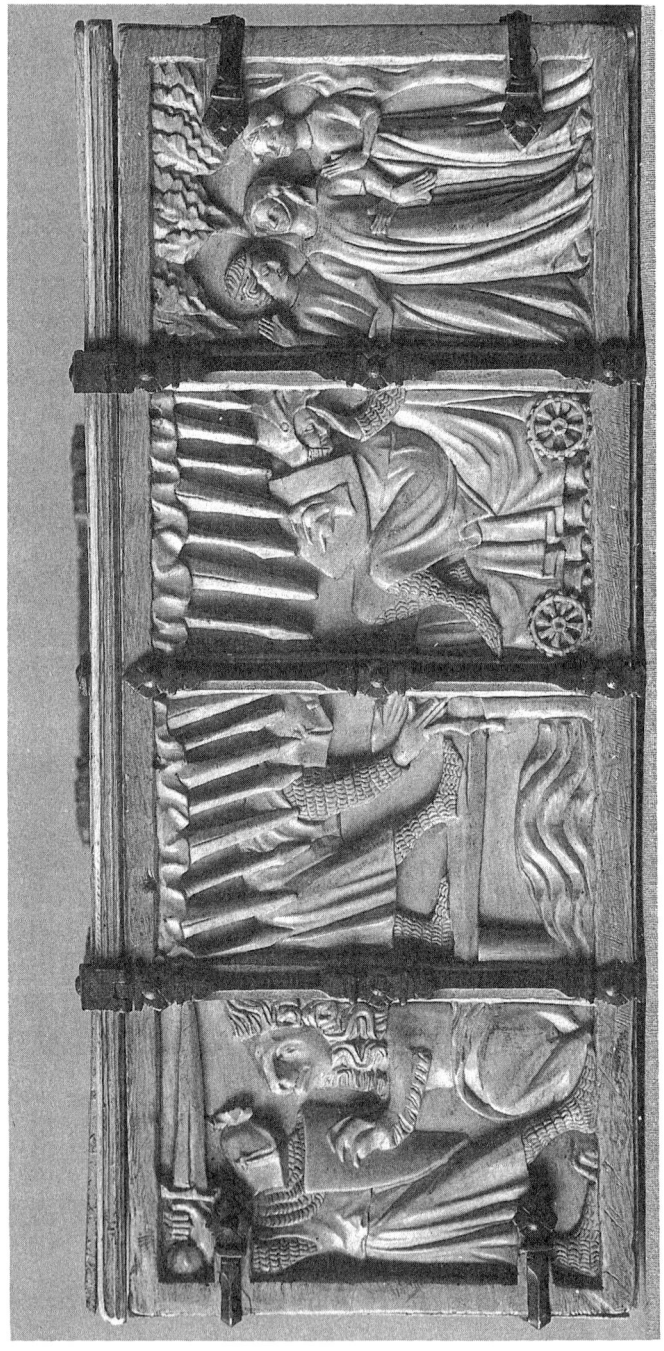

PLATE 9. Lancelot and the Sword Bridge/Gawain and the Perilous Bed (Ivory casket. Metropolitan Museum of Art, Parisian, c. 1325). The Metropolitan Museum of Art, Gift of J. Pierpont Morgan, 1917 (17.190.173). All rights reserved. The Metropolitan Museum of Art.

number of instances. Lancelot rescues Guinevere (with Gawain's help) after a series of adventures that involve an underwater bridge. As mentioned above, the story of the "Beheading Game," as in *Sir Gawain and the Green Knight*, was attributed to Lancelot in the *Perlesvaus*.[91]

In the Vulgate Cycle, Gawain joins his family in the feud against Lancelot only after the death of his favorite brother, Gareth.[92] In the Post-Vulgate Cycle, however, Ban's family is feuding with Arthur's knights well before Gawain quarrels with Ector.[93] There seems to be some intimate rivalry between the two factions that goes deeper than the simple vying between their leaders for the supremacy of the Round Table. The result of this feud is that the knights of Ban's clan, particularly Lancelot, slaughter most of the Round Table in a manner not unlike that in which Batraz slaughters most of the Narts. In addition Gawain's blind insistence on battling Lancelot to the death and the resulting slaughter of many of Lancelot's forces, followed by Gawain's lingering death and subsequent appearance in Arthur's dream, seem to reflect Batraz's insistence on continuing the slaughter of the Narts to the point that his bloodshed offends God, who shortly thereafter causes him to suffer a lingering death, after which the Narts have trouble convincing his corpse to let them lay it in a tomb.

Erec

Perhaps best known from Chrétien's *Erec et Enide* (ca. 1170),[94] Erec appears early in Arthurian tradition. He is the son of King Lac in Hartmann von Aue's *Erec*.[95] Hartmann was born and raised in the Upper Rhine region, which was heavily settled by Alans, and he was educated at a monastery, possibly Reichenau (see chaps. 8, 9, and 10), which was famous for its relic of the Holy Grail. The major importance of Erec to the Arthurian legends is his death. Following the Quest for the Grail, Lancelot's half-brother Ector accuses Gawain of treason for slaying Erec and Palamedes; Arthur and Lancelot intervene to stop the fight.[96] Much of the tension and conflict in the last days of the Round Table derives from this incident.

Bromwich proposed that the name Erec in Chrétien's tale referred to Gwerec or Werec, count of Vannes in the sixth century, and that the name Enide was an eponym for Vannes.[97] She argued that the names later became attached to the Dumnonian tale of Gereint and Enid.[98] In any case the name Gwerec (or Guérec) is probably the same as that of Goeric (Bishop Abbo), who was unquestionably an Alan. Given this fact, the sixth-century date, and the number of counts Alan of Vannes, it is highly probable that Gwerec of Vannes was also an Alan.[99]

Although some of the continental Arthurian material exhibits a knowledge of Welsh geography, such works as *Erec* and the Lancelot texts do not. Marx argues that Dumnonian emigrants told the Arthurian tales in the bilingual courts of Armorica (where French legends were attached) and then transmitted these stories back again to Cornwall, along with the French elements.[100] We find it easier to believe that the Celtic bards learned tales already extant at these courts (such as that of Gwerec/Erec), then transmitted them to Cornwall.

Tristan

The story of Tristan was extremely popular throughout the Middle Ages and the Renaissance.[101] He appears on hand mirrors, combs, brushes, quilts, frescoes, floor tiles, stained-glass windows, jewelry boxes, tapestries, and a variety of other personal and decorative items in addition to manuscript covers and illuminations.[102]

The prose *Tristan* preserves many ancient, authentic elements;[103] however, the story of Tristan and Isolde, wife of King Mark, is not found in Celtic sources that predate the twelfth- and thirteenth-century Arthurian romances.[104] Thomas d'Angleterre's *Tristan* (ca. 1150–1200), written in Old French, was one of the most influential English Arthurian romances.[105] Thomas's *Tristan* was translated into Norwegian as *Tristrams saga ok Ísöndar* (1226), which in turn influenced the Icelandic ballad "Tristrams Kvæ5i."[106] Béroul's Anglo-Norman romance *Tristan* (late 1100s) belongs to a noncourtly, primitive stage of the

Tristan legend.[107] The thirteenth-century *Palamedes* predates the cyclic version of the prose *Tristan*.[108] The *Tristrant* (ca. 1170–1190) of the Oberg region is a Middle High German adaptation by Eilhart von Oberge of a French original, probably the so-called *Estoire*.[109] Some scholars believe that Eilhart came from the Middle Rhine area instead of from Oberg near Braunschweig.[110]

Like the love affair between Lancelot and Guinevere, the romantic liaison between Tristan de Lyonesse[111] and La Belle Isolde does not exist in Celtic sources earlier than the twelfth or thirteenth century.[112] Hollister made the astute observation that "although the conduct of Tristan and Lancelot would have been regarded by earlier standards as nothing less than treasonable, both men are presented sympathetically in the romances."[113] Actually the "treasonable" behaviors exhibited by both heroes can be seen in this light only if interpreted by medieval moral standards. If judged, say, by the culture of the ancient Alans, both men had defendable claims to the women they took as lovers, since they had successfully acquired these women in combat—whether or not the action was undertaken in someone else's name.[114]

As with Gawain and Arthur there was a sense among the medieval storytellers that Lancelot and Tristan somehow belonged together. In several instances, such as the Italian cantare "La Vendetta che fe Messer Lanzelloto de la Morte di Miser Tristano" ("Sir Lancelot's Vengeance for the Death of Sir Tristan"), Lancelot is the avenger of Tristan's death (see plate 10).[115] This "avenging" connection extended to their families as well. The shortened *Merlin*, which follows the *Queste* of the Spanish and Portuguese *Demandas*,[116] tells that Mark, after killing the Archbishop of Canterbury, was slain by "Paulars, a knight of Ban's lineage."[117]

In addition to Tintagel, King Mark is frequently said to reside at Castle Dore, an earthwork fort near Fowey in Cornwall.[118] Inhabited from the third through the first century B.C.E. but abandoned during the Roman period, it was occupied again by a royal household in the fifth century. Outside Fowey is a monument that originally stood closer to Castle Dore, inscribed as the grave of "Drustanus, son of Cunomorus." The name Tristan has often been said to derive from Drostan or Drest, a

PLATE 10. Mark Slays Tristan (MS Paris, Bibliothèque Nationale f.fr. 101, fol. 383v). Photograph courtesy of Bibliothèque Nationale, Paris.

common name for Pictish chieftains that also occurs among the Celts of Britain.[119] This Arthurian hero might have acquired his name from contact between the Iazyges and the Picts and Celts of the region around Hadrian's Wall. In any case the name Drustanus can be read as Tristan, with Cunomorus being the Latinized form of Kynvawr, a king who reigned in Cornwall during the first half of the sixth century.[120]

Another historical figure who contributed to the portrait of Tristan is the sixth-century count Alan Judual of Vannes (see map 16), who was exiled from Dol[121] to the court of Childebert I by King Mark Conomor of Armorica and Cornwall (d. 560).[122] Half-Alan, half-Celt, and perhaps descended from an offshoot of Goar's tribe, Alan Judual was imprisoned by Childebert I (r. 534–558).[123] Alan Judual's father, Jonas,[124] was murdered by King Mark near a place called Dol, just as Tristan is murdered by King Mark at Dol in the legends. Alan Judual, however, was freed by Childebert's brother, Chlothar I (r. 558–561), following Mark's death in battle.[125] The count returned to Vannes where he became the ancestor of a line of counts and dukes of Brittany, many of whom bore the name Alan.

This mixture of legend and history with parallels to tales of Northeast Iranian derivation and to the history of the Alans and Sarmatians is common among the male characters of the Arthurian tradition. The women in the Arthurian legends have not had as much historical influence on their characters as their male counterparts, and, as we shall see in the next chapter, have even closer parallels to the Northeast Iranian traditions as a result.

NOTES

1. E.g., Goeric of Albi and Alan Judual of Vannes, respectively.

2. E.g., Lacy et al. 1986:206–208. Cai (Kay) is mentioned several times in the *Lebor Gabála* (e.g., Macalister 1939, 35:119).

3. The earliest manuscript to include this poem is the thirteenth-century *Black Book of Carmarthen* (Wilhelm and Gross 1984:15–16; Jones 1967).

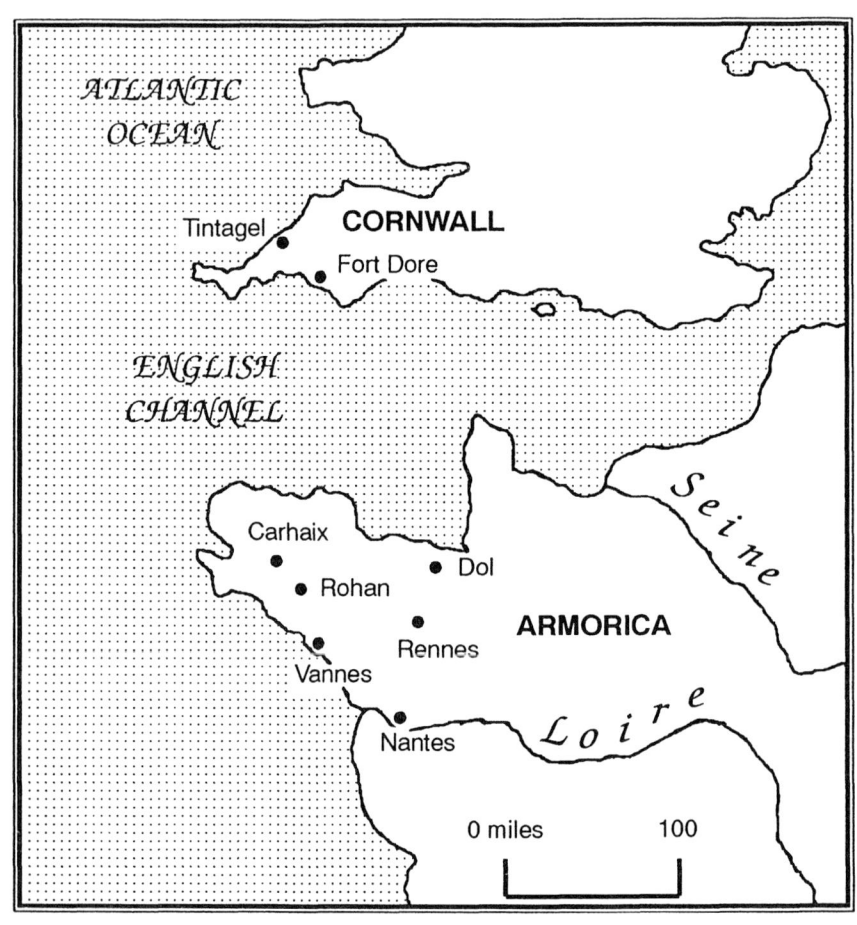

Map 16. Sites Associated with the Legend of Tristan

4. Cavendish 1978:25.

5. Rhys 1928:65.

6. Wace in Rhys 1928:109; Layamon in Rhys 1928:257 gives the name as Kinun.

7. I.e., the region of Gaul that became Normandy; Rhys 1928:65, 86.

8. Cf. Allainville-en-Beauce; Bachrach 1973:62.

9. Rhys 1928:109, 258. Malory has Bedivere enter a monastery and stay there until his death; cf. the custom of Alans becoming clerics late in life.

10. Lloyd-Morgan (personal communication).

11. This is the historical son of the king of Cornwall and a prototype for Tristan.

12. Nickel 1975a:12. Examples of this use of Kai include the legendary Iranian warrior-king Kai Khosraw, founder of the warlike Kayanid dynasty as described in Firdausi's *Shāh Nāma* (*Book of Kings*); Levy 1967:99 ff.; cf. Puhvel 1987:117–125. The name of the scribe of what appears to be the oldest manuscript of the Post-Vulgate *Queste del Saint Graal* is Walterus de Kayo (a place-name that has never been satisfactorily translated but that is presumably Caix, Somme). "Kayo," however, may well be a "Latinized" form of *kai*, making this scribe's name something like "Walter of the Warrior" or "Walter of the Place of the Warriors." This same manuscript also contains the *Estoria del Noble Vaspasiano* (*The History of the Noble Vespasian*) and an extensive account of the story of Alain. Alan settlements were known in both the region of the scribe's origin and that of the composition of the manuscript.

13. Littleton and Thomas 1978:518.

14. Miller 1989:64–65.

15. Miller 1989:57–58.

16. There is perhaps even a counterpart of the evil Mordred in the Ossetic trickster-figure Syrdon, the sworn enemy of Batraz and his followers. For a discussion of Syrdon's role in the Nart sagas and of the extent to which he presents some interesting parallels to the Norse trickster figure Loki see Dumézil (1986).

17. E.g., Cowen 1969, 1:233–234; Dumézil 1986:142–143.

18. E.g., Geoffrey of Monmouth, Bk. 9, passim; Thorpe 1966:212–236.

19. Rhys 1928:86.

20. Markale 1985:126.

21. Variants of the name Perceval include Perchevaus (Williams 1922–1925, 1:passim), Percheval (Williams 1922–1925, 1:144–145, ll. 4683–4712; 149, ll. 4859–4861; 214–215, ll. 6996–7020; 2:76, ll. 9356–9363; 165, ll. 12,306–12,312; 3:34–35, ll. 15,045–15,058; 93, ll. 16,970–16,979; Potvin 1865–1873, 5:151–152, ll. 34,956–34,990), Perchevax (Williams 1922–1925, 3:5, 67, 89), Pierchevaus (Potvin 1865–1873, 4:267, ll. 28,226–28,235; 5:144, ll. 34,756–34,775; 151–152, ll. 34,956–34,990; 153, ll. 35,023–35,030; 158–159, ll. 35,159–35,177; 6:120, ll. 44,315–44,318; 132–133, ll. 44,680–44,719), and Piercheval (Potvin 1865–1873, 6:146–147, ll. 45,097–45,114).

22. Weston 1906–1909, 1:172. See also M. Yoshida 1994.

23. E.g., the Didot-*Perceval* and the *Perlesvaus*.

24. Woods-Marsden 1988:29.

25. Lacy et al. 1986:541.

26. Lacy et al. 1986:540.

27. Coyajee 1939:29–33.

28. Coyajee 1939:32.

29. Duval 1979:16.

30. Closs in Matthews 1984:41. Wolfram von Eschenbach's *Parzival* (ca. 1200–1210; Lachmann 1833; Leitzmann 1902–06, 5 vols.; Deinert 1965; Schröder 1978; Hatto 1980; Bumke 1981; Poag 1972; Sacker 1963) is a reworking, expansion, and completion of Chrétien's *Conte del Graal*. Wolfram claims that a certain Kyot, a Provençal, provided the true story of the Grail, a tale written in Arabic in a discarded manuscript by Flegetanis (a part-Jewish astronomer from Toledo who read about the Grail in the stars), and that he also found the story in Latin chronicles of Anjou. Closs (Matthews 1984:41) believes that this is a "patently . . . fantastic fabrication to impress the gullible and to delight the cognoscenti in Wolfram's audience."

31. The identification of Gales as Wales was originally made by Loomis (1949:483). In actual usage in Old French, however, the word *galles* more frequently referred to a foreigner than to a Welshman.

32. E.g., the Holkham Bible Picture Book, ca. 1326–1331; see Malcor 1991:83.

33. Loomis 1963a:272.

34. Usually via the Crusades; e.g., Faugère 1979:198–205.

35. E.g., Junk 1912:15–16.

36. Junk 1912:39.

37. Junk 1912:63.

38. Junk 1912:46–7.

39. Junk 1912:18.

40. Ringbom 1951:485–489; Wikander 1941:232; von Suhtschek (Ringbom 1951:485) also translates *gôhär, gôhr, gohr, ghr*, as "Perle" or "Edelstein." See also Chavannes and Pelliot 1911:563.

41. This is a variant of Perceval's name that includes the forms Perlesvaus and Perchevaux.

42. Cf. Parsifal. Bergmann (1870:30) has provided the most plausible etymology for Parsifal (Parzival), deriving the name of Wolfram's hero from the Persian *fârisi-fâl* ("ignorant knight"). Perceval's half-brother in Wolfram's *Parzival* is Feirefiz (Prester John). The name Feirefiz has been said to mean in French *fils pie* ("pious son") and *vrai fils* ("true son"). This may or may not be corroborated by the Ethiopian *Kebra Nagast* (*Book of the Glory of God*), in which a young prince descended from Solomon bears this title. See Adolf (1947) and Ponsoye (1957:97–98).

43. Golther 1925:250; Evola 1967:95.

44. Burgundians, the *bacaudae* (or rebellious peasants) of Armorica, and Franks flanked these Alans. Gregory of Tours 2.7 in Thorpe 1974:116–118; Wolfram 1988:177–178; Wenskus in Beck et al. 1881:123; Bachrach 1973:68.

45. Randers-Pehrson 1983:190.

46. Marx 1965:42–3.

47. By this same logic the scribes associated with Poitou were simply foreigners.

48. Bryant 1978:20.

49. Wolfgang 1976:9, 30. Bruce (Wolfgang 1976:30) feels that these names are derived from Perceval. Pellinore appears as Perceval's father in the prose *Tristan* and the Huth *Merlin*, and as both Perceval's father and the Maimed King in the *Livre d'Artus* (Wolfgang 1976:30).

50. Nitze 1927; Roach 1956:313–342.

51. Roach 1941.

52. Foerster 1877:83, ll. 2604–05.

53. Roach 1941:7–8, 309–313.

54. Wolfgang 1976:17, 22.

55. Evans 1898:7–8. Bayer (1983:26; Charvet 1967:25) also suggested that Alain in Robert's works was a tribute to Alanus ab Insulis.

56. Wolfgang 1976:38–40, n. 129, 42–46, 163. Gomeret is given in some French verse romances as the kingdom of Ban (either Perceval or Lancelot's father). Gomeret has been identified by several scholars (e.g., West 1969:76; Brugger 1927:227–229, 463–464 n. 3) as the city of Vannes, the rulers of which have frequently borne the name Alain.

57. Wolfgang (1976:46) concludes that, for all the discussion trying to turn Bliocadran into a Celtic reflection (e.g., Bran), the only true parallel between these figures is "the strength of the warrior [a commonplace]."

58. Cf. Bachrach 1973:86–92.

59. Dumézil 1930:66.

60. Nitze 1949:301.

61. Paton 1903:194–195. In the *Perlesvaus* Perlesvaus (Perceval), not Lancelot, becomes connected with water-fairies, just as Arthur, not Lancelot, is connected with the Lady of the Lake in Malory's *Le Morte Darthur*. Malory's decision to assign the Lady of the Lake to Arthur rather than to Lancelot had been attributed to an identification of his French source as the *Mort le roi Artu*, the final section of the prose *Lancelot*.

The author of the *Perlesvaus* (ca. 1203–1213) likely came from the north of France, where many Alans and some Sarmatians are known to have settled. This author may have been a chaplain or secretary for a noble household (Kelly 1974:19) of northern France or Belgium (Nitze 1937, 2:10). He had access to an excellent library that included most of the Arthurian works of the day (Kelly 1974:19). Loomis (1963a:99) attributes the author's knowledge of the story of Ban and Claudas to an early form of the beginning of the prose *Lancelot*, which may have ultimately derived from legends told by the Alans and Sarmatians who settled in northern Gaul.

62. Dumézil 1930:75–77.

63. This is an odd attitude for the Cistercians in particular, who were busy preaching the Crusades, but perhaps they felt that the hero should have become a cleric instead of a knight.

64. Even the medieval monks were guilty of dozing until the storytelling turned back to the Knights of the Round Table, as Matarasso (1969:10) has pointed out.

65. Campion and Holthausen 1913; Rodriguez 1976; Fowler 1975:5–20. Perceval was displaced in the Grail legends by Galahad (Wolfgang 1976:30).

66. Several Arthurian figures are described as a "son of a widow" (e.g., Arthur, Lancelot, Perceval, Bors, Lionel, Gawain, Agravain, Gaheris, Gareth, Mordred). Although Weston (1906–1909, 2:306) equates this epithet with "initiates" (apparently into some secret rite), another explanation seems likely. It is interesting to note that Batraz, in contrast, is originally the son of a "widower" (i.e., Xæmyc; just as Tristan is the son of the widower Meliodas), but by the time he avenges his father's murder he is also the son of a widow, namely, his stepmother.

67. E.g., Jenkins 1975:75; Dumézil 1930:61–68.

68. Potvin 1865–1873, 3:117–221, ll. 12,451–15,795; Weston 1906–1909, 1:309–311. According to Geoffrey of Monmouth (Thorpe 1966:135–141) Caradoc was the duke of Cornwall under Maximin (Maximus) and a contemporary of Conan Meriadoc.

69. Cf. the Iranian hero Rustram; Puhvel 1987:122; Levy 1967:73–80.

70. Note the similarity between this tale and the story of Xæmyc, Batraz's mother, and Syrdon. Also note parallels to the tale of Uryzmæg and Puk (Dumézil 1930:48–49).

71. Cf. Loki.

72. Potvin 1865–1873, 3:117–221, ll. 12,451–15,795; Lacy et al. 1991:72. A variant of this adventure is found in Biket's *Lai du Cor* (Erickson 1973), which may have connections to the Grail tradition.

73. Roach 1949–1983.

74. This story is told by William of Malmesbury, *Gesta Regum Anglorum* (1125; *Willelmi Malmesbiriensis Monachi de Gestis Regum Anglorum Libri Ouinque*, Stubbs 1887–1889).

75. Lacy et al. 1986:259.

76. Lacy et al. 1986:259.

77. Lacy et al. 1986:259. The earliest appearance of the name Gwalchmai probably occurs in the *Stanzas of the Graves* (Wilhelm and Gross 1984:16).

78. E.g., Wilhelm and Gross 1984:16.

79. Coyajee 1939:14; Puhvel 1987:106.

80. Coyajee 1939:40–41.

81. Cf. Chambers 1927:151.

82. Loomis 1963a:272.

83. Just as the Latin Artorius become Arthyr in Welsh.

84. Markale 1985:122–123. The "cooling" of the young Cūchulainn in several vats of water in one episode of the *Táin* (Kinsella 1969:82) has been often cited as parallel with the "cooling" of Batraz at his birth (e.g., Dumézil 1930:51; Markale 1985:123–124).

85. Markale 1985:122–123.

86. Lacy et al. 1986:259. The spelling Walwanus is first found in William of Malmesbury (Lacy et al. 1986:259). Gawain and Wavain were knighted on the same day, according to Wace (Rhys 1928:57), and conflation between these two names probably accounts for Walwanus and similar forms.

87. In Wace, Arthur gives Norway to Gawain's father, Lot (Rhys 1928:57). Here (Rhys 1928:65) Gonfal is listed as jarl of Orkney in Wace, right after the description of Lot as king of Norway, and some scholars have suggested that a corruption of this text resulted in the form "Lot of Orkney." The connection between Arthurian heroes and Norway persists in Gottfried von Strassburg's *Tristan* (ca. 1200–1210), in which Tristan is kidnapped from his foster-parents by Norwegian merchants and washes up in Cornwall following his release (Ganz 1978; Hatto 1967; Batts 1971; Jackson 1971; Jaeger 1977).

In other works Lot is said to receive Lyonesse (the traditional homeland of Tristan). Wace (Rhys 1928:53) refers to Lot of Lyonesse (rather than of Orkney). Although this land has been viewed as the semimythical Lyonesse, the name may simply be a rendering of Lyons (ancient Lugdunum and the capital of Lyonnais, a historical region of France now covered by the departments of Rhône and Loire), and at least one duke of Alençon was buried at Lyons (Saintsbury 1922, 5:143, n. 1).

88. The German portraits are less harsh than the French; Lacy et al. 1986:259.

89. This work has been dated from as early as the last quarter of the twelfth century to as late as the last quarter of the thirteenth century (Lacy et al. 1986:131–132).

90. Day 1984.

91. E.g., Loomis 1959:265–266.

92. This feud begins with a quarrel between Gawain and Lancelot's half-brother Ector de Marys.

93. Bogdanow 1966:146, 193–196.

94. Roques 1952, 1958, 1960; Micha 1957; Frappier 1957; Haidu 1968; Kelly 1976; Lacy 1980; Topsfield 1981; Foerster 1884, 1890; Doutrepont 1939:261–264; Lathuillère 1966. This tale was translated into

Welsh as *Gereint and Enid* (Jones and Jones 1949; Jarman and Hughes 1976).

95. Leitzmann 1972; Thomas 1982; Benecke and Lachmann 1968; McConeghy 1984; Neubuhr 1977; Wapnewski 1962.

96. Bogdanow 1966:140 ff.

97. Bromwich 1960:464–466; cf. Marx 1965. Werech (or Waroch) was the legendary king of Bro Erech, the most historically verifiable of the three kingdoms that supposedly comprised Armorica when the name changed to Brittany. The other two kingdoms were Dumnonia and Cornouaille (Chadwick 1970:81–83).

98. The Dumnonii were a Celtic tribe that ruled lands in southwestern Britain who also had a strong presence in Brittany (Chadwick 1970:81–83).

99. Cf. Gueric of Igny; Leclercq 1968:208–209. Gueric of Igny (d. 1157) was a student of St. Bernard at Clairvaux, where he spent fifteen years after his conversion in 1125. He served as master of the cathedral school of Tournai before he was appointed to the diocese of Reims. In addition to Gueric's Alan-style name it is interesting to note that both Tournai and Reims produced several images that contain the Chalice at the Cross motif during his tenure. On a related note Marx (1965:274 ff.) discusses the legends of a certain Guerrehés, which may be yet another variant of this name.

100. Marx 1965:81.

101. Tristan was still popular at the time of the Medicis and a favorite subject with members of that family (Joanna Woods-Marsden [personal communication]).

102. Loomis and Loomis 1938.

103. Marx 1965:81–82.

104. Lacy et al. 1986:255. The text of the legend of Diarmaid and Gráinne (MacCana 1970:109–113) dates to the twelfth century (Puhvel 1987:186); we have no knowledge of the content of the text of the same name, the title for which appears on "a tenth-century saga list" (MacCana 1970:110), the same period as the texts for the Tristan legend. Even so Loomis and Loomis (1938:42) felt that this Irish tale, like the Arabic love story of Kais and Libna, influenced the Tristan legend only after the core story had formed. For Loomis and Loomis this core story is the tale of a fight between Drust, son of Talorc, (supposedly king of the Picts ca. 780–785) and the Morhaut. There is nothing in all of this to prevent the continental tales of Mark Conomor, Drustan, and Alan Judual from conflating with the insular stories of Drust and of Diarmaid

at a later date. That the legend of Tristan first appears in its Arthurian form in both manuscript and visual-art traditions on the Continent argues strongly for the Alan Judual core to the story. The tale of Kais and Libna would have been in easy proximity to this legend, and the story of Drust and the Morhaut would have been attracted easily to the tale because of Drustan's name. The story of Diarmaid may have contributed the final juggling of relationships between the principal characters so that Mark became Tristan's uncle rather than his father.

105. Wind 1960.

106. Lacy et al. 1986:583–584; Leach 1921; Schach 1973; 1965:63–86; Kölbing 1878; Helgason 1962–1965; Hill 1977:29–38; Ólason 1982:213–220; Schach 1964:281–297; Leach 1921.

107. Muret 1962.

108. *Gyron le Courtoys* 1501; Pickford 1977b; *Meliadus de Leonnoys* 1528.

109. See Buschinger 1972, 1976; Bussmann 1969; Thomas 1978. This text is probably not the thirteenth-century Vulgate *Estoire del Saint Graal* or the *Estoire de Merlin* since both Eilhart's *Tristrant* and Béroul's *Tristan*, which are both based on this *Estoire*, date to the late twelfth century (Lacy et al. 1986:45, 146–148, 609–614).

110. His identity and origins remain uncertain. In one of the few instances in which an Arthurian legend can be documented as diffusing to the area covered by the former Soviet Union the sixteenth-century *Povest O Trištanu I Ižoti* is a Russian/Serbo-Croatian prose version of the Tristan story based on the French prose *Tristan* but with additional episodes (Veselovski 1888). This tale was probably transmitted by thirteenth-century Dominican missionaries well after the Arthurian legends had become popular in Europe.

111. This name is often rendered in the texts as Leones, which was the name of a Roman legion (Seeck 1876:xxiv, 116).

112. Lacy et al. 1986:255.

113. Hollister 1982:276.

114. This was probably a medieval attempt to explain these bizarre stories, which appear in other forms as well. For example, in one version of the Tristan story (discussed by Bogdanow 1966:20) both Tristan and Mark were in love with the wife of a man name Segurades, a tale intended to establish a motive for Mark's hatred of Tristan.

115. Branca 1971:289–305.

116. The Spanish *Demanda Mort Artu* and the Portuguese version derived from the *Mort Artu* of the Post-Vulgate Cycle. Only two

fragments of the Post-Vulgate *Mort Artu* have been preserved in French, in MS B.N. fr. 340.

117. Bogdanow 1966:40. In Malory this role is played by Bellangere le Beuse; cf. Allainville-en-Beauce and Bedivere of Beauce. Mark's death is not recorded in the extant manuscripts of the prose *Tristan*, although Gardner's translation of the Italian *Vita di Merlino* has Bors slay Mark for burning Lancelot's corpse. An Italian manuscript has Mark forced to eat himself to death in a cage in a tower that stands near Tristan's tomb, and a Spanish manuscript has Mark die of natural causes after abdicating in favor of Tristan's son.

118. Ashe in Lacy et al. 1986:85–86; see map 16.

119. Rendered Drystan or Trystan in Welsh; Ganz 1978; Hatto 1967; Batts 1971; Jackson 1971; Jaeger 1977.

120. I.e., Mark Conomor; cf. the legendary genealogy of the legendary Tristan in appendix 2.

121. Dol was closely tied to the Alan-ruled cities of Vannes and Rennes from Gallo-Roman times (Markale 1983:55, 58).

122. Fawtier 1912:149–153; Gregory of Tours 4.3 in Thorpe 1974:197–198; Morice 1750–1756, 1:50; Bachrach 1973:80; Chadwick 1965:279–280; 1969:212 ff.

123. Bachrach 1973:84; cf. Chadwick 1969:225–237.

124. Meliodas is Tristan's father in the legends.

125. Mark fought for Chramm, son of Chlothar, in this attempt to usurp the Merovingian throne (Coghlan 1991:154), which may account for Chlothar's change of heart toward Alan Judual.

CHAPTER 5

Women, Water, and Warriors

In this chapter we will look at the female characters of the Arthurian legends, concentrating on the Dame du Lac, and the vast number of parallels between these women and the preeminent female figure of the Nart sagas, Satana. We will also consider the otherworld that the Dame du Lac calls home, its parallels to the Iranian otherworld, the nature of the people who comprise her court, and their similarities to figures in the Nart sagas. Finally we will attempt to determine whether these parallels result from transmission from the Celtic tradition, from a common Indo-European heritage, or from transmission from the Sarmatian and Alan tribes that settled in Britain and Gaul.

The most famous woman of the Round Table, Guinevere, emerges as probably the only major female figure of the Arthurian tradition who is an almost completely Celtic intrusion into what otherwise appears to be a cycle of largely Alano-Sarmatian origin with a Celtic overlay. At base Arthur's queen is Finnabair, the daughter of Medb of the *Táin Bó Cuailgne* of Ireland, a fertility-goddess in her original form and the goddess with whom the king must mate to receive sovereignty over the land. Markale argues that the love affair between Lancelot and Guinevere is parallel to the affair between Batraz and Satana at the hypothetical Indo-European level.[1] There is, however, no evidence for such an affair in the early legends of Lancelot as described in Ulrich von Zatzikhoven's *Lanzelet*.[2] Not much more needs to be said about Guinevere in the context of this book. Yet several other women in the Arthurian legends do have significant implications for our hypothesis.

The Dame du Lac

One of the most prominent female figures in the Arthurian legends is the woman from whom the hero obtains his sword. This figure may be the hero's mother, as in the case of Perceval, but she usually appears as the Dame du Lac, the "Lady of the Lake" (see plate 11). Although she is closely connected with Lancelot in the early legends, in later versions of Arthur's story she gives the British king one of his swords as well.

The Dame du Lac has received little attention from scholars since Lucy Allen Paton's *Studies in the Fairy Mythology of Arthurian Romance* (1903). Yet in her early manifestations this water-woman figured as one of the prime movers of the action in the legends of King Arthur and the Knights of the Round Table, particularly in the legends of Lancelot.

The Dame du Lac of the Arthurian tradition is first mentioned in 1179 by Chrétien de Troyes in the *Conte de la charrette*.[3] Chrétien explains that she was a fairy who raised Lancelot and gave him a ring, the stone of which enabled him to break enchantments. Lancelot could also use the ring to summon her to his aid.[4] These details generally recur in some form in the majority of the early stories of the Dame du Lac. In addition to the *Conte de la charrette* by Chrétien she appears in the *Lanzelet* (ca. 1194–1205) by Ulrich von Zatzikhoven, the Vulgate *Merlin* (ca. 1215–1235), the prose *Lancelot* (ca. 1215–1235),[5] and the thirteenth-century prose *Prophécies de Merlin*.[6] In only two of these works does a name for this character occur more than once.[7] This name is the Dame du Lac, and at its second appearance the name is sometimes replaced with the description of the Dame du Lac as a white serpent.[8] Among the other works containing this character[9] there is no consensus regarding her name. She is an anonymous *fée* ("fairy") in the *Conte de la charrette*, an equally anonymous *merminne* ("love from the sea") or *merfeine* ("sea-fairy")[10] in the *Lanzelet*, and Niniane or Viviane (depending on the manuscript) in the Vulgate *Merlin*, where her name is glossed as "she who was never without a sword."[11] She is also called Nimué in Malory.[12]

The authors of the romances were equally divided regarding the nature of the Dame du Lac. She is an ordinary fairy,

Women, Water, and Warriors

PLATE 11. The Dame du Lac (MS Paris, Bibliothèque Nationale f.fr. 113, fol. 156v). Photograph courtesy of Bibliothèque Nationale, Paris.

a wise sea-fairy, a treacherous and ungrateful woman, a woman who understands charms, or a great prophetess. She can be the Queen of Fairyland, the queen of a mortal kingdom, the Queen of Ladies, or no queen at all.

Among scholars who prefer the Celtic-origin hypothesis for the Arthurian legends the interpretation of the Dame du Lac as a fairy, derived from a Celtic goddess of sovereignty, prevails. According to Nutt the Dame du Lac "appears . . . in every form and at all periods of Celtic mythic literature, and forms one of the most distinctive and characteristic personages of that literature."[13] She is "the supernatural woman who instructs a young hero in the manly exploits—skill in arms or the chase— that fit him for some special purpose."[14] Paton contends that "in the case of the Dame du Lac her title at once betrays her fairy nature; for the Celtic imagination placed the Otherworld not only beyond the sea, but also beneath the sea."[15] The Irish Macha came to this world from such a land,[16] and in the prose *Perceval* Grail maidens arise from a spring with food and drink. Paton uses Tydorel (from the lay *Tydorel*) as an example of a being dwelling beneath the waves, but he is most likely a water-nix.[17] Likewise Nutt merely describes an Indo-European figure in its Celtic reflex.[18] There is absolutely nothing in Nutt's evidence that indicates that the Dame du Lac herself is Celtic. In fact, of all the motifs associated with the Dame du Lac, only her one appearance as a transformed hag in the prose *Prophécies de Merlin* can be traced with any certainty to the Celtic tradition. In addition Spanish, Teutonic, and even modern Ossetic water-fays are well known, but the Dame du Lac seems to be something more than simply one of these fairies.

Except in the Vulgate *Merlin*, in which Viviane appears once wearing green, the Dame du Lac wears white, and she insists that her court and her protégés wear white as well. She gives instructions that Lancelot be knighted while wearing the white clothes she has given him. The wearing of white, however, does not automatically indicate that a figure is Celtic or that this figure is from the Celtic otherworld. Satana of the Nart sagas also has a connection with white cloth and water.[19] She appears washing her linen in a river in tales of the birth of Sozryko.[20] A similar motif in Celtic tales[21] is generally connected with stories of death, whereas the tale of Satana combines with a tale similar to that of Athene and Hephaistos from Greek mythology,[22] which leads into accounts of how Satana raised the infant warrior in the otherworld. This is far closer to the tales of the Dame du Lac and the raising of Lancelot than to those of the Morrĩgan and her prophecies of death.

The Dame du Lac's continental origin, tendency to appear with a male escort, connection with the dead, and preference for wearing white have all have been used to argue that she is of Celtic origin.[23] The main thrust of this argument is that in Celtic myth women generally appear as the consorts of gods on the Continent whereas they appear as individual goddesses in insular traditions.[24] It is, however, interesting that women in the Nart sagas figure primarily as consorts as well. Satana, who was born in a tomb and who wears white, appears as the wife of Uryzmæg.[25]

In most of the stories the Dame du Lac possesses foreknowledge. In those cases where the foreknowledge is unlimited she never prophesies. In the earliest stories she is able to act upon her unlimited foreknowledge to change the future. In later works she is prohibited from taking any action based on her foreknowledge, since anything she might do would cause more deaths than would normally occur. In some stories her foreknowledge is limited, particularly with regard to her own death. In the prose *Prophécies de Merlin* she asks Merlin to prophesy about her death for her. In the stories in which her foreknowledge is limited she sometimes prophesies herself, but she usually passes on the prophecies she heard from Merlin. And on at least one occasion she interprets a prophetic dream for Guinevere. Curiously, Satana, the Wise Woman of the Narts, also exhibits these prophetic skills, whereas otherworldly women of the Arthurian tradition who boast hypothetical Celtic origins (e.g., Guinevere and Morgan Le Fay) do not.[26]

Rarely the Dame du Lac (usually in her incarnation as Niniane) is said to learn her magic from Merlin; but in most stories she has learned her magic on her own, or the magic is attributed to her fairy nature. The Dame du Lac specializes in a magic of opposites: changing youth to age, age to youth, courage to cowardice, cowardice to courage, enchantment to disenchantment, disenchantment to enchantment, sorrow to joy, joy to sorrow, health to injury, injury to health, life to death, and death to life. Her favorite magic is that of healing and of causing joy. She favors such magic items as rings and usually employs these for the benefit of Lancelot. In the *Lanzelet* she sends a mantle to Arthur's court to test the chastity of Lancelot's favorite wife, Iblis.[27] She uses magic shields to aid Lancelot in battle. She also uses a magic shield and sometimes a magic salve to cure his madness. On one occasion she gives one of her spell-breaking rings to Uriens, Morgan's husband. On another occasion Uther Pendragon sends the Dame du Lac four rings that contain four teeth from a great serpent he had killed. At the end of the *Mort le roi Artu* the Dame du Lac receives Excalibur from Arthur when Lancelot cannot be located to claim the sword. And on one occasion the Dame du Lac enables her second-in-command, Saraide, to change Lionel and Bors into greyhounds by using magic wreaths and collars.

The Dame du Lac rarely leaves her own land. When she does so, she is usually drawn forth by the death of a king.[28] In the prose *Lancelot* she appears at the death of King Ban and steals the infant Lancelot, thereby preventing the child's death at the hands of Claudas.[29] She appears shortly after the death of King Bors (or she sends Saraide) to take Lancelot's cousins, Bors and Lionel, into her protective custody.[30] In Malory she appears with Morgan at Arthur's death to take Arthur's body away in a boat.[31] Once she is said to cause a death of a prince (Dorin, son of Claudas). Twice she sends a messenger to give instructions about burial and conduct during mourning to the survivors of a deceased monarch. And in Lancelot's case she will sometimes appear in order to prevent the death of a king (Lancelot himself). In the earliest extant story of the Dame du Lac, the *Lanzelet*, she is the mother of Mabuz, lord of Castle Death, and she is the builder of the magical Castle Death, which turns brave men into cowards and the cowardly Mabuz into the bravest of all men.[32]

The Dame du Lac usually communicates with the world beyond her home through female messengers. If her messengers are ignored, then the Dame herself will appear and enforce her will. The only other event that will cause the Dame du Lac to leave her home is the investiture of a young knight, particularly one of her protégés. She gives Arthur specific instructions for the knighting of Lancelot, threatening dire consequences if her every word is not obeyed or if Lancelot fails to be knighted in the special white outfit she provides for him. She alone can declare the time at which her protégés will be knighted, and she stands the night-long vigil with Lancelot, Lionel, and Bors on the three occasions she requests knighthood for one of her protégés.

There are three types of Dame du Lac stories, those in which she functions as the guardian of Lancelot, as the opponent of Morgan Le Fay, and as the lover of Merlin. The first class is the most important, because the other two result from later influence. With the possible exception of the *Lanzelet* no early example of the first group has survived.[33]

The Guardian of Lancelot. In the earliest surviving tales the Dame du Lac is the mortal enemy of a powerful knight, originally Iweret of the Fair Forest Befort and lord of Castle Dodone, who threatens to kill her cowardly son and take away his inheritance.[34] In later stories the Dame du Lac appears as the enemy of Claudas de la Deserte, who threatens to kill the infant Lancelot (the Dame du Lac's foster-son) and take away his inheritance (probably a collapsed version of the earlier tales). In the earliest works the Dame du Lac appears solely as the foster-mother of Lancelot. She either has him trained in the use of arms or gives him a lecture on their use without any practical training to back up her words. She showers Lancelot with gifts: a white horse,[35] white armor (which may or may not have gold bells), a shield,[36] a white lance that can pierce steel, a white sword "forged with evil intent by the enemies of the Lady" that can "cut iron and steel,"[37] a magic ring that enables Lancelot either to detect or to break magical enchantments, a magic tent that can change size as well as cure wounds and sorrow, and a magic mirror that enables Lancelot to see the one he loves most.[38] The Dame du Lac usually withholds Lancelot's name, eventually revealing it in the presence of a woman who stands in a graveyard where Lancelot finds himself after winning a major fight and having a conversation about tombs with an old hermit in a nearby chapel.[39]

The connection with graves continues from Lancelot and the Dame du Lac to Galahad, whose stories seem to preserve some even more ancient aspects of this connection. In the Irish translation of the *Queste del Saint Graal* (*Logaireacht an tSoidigh Naomhtha*) Galahad comes upon a grave that is burning.[40] He lays his hand on the grave, at which point the flames die away and the dead knight speaks to him. This scene may reflect the Scythian and Sarmatian (and possibly Alanic) practice of building a hearth on a grave,[41] a ritual performed in honor of the goddess of the hearth,[42] who is represented in the Nart sagas by Satana and who in turn appears to be derived from the same prototype as the Dame du Lac.[43]

The Opponent of Morgan Le Fay. Morgan Le Fay belongs primarily to the legends of Arthur as they were known in Britain, although she appears in some of the continental material as well. In these stories she generally figures as the opponent of the Dame du Lac.[44] The conflict between these two women usually arises as they vie for control of Lancelot. A side product of this rivalry is the Dame du Lac's friendship with Guinevere, which develops in the stories in which Lancelot falls in love with Arthur's queen. In these tales the Dame du Lac attempts to aid Guinevere in her love affair with Lancelot, while Morgan Le Fay struggles to expose the affair. In Malory the Dame du Lac became the protectress of Arthur,[45] which is the only medieval version of the Arthurian tales in which Arthur gets Excalibur from the Lake. In contrast Malory depicts Morgan as Arthur's plotting half-sister (through his mother, Igraine), who, among other mischievous activities, arranges to have Excalibur stolen and replaced with a nonmagical replica. Both women exhibit an inconsistency in their relationships with Arthur. In Malory, after spending the bulk of the story antagonizing her half-brother, Morgan appears as one of the three queens to take the mortally wounded king away to the safety of Avalon. The Dame du Lac's ambiguous relationship with Arthur in the Vulgate Cycle seems to arise from Lancelot's love for Guinevere.[46] This love affair sometimes causes the Dame du Lac to work against Arthur, whereas she usually employs her power in his support. Morgan, in contrast, serves primarily as the "gadfly" of the Round Table, always challenging Arthur's knights with magical creations, such as the Green Knight.

Both Morgan Le Fay and the Dame du Lac are absent from most of the Grail material. A Sicilian legend of Arthur places the king with Morgan inside Mount Etna,[47] where she keeps him eternally young after his "death" and where he is fed every year by the Grail. This is essentially Morgan's only connection with the Grail legends. Loomis tries to tie her more closely to the Grail cycle by identifying her with Elaine Sans Pere.[48] The bulk of his argument, however, is based on his interpretation of Pelles, Elaine's father, as the Grail Keeper and Morgan as the possessor of a horn of healing—a weak argument at best.

Morgan is not a definite antecedent to the Dame du Lac, as some would have us believe.[49] These scholars feel that Morgan Le Fay developed from the Celtic war-goddess, Morgana (the Morrīgan).[50] Attempts to present her as the source of the figure of the Dame du Lac have drawn on the connection of a war-goddess with warriors and of the Dame du Lac's training of Lancelot and his cousins in the arts of war. Although the training of warriors by women is well known in the Celtic materials,[51] fighting women are also found in Scythian and Alan-Sarmatian material.[52] The legends of the Amazons developed from observations by Greeks of the female Scythian warriors.[53] Sarmatian women were said to be descended from the Amazons and the Scythians, and they fought in armor on horseback, as did the men.[54] Archaeological evidence is surprisingly abundant for the presence of women warriors among the "Sauromatians."[55] Some of these women may have been priestesses as well as warriors, a dual class that could easily be reflected in such figures as the Dame du Lac, with her ties to the otherworld.[56] Some of the altars that are found in the graves of these "Sauromatian" warrior-priestesses (or shamans) are decorated with wolves or dogs in the Scythian animal-style,[57] and this aspect of the religion might be reflected in the tale of Saraide using the Dame du Lac's magic to turn Lionel and Bors into dogs.[58] Very often bronze rings, white paint, and lumps of charcoal are found in these "Sauromatian" burials as well, items that may be reflected in the Dame du Lac's penchant for magic rings and for wearing white as well as in stories of Lancelot's family and burning graves.[59] Fighting women are also noted among the Alans who invaded Gaul in the fifth century.

Paulinus Pellaeus indicates that Alan women fought alongside their men at Bazas.[60] In any case the warrior aspects of the Dame du Lac do not link her to the Celtic Morrīgan any more than Morgan Le Fay's name links her to the war-goddess.[61]

Other scholars, attempting to find a Celtic source for Morgan, have turned to the Welsh *Dialogue with Glewlwyd*, in which she appears as the daughter of King Aballach.[62] In this story Morgan lives on an island with her father and sisters.[63] Some scholars have argued that the confusion between this island belonging to Avallach and Manannán's Hesperides-like island of Celtic legend (traditionally the Isle of Man) may have led the Bretons to create the isle of Avalon and to change Morgan's name to that of the Welsh Modron. This detail of Morgan's island homeland has been used to argue that she served as the source for the figure of the Dame du Lac. The Dame du Lac's homeland, however, is never made up of her sisters, and in many cases the Dame du Lac does not come from an island.[64] The Morgan of the Welsh Triads and the Modron of the *Mabinogi* differ in some extremely important ways from the Morgan Le Fay of the Arthurian tradition. These differences can perhaps be seen best when the character of Morgan and that of the Dame du Lac are compared in their relationship to Lancelot.

Both women are extremely well defined in the legends, and several details throw them into sharp contrast with each other when they appear in the same tale. In *Prophécies de Merlin* (1270s), when the Dame du Lac and Morgan are pitted against Lancelot, Arthur, Guinevere, and Merlin in turn, the differences between the two characters become readily apparent. Perhaps the most dramatic example is that while Morgan seeks to harm Lancelot, the Dame du Lac protects him. These differences carry over to the other Arthurian legends as well (see fig. 8).

Thus the differences between the Dame du Lac and Morgan Le Fay seem to indicate that these female characters derived from different sources, rather than from a common Celtic source. We suggest that the source for the Dame du Lac was a prototype of the figure that developed into the Wise Woman of the Narts, Satana, as well.[65] We also suggest that Morgan Le Fay derived either directly from a Celtic source or

DAME DU LAC	MORGAN LE FAY
Lives beneath lake	Lives on Avalon
With court of women	With sisters
Teaches manners and love	Trains warriors
Gives sword	Steals sword
Mother of a coward	Mother of a hero (Owain/Yvain)
Protective magic:	**Destructive magic:**
tent to shelter	cloak with acid to destroy
transforming castle (courage/coward)	[no equivalent]
magical ring to break spells of deception	false Excalibur (non-magical designed to deceive)
spells of peace and congeniality	spells of deceit
Requires return of magic items	Does not require return of magic items
Heals Lancelot	Enables Arthur, still injured, to live as "Once and Future King"

FIG. 8. The Dame du Lac and Morgan Le Fay (based on the analysis in Paton 1903)

that she developed from the same prototype as the Dame du Lac but has been subjected to such a heavy Celtic overlay that her origins are all but obscured.

The Lover of Merlin. In the stories in which the Dame du Lac learns her magic from Merlin she is usually said to be his lover as well. Her name in such instances is often given as Niniane or Viviane.[66] Even in these works, however, Merlin is not the only lover of the Dame du Lac. Meliades, a knight whom either the Dame du Lac or her mother raised from birth, figures as the Dame's lover, sometimes before and in most cases after Merlin's imprisonment in the tomb. In those works where Meliades does not appear, such as the prose *Lancelot*, a nameless lover always accompanies the Dame du Lac when she leaves her home or travels through her forest with her court.[67] In Malory she is said to marry yet another lover, Pelleas, after her betrayal of Merlin.

In later stories the Dame du Lac, in her guise as Viviane/Niniane/Nimué, imprisons Merlin in a tomb, tree, or cave. On several occasions she is said to talk to Merlin's spirit, and once she enables her lover, Meliades, to visit the tomb and speak with the dead prophet. Perhaps these tales developed from other stories of the prophetic skills of the Dame du Lac.

In spite of her connection with lovers the Dame du Lac, in her manifestation as Niniane/Viviane, appears to be closely connected with the huntress-goddess of several Indo-European peoples, such as the Greek Artemis, the Roman Diana, and the Scythian Diana.[68] Artemis was the virginal sister of Apollo, the god of prophecy, and she sometimes shared his prophetic powers. Artemis is also sometimes identified with Hecate, teacher of witchcraft and goddess of the dead, just as the Dame du Lac seems to have some special connection with tombs and the dead. The Dame du Lac shares Artemis's concern for chastity (if not for virginity), a trait that also appears in tales of Diana.

Viviane in particular seems to have close ties to Diana. Viviane's mother's name was Diane, and Viviane herself lives beside Lake Diane.[69] Viviane usually appears, like Diana, riding through the forest, hunting, or bathing in a lake or river. Viviane's cruelty toward Lancelot's mother, Elaine, echoes the attitude of the Scythian Diana toward other women.[70] Diana was the protectress of the young, especially maidens, just as the Dame du Lac protects the infant Lancelot and his young cousins. And the dog, the form Saraide uses to hide Bors and Lionel, was particularly sacred to Diana.

The Lake. Concerning the home of the Dame du Lac the authors of the romances were as divided on its location as they were on the Dame du Lac's name. Her home is in the sea, over the sea, on an island in a lake, in a rock in a lake,[71] beneath a mirage of a lake, in a valley from which no man can return, in a forest beneath a lake, in a forest beside a lake, or simply in a forest. She lives in a crystal ball atop a mountain, in a magnificent palace, in a luxurious manor, in a simple hut, or in a rock.

The characteristics of her land vary as well. It is usually a place of eternal spring. Often it has only one gate. It is usually a place of eternal joy, which may include eternal youth and eternal health. Sometimes the land has the power to abate anger.[72] Sometimes the land is described as wide and deep. Sometimes the Dame du Lac's home is called the Land of Maidens. And on at least one occasion the land is associated with the Black Chapel (also known as the Chapel Nigramous) that figures so consistently in the adventures of Lancelot.[73]

Coyajee believed that the emphasis on lakes in the Arthurian tradition stemmed from the connection between water and the Iranian *Xvarīnah* ("halo, nimbus, glory"),[74] most likely via direct diffusion to Europe.[75] Gallais equated the water symbolism of the Grail legends with the Iranian legends of Anāhitā, although he saw the parallel as occurring at the hypothetical Indo-European level.[76] Yet, given the presence of Alans in the regions where the legends of the Dame du Lac developed in medieval Europe, it is more likely that these Northeastern-Iranian-speaking people were responsible for this type of female figure's presence in Gaul and surrounding regions.

The people who comprise the court of the Dame du Lac were, with the exception of Lancelot, originally all women. The Celtic "Elysium," according to MacCulloch, was a Land of Women, usually on an island.[77] In later stories men appear in her home as frequently as the maidens. This later version of the Dame du Lac's kingdom is much closer to the Ossetic version of the otherworld, which is found under the sea, where young heroes are raised.[78] It is interesting to note that Satana's mother came from an otherworld beneath the sea, which was peopled by both men and women.[79] Indeed, as Colarusso points out, Satana is closely linked with water and is "credited with the discovery of water's 'life force.'"[80]

In most instances the People of the Lake wear white garments. They travel by riding white mules or white horses, piloting boats without oars, or driving carts. The People of the Lake can use magic to create tents, houses, and even castles, but only Saraide can use magic for other purposes.[81]

The maidens of the Grail, the only women to retain much in the way of an important role in the works of Robert de Boron and in the *Perlesvaus*, have a similar description: they are maidens who come as messengers dressed in white, who ride white horses and white mules, drive in carts, heal injured knights, and occasionally appear in connection with water. These women sound like the maidens of the lake, the messengers of the Dame du Lac. Yet in Robert's works they come from the Grail Castle and the Maimed King rather than from the Dame du Lac. What happened to their queen? The answer probably lies in the *Perlesvaus*, the attempt to Christianize the legends of Lancelot. For some reason the Dame du Lac could not be Christianized, so the authors simply removed her from the story—except in her negative appearance as Viviane. The two traditions of Lancelot (with and without the Dame du Lac) continue side by side on the Continent, and when the legend traveled to Britain in the fourteenth century the stories with the Grail and without the Dame du Lac traveled first. In the fifteenth century the last portion of the prose *Lancelot* traveled to Britain and was used by Malory when he composed *Le Morte Darthur*.[82] Since the Dame du Lac appears mainly in the company of Arthur, especially at his death, in the *Mort le roi Artu*, Malory linked his Lady of the Lake to Arthur instead of to Lancelot, and the Arthurian tradition as it is best known today was born.[83]

Other scholars have argued that the propensity of the People of the Lake for wearing white indicates that they are from the Celtic Land of the Dead. This is an otherworld similar to that inhabited by the Dame du Lac. This otherworld is also heavily associated with the color white. Otherworldly figures in Ossetic legend (e.g., St. George) prefer the color white as well, and Satana in particular is connected with the dead.[84] It is as probable, then, that the Dame du Lac derived from an Alanic source as it is that she derived from a Celtic source. The reference to the Dame du Lac as the queen of a Land of Women may show Celtic influence, but the idea for such a land appears in the traditions of other Indo-European peoples (e.g., the Greek island of the Hesperides).

The Absence of the Dame du Lac. As interesting as the works in which the Dame du Lac appears are those in which she is absent. The Dame du Lac does not appear in the legends of Lancelot prior to 1179, nor does she figure prominently in any of the works concerning the Holy Grail. In the Vulgate *Queste del Saint Graal* the Dame du Lac rides through the forest twice on her white horse. In the remainder of the prose *Lancelot* and the *Mort le roi Artu* she is a major figure, battling Morgan for control over Lancelot's life. What happened to her character in the Grail stories of Lancelot?

The works in which the Dame du Lac does not appear and which contain either Lancelot or Merlin are Robert de Boron's *Joseph*, the Vulgate *Estoire del Saint Graal*, the Vulgate *Merlin* (which contains only a very sketchy picture of Viviane);[85] the Vulgate *Queste del Saint Graal*; and the *Perlesvaus*, whose author remains anonymous. In the rest of the works that do not include the Dame du Lac Lancelot is absent as well or appears only as a name on a list of the knights of Arthur's court. But in these four major adventures of Lancelot and Merlin the Dame du Lac manifests herself only once, and then as the evil Viviane, who imprisons Merlin in a tomb, instead of as the protective foster-mother of Lancelot. A quick look at the works of Robert, the Vulgate, and the *Perlesvaus* reveals another interesting fact: the women, including Guinevere, have almost vanished. This fact leads us to conclude that he knew the tradition of the Dame du Lac but simply edited her out of the story in the same manner in which he removed all but traces of the other women of the Arthurian tradition. This is why these women do not appear in those portions of the Vulgate and the *Perlesvaus* that follow Robert de Boron's texts. Viviane remains in the *Merlin* to provide an example of what women should not be. In the *Perlesvaus* Guinevere dies before Lancelot ever gets a chance to appear in the same scene with her. Lancelot spends a night in Guinevere's tomb,[86] and the rest of the romance is devoted to converting Lancelot from his pagan ways to Christianity.

The Grail tradition is for the most part clerical in origin and transmission,[87] and most of the women in the Arthurian legends have been edited out of these stories. Powerful figures, such as the Dame du Lac and Morgan Le Fay, were particularly subject to removal from the stories by the monks.[88] This alone could account for the absence of the Dame du Lac from these tales.

The Female Sword Bestower. Another form of female character connected with the Dame du Lac also appears in the traditions of several Indo-European peoples. This is the figure Littleton has identified as the "Female Sword Bestower."[89] Usually a water-nymph or a goddess, she is a close relative of a hero, whom she helps to procure a weapon that has been forged in the otherworld (see chap. 7). Examples can be seen in the Greek Thetis (mother of Achilles), the Ossetic Satana (aunt of Batraz), and the Welsh Aranrhod (mother of Lleu Llaw Gyffes).[90] The Dame du Lac is the aunt of Bors and Lionel (the sons of King Bors and Evaine). By extension she must be Lancelot's aunt, since King Bors and King Ban were full brothers and Evaine and Elaine were full sisters. In several versions of Lancelot's story the Dame du Lac is directly responsible for the forging of his sword.

But the Dame du Lac goes far beyond these basic functions in her relationship to the young warriors. She stands the nightlong vigil with all three of her protégés. In the *Lanzelet* she supplies specific instructions for the use of Lancelot's sword. She also supplies Lancelot with his lance, shield, armor, horse, tunic, and replacements for those parts of his weapons and armor that he loses or breaks.

Many of these characteristics can be seen in Satana, the Wise Woman of the Narts. In the Nart sagas Satana is associated with water. She not only helps Batraz obtain his magical weapon but also teaches him to use it effectively. Thirsting for vengeance against Sajnæg Ældar, his father's murderer, Batraz turns to Satana for help.[91] She tells him to seek Sajnæg Ældar, gain his confidence, and ask to see his famous sword—one that was made by Safa, the god of weapons—on the pretense that he would like to have a copy made. Ordinarily, Satana warns Batraz, Sajnæg Ældar extends the weapon point first, even to show it off; the only way the hero can prevail is to trick his enemy into extending the sword hilt first. With the help of his loyal steed, Durdura, who had also served Xæmyc, his father, Batraz follows his aunt's instructions to the letter. When Sajnæg Ældar, who does not recognize the son of the man he had killed, finally does extend the wondrous weapon hilt first, the Nart leader grabs the hilt, dispatches his father's murderer, and assumes possession of the sword.[92]

Because of this story and other tales Markale sees Satana as an Indo-European parallel of the female figures who train such warriors as Cūchulainn.[93] But the detailed parallels between this Ossetic female figure and the Dame du Lac are closer than simple analogs of Indo-European derivation. Uryzmæg's wife, Satana, mother of the dominant clan of Narts, bears a fairly close resemblance to the Lady of the Lake, whereas she shares few if any of Morgan's evil qualities.

In conclusion the Dame du Lac belongs to a pre-Christian tradition of hypothetical Indo-European origin. The manuscripts in which her story appears were composed in regions that were directly influenced by Celtic, Teutonic, Roman, and Scythian traditions and indirectly influenced by the Greek tradition through the possibility of scholarly borrowing.[94] She may be a composite figure who has her roots in several of these traditions. Since the Dame du Lac appears in the works of a secular nature[95] and is generally absent from those that include the Holy Grail, we are more inclined to believe that her character had its origin in a popular rather than a scholarly tradition. In light of the other evidence presented in this book we believe that this popular tradition was of Northeastern Iranian derivation and was carried into Gaul by the Alans and Sarmatians who settled in that region. The subsequent fusion of the Northeast Iranian and Celtic traditions resulted in the polar opposition of the Scythian-influenced Dame du Lac and the more Celtic Morgan Le Fay.

NOTES

1. Markale 1985:137–138. This love affair between Batraz (Pataraz) and Satana (Satanaya) is found in the Circassian Nart sagas (Colarusso [personal communication]).

2. Nor is Lancelot (see chaps. 3 and 4) by any means Guinevere's only lover. The French romance *Yder*, which contains an unfavorable

portrait of Arthur, tells how Yder, the lover of Guinevere, kills a bear (Adams 1983).

3. As will be noted in the list of manuscripts that follows, all of the authors of the early legends of the Dame du Lac wrote in France (in a variety of dialects of Old French). One exception is Ulrich von Zatzikhoven, who wrote his *Lanzelet* in Thurgau, Switzerland, but who claims as his source a French manuscript brought to Thurgau by Hugh de Morville. A second exception may be the prose *Lancelot*, which is signed by the Welsh cleric Walter Map, whose authorship has been called into doubt by recent scholarship. For more information on the origins of the Lancelot legend see Webster 1934.

4. The Old French reads:

> Mes cil don plus dire vos doi
> Avoit un anel an son doi,
> Don la pierre tel force avoit
> Qu'anchantemanz ne le pooit
> Tenir puis qu'il l'avoit veue.
> L'anel met devant sa veue,
> S'esgarde la pierre et si dit:
> "Dame, dame, se Deus m'ait,
> Or avroie je grant mestier
> Que vos me venissiez eidier!"
> Cele dame une fee estoit,
> Qui l'anel done li avoit,
> Et si le norri an s'anfance;
> S'avoit an li mout grant fiance
> Que ele, an quel leu que il fust,
> Secorre et eidier li deust;
> Mes il voit bien a son apel
> Et a la pirre de l'anel,
> Qu'il n'i a point d'anchantemant,
> Et set trestot certainnemant
> Qu'il sont anclos et anserre. (Foerster 1899:84, ll. 2347–2367).

5. There has been much debate over the authorship of the prose *Lancelot*. Carman (1973:129–131) suggests that the first and fourth volumes, the *Estoire* and the *Queste*, were written by one set of authors, and another group of authors worked on the second, third and fifth volumes (i.e., *Merlin*, *Lancelot*, and *Mort le roi Artu*). Carman (1973:23–26) attributes the similarity among these last three parts, and especially the emphasis on the Dame du Lac in the *Merlin* and the *Lancelot* to the

patronage of Eleanor (Aliénor) of Aquitaine, who died before the *Mort le roi Artu* was completed (which may explain the relative absence of the Dame du Lac from this final section). The *Mort le roi Artu* ends with the words: "Here Master Walter Map ceases to tell the *History of Lancelot* . . . ;" Carman (1973:108–109) suggests, however, that this line was added during the final compilation of the Vulgate Cycle. The presence of the Grail material and absence of the Dame du Lac in the first and fourth volumes also has led to the conclusion that Robert de Boron (or someone familiar with his work) was responsible for composing this portion of the Vulgate Cycle. For more information see Carman (1973).

6. Attributed to Maistre Richart d'Irlande.

7. The Dame du Lac first appears in the Vulgate Cycle in the early thirteenth century and does not appear again until the prose *Prophécies de Merlin* of the late thirteenth century.

8. Paton 1926, 1:169, 171. Guinevere is also symbolized by a white serpent (Paton 1926, 2:242–243).

9. I.e., a woman who is connected with either Lancelot or Merlin in the same manner as the Dame du Lac of the Vulgate Cycle or the Dame du Lac of the prose *Prophécies de Merlin*; Paton 1926.

10. Translations of *merminne* and *merfeine* were provided by Donald Ward (personal communication).

11. Some of the editions of the Vulgate *Merlin* use Niniane and some use Viviane, depending on the manuscript source (with the variance probably deriving from the difficulty of distinguishing between V and N as the initial letter), as the name of the woman who traps Merlin in his tomb. Some scholars have attempted to determine which was the original form; however, Paton (1903:240–247) pointed out that the name Niniane (Viviane) does not appear in Arthurian literature prior to the development of the tale of Merlin. While the figure of Niniane may have been influenced by that of the Dame du Lac, attempts to link the names of these two women have been convoluted at best. Any connection they do have does not appear to be at the onomastic level.

12. Cowen 1969.

13. Nutt 1881:32.

14. Nutt 1881:32.

15. Paton 1903:167.

16. A Celtic fairyland beneath the waves; Paton 1903:167.

17. Paton 1903:168; cf. Ward 1981. Aalardin du Lac (in the First Continuation of Chrétien's *Perceval*) parallels Tydorel's father.

18. Nutt 1881:32.

19. Cf. the hunt for the white animal.

20. Dumézil 1930:75–77.

21. Cf. the Morrīgan's washing of armor at a river where she prophesies the death of a king; Ross 1967:245–246.

22. A shepherd spills his "seed" on a stone to produce the warrior Sozryko. Hephaistos, upon seeing Athene, performs the same act and produces a "serpent-footed" child; see chap. 7.

23. The connection with water may link the Dame du Lac with the Celtic otherworld, as may the references to her wearing white. We are puzzled, however, by scholarly insistence that figures surrounded by white belong to a Celtic otherworld. The Christian tradition of clothing angels and saints in white would have been equally familiar to the medieval authors of Arthurian romance, and Welsh descriptions of the otherworld, such as *The Dream of Rhonabwy* (Gantz 1976:177–191), include an extraordinary variety of colors.

24. Ford (personal communication); cf. Ford 1976:379–390.

25. Hübschmann 1887:556–557; Dumézil 1930:24–25.

26. In contrast the Morrīgan of the Celtic tradition does exhibit prophetic skills with respect to the outcome of battles.

27. In the other accounts of the adventures of Lancelot he usually appears as a bachelor or in a forced marriage to Elaine, daughter of Pelles. In the *Lanzelet*, however, Lancelot marries an unnamed woman, deserts her, marries Ade (whose brother reclaims her when Lancelot appears to be a coward in Mabuz's castle), marries Iblis, wins the right to marry Guinevere, is forced into marriage by the Queen of Pluris, and wins the right to marry Elidia. Iblis stands foremost in Lancelot's affections, but he maintains the vast tracts of land he acquired through marriage to his various wives and presumably maintains the wives as well. Iblis passes the chastity test when all the other women of the Round Table, including Guinevere, fail.

28. This is the trait that has most frequently led to her identification as a Celtic personification of Sovereignty.

29. Colarusso (lecture, June 23–26, 1992, "The Nart Hero as Victim and Avenger," Maikop, Adygheya) has identified the pattern of a nurse taking a dangerous baby away from its surviving parent and placing the child in a body of water as a common element in Nart hero tales.

30. The Dame du Lac raises Lancelot, Bors, and Lionel for two reasons: to prevent their deaths at the hands of her enemy Claudas and to use them basically as assassins against her foes, with Lancelot always pitted against the most powerful of them.

31. MacCulloch 1918, 3:194.

32. Lancelot gains access to this castle by crossing a sword bridge. It is interesting to note that in one of the adventures of Batraz (Dumézil 1930:61–68) he gains access to a castle surrounded by an impassable moat by having the Narts shoot him either from a cannon or a bow, i.e., by means of a weapon.

33. Paton 1903:170.

34. This is the motivation for her theft of and raising of the brave Lancelot.

35. This horse may be either a mare or a stallion. In the *Lanzelet*, which makes the earliest reference to Lancelot's receiving a mount from his foster-mother, the horse is a mare (ll. 352–353; Hahn 1965:9; cf. Webster 1951:29–30; cf. Dumézil 1930:72–73). In the prose *Lancelot* he receives a warhorse, which is most likely a stallion. In the prose *Prophécies de Merlin* the horse's sex is never determined. In the *Perlesvaus* the horse is a mare. Outside of the Arthur of the Welsh tradition Lancelot is one of the few knights, to our knowledge, who uses a mare for a warhorse. Most of Arthur's knights preferred the more aggressive—and less likely to become pregnant—stallion as a mount. Cf. Puhvel's discussion (1987:273–276) of Giraldus Cambrensis's (Gerald of Wales; ca. 1185) description of the Irish sacrifice of a white mare during the coronation ceremony for a king. Although this practice may have been widespread among the Celtic peoples, Lancelot's mare is not sacrificed nor does he become a king upon receiving her. Therefore it is unlikely that Lancelot's white mare had her origins in this ancient Celtic ceremony (cf. Weston 1901a and Paton 1903).

36. This shield can be plain white; white with an eagle; white with one, two, or three beads of unspecified color, which increase strength; white with a knight and a queen, split in two and held together by leather straps, which cure sorrow when joined into a solid shield; and colorless, which cures madness.

37. Recall that "Cut Steel" has been proposed as the name of Excalibur, and Caliburnus has been translated as "cut steel" in Malory (Ackerman 1952:48). This makes Lancelot's sword Excalibur's twin—which may explain why he is the only knight of the Round Table who has the right to wield Excalibur.

Lines 365–369 of the *Lanzelet* vary according to the manuscript and appear in similar forms in other sources in which Lancelot receives his sword from the Dame du Lac. In some versions of the *Lanzelet* the destructive power of Lancelot's sword comes not from the "evil intent" with which it was forged but from the "wrath" in which Lancelot wielded it. This wrath is not normal anger; it is a rage peculiar to Lancelot, similar to the battle rage of Cūchulainn, during which only the Dame du Lac dares to face her protégé. Lancelot's madness, which extends into every aspect of his life, including his *folle* (insane) love for Guinevere, would provide an interesting study in itself (Owen, diss., 16–21).

38. This lover is thought to be the Dame du Lac in the original version of the story, but later is interpreted as Guinevere.

39. This pattern seems to form the heart of the stories of Lancelot and has been noted by numerous scholars, including Paton (1903), Weston (1901a), and Webster (1934 and 1951).

40. ll. 3981 ff.; Falconer 1953:280–281.

41. Abaev 1980:12; Sulimirski 1970:34, 40–41, 86; cf. Siegfried (Sigur5r) finding Brunhild (Brynhildr) on a rock, asleep, surrounded by flames.

42. Herodotus 4.59–62 glosses this goddess as "Hestia"; de Sélincourt 1972:289–290.

43. In any case this does not seem to have been a common Celtic practice.

44. By the time of Malory, Morgan appears simply as the antagonist of Lancelot rather than of the Dame du Lac, since Lancelot's protectress was all but eliminated from Malory's version of the story when the author attached her to Arthur instead of to the continental knight.

45. Paton 1903:187.

46. Paton 1903:197.

47. This story is found in the thirteenth-century French *Floriant et Florete* and Guillem de Torrella's *La Faula* (ca. 1350–1380); cf. Gervais of Tilbury's *Otia imperialia* (1211) and Caesarius of Heisterbach's *Dialogus miraculorum*; Gardner 1930:12–15. A similar legend is told of the German Tannhäuser (a historical figure who lived ca. 1228–1265) and Venus (Ward 1981, 1:157–158, 366–367). Sozryko of the Circassian Nart sagas also lives in a cave after he receives a mortal wound (Colarusso [personal communication]).

48. Loomis 1963b:159–160.

49. Cf. Loomis 1963b:159–161.

50. Still other scholars (e.g., Loomis 1963b:160) argue that Modron (whose son, Mabon, is a famous prisoner in the *Mabinogi*; Ford 1977:146–149, 193) is the Welsh prototype of Morgan. However, Owain (Ywain), Morgan's son by Uriens in the Arthurian tales, is famed for his connection with ravens (or with a lion in the continental variant in which he appears as Yvain) rather than from his status as a prisoner. A Celtic derivation for Morgan or even for her name has been called into serious question in recent years (Hale 1984:36).

51. Matthews and Stewart 1987:79–82, 86–90.

52. Newark 1989:9–30.

53. E.g., in the writings of Suetonius and Hippocrates; Walker 1983:24–27; cf. Sulimirski 1970:34; Wolfram 1988:28.

54. Herodotus 7.110–117; de Sélincourt 1972:306–308; Sulimirski 1970:33–34; Newark 1989:14.

55. Sulimirski 1970:34; Rolle 1980.

56. Sulimirski 1970:34.

57. Sulimirski 1970:35; Newark 1989:18–19; cf. Wenskus in Beck et al. 1881:122.

58. In the Ossetic tales Satana turns Uryzmæg into a dog (Dumézil 1930:26–28). In another story Arthur's hound, Cabal, left his pawprint in a stone (Nennius, *Historia Brittonum*, chap. 73; Brengle 1964:6). The Kabardians tell this same folktale about Sozryko's horse (Dumézil 1930:4), and it also appears in the Carolingian cycle, with Sir Hugo's camel leaving its print in the stone (Stein 1988:38).

The legends of Sir Hugo seem to be particularly Sarmatian in character. This Carolingian knight supposedly tied a Holy Blood relic (which was concealed in a cross-shaped reliquary) onto the back of a camel and set the beast to wander. The camel came to rest at a nunnery, which was thus granted the care of the relic. This connection between camels and women seems to stem from Sarmatian tradition. For instance, the skeleton of a camel was found in the grave of a female Sarmatian (Sulimirski 1970:106), and a camel figurine was found in the grave of another Sarmatian woman (early 100s C.E.; Sulimirski 1970:147). Camels themselves were perhaps better known to the steppe peoples, such as the Alans and the Sarmatians, than to the Carolingian knights. In the Franciscan friar William of Rubruk's description (quoted by Lamb 1943:42–43) of the Mongols (ca. 1250) we find this passage: "Their household goods and treasure they put in chests upon higher carts hitched to camels that can cross rivers without harm." It is remotely possible that the name Camelot has some connection to camels as well, either through the Latin *camelus* ("camel") or the Arabic *khamlat* ("pile, nap"), via the French *camelot* ("a costly eastern fabric"; Simpson and Weiner 1989, 2:803–805, 807).

59. Among other items; Sulimirski 1970:34. Jones-Bley (personal communication) suggests that the "white paint" might be chalk.

60. White 1921:335.

61. Morgan Le Fay, aside from taking an occasional warrior as a lover and from making attempts to force Lancelot to be her lover, has few if any connections to the functions of the Morrīgan.

62. Triad 70; Bromwich 1961. This name also is used as an alternative name for the isle of Avalon; hence some scholars draw a connection between Morgan and this island. This may in part be the reason that she appears as one of the three queens who take Arthur to this island in some versions of the story of his death.

63. The important point of this argument seems to be that Morgan is associated from the first with at least one sister, who appears in the Arthurian legends as Morgawse, the matriarch of the Orkney clan. Morgan, daughter of Aballach, was intimately connected with her sisters, and in *The Dream of Rhonabwy* (Gantz 1976:177–191) Modron and her sister bring victory to Owain (Morgan's son by King Uriens, one of Arthur's oldest supporters) through a "flight of ravens," a sign that connects her once again with the Celtic Morrīgan.

64. In early tales it is peopled exclusively by women, but even then Lancelot and his male cousins dwell in this land; and in later legends both men and women are said to live there.

65. According to Colarusso (1989:4) the name Satana (or Satanya) is derived from Iranian **sata-* ("[one] hundred"), a Northwest Caucasian form, *na* ("mother"), and an attributive suffix *-ya* (or *-a*). She is thus literally the "Mother of a Hundred Sons" (i.e., the Narts).

66. This variant of the Dame du Lac is often called Nimué by modern authors. Medieval authors preferred the forms Niniane and Viviane, although Malory (1469) did use the form Nimué.

67. The only story in which this lover is named is Malory's *Le Morte Darthur*, where he is called Pelleas; however, this is a very late and extremely reworked version of the tales of the Dame du Lac.

68. Markale 1975b:133–138.

69. The prose *Lancelot* (1488) gives the name of the lake into which the Dame du Lac carries the infant Lancelot: "that lake was called in

Pagan times the lake [Dyane]" (Pickford 1977a:chap. 3). Lake Dyane is also found in the Huth *Merlin* (Paton 1903:219–240).

70. Markale 1975b:136.

71. MacCulloch 1918, 3:194. The underwater kingdom in the Nart sagas is entered through a stone on the floor of the sea (Dumézil 1930:20).

72. A power that fails miserably when it comes to controlling Lancelot's rages.

73. E.g., the Chapel Perilous of the Castle Nigramous; Cowen 1969, 1:220–224.

74. Puhvel 1987:106.

75. Coyajee 1939:12.

76. Gallais 1972:248–249.

77. MacCulloch 1964, 3:114–123.

78. E.g., Dumézil 1930:20–24.

79. Dumézil 1930:20–24.

80. Colarusso 1989:5.

81. Saraide acquires this magic from the Dame du Lac in the form of collars for the purpose of turning Bors and Lionel into greyhounds to save them from Claudas. Saraide's use of magic collars in the prose *Lancelot* to transform Bors and Lionel into dogs belongs to Aarne-Thompson Tale Type 325, *The Magician and His Apprentice*, Section III, *Man Transformed into Dog; Tabu Against Selling Collar*. Although some scholars have argued that the story indicates the Dame du Lac's Celtic origin, the story is found from Indonesia to Ireland, Spain to Finland, India to Russia, and the Bahamas to Ecuador.

82. This notion appeared in several of the works we read and would account for Malory's references to a "French Book" as his source. The alternative is that the continental and insular traditions both had stories of a warrior whose arms were supplied by and whose career was guarded by a water-fairy, with the continental authors calling this warrior-figure Lancelot and the insular authors calling him Arthur.

83. Cf. Markale 1975a:123–124, 136, 138, 220.

84. She was born from her dead mother inside a tomb; Dumézil 1930:24–25.

85. Robert de Boron composed the poem on which the first 504 lines of the Vulgate *Merlin* are based. It is uncertain how much other material he contributed to this work (Lacy et al. 1986:457).

86. This is not an unusual pastime for Lancelot, who seems to spend much of his time in graveyards and tombs.

87. Malcor 1991.

88. However, clerically trained scribes, such as Chrétien de Troyes and Ulrich von Zatzikhoven, used these women frequently.

89. Littleton 1982a:53–65; 1983:47–57.

90. Ford 1977:189.

91. Dumézil 1930:62.

92. Dumézil 1930:63.

93. Markale 1985:137–138.

94. Bachrach 1973; Vernadsky 1963:401–434; Peterson 1985.

95. E.g., Chrétien's *Conte de la charrette*, Ulrich's *Lanzelet*, and the secular portions of the prose *Lancelot*.

PART III

Themes and Images

CHAPTER 6

The Sword in the Stone

The Sword in the Stone episode, wherein the young Arthur, not yet a king, pulled a naked sword from a stone, and thereby demonstrated his right to the British throne, is among the most famous episodes in medieval European romance (see plate 12). Although absent in the early Welsh literature about Arthur, such as *Culhwch and Olwen* and *The Spoils of Annwn*, as well as in Geoffrey of Monmouth's *Historia Regum Britanniae* and in the closely related accounts of Wace and Layamon,[1] the story of the Sword in the Stone is to be found in almost every other medieval Arthurian text, from Robert de Boron's *Merlin* (ca. 1191–1202) and the Didot-*Perceval* (ca. 1200) and the *Queste del Saint Graal* to Sir Thomas Malory's *Le Morte Darthur*.[2] The image of a sword embedded in a stone has long since become a concise metaphor for the Arthurian tradition as a whole, as evidenced by the title of T.H. White's well-known novel *The Sword in the Stone*.[3]

Yet the episode itself remains enigmatic and has few if any clear parallels elsewhere in legend and saga. In the Motif Index of Folk Literature Stith Thompson classifies it under two headings: motif H31.1 "Recognition by unique ability to dislodge sword" and motif D1654.4.1 "Sword can only be moved by right person." He cites only three examples: (1) the Sword in the Stone tale from the Arthurian legends, (2) the "sword in the tree" from the *Vlsunga Saga*, and (3) an oral tale from Uttar Pradesh in India.

In spite of the fame of this episode in connection with Arthur, no family is a bigger practitioner of thrusting weapons of war into stone and withdrawing them to prove their right to do something than the knights of Lancelot's clan. Galahad's withdrawal of Balin's sword from a floating stone is the best

181

PLATE 12. The Sword in the Stone (MS Paris, Bibliothèque Nationale f.fr. 95, fol. 159v). Photograph courtesy of Bibliothèque Nationale, Paris.

known example, with the tale found in the Vulgate *Estoire de Merlin* and *Queste del Saint Graal* and in Malory.[4] Lancelot, however, also secures a sword from the stone altar of the Chapel Nigramous,[5] and, in the *Perlesvaus*,[6] he repeatedly draws bolts and spears from pillars to prove his right to pursue a quest, even though his original sword is handed to him by the Dame du Lac. In addition the hilts of the swords in the Perilous Cemetery of the Lancelot/Grail tradition are said to be embedded in the marble headstones of the murdered brothers of Chanaan (Canaan). Thus the Sword in the Stone and its equivalents are widely represented in medieval Arthurian literature, and this implies that the motif is not simply a late and perhaps fortuitous addition but rather an integral element of the tradition that flowered in the medieval French, and eventually English, romances.

Some years ago Bruce asserted that the origin of this seemingly unique motif is to be found "in the legends of Theseus and Siegmund,"[7] and, to be sure, there are some superficial resemblances here. As a young man Theseus recovered his father's sword from under a rock.[8] The *Vülsunga Saga*, in which Odin, in the guise of an old man, drove a sword into a tree,[9] a sword that only Siegmund was strong enough to withdraw, provides a much closer parallel.[10] While Theseus's sword is simply hidden, Siegmund's blade, like Galahad's sword in the floating stone, is found by the hero when he is unarmed and in need of the weapon. Although these last three stories do not carry the same "right to rule" implications that Arthur's withdrawal of Excalibur from a stone does, the fact that Siegmund's blade is found embedded in wood is closer to an Alanic tradition of thrusting blades into piles of wood on the ground, from which we believe this motif derived, than are any of the other legends. However, whether the *Vülsunga Saga* took the motif from the Arthurian legends, or vice versa, or whether both traditions acquired the motif independently from the Alan invaders of the Rhine and Gaul will probably never be determined with any certainty.

Like Geoffrey's *Historia* and the Welsh texts the Nart sagas do not include a Sword in the Stone episode. They do associate Batraz with a magical sword, however; and here a basic distinction must be made between the *two* swords that figure so prominently in the legends about Arthur. In the Alliterative *Morte Arthure* Arthur possesses two swords: War and Peace, Clarent and Claris.[11] Elsewhere in the legends these two swords are both called Excalibur.[12] According to the tradition Caliburnus[13] was broken when Arthur used the blade in a fight with a knight who anonymously defends a fountain.[14] Merlin instructs Arthur to throw the pieces of the sword into the water. Arthur does so, whereupon he is presented with Excalibur by the Lady of the Lake. The most likely explanation for the names of the two swords is that the original story of Arthur's second sword involved a reforging of the broken Caliburnus[15]—à la Siegfried's reforging of Siegmund's sword and Perceval's rejoining of the pieces of the broken Grail sword—making Excalibur *ex Caliburnus*, "from Caliburnus."[16] It is this second sword that has a strong counterpart in the Ossetic tradition.

Batraz like Arthur gained possession of a magical sword with the aid of his stepmother.[17] It was this sword that the Narts reluctantly threw into the sea, just as Excalibur, which was given to Arthur by the Lady of the Lake, was eventually returned to the water by Bedivere. Indeed this Excalibur (or Caledfwlch,[18] Caliburnus, etc.), which Geoffrey of Monmouth claims was "forged in Avalon," is mentioned prominently in *all* of the Arthurian texts, including the early Welsh ones.[19] *The Dream of Rhonabwy* describes the hilt of Arthur's sword as "graven with two serpents from whose jaws two flames of fire seemed to burst when it was unsheathed," which, for all of Paton's insistence that this describes a Pan-Celtic sword, sounds just as Sarmatian as it does Celtic.[20]

But what of the Excalibur that was embedded in the stone that so miraculously appeared in the churchyard and that Arthur alone was able to draw forth? From Ammianus Marcellinus (31.4.22) we know that the Alans' "only idea of religion [was] to plunge a naked sword into the earth with barbaric ceremonies, and they worship that with great respect, as Mars, the presiding deity of the regions over which they wander."[21] Sulimirski suggests that sword worship of this sort was common among all of the Iranian-speaking steppe peoples and cites Herodotus's statement to the effect that among the Scythians of the North

Pontic region the iron sword, or "scimitar," was thought to be an image of the war-god—the "Scythian Ares."[22] Claudius Marius Victor, a fifth-century rhetorician from Marseilles, also comments on the "primitive" religion of the Alans in his poem *Alethia*.[23] He states that the Alans offered sacrifices to the spirits of their ancestors and mentions that swords figured prominently in the religion of the ancient Alans as well. As we noted in chapter 1, Herodotus lists the three primary gods of the Scythians as Hestia (Tabiti), Zeus (Papaeus),[24] and Earth (Api), the wife of Papaeus.[25] The other important gods of the Scythians were Apollo (Oetosyrus), the Celestial Aphrodite (Argimpasa), Herakles, and Ares. The Royal Scythians alone worshiped Poseidon (Thagimasadas). Herodotus went into great detail concerning the ceremony for honoring Ares, since it was so different from the sacrifices offered to the other gods of the Scythians.[26] This ceremony was conducted at the temple to Ares, which was located at each Scythian capital. These temples consisted of heaps of brushwood that were piled up, flat on top, steep on three sides, and sloped on the fourth. At the top of this pile of sticks an ancient iron sword was planted as an image of the god. There

> annual sacrifices of horses and other cattle are made to this sword, which, indeed, claims a greater number of victims than any other of their gods. Prisoners of war are also sacrificed to Ares, but in their case the ceremony is different from that which is used in the sacrifice of animals: one man [i.e., prisoner] is chosen out of every hundred; wine is poured on his head, and his throat cut over a bowl; the bowl is then carried to the platform on top of the woodpile, and the blood in it poured out over the sword.[27] While this goes on above, another ceremony is being enacted below, close against the pile: this consists in cutting off the right hands and arms of the prisoners who have been slaughtered, and tossing them into the air. This done, and the rest of the ceremony over, the worshippers go away. The victims' arms and hands are left to lie where they fall, separate from the trunks.[28]

The veneration of swords as divine symbols seems to have been deeply rooted in the steppe cultures. As Bachrach points out, even the non-Indo-European Huns seem to have picked up the sword cult from their Alano-Sarmatian neighbors.[29] The cult was carried westward by the Alans, who, in the fifth and sixth centuries C.E., settled in various parts of Western Europe.

Batraz exhibits several characteristics that link him to the Scythian Ares. In Tale 18 of the Nart sagas, "How Batraz Avenged the Death of His Father Hamyc [Xæmyc]," Batraz kills his father's murderer and takes the man's right arm to his own stepmother as proof.[30] His stepmother makes him take the arm back to his victim because "it is not the custom among the Narts to bury illustrious personages" whose corpses are not intact.[31] Elsewhere the proper offering to Batraz is said to be piles of wood.[32]

Admittedly, in Ammianus's account, the emphasis is upon the plunging of the sacred sword into the earth, whereas in the medieval European romances it has shifted to the act of removing it by a qualified person. However, from what we know of the way in which Alanic and Sarmatian chiefs were selected—they were regularly chosen from among the best warriors—it can cautiously be suggested that the act of removing the sword played an important part in the "barbaric ceremonies" alluded to by Ammianus.[33] Perhaps he simply failed to see (or hear about) this aspect of the matter, which, after all, would not have been as obvious or as frequent as the mere presence of divine swords in the ground.

In any event we suggest that in the motif of the Sword in the Stone that first appears in Robert de Boron's *Merlin* it may be possible to detect the reflection not only of the Alano-Sarmatian sword cult per se, but also perhaps of an as yet unattested Alano-Sarmatian (or at least Alanic) ritual in which young men proved themselves worthy of being members of the war band.[34] Arthur, it will be recalled, was barely past puberty when in the company of Kay and his guardian[35] he rode to the site where the miraculous sword had appeared.[36] When, almost by chance, Arthur managed to remove the sword from the stone, something that others had failed to do, he not only demonstrated that he was the legitimate heir to Uther Pendragon's throne but also that he was ready for knighthood. In the case of Galahad the emphasis seems to be on this latter aspect, as he does not become a king. His subsequent role as the Grail Knight, however, which

The Sword in the Stone

elevated him above all his companions (including Arthur), may have been validated by the sword he pulled from the floating stone.

We should emphasize once again that no such Alano-Sarmatian rite of removing a sword from the earth is actually attested. But the presence of the Sword in the Stone motif in the Arthurian tradition permits us to reconstruct an aspect of the sword ritual not reported by Ammianus. Colarusso (personal communication) has pointed out that such extractions of a sword or spear (from the earth, a tree, and/or particularly the anvil of Tlepsh[37]) are found in the Circassian Nart sagas as well.[38]

The medieval version of the motif is a postpagan one. As far as the sword is concerned, the symbolism of the war-god had long since given way to that of the Christian Cross, suggested by the cruciform shape of the weapon's hilt. And, as Bachrach points out, "the stone, or more exactly, the rock is the church which holds the sword, a symbol of secular rule, and will only permit the rightful king to wield it."[39] Yet if we strip away the veneer of Christian symbolism here, we find, at bottom, the image of a ritual that is congruent with what we know about pre-Christian Alano-Sarmatian religion, one that involves an intense concern with the supernatural power represented by a naked sword. That this sword is embedded in a stone rather than in the ground does not detract from this congruence. It may also have represented a sort of *axis mundi* ("world axis"), a sacred reference point in terms of which the tribe oriented itself. If our analysis is correct, the act of removing the sacred sword firmly associated the warrior who did so with that sacral center. It also imbued him with the supernatural power inherent in the weapon itself, and thus fit for inclusion among the ranks of full-fledged warriors.

There remain, however, two important matters that need to be discussed if we are to obtain a clear picture of the meaning and origin of the Sword in the Stone.

First, in most of the Arthurian romances the sacred sword is actually embedded in an anvil, which in turn is embedded in a stone.[40] Why an anvil? Here an interesting bit of syncretism has occurred. In the oral and literary traditions derived from the *Nibelungenlied*[41] the hero Siegfried gains the use of a magical sword with the help of a divine smith called Mime, who teaches him the secret of metalworking.[42] He forges his own weapon and by doing so validates his legitimacy as a warrior.[43] A warrior's ability to forge his own sword is proof positive that he has achieved full mastery of his profession.[44] By drawing the sword from an anvil, the symbol of the smith's craft, Arthur also in effect "forges" his own sword and thereby, like Siegfried, demonstrates the degree to which he has mastered his trade.[45] It is possible that the Alans and Sarmatians shared in this tradition.

Second, there is the question of why the Sword in the Stone episode is absent from British chronicles, as well as from Geoffrey's *Historia*. No answer to this question is as yet possible. The archaeological excavations at Ribchester and other sites associated with the Sarmatians have so far failed to yield evidence relating to swords in the earth.[46] Perhaps the Iazyges themselves had abandoned this aspect of the sword cult before they were defeated by the Romans and impressed into the legions.

As we have seen, this particular tribe of Sarmatians was the first to cross the Don River, and, from the beginning of the Middle Sarmatian period (ca. 200 B.C.E.–50 C.E.), they lived somewhat apart from the rest of the Sarmatian tribes.[47] Their separation from the mainstream of Alano-Sarmatian culture was effectively complete after they were settled in Britain. Thus, after two and a quarter centuries of intimate association with the Roman military establishment and with the local Celtic population, even if our reconstructed rite of passage had been part of the Iazygian culture in 175 C.E., it might very well have disappeared by the time of the historical Arthur (ca. 500).[48]

It is interesting that the earliest appearance of the Sword in the Stone is in the "continental" (i.e., French) Arthurian romances in regions that were settled by Alans, specifically the eastern part of what became Brittany and the western portion of the Orléanais, where the sword cult was probably still very much alive. In Brittany and elsewhere in France, by the time Robert de Boron and other authors began to weave their tales about Arthur, Merlin and the Grail, this specifically Alanic element, a Christianized version of the embedded sword, had probably long since become part of the oral traditions about

Arthur, Lancelot, and their exploits. Eventually this element conflated with the anvil theme, and in the late thirteenth century, thanks to the growing popularity of the French romantic literature, the episode diffused to England, where it surfaced for the first time in *Arthour and Merlin*.[49]

NOTES

1. Both chroniclers seem to have drawn on essentially the same sources as Geoffrey of Monmouth. Ford 1977:119–158; Loomis 1941:884–936 (cf. *Annwfn*); Rhys 1928; Thorpe 1966;.

2. De Gentil in Loomis 1959; Sommer 1908–1916, 6:81–85; and Wilson 1961:7–11. Another early manifestation of the Sword in the Stone episode is to be found in the so-called prose *Merlin*, a mid-thirteenth-century redaction of Robert's poem; see Brengle (1964).

3. White 1938.

4. Sommer 1908–1916, 2:6–7; Pauphilet 1923; Wilson 1967:759; Cowen 1969, 2:245–246.

5. Cowen 1969, 1:222. This sword is not embedded in the altar in Malory, but other versions of the Lancelot story are not so clear.

6. E.g., Bryant 1978:218.

7. Bruce 1958:145. Micha (1948:37) attempted to derive this motif from a passage in Virgil's *Aenead* (6.145–148), in which the Sibyl tells Aeneas that he must fetch a "golden bough" before he can visit the Land of the Dead. But this is by no stretch of the imagination the same thing as pulling a sword from a stone (or even a tree) so as to demonstrate one's right to rule or one's physical prowess. Some scholars (e.g., Micha 1948:38) have also sought to connect the episode with Near Eastern legends, including the tale of how the Persian king Darius was "chosen" by the actions of a horse—again, a far cry from the Sword in the Stone!

8. Rose 1959:264.

9. This tree was Branstock, the central pillar of the Vulsungs' castle.

10. Davidson 1964:49. Colarusso (personal communication) suggests that this is a conflation of an old Iranian motif of a sword in

nine layers of earth with a tale that survives in Circassian tradition in which a hero takes a sword down from the World Tree.

11. E.g., Ackerman 1952:59.

12. For critical editions of the Alliterative *Morte Arthure*, see Hamel 1984, Perry 1865, and Krishna 1976.

13. Caliburnus is Arthur's first sword, which he acquired from a stone. Although at least one late thirteenth-century English text, *Arthour and Merlin* (Turnbull 1838), explicitly calls the Sword in the Stone Excalibur (Newstead 1967:38), the weapon that validated Arthur's right to rule is otherwise distinct in function, if not always in name, from the wondrous Excalibur, which in Malory (Cowen 1969, 1:64) he subsequently received from the Lady of the Lake and which remained in his possession until his death (see chaps. 2 and 5).

14. Twentieth-century Arthurian tradition (as exemplified in the play *Camelot* [1960] and the movie *Excalibur* [1981]) asserts that this battle was against Lancelot, who is anonymously defending a river or a stream. This may reflect influence from the famous battle between Robin Hood and Little John in the legends of Robin Hood, in which the leader of a group of warriors is defeated by a stranger who then joins the band (Holt 1982:167).

15. Glare 1982:302; Lacy et al. 1986:176; Nickel 1975a:11.

16. The sword that Lancelot receives from the Dame du Lac is said to "easily cut iron and steel" (Webster and Loomis 1951:30). Cf. the proposed etymology of Excalibur.

17. Dumézil 1930:61–63.

18. Ford (1983:271) derives Caledfwlch from Welsh *caled* ("hard") and *bwlch* ("point"). Zimmer (1890:516–517) discusses the origin of Caledvwlch (Caledfwlch), the name of Arthur's sword, from Caladbolg, the name of Fergus's sword.

19. Thorpe 1966:217. This is echoed by Wace (Rhys 1928:43).

20. Gantz 1976:177–191; Paton in Rhys 1928:xvi; cf. Rolle 1980:125.

21. Rolfe 1939:395.

22. Sulimirski 1970:36; Herodotus 4.62; de Sélincourt 1972:290.

23. Schenkl 1888:335–498, ll. 189–200; Bachrach 1973:31–32; Courcelle 1948:221. Werner (1956:16) discusses the evidence for Alan burials at Marseilles.

24. I.e., "Father"; Nausicaa in the *Odyssey* addresses her father as "Pappa," and there was a native god whom the Greeks called Zeus Papa also in northwest Asia Minor.

25. Herodotus 4.59–62; de Sélincourt 1972:289–290.
26. Here is the description of the usual sacrifice:

> The victim has its front feet tied together, and the person who is performing the ceremony gives a pull on the rope from behind and throws the animal down, calling, as he does so, upon the name of the appropriate god; then he slips a noose round the victim's neck, pushes a short stick under the cord and twists it until the creature is choked. No fire is lighted; there is no offering of first-fruits, and no libation. As soon as the animal is strangled, he is skinned, and then comes the boiling of the flesh. This has called for a little inventiveness, because there is no wood in Scythia to make a fire with; the method the natives adopt after skinning the animal is to strip the flesh from the bones and put it into a cauldron—if, that is, they happen to possess one: these cauldrons are made in the country, and resemble Lesbian mixing-bowls in shape, though they are much larger—and then make a fire of the bones underneath it. In the absence of a cauldron, they put all the flesh into the animal's paunch, mix water in it, and boil it like that over the bone-fire. The bones burn very well, and the paunch easily contains all the meat once it has been stripped off. In this way an ox, or any other sacrificial beast, is ingeniously made to boil itself. When the meat is cooked, the sacrificer offers a portion of both flesh and entrails by throwing it on the ground in front of him. All sorts of cattle are offered in sacrifice, but most commonly horses. (Herodotus 4.59–62; de Sélincourt 1972:290)

27. This practice may have influenced the legends that developed into the stories of the Holy Grail in its form as a cup or bowl filled with blood (cf. chaps. 8 and 9).

28. Herodotus 4.59–62; de Sélincourt 1972:290–291.

29. Bachrach 1973:111.

30. Dumézil 1930:61–68.

31. Dumézil 1930:63.

32. Dumézil 1930:64. For all their warlike tendencies, however, Batraz of the Boratæ clan (the clan of Narts that is associated with the

Third Function) and Lancelot of the lineage of King Ban come from families closely associated with ideas of fertility rather than with ideas of war.

Why an image of the sword ritual fails to persist among the Ossetians, who otherwise preserve much of their Alano-Sarmatian heritage, is not clear, for their ancestors practiced it (c.f. Ammianus Marcellinus 31.4.22; Rolfe 1939:395).

33. Ammianus Marcellinus 30.2.22–23; Rolfe 1936, 3:392–395; Bachrach 1973:21–22.

34. Littleton 1982b:58–59.

35. This guardian is listed as either Antor or Ector, depending on the source.

36. Both Robert and Malory name London as the site. Geoffrey of Monmouth (9.1), however, states that Arthur was crowned at Silchester and that Dubricius, who performed the ceremony, was archbishop of "the city of the Legions," which has variously been identified as York and Chester, as well as London (Thorpe 1966:212).

37. Tlepsh (λapš; "god of the forge"), who appears as Kurdalägon in the Nart sagas of Ossetia, was a god of blacksmiths among the Caucasian peoples. His name may derive from *klupš or *kalups-, "steel" (Colarusso [personal communication]; cf. Latin *chalybs* [Glare 1982:308]; cf. also the Kalybes, a Caucasian tribe of smiths; Lewis and Short 1907:324; Magne 1953:330; Vinaver 1958:516, Nickel 1975a:11).

38. In one story from the Circassian Nart sagas three brothers supply Tlepsh with ore from which he forges a sword. The brother who successfully pulls the sword from the anvil gets to keep the weapon (Colarusso [personal communication]). Stories of Tlepsh are also found among the Cherkess.

39. Bachrach 1973:111.

40. Cowen 1969, 1:16. The principal exception is *Arthour and Merlin*, which makes no mention of an anvil. Rather it simply describes the scene as follows (ll. 27–29; see Weston 1910a:119):

> A great stone standing on the ground,
> 'T was long and high, the sooth to say,
> Therein a right fair sword lay.

41. I.e., the so-called *Nibelungen Stoff* (*Nibelungen* material).

42. We are indebted to our colleague Udo Strutynski (personal communication) for calling to our attention the isomorphic elements in the Siegfried tradition.

43. More specifically he repairs the sword that his father, Siegmund, had pulled from a tree, as the weapon had been broken in two by Odin's spear; see Davidson (1964:49). Cf. the broken sword of the Arthurian tradition that is repaired by Perceval and the broken Excalibur that is replaced for Arthur by the Lady of the Lake.

44. Although pre-Christian in origin, this particular aspect of the matter does not appear to be specifically Alano-Sarmatian. Rather it would seem to reflect a widespread Northern European concern with smiths and smith symbolism, which also appears in the story of Wayland the Smith, the Finnish *Kalevala*, and a host of other tales in which divine or semidivine smiths serve as repositories of the magical lore associated with the transmutation of ore into metal and with how this knowledge can be put to practical use by warriors.

45. In a sense Perceval "reforges" the broken Grail sword by joining the pieces together.

46. E.g., an iconographic image of a sword in the ground; Richmond 1945:16–29; Sulimirski 1970:175–176, Littleton and Thomas 1978:520–523.

47. E.g., the Roxolani and the As (the ancient Ossetians). See Sulimirski 1970:171–172.

48. I.e., the *dux bellorum* ("war leader") mentioned in chap. 2.

49. Weston 1910a:119; Turnbull 1838. Other swords (besides those embedded in stones) figure prominently in the Arthurian legends as well. The Sword of Solomon figures in the Grail legends. This connection with Solomon is interesting, since the *Biblioteca Sanctorum* (1961:col. 651) suggests that St. Alanum, which would have appeared as "S. Alanum" in church records, was corrupted to "Salamun" (Solomon) in medieval Brittany. Sword cults were popular throughout Iron Age Europe as well as in other regions. Obayashi and A. Yoshida (1975) compare and contrast the Scythian sword cult to several sword cults that are characteristic of many cultures (e.g., that of the Huns) from Central Asia to Japan. Indeed the traditional Japanese reverence for swords and swordsmanship may derive from the same source that gave rise to the ritual underlying Arthur's actions in that fateful churchyard;for discussions of this possible connection, as well as of the possibility that Japanese legendry per se contains a number of "Arthurian" figures and themes (e.g., the legends surrounding the hero Yamato-takeru, who dies shortly after giving up his magical sword), see Littleton 1982a: 258-261; 1983; 1995.. Several lakes filled with finely crafted swords have been found (e.g., Clark and Piggott 1965:329; Glob 1969:188; Megaw 1989:130–131). This last phenomenon may have been in part responsible for the Arthurian stories of swords that are connected with the Lady of the Lake.

CHAPTER 7

The Serpent Image

Among the many striking images associated with the Arthurian and Grail romances is that of the serpent or dragon. In a famous illuminated manuscript of 1290 Arthur is depicted in battle under a windsocklike banner in the shape of a serpent (or dragon).[1] Frequently echoed in illuminations of medieval horsemen (see plate 13), this image has some remarkable parallels in the ancient Sarmatian tradition, both in the steppes and in Britain.

As we have seen, the name of one of the several Sarmatian tribes noted in antiquity by Herodotus, the "Sauromatae," seems to have meant "Lizard People,"[2] and the name Sarmatian itself most likely derives from a similar reptilian epithet, applied generally by the Greeks to this "Scythian" nation.[3] *The Oxford English Dictionary* derives the Latin word *Sarmatæ* from the Greek Σαρμάτης ("Sarmates") and Σαυρομάτης ("Sauromates," i.e., "Sauromatae"), "whence the form Sauromatian."[4] This latter term is probably connected to the Greek σαῦρος ("lizard"), and the name may be derived from the serpentine dragon banner that was carried by these people. The lizard (or dragon) seems to have been an important Sarmatian symbol, one that served as a type of tribal "totem." A similar flexibility can be seen in the medieval notion of "serpent" as well, which seems to have included all forms of reptiles.[5]

Serpents and dragons turn up frequently on Sarmatian artifacts, including the sacred *tamgas* that identified clans and subtribes.[6] Such artifacts belong to the "animal style" (see plate 2) characteristic of steppe cultures.[7] One widespread motif from this style is the coiled snake, sometimes depicted with its tail in its mouth. An example is found on a well-known golden plaque,

PLATE 13. Mounted Horsemen from the Golden Psalter (Codex 22, fol. 140, Zumbül-Album, St. Gallen, Stiftsbibliothek). Courtesy of the Stiftsbibliothek St. Gallen.

which shows a wolf (or some wolflike animal) battling a coiled serpent.[8]

Similar reptilian images abound in the Arthurian tradition. In one manuscript of the Vulgate *Estoire del Saint Graal/Merlin* Merlin appears bearing a snakelike banner identical to the banner carried by a Sarmatian warrior on a grave stele from Chester (see plate 14).[9] Another illumination in the same manuscript depicts a knight with the dragon/serpent banner.[10]

Recall that in Elis Gruffydd's *Chronicle*, Arthur and Mordred both have creatures perched on their helms when they meet at the final battle.[11] These creatures are described as *preves* (see chap. 2). These flying, serpent-like creatures are related to the Middle English word "adder."[12] The adder was considered to be a Spanish serpent related to the Latin *vermis*, which became *wyrmis* in Middle English.[13] This creature was thought to be a wingless dragon. In this battle the creatures "leap" and "jump" at each other, to prove the prowess of the combatants.[14] What we may actually have here is a reference to serpentine devices worn on the helmets of the leaders, not unlike the banners carried by Sarmatian warriors.[15] Somewhere in this tale may also be the seeds of Malory's story of a serpent biting the heel of a knight as the cause of the last battle between Mordred and Arthur.

One of the stranger legends in the Arthurian tradition is that of the boy who kisses a snake to turn her into a woman. This story appears in twelfth-century Wales.[16] In the *Lanzelet* Lancelot is required to go into a forest and kiss a snake.[17] This snake turns out to be a beautiful woman, and in later works she appears as the cunning and devious Elaine. It is interesting to note that in the Irish *Lebor Gabála Érenn* the Fir Bolg carry bags of earth as protection, against venomous reptiles in particular.[18] Later the same text mentions that Irish earth is sold in Greece as protection against venomous reptiles.[19] This fascination with snakes in the legend, however, may have arisen just as easily from contact with a Sarmatian tribe, such as that at Bremetennacum Veteranorum, as from any exclusively Celtic source.

The connection among women, snakes, and Scythian royalty is also well documented. One Scythian myth gives Herakles and a serpent-footed goddess as the progenitors of the line of Scythian kings.[20] Rostovtzeff includes the detail that the

198 From Scythia to Camelot

PLATE 14. Merlin with the Pendragon (MS Paris, Bibliothèque Nationale f. fr. 95, fol. 327v). Photograph courtesy of Bibliothèque Nationale, Paris.

sacred beasts of this goddess were the raven and the dog, and the Dame du Lac appears to have some connection with dogs.[21] The legend of the birth of Sozryko of the Narts tells of how the hero was born from a stone after an old shepherd spilled his seed on the rock upon viewing the beautiful princess Satana, the Wise Woman of the Narts, the same story that is told of Hephaistos and Athene, a "union" that resulted in the birth of a "serpent-footed" child.[22]

The connection between a woman and a snake in the Arthurian legends centers on the Dame du Lac, Lancelot's foster-mother. In the *Prophécies de Merlin* the Dame du Lac is sometimes euphemistically referred to as a white serpent.[23] Like the Dame du Lac, Artemis is sometimes associated with a serpent (Pythian Artemis). On one occasion Uther Pendragon sends the Dame du Lac four rings, each of which contains a tooth from a great serpent he had killed, and the White Serpent (the Dame du Lac) identifies the rings as having great magical properties. In a similar Welsh story Peredur meets a group of warriors who are waiting for a serpent to die before they claim the magic ring on which the reptile is sitting.[24] In the Nart sagas Xæmyc acquires a tooth from a woman that enables him to force another woman who lives in a forest to change into serpent form until he agrees to marry her.[25] Similarly in one tale from the *Lanzelet* Lancelot, who inherits one of the rings made with the teeth of the serpent that Uther had given the Dame du Lac, enters a forest, where he kisses a serpent, which then transforms into a woman.

Such a connection between women and serpents can also be seen in the legends of Caradoc of Vannes. Weston pointed out that the "*Book of Carados* [Caradoc]" in the First Continuation of Chrétien's *Conte del Graal* is "considerably older" than the rest of the work.[26] Caradoc's encounter with the serpent occupies a significant place in the story, and it is interesting to note that he is freed from the serpent by the faithful Guimier.[27] Harper noted parallels between the serpents of this section and popular traditions about serpents in Scotland.[28] Gaston Paris contended that the core of *Caradoc* was of Irish origin, but Lot disagreed, tracing the tales to North Britain with perhaps a Scottish (but not Irish) origin.[29] Remember, however, that the Sarmatians who flew the serpent banner and who patrolled Hadrian's Wall were settled in North Britain. In addition, given the parallels between Caradoc and Batraz and Weston's belief that Gawain (who also closely parallels Batraz) was the original hero of the tale, it is highly probable that the story came from a Sarmatian rather than from a Celtic source.[30]

The serpent image figures strongly in some of the Grail works as well. Lovelich's verse translation (ca. 1450) of the *Grand Saint Graal* (or the *Lancelot Grail*; ca. 1200–1210) uses the serpent motif. In this story Nascien dreams of a serpent attacking him,[31] after which a serpent kills a tree:

> And besied this Tre Cam Owt A Serpent,
> that there flawmes of fyr out Caste cerament,
> and waster this faire tre Anon,
> And Alle the flowres [th]ere Everichon:
> thanne Anon After, I the plyht,
> Al this was past Owt of the kynges syht.[32]
>
> [And beside this tree came out a serpent,
> that there flames of fire out cast certainly,
> and wasted this fair tree soon,
> And all the flowers [th]ere every one
> then soon after, I swear to you,
> All this was passed out of the king's sight.][33]

This serpent is identified both as "the death of the soul of men" and as "the pricks of death."[34]

Serpents figure in other Arthurian legends as well. Waite relates an odd passage from the Huth *Merlin* in which "Orpheus, a certain enchanter, is doomed to remain in the Castle of the Holy Grail, with two snakes about his neck, until the Quest has been achieved."[35] This figure, however, as Waite points out, is completely neglected in surviving versions of the *Queste*. And, as we have seen, when Guinevere is abducted by Valerin in the *Lanzelet*, he keeps her in a castle surrounded by snakes, a barrier that Lanzelet cannot pass.

Markale has argued that St. Michael's dragon is the result of a translation of the myth of Pythian Apollo to a Christian milieu.[36] Markale sees Perceval's association with serpents in the *Queste del Saint Graal* and other legends as the result of a similar translation of a local Gallic myth. Given the number of Sarmatian settlements in the region, however, it is equally possible that the myth behind these legends was of Sarmatian origin.[37] Markale links the Black Serpent of the *Queste* (ca. 1215–1235) with the serpents in the Welsh *Peredur* (ca. 1300–1325)[38] because these reptiles both appear atop stones.[39] His argument returns to firmer ground when he links the serpents in the Perceval legends with the Philosopher's Stone through alchemic iconography and through the motif of the subterranean treasure guarded by a dragon (serpent).[40] Both the Welsh author of the *Peredur* and the French romancers probably drew from a common, most likely French, source.[41] Such a source could have been in either oral tradition or the visual arts. Pauphilet argued that the motif of the Serpent with the Chalice at the Cross from the plastic arts served as the source for the serpent motifs in the *Queste del Saint Graal*.[42] The medieval images of the Serpent at the base of the Cross in Crucifixion scenes and the Mi5gar5-serpent coiled at the base of the World Tree with Odin hanging above have been cited as examples of the use of mythological motifs by Carolingian artists.[43] The direction of the diffusion of this image, however, is still unclear. In a related image from a legend of Buddha, cited by Heinrich Zimmer, a serpent coils itself around his body seven times.[44] The same motif appears in the effigies of the Mithraic Chronos and in the Bethlehem cave of southern France.[45] Teichmann proposed that the connections in Christian imagery between the Tree of Life and the Cross and between water, especially from a stone, and the Serpent at the Cross derived from the Egyptian cult of the dead as it was transmitted to the Caucasus region, then to Spain, France and finally Germany.[46] There is at least one Egyptian representation of a snake at the base of a tree in connection with a sun-god, a type of deity that among the Alans, was symbolized by a cup.[47] The combination of these two motifs may be responsible in part for the motif of the Serpent with the Chalice at the Cross.[48] However, as seen in the case of other elements of the Arthurian tradition, the area of diffusion (i.e., the Rhine and the Pyrenees) for the image of the Serpent at the Cross is precisely that which is reflected in the Alan and Sarmatian settlements, and it is at least as likely, if not more so, that the image arose from an Alanic source as it is that the image was spawned by an Egyptian cult.

While the Christian connection between Eve and the Serpent beneath the Tree of the Knowledge of Good and Evil in the Garden of Eden may have had some effect on this connection between serpents and trees and between serpents and women as these stories are found in the Arthurian tradition, the positive overtones in several of these legends (e.g., the Dame du Lac) suggest that another, non-Christian source provided the serpentine influence on the tales of King Arthur and the Knights of the Round Table. A Christian interpretation of such images as that of Arthur fighting beneath a serpent banner, or wearing a serpent device on his helm, makes no sense, whereas both emblems would be quite appropriate for a Sarmatian king.

NOTES

1. B.N. fr. 95, fol. 173v. Loomis and Loomis 1938:95–97, fig. 236; cf. plate 4.

2. Colarusso (personal communication) points out that in the Circassian Nart sagas Arkhan Arkhozh is a villain who is "a 'lizard man,' all covered in scales."

3. Cf. Sulimirski 1970:21.

4. Simpson and Weiner 1989, 14:487.

5. Lewis and Short 1907, part S:467–468.

6. Phillips 1965:99. Cf. Nickel 1975a:12, for a discussion of the Polish *wappen* ("coats of arms").

7. Wenskus in Beck et al. 1881:122.

8. Phillips 1965:97, fig. 107.

9. B.N. fr. 95, fol. 327v, "Merlin Carries the Pendragon," ca. 1290; Loomis and Loomis 1938:95–97, fig. 224. See Sulimirski 1970:pl. 46; cf. plate 3.

10. B.N. fr. 95, fol. 173v, "Arthur in Battle"; Loomis and Loomis 1938:95–97, fig. 236.

11. National Library of Wales, MS 5276D and Mostyn MS 158.

The Serpent Image

12. Old English *nædre*, "a dragon or flying serpent" (Simpson and Weiner 1989, 1:142).

13. Old English *wyrm*, derived from **wurmi-z* (Simpson and Weiner 1989, 20:562).

14. The description of this battle was provided by Lloyd-Morgan (personal communication).

15. Cf. the etched images on the helm of the "Golden Man"; see frontispiece.

16. Owen 1968:82.

17. Paton 1929:5–19.

18. Macalister 1940, 39:147.

19. Macalister 1940, 39:153. This later legend may be tied to tales of St. Patrick banishing the snakes from Ireland.

20. Herodotus 4.9–13; de Sélincourt 1972:273–274; Rolle 1980:125.

21. Rostovtzeff 1922:107–108.

22. I.e., Erichthonios. Rose 1959:110; cf. Dumézil 1930:75–77. See chap. 5 n. 23.

23. Paton 1926, 1:169, 171; cf. Guinevere as a white serpent (Paton 1926, 2:242–243).

24. Goetnick 1975:3; cf. Fafnir the dragon in Wagner's *Ring* cycle.

25. Dirr 1925:197–199.

26. Weston 1906–1909, 1:314.

27. Weston 1906–1909, 1:309–311. Cf. the Germanic myth in which Loki's faithful wife catches the venom from the serpent that is set to drip on him (motif Q501.3 "Punishment of Loki"). Although the Loki story is now no more than an etiological tale for the origin of earthquakes, it shares the motifs of the faithful wife/wife-to-be (motif T210 "Faithfulness in marriage"), the serpent (motif R41.3.1 "Prison filled with snakes" and a variant of motif B765.4.1 "Snake attaches itself to a woman's breast and draws away her milk while she sleeps"), the cup (motif D1380 "Magic cup"), and the prisoner (both of whom are eventually freed; motif R152 "Wife rescues husband"), with the story of Caradoc.

28. Weston 1906–1909, 1:314.

29. Paris 1899:212; Weston 1906–1909, 1:314; cf. Lot 1899:568.

30. Weston 1906–1909, 1:316.

31. Lovelich 1874–1905, 1:417.

32. Lovelich 1874–1905, 1:427, ll. 231–236.

33. This translation is our own.

34. Lovelich 1874–1905, 1:432–433; Malcor 1991:77. Later in the text a black man is called the "Wise Serpent" (Lovelich 1874–1905, 2:44). This figure is later identified as the Devil (Lovelich 1874–1905, 2:50; Malcor 1991:77). Still later a great serpent is killed by the Rose Man (Lovelich 1874–1905, 2:142). This creature is either Death or the Devil (the French encompasses both ideas), who is defeated by Jesus (Lovelich 1874–1905, 2:147; Malcor 1991:77).

35. Waite 1933:199.

36. Markale 1982:139.

37. Grenier 1931, 5:398 ff.; Stein 1949–1959, 1:264; Bachrach 1973:59.

38. Goetnick (1975:1, 36) dates the *Peredur* to the twelfth century, but most scholars now agree that the *Queste* predated the passages that the two legends seem to have in common, hence our later date (taken from the *Llyfr Gwyn Rhydderch*) for this version of the serpent image.

39. Markale 1982:62.

40. Markale 1982:62-63.

41. Loomis 1956:28; Frappier 1953:i, 40; Jones and Jones 1949:xxix; Roques 1910:385; Loth 1913:53 f.; Marx 1960:92-93; Lewis 1957:xi; Thurneysen 1912:189; Bruce 1923, 1:347; Chambers 1927:155; Fourquet 1938:30, 110; Foerster 1887:xxix f.; Nelli 1951:119; Vendryes 1950:24; Williams 1909:121; Zenker 1923:241–242; Windisch 1912:192, 273, 280; Schofield 1895:153; Jones, G. 1926: 83, 86; Kittredge 1916:262; Rivoallan 1957:135–136; Jones, R. (1957: 225; 1960:xvi); Jones, W. 1907–1927, 1:253; Goetnick 1975:2.

42. Pauphilet 1921:116; see also Malcor 1991, chap. 3, passim.

43. The Cross was seen as the *axis mundi* by medieval theologians; see Cirlot 1983:69. See Malcor 1991:74–75 for a discussion of these parallel images. Cf. Schiller 1972, 2:107. In legend this serpent lies at the bottom of the sea (which is thought to encircle the world), biting its own tail. The World Tree (the ash tree Yggdrasill) has roots in the three realms of Niflheimr, Mi5gar5r, and Asgar5r. So, technically, the Mi5gar5-serpent encircled only one of Yggdrasill's three roots. In art, however, this concept is generally depicted by a serpent coiled at the base of a tree. There may also be a correlation between the blindness of Hö5r and that of Longinus in the Crucifixion images. Cf. Peebles 1911, passim.

44. Cirlot 1983:287; Zimmer 1946.

The Serpent Image

45. Birks and Gilbert 1987:34. This cave was supposedly a site for Cathar worship services and initiations. Whether this "serpent" is a Mithraic etching, Cathar painting, or natural lines in the rock is anyone's guess (Malcor 1991:75).

46. Teichmann 1986:138–145. Teichmann also proposes the alternative route of Africa to Spain to France to Germany, with a separate distribution to the east.

47. From the *Book of the Dead*; Teichmann 1986:142, pl. 84.

48. Malcor 1991:70–77.

Part IV

The Holy Grail

CHAPTER 8

The Holy Grail, the Cauldron of Annwfn, and the Nartamongæ

This chapter explores the parallels between the legend of the Holy Grail, which is inextricably bound up with the Arthurian tradition, and the Ossetic accounts of the Nartamongæ, or "Revealer of the Narts," a magical vessel that plays an equally significant role in the Nart sagas.[1]

The Holy Grail

The traditional story of the Holy Grail as it was outlined by Robert de Boron in his *Joseph* (see map 17) and in the various forms of the *Estoire* and *Queste*, portrays the Grail as the Chalice of the Last Supper, which Joseph of Arimathea used at either the Crucifixion or the Deposition to collect the blood of Jesus. In this version of the Grail story Joseph is imprisoned for a while and is fed by a mannalike substance produced by the Grail. Joseph then takes the cup and in the company of other followers of Jesus, such as Lazarus and Mary Magdalene, performs missionary work in the Orient. Here he meets Evelake and Seraphe, two pagan kings, who are baptized under the names Mordrains and Nascien. Joseph then takes the Grail west, landing at Marseilles. He crosses Gaul and travels to Cornwall, where he is imprisoned again. This time Mordrains and Nascien come to his rescue, the troops being fed by the Grail. Mordrains is maimed by the power of the Grail, and Nascien is blinded. Nascien ascends to heaven, but Mordrains is doomed to live until the Grail Knight from Arthur's court comes to visit him. The Grail passes from Joseph into the care of his son.[2]

The Holy Grail appears in many forms in the Arthurian tradition, of which the Chalice of the Last Supper is only one. While Cavendish argues that William of Normandy's minstrels learned the legends of Arthur after the Battle of Hastings (1066) and took these tales home with them to the Continent, there is evidence that the Grail legend, in the form of the Chalice at the Cross at the very least, was already known in the Rhine region as early as 516.[3] The other forms of the Grail, described primarily in twelfth- and thirteenth-century literature, include everything from a nebulous light to a stone. Manessier differs from Chrétien by giving the detail of the *"riche"* Grail with its food-providing qualities. Chrétien could have drawn on any of a number of food-producing vessels from folk tradition (motif D 1472.1.19 to D 1472.1.33). Markale cites the nutritive properties of the Grail as coming from a Celtic source.[4] In *Sir Gawain at the Grail Castle* the Grail actively serves, without human intervention, the people at the feast.[5] In the Irish translation of the *Queste* Joseph of Arimathea uses the Grail to duplicate the miracle of the multiplying of the loaves (St. Matthew 15:36–39; St. Mark 8:1–10).[6]

Marx argued that the difference between two of the forms of the Grail, the cup and the stone, depended on which ancient Celtic source an author used.[7] For Marx the Grail represents the Sovereignty principle (see plate 15),[8] and he saw the medieval authors as drawing on either the Great Fâl[9] or the chalice-bearing Female Personification of Sovereignty for their imagery. There are, however, other possible explanations for these forms than a Celtic origin, and it is the Grail in its form as a chalice or other *gradalis* ("vessel") with which we are concerned here.

The chalice form of the Grail has been heavily influenced by the Christian communion ceremony.[10] This influence has led scholars, such as Loomis, to search for other examples of this Christian overlay in many aspects of the Grail tradition. For instance, Loomis discussed the derivation of "Corbenic" (the name of the Grail Castle) from a combination of *cors* and *benoiz*, i.e., "blessed cup."[11] Although his etymology is not generally accepted, the notion that the legends of the Grail are somehow related to the Christian communion feast is well known and

The Holy Grail 211

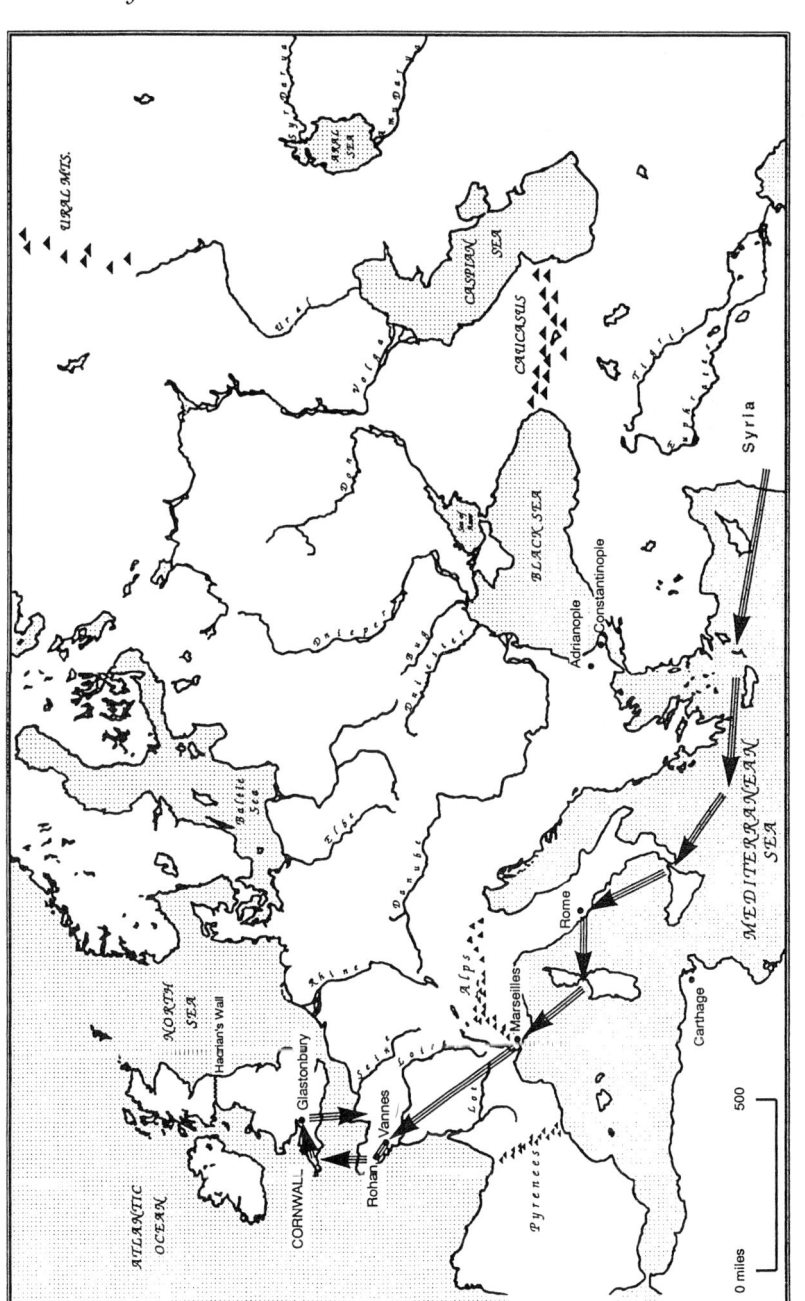

MAP 17. The Travels of Joseph of Arimathea

PLATE 15. Ecclesia with the Grail ("Book of Pericopes of Heinrich II," originally from Reichenau [ca. 850]; Munich, Bayerische Staatsbibliothek, clm 4452). Courtesy of the Bayerische Staatsbibliothek.

widely accepted among Grail scholars.[12] The only major difference of opinion arises over the question of whether the communion feast actually inspired the Grail legends or whether the legends have simply been overlaid by details from the feast.[13]

The connection between the Grail and the Chalice of the Last Supper was often implied in some medieval manuscripts even when it was not explicitly stated by the text. An illumination in B.N. fr. 99, fol. 563, from *Li Roumans du bons chevalier Tristan*, shows the Grail above Galahad as he sits in the Siege Perilous at a table. Except for the fact that the Chalice is in the air instead of at the table and that the men sitting at the table are dressed as medieval nobles instead of as Jesus and the apostles, the illumination looks almost exactly like traditional medieval depictions of the Last Supper.[14] The appearance of the Grail at a feast without a bearer is, as we shall see, a much more Ossetic than Celtic image.

The idea that the Grail legends came from the East has recurred frequently in Arthurian scholarship.[15] There is a persistent notion among some scholars that these legends originated somewhere near the Caucasus Mountains, or at least passed through these mountains at some point in time. Cooper-Oakley says that the Grail tradition came from the Ganges "in . . . land of Tribalibot . . . spread . . . over the Caucasus . . . over the mountains Agrimontin."[16] Schroeder advanced an Indo-Oriental hypothesis for the origin of the Grail, while Iselin argued for a Syriac origin.[17] Franz Kamper traced the Grail legend to "Oriental myth and Arab legends."[18]

The ancient Sarmatians spoke a Northeast Iranian dialect, and, as Phillips and others have pointed out, they shared a number of fundamental beliefs with their fellow Iranian-speakers in Persia and elsewhere.[19] And a few scholars have long maintained that there are some "Persian" (if not Sarmatian or Scythian) overtones in the legends. Abegg suggests that one of the names for Parzival's father, Gharmet, derives from Gayomart, the primeval human being in the *Avesta*.[20] Also drawing on Persian materials, von Suhtschek attempted to demonstrate that Wolfram von Eschenbach's *Parzival* is derived from an Iranian epic entitled *Barzu-Name* and suggests that one of the names for the Grail Castle, Monsalvatsch (or Montsalvat), can be equated with *sal-wadsche*, a famous Parsee holy place, while Faugère discusses the hypothesis that the Grail legends were somehow transmitted to Europe at the end of the eleventh century, most likely by Crusaders.[21] The major problem with this argument is that there is evidence of the Arthurian legends, particularly of the Grail cycle, in Europe prior to the dates for the Crusades.[22] However, all the Germanic Grail legends exhibit a marked Iranian influence.[23] Although these "Persian" connections are admittedly tenuous, they may reflect yet another independent development from a common Iranian tradition about the quest for the sacred that may have reached Europe in the early Middle Ages. This would not affect the suggestion that the core of the tradition arrived a millennium earlier and reflects a Northeast Iranian rather than "Persian" provenance.

Wolfram claimed in his *Parzival* (ca. 1200–1210; 16.827.1–2) that Chrétien de Troyes had failed to present the "true" story of the Holy Grail. While Wolfram's narrative differs in many details from Chrétien's, the differences between these and other continental Grail narratives can be accounted for through the effect of historical events upon a single tradition that was shared by the Alans. Wolfram drew heavily on sources from southern Gaul for his Grail material.[24] In addition to place descriptions and personal names, it is quite likely that he took his patterns for his story from the south as well. In *Parzival* the Grail is described as a rock on which the names of the guardians, who are called "Templars," appear. The Knights Templar, who supplied the name for these guardians, are the traditional heirs of the treasure of the Temple of Solomon following the demise of the Cathar heresy.[25] Some of the Templars were associated with the Alan families of southern Gaul, just as the Cathars were.[26] It is likely that Wolfram's source was a variant of an Alanic story preserved by these descendants of the Alans of southern Gaul.

Markale sees strong parallels between Wolfram's *Parzival* and the Iranian *"Conte de la Perle,"* which is Manichaean in character.[27] He believes that this similarity is lacking in other Grail legends, and he proposes that Wolfram made a conscious substitution of the stone for the vessel with blood or for Chrétien's "deep dish."[28] Wolfram's Grail has been repeatedly described as "Germano-Iranian," and attempts to explain this connection have ranged from influence through the Cathars in the south of France to oriental tales brought back to Europe by Crusaders.[29] Friedrich von Suhtschek "maintained the Arthurian cycle to be of Iranian origin and Wolfram's *Parzival* and Gawain romance a free translation from the Persian," and Closs argued that instead of a direct translation, the story of the Grail had been supplied by "a long forgotten source" of Persian origin.[30] Closs also maintained that the Grail had its origin on the "borders of Persia and Afghanistan," citing in partial support the connection between Wolfram and Manichaean beliefs.[31] Closs credited Arabs and Crusaders with the transmission of the legends, with the Albigensians providing a fertile ground for such legends to take root.[32] Markale felt that Wolfram's *Parzival*, which claims the mysterious Kyot as its source, is the only Grail romance that exhibits Cathar-like thought.[33] Waite went farther with this notion, claiming that this reference to Kyot is the only literary remnant of the Grail tradition of southern France.[34] Wolfram does not use the prologue, which links Parzival's family to the Orient on the father's side, but he does link the line of Gahmuret, which is from the East, to the House of Anjou.[35]

The paradise described by Albrecht in *Titurel* (ca. 1270) is decidedly oriental in character, and it even employs a Grail Knight from India.[36] The connection between the Iranian paradise and the otherworld of the Arthurian legends has been noted by several scholars.[37] These similarities have been generally ascribed to the common Indo-European heritage of the cultures involved.[38] Weston made the astute observation, echoed by Closs, that "visits to the Otherworld are not always derivations from Celtic fairy lore."[39] In short the oriental concept of the underworld influenced the legend of the Grail Castle more than the Celtic otherworld did.[40]

According to Owen, Robert de Boron added the light-giving quality to the Grail, which Wolfram later attributed to the bearer.[41] Robert supposedly took this motif from the apocryphal *Gospel of Nicodemus*, and the motif was subsequently used by the authors of the Second Continuation of the *Conte del Graal*, the *Perlesvaus*, and the prose *Lancelot*.[42] Some scholars, however, have noted an alternative source for this motif. They have commented on the light of the Grail as apparently having its root in an oriental myth.⁴³ The motif of heavenly light appears in many relic legends, particularly in legends from the East.⁴⁴ Recall that some scholars have suggested that the Grail is the alchemical symbol for *mercure igné*, a symbol of the *Xvarīnah* ("halo, nimbus, glory")⁴⁵ of ancient Persia, which supposedly spread to the West through Shî'ite sources.⁴⁶ Ringbom sees two ideas attached to this concept in Christian art: (1) the *Xvarīnah*, or "light," and (2) the Serpent (the second of which he feels was introduced into Germany by an Egyptian mystery cult in Merovingian times).⁴⁷ Ringbom also proposes the word *Perle* as the source of Wolfram's strange Grail variant, since *Perle* also translates as "jewel." Fuehrer points out that in several manuscripts of Chrétien's *Conte del Graal*, "The Grail is full of precious stones."⁴⁸ Faugère concurs with Ringbom regarding the connection between Wolfram's Grail and the Iranian *gohar* (literally, "innermost soul") and regarding the previously noted identification of the *gohar* as the German *Perle* (see chap. 4), both of which refer to the "fire" in the water.⁴⁹ Gallais also discussed the connection between the Grail and the *Xvarīnah*, pointing out that the Iranian *Xvarīnah* corresponds to all three Dumézilian functions, culminating with the "*xvarnah royal*."⁵⁰ The "*xvarnah céleste*," in particular, corresponds to the combined idea of the light of the Grail and of the Grail maiden.⁵¹ He also parallels the Grail as a chalice to the cup of Jamshid (or Yima; cf. the Indian Yama) and the legends of Kai Khosraw.⁵² Gallais argues that these similarities exist because of the common Indo-European heritage of Ireland and India.⁵³

Several cups that test honesty appear in the legends of Kai Khosraw.⁵⁴ Coyajee attributes these and other similarities between the Indo-Iranian myths and legends and the Arthurian legends to a common "Aryan" heritage.⁵⁵ Granted, many forms of magic vessels appear in the folklore and myths of the Celts; however, these same motifs can be found in folkloric narratives worldwide.⁵⁶ Coyajee saw parallels between the Grail tradition and Iranian tradition in "(a) the Nature of the Grail and the Glory [*Xvarīnah*], (b) the virtues attributed to them, (c) the 'treasures' and 'talismans' connected with the Holy Grail, and the Glory, (d) the exploits of the heroes who pursued the quest of the Grail and the Glory, as illustrated by the 'Vengeance quest,' the story of the Fisher King, the hero's acquisition of the Kingship and the 'Great Fool' tale."[57]

For all of these Eastern-origin hypotheses, however, many scholars still seek a Celtic source for the Grail in, among other magical vessels, the Cauldron of Annwfn.

The Cauldron of Annwfn

Goetnick has argued that the Grail, while undoubtedly a religious object from the first, was not originally associated with the Christian religion.[58] For example, the notion that the Grail hero was not Christian appears in the Welsh *Peredur* (ca. 1300–1325), where the hero is unable to answer Kay's (Cai's) questions because he has made a vow not to speak to Christians.[59] Goetnick saw the vessel as the possession of the Celtic "god of the sun."[60] Goetnick's sole proof that the Grail is of Celtic derivation is the presence of other food-producing vessels in Celtic tradition. Such vessels exist in several folkloric traditions, however, and, as we shall see, in Alanic tradition as well, and there were certainly enough Alans in Gaul to have transferred their motif to the tradition that a Celtic origin should not be presumed on the basis of this argument alone.[61]

Goetnick identified the Grail maiden as the Sovereignty figure. The problem with identifying every maiden who bears a chalice as the Celtic Sovereignty figure is that the Ecclesia tradition[62] was well known and in wide distribution well before the first appearance of this allegorical figure of Sovereignty in any manuscript. This is particularly true in the case of a chalice that is borne at the Cross.[63] This motif was employed by the clerics and clerically trained scribes who wrote and copied the Grail manuscripts. Weston says that on the occasion of Bors's visit to Castle Corbenic, Elaine's father explains that she is crying because she lost her virginity and can no longer be the Grail Bearer.[64] Weston speculates that in the original version Elaine would have been crying for a slain knight. Elaine may have indeed been the original Grail Bearer, but until we can locate Weston's source (which she does not identify), we are unable to advance the argument farther.

The proponents of the Celtic origin of the Grail tend to rely on the tenth-century Welsh poem, traditionally attributed to the sixth-century poet Taliesin, entitled *Preiddeu Annwn* (i.e., *Annwfn*), or *The Spoils of Annwn*. In this poem Arthur, not yet described as a king, leads a raid on Annwfn, the Isle of the Dead, and there obtains a magical cauldron:

> In the Four-Cornered Fortress (Kaer Pedryvan), four-sided,
>
> My first utterance, it is from the cauldron that it was spoken,
>
> By the breath of nine maidens it [the cauldron] was kindled,
>
> Even the Chief of Annwn's cauldron, what is its nature?
> Dark blue [enamel] and pearls are round its rim.
> It will not boil the food of a coward [or one forsworn]; it has not been destined.[65]

The similarities between this poem and the Second Branch of the *Mabinogi*, "Branwen daughter of Llŷr," have often been pointed out: Both texts describe an expedition from which only seven warriors return, and although the story of Branwen involves an expedition to Ireland rather than to the netherworld, it does include a magical cauldron that regenerates the dead.[66] Arthur plays no part in the story.

A Welsh tale that involves both Arthur and a cauldron is *Culhwch and Olwen*. Here Arthur leads an expedition to Ireland and obtains a magical cauldron, one that appears similar in its properties to the Cauldron of Annwfn. Both Barber and Ford suggest that *Culhwch and Olwen* may be a later, euhemerized version of *The Spoils*.[67] Geoffrey Ashe has argued that *Culhwch and Olwen* presents a Welsh Arthur who "had developed in popular imagination shortly before Geoffrey [of Monmouth]" and that no "Nart saga [can] explain it."[68] However, at base the story of *Culhwch and Olwen* is simply the tale type known to folklorists as "The Ogre's Daughter" (Type 313: *The Girl as Helper in the Hero's Flight*), in which magical helpers aid a hero in the completion of a set of impossible tasks demanded of him by a giant in exchange for the daughter's hand in marriage. These magical helpers can be anything from talking animals to jinn, and we propose that in this variant of the tale the original helpers who would have appeared in the Welsh story have been replaced by Arthur, Kay (Cai), Bedivere (Bedwyr),[69] Guinevere (Gwenhwyvaer), and other denizens of the court of Camelot, as well as by historical figures like Gildas, mythological figures like Gwyn son of Nudd, and legendary figures from non-Arthurian material like Creiddylad daughter of Lludd. The choice of the Arthurian characters as the replacements for the original Welsh magical helpers may have presented itself to the master storyteller who created *Culhwch and Olwen* in its present form, simply because of the popularity of the stories of the Round Table in the Middle Ages.[70] We see *Culhwch and Olwen* as a masterful Welsh variant of a common folktale with an Arthurian overlay rather than as the story of any original Welsh Arthur.

Waite argues that the Celtic church bore definite traces of eastern influence, and that this accounted for the oriental influence in the Grail legends.[71] Still this does not make the ultimate source of the Grail tradition Celtic. Some scholars have asserted that the oriental character of the Celtic church was transmitted to Ireland through the Visigoths of Spain and southern France.[72] But this same region was heavily settled by Alans as well, and a case can be made for Alans getting to Ireland.[73] The Celtic church itself was either Romano-British or colonized *de novo* from Gaul.[74] There was historical missionary work from Gaul to Britain.[75] Fictional missionary work is also attested, such as the Irish translation of the *Queste*, in which the missionaries from Gaul, Joseph and Josephe, were imprisoned by the British king Crudel.[76] The continental kings Mordrains and Nascien raised an army and attacked the forces of the British king. Crudel was killed, and the missionaries were released. In this story oriental ideas, particularly from Egypt, are carried to Britain by the missionaries. In actuality there is evidence, beginning in the fifth century, that real Gallic missionaries had been exposed to such notions prior to their work in Britain, possibly through the transference of the Johannine Rite to southern Gaul.[77]

Gnostic thought, which originated in the East, flourished in Rome and Alexandria, then spread to Wales, where it appeared in the writings of Taliesin.[78] This influx of Gnostic thought into the British Isles and Ireland influenced the form of Christianity adopted by the Celtic church, which, for this and other reasons, took on a particularly anti-Roman character.[79] But the hypothesis that this form of Gnosticism influenced the Grail legends does not make sense, since the Arthurian legends are almost without exception pro-Roman.[80] It is interesting to note that the Alans who settled in southern Gaul and Armorica, as well as the Sarmatians posted to Hadrian's Wall, were all pro-Roman. Weston proposed that the Grail tradition had its origin in "Hellenistic-Oriental mystery religions ultimately sublimated to a Christian gnosis, . . . transported by the foreign legionnaires to the furthest bounds of the Roman Empire."[81] Some scholars have argued that Catharism arose from a Gnostic cult that spread through the Roman Empire in the third century.[82] Marx saw the legends of the Grail as influenced in part by the transformation of the initiation rituals from an eastern mystery religion of agrarian character.[83] Still others have argued that the Grail derived from a Mithraic source.[84] While any or even all of these sources may have influenced the Grail legend at one time or another, we still hold that the core of the legend as we know it was most likely carried to Britain and Gaul by the Sarmatians and Alans who settled in those regions.

In addition to possible influence from an eastern religion Celtic sources for the Grail have been proposed in Irish folklore. A series of magical cauldrons in Irish texts have often been cited as prototypes of the Grail.[85] There is the famous cauldron associated with the Dagda, which never runs out of nourishment. Recall the three cauldrons in which the young Cūchulainn was dipped to "cool" his anger.[86] Yet these Irish vessels lack one important feature shared by the Cauldron of Annwfn, the Grail, and the Nartamongæ: the capacity to accept or reject the person who would possess them. The idea of a magical vessel, especially one that provides an endless supply of food or drink, is widespread, at least among the ancient Indo-European-speaking communities (see motifs D1171.8 "Magic cup" and D1472.1.14 "Magic cup supplies drink"). All but one of the attestations Thompson cites are Indo-European, and it is therefore possible to suggest that all of the magical cups discussed in this chapter are ultimately derived from a common, albeit very ancient, Indo-European prototype. However, by the time the Iazyges arrived in Britain that prototype, if it existed, had long since given rise to a number of otherwise distinct traditions, among them the one that links the three vessels in question. Thus the Irish cauldrons would seem to reflect a separate development from this assumed Indo-European prototype. Newstead identifies the prototype of the Grail as a vessel that she speculates belonged to the Celtic sea-gods, such as Manannán and Bran.[87] What she was possibly alluding to here was the fact that the Grail is occasionally associated with the sea. At one point in the *Estoire* Josephe carries the Grail into the sea.[88] This ceremony, however, has many biblical reflexes and could also derive from such practices as the bathing of the statue in the religion of the Dea Syria or the carrying of the image of Nerthus into the water in Germanic religion—none of which is even remotely Celtic.[89] Gallais noted the water symbolism of the Grail, which he compared with Anāhitā and other Third Function symbolism used in the *Continuation-Gauvain*, *Conte del Graal*, and *Elucidation*.[90] This notion makes much more sense than Newstead's hypothesis. In Alanic religion the deities associated with the Third Function are the goddess of the hearth and the god of water, represented in the Nart sagas by Satana and Batraz/Don Bettyr.[91] And Batraz is connected to both water[92] and to the magical Nartamongæ.

The Nartamongæ

The Ossetic texts recorded by Dumézil describe the vessel as a large, magical cup that appears at the banquets of the Narts and that refills itself when it is empty. This Cup of the Narts magically elevates itself to the lips of the hero who is above reproach, a hero "without flaw," and thus there were inevitably disputes over who was best qualified to be its guardian.[93] In one tale,

> The Narts are quarrelling among themselves about the Nartyamonga [Nartamongæ]. "I," said Uryzmag [Uryzmæg], "I have supported your expeditions; without me

you would have achieved nothing, so the cup returns to me." But Soslan, Sozyryko, and Batraz respond: "No, we will not give up the cup so easily. We will give it only to him among the Narts who lives as a hero without flaw [blemish].

Then Uryzmag says: "Truly, among the Narts I am the hero without flaw!" "No," said Batraz, "that is not true: one day a vulture lifted you from the place where the Narts were having a discussion, carried you over the sea, and deposited you on an island; how can you pretend that you are a hero without flaw?"

Then Soslan says: "I am among the Narts the hero without stain!" "How dare you pretend that?" replied Batraz. "One time you lay down across the sea, and the army passed from one shore to the other on you as on a bridge. But your back became tired by the hooves of the horses, you sagged, and everyone fell into the sea!"

Then Sozyryko says: "But it is I among the Narts who am without flaw!" "No," said Batraz, "When Barsag's Wheel [Barcädžy calh], rolling toward you, cried to you: 'Sozyryko! I come to you; receive me!' you asked it: 'How must I receive you?' The Wheel responded to you 'With your front!'—and when you received the Wheel on your front, your eyes blinked. How dare you pretend to be the Nart without flaw? Isn't that a flaw, a proof of faint-heartedness?"

After that, Batraz said: "It is I, I alone who am, among the Narts, the hero without flaw, isn't that true? What reproach can you make toward me?" The Narts found nothing to say, and the cup was awarded to him.[94]

Thus Batraz established his claim to the Nartamongæ, although he was not a member of the Alægatæ,[95] the Nart clan in whose collective care the cup had originally been placed.[96] Batraz unites the three clans by being of the blood of the Boratæ, by becoming a superior warrior to any member of the Æxsærtæghatæ,[97] and by securing the cup of the Alægatæ. The Grail legends of the Continent tell of a family that is associated with the fertility of the land and that brings forth a preeminent warrior who becomes the sovereign of the Grail Castle and guardian of the Grail.

In other contexts the Nartamongæ acts as a "lie detector," and its appearance at the lips of a speaker, especially one who is describing a bold adventure, is thought to be proof positive of his veracity.[98] In Tale 16 the Narts, as usual, were drinking and boasting, and one of them, who was jealous of Batraz, taunted Xæmyc, Batraz's father, daring him to relate some recent adventure of his "monstrous son," the implication being that the cup would not verify it.[99] At that moment Batraz arrived. He immediately launched into an account of his recent exploits, adding that, "if I speak correctly, the cup will transport itself to the mouth of Hamyc [Xæmyc]!" Whereupon it did so, and the company knew that Batraz had indeed spoken the truth.

There is a possible onomastic connection between the two stories, as Chrétien de Troyes calls the brother of Amfortas (the wounded Fisher King) Amagnon (or Magnon).[100] In his Continuation of Chrétien's *Perceval* Manessier uses the variants Margon, Mangon, and Magnon interchangeably for this character.[101] A similar name, Amangon, occurs in other Grail texts, although not necessarily associated with the Fisher King or his immediate family.[102] Markale notes that in the *Elucidation* hill-dwelling maidens offer refreshment to travelers until a king by the name of Amangon tries to steal one maiden's golden cup.[103] Moreover, in the Arthurian romance *Fergus et Galienne* (1200–1233) by Guillaume le Clerc, a character swears by the name "St. Mangon."[104] And in Biket's *Lai du Cor* (ca. 1150),[105] which can be considered a precursor to the fully developed Grail story, the magician-king Mangon of Moraine sends a drinking horn to Arthur's court. The contents of the horn are successfully imbibed by Caradoc, whose wife exhorts him to be brave. This tale is closer in spirit to the legend of the Nartamongæ than to the later Grail tradition, which, as we have seen, focuses on the purest rather than the bravest knight. In his discussion of the various Amangons in Arthurian literature Thompson makes no mention of the Nartamongæ as a possible source for the name, and Rhŷs identifies Amangon "with the Celtic hero Amacthon, son of Don."[106] In any case, although neither the Fisher King nor his brother has an exact counterpart in the Ossetic sagas, the similarity between the names Amonga and Amagnon/ Magnon/Amangon/Mangon[107] is certainly suggestive.

In short, as both Dumézil and A. Yoshida have suggested, the role played by the Nartamongæ in the Nart sagas is clearly analogous to that played by the Holy Grail in the Arthurian legends.[108] In both traditions a band of heroes vies for access to or control over a sacred cup, one that appears at feasts and confers supernatural benefits upon those fortunate enough to possess it. Furthermore, in both traditions, it is only the purest of the pure, the hero "without flaw," who achieves that honor; the others are precluded for one reason or another. In the Arthurian tradition Lancelot, despite his consummate courage and ability as a warrior, is denied physical contact with the Grail as a result of his well-known indiscretions with Guinevere, just as Sozyryko's behavior when confronted with Barsag's Wheel disqualifies him from being the guardian of the Nartamongæ.

There are some fundamental differences between the Ossetic and medieval European traditions of the Sacred Cup. It hardly needs to be said that the Holy Grail, almost by definition, is a Christian symbol: the Chalice of the Last Supper, brought to Britain by Joseph of Arimathea and deposited at Glastonbury.[109] There is no specifically Christian symbolism attached to the Nartamongæ. It remains a "pagan" talisman, despite the fact that many Ossetians have been Eastern Orthodox Christians (others are Muslim) for over a millennium. The reasons why Lancelot is precluded from the communion table of the Grail are much more sophisticated than those that preclude Uryzmæg, Sozyryko, and Soslan from being awarded the Nartamongæ; in Lancelot's case it is a function of his humanity rather than any failure to exhibit physical courage. It should also be noted that the Nartamongæ is not accompanied by "Hallows" (other sacred objects; see chap. 9) as is the Grail in many of the Arthurian legends.

Nevertheless, the similarities between the two vessels are such that, like the rest of the Arthurian and Ossetic sagas, the traditions surrounding them almost certainly stem, at least in part, from the common Alano-Sarmatian culture, in this case a concern with magical cups and cauldrons. As Sulimirski has demonstrated, this concern is clearly evident in the archaeological sites associated with the Sarmatians in south Russia and elsewhere in Eastern Europe.[110] It is particularly interesting to note that the cauldrons are found almost exclusively in the graves of Sarmatian women in Siberia and that the Grail of the Arthurian tradition is almost always borne by a woman.[111] Magical vessels seem to have played an important role in the myths and rituals of the steppe peoples; one need only cite the Scythian origin myth wherein a cup falls from the sky and is recovered by Kolaxaïs, youngest son of the primeval being Targitaos. The cup here is the prime symbol of sovereignty, and Kolaxaïs's possession of it is essential to his establishment of the royal lineage, just as Batraz's stewardship of the Nartamongæ serves to reflect his sovereignty over the Narts.

The story of the quest for the Holy Grail, to say nothing of the accounts of the Cauldron of Annwfn and the Nartamongæ, seems in large measure to be rooted in the ancient Northeast Iranian traditions surrounding a magical cup that presents itself only to the bravest of the brave[112] and that provides a feast for the heroes of a war band. These war bands themselves, as Colarusso (personal communication) has pointed out, "define much of their structure by feasts." The only time that the Narts or the knights of the Round Table seem to get together is for a feast.[113]

Some important problems, however, remain to be resolved if one assumes that elements of what was to become the Grail theme were introduced to Britain by the Iazyges in the second century. One is that by the time the theme crystallized in the twelfth century it had long since evolved far beyond its Ossetic cognate. There are a great many reasons for this, some of which will be explored in the next chapter, where we will delve into another important dimension of the Grail legend, one that will take us from Jerusalem to Rome and thence to the south of France in the company of that other tribe of Northeast Iranians gone West, the Alans—the same continental Alans whose folk hero, the previously discussed "Alan of Lot" (i.e., Lancelot), so closely resembles both Arthur and Batraz.

NOTES

1. Dumézil (1978:228–236) translates this word as *Revelatrice*.
2. This son is called Josephe or Alain, depending on the source.
3. Cavendish 1978:27; cf. Malcor 1991:42.
4. Markale 1989:278.
5. Weston 1903:21.
6. Falconer 1953:217, ll. 1599 ff. Like the Grail, Joseph of Arimathea's body is carried to another country, where it stops famine (Lovelich 1874–1905, 1:323).
7. Marx 1952:254–255.
8. Even though the allegorical figure of a woman bearing a chalice more likely derives from the figure of Ecclesia; Malcor 1991:128–185; see plate 15.
9. A stone that shrieked under the true king of Ireland; Rees and Rees 1961:29.
10. Malcor 1991.
11. Loomis 1956:243.
12. E.g., Ashe in Lacy et al. 1986:306–307.
13. With the majority of scholars taking this latter view; e.g., O'Gorman in Lacy et al. 1986:259.
14. E.g., Lozachmeur and Sasaki 1984, 1.4:21.
15. E.g., Sterzanbach 1908:10.
16. Cooper-Oakley 1900:148–149.
17. Schroeder 1910; cf. Iselin 1909; Evola 1967:18.
18. Closs in Matthews 1984:33.
19. Phillips 1965.
20. Jung and von Franz 1986:14–15.
21. Matthews 1984:41; cf. Faugère 1979:198–205.
22. Malcor 1991.
23. Markale 1982:151.
24. Poag 1972:56–67.
25. Baigent, Lincoln, and Leigh 1982:29–59.
26. I.e., through Goeric and the other Alanic counts of Albi.

27. Markale 1982:156–157.
28. E.g., the Cistercian version found in the *Queste del Saint Graal;* Markale 1982:157–158.
29. Markale 1986:268–270; Evola 1967:69 f.
30. Closs in Matthews 1984:41–42.
31. Matthews 1984:41–42.
32. Matthews 1984:43.
33. Markale 1982:159–160.
34. Waite 1933:375.
35. Markale 1982:164.
36. Staerk 1903:48.
37. E.g., Glück 1923; Closs in Nelli 1951:54.
38. Closs in Nelli 1951:54.
39. Closs in Matthews 1984:30.
40. Peebles 1911:196.
41. Lot-Borodine 1919:77.
42. Owen 1968:173.
43. Delcourt-Angelique 1984:91.
44. Staerk 1903:6.
45. Puhvel 1987:106.
46. Duval 1979:181.
47. Ringbom 1951:315–316. It is more likely, however, that the affinity for serpents could have been introduced to this region by Sarmatians.
48. Fuehrer 1970:142.
49. Faugère 1979:61; Ringbom 1951:484, 492.
50. Gallais 1972:113.
51. Iranians use Daena to symbolize this same concept (Gallais 1972:113).
52. Gallais 1972:113; Levy 1967:99 f.
53. Gallais 1972:249.
54. E.g., the Upamsu cup, the Agrayana cup, and the Ukthya cup; Coyajee 1939:72.
55. Coyajee 1939:90.
56. Cf. Vendryes in Nelli 1951:78.

57. Coyajee 1939:87–88.

58. Goetnick 1975:295–297.

59. Goetnick 1975:16, 36.

60. There was no such divinity in Celtic mythology (MacCulloch 1918, 3:7–213).

61. The Alans, Vandals, and Suevi who crossed into Spain in 409 numbered at least 200,000. By 411 some 30,000 Alans were in Lusitania alone. Between 70,000 and 300,000 barbarians were with Athaulf, at least one contingent of which was Alanic. See Keay 1988:204.

62. Ecclesia is the female personification of the Christian church that was created at Reichenau and that spread rapidly throughout Europe. For a discussion of Ecclesia in the Arthurian tradition see Malcor 1991:128–171.

63. Malcor 1991.

64. Weston 1903:84, note to p. 62. Weston (1920:77; cf. Waite 1909:603; 1933:574) saw a connection between the Grail and the Suit of Cups (the modern Hearts) of the Tarot. In declaring that the Tarot traveled from the East to Europe, she cites De la Hoste Ranking's conclusion (Weston 1920:79) that the Tarot was created by people who spoke an Indian dialect and that the cards show "the influence of the Orthodox Eastern Faith" (with some of the dress being decidedly Russian). It is quite possible that these people were related to the superstitious, fortune-telling Alans.

Note that in the Esclarmonde legends of the Pyrenees the Lady in White, a synthesis of the fairy of mythic ancient times and the Cathar abbess, does not die but is miraculously transported to the mountains of Asia (Markale 1982:162), the homeland of the Alans. The wanderings of the Alans and the influence of their religion could have accounted for the effects noted by all these hypotheses.

65. Loomis 1941:889–91.

66. Ford 1977:58–59.

67. Barber 1972:75–76; Ford 1977:58.

68. Ashe 1985:160–163.

69. Bedivere is often said to be Arthur's "cupbearer" (butler) in the early tales of the Round Table (see chap. 4).

70. These helpers may easily have been talking animals, such as the birds in the legend of Connaire Mor, given the Celtic love of zoomorphism.

71. Waite 1909:434.

72. E.g., Chadwick 1962; Marx 1965:8–9.
73. Littleton and Malcor, unpublished paper.
74. Waite 1909:448.
75. Waite 1909:448.
76. Falconer 1953:196, ll. 705–724.
77. Waite 1909:448.
78. Barthélémy 1987:256.
79. Barthélémy 1987:256.
80. E.g., the Roman generals in Arthur's family and the attempts to make Arthur the Roman emperor.
81. Weston 1920; Matthews 1984:30.
82. E.g., Meyer 1956:124–125.
83. Marx 1952:272.
84. E.g., Coyajee 1939.
85. E.g., Corcoran 1968:232.
86. Kinsella 1969:92. This cauldron was known throughout the ancient Celtic domain. There is archaeological evidence of such vessels from Gaul and Britain, as well as references to them by Strabo (Markale 1982:188–189).
87. Newstead 1939:43.
88. Hucher 1875–1878, 3:130–131.
89. The Dea Syria was described by Lucian; Attridge and Oden 1976:53. Nerthus was described by Tacitus; Mattingly 1970:134–135.
90. Gallais 1972:248; cf. Dumézil 1958:86–89.
91. Abaev 1960:12–14.
92. In which he is cooled both following his birth and when he becomes the Steel Man.
93. Dumézil 1930:59. This cup is also referred to as the Wac[y]amongæ.
94. Dumézil 1930:136–137. This translation is our own. The French reads:

> Les Nartes se querellaient au sujet du Nartyamonga. «Moi, disait Uryzmag, je vous ai appris à faire des expéditions; sans moi vous n'auriez pu, la coupe me revient». Mais, Soslan, Sozyryko et Batraz répondirent: «Non, nous ne donnerons pas si

facilement la coupe. Nous la donnerons seulement à celui des Nartes qui vit en héros sans tache.»

Alos Uryzmag dit: «Justement, je suis, parmi les Nartes, le héros sans tache!»—«Non, dit Batraz, ce n'est pas vrai: un jour un vautour t'a enlevé de la place où discutaient les Nartes, t'a porté au-dessus de la mer et t'a posé dans une île; comment peux-tu prétendre que tu es un héros sans tache?»

Alors Soslan dit: «Moi, je suis, parmi les Nartes, le héros sans tache!»—«Comment oses-tu prétendre cela? riposta Batraz, Une fois tu t'es couché en travers de la mer, et l'armée passait d'une rive à l'autre sur toi comme sur un pont; mais ton dos fut lassé par le poids des chevaux, tu te plias, et tout le monde tomba à la mer!»

Alors Sozyryko dit: «C'est donc moi qui suis, parmi les Nartes, le héros sans tache!»—«Non, dit Batraz. Quand la Roue de Barsag . . . roulant vers toi, te cria: Sozyryko! je viens à toi, reçois-moi! tu lui demandas: comment dois-je te recevoir? La Roue te répondit: avec ton front!—et quand tu tu reçus la Roue sur ton front, tes yeux clignèrent. Comment oses-tu prétendre être le Narte sans tache? N'est-ce pas là une tare, une preuve de pusillanimité?»

Après cela, Batraz dit: «C'est moi, moi seul qui suis, parmi les Nartes, le héros sans tache, n'est-il pas vrai? Quel reproche pouvez-vous me faire?»—Les Nartes ne trouvèrent rien à dire et la coupe lui fut adjugée.

95. Colarusso (personal communication) sees this as deriving from *ārya-kāta* ("Aryan-adjective-plural"), hence "Aryan Ones."

96. Dumézil (1978:44–49) notes that the hero of the legends of the Nartamongæ pursues his quest while incognito. The Grail heroes, notably Perceval, Galahad, and Lancelot, are also incognito while they pursue the Grail.

97. Colarusso (personal communication) sees the first element in this name as *xšarta-* (cf. Sanskrit *kṣatriya*), with the entire name meaning something like "warrior group."

98. This is the same idea behind magical drinking cups in the Arthurian tradition, such as the horn in Biket's *Lai du Cor*, that detect whether or not a woman is faithful to her husband.

99. Dumézil 1930:58–59.

The Holy Grail

100. Loomis 1949:248.

101. Ivy 1951:80, 89, 91, 93, 97. This name may or may not be related to the Breton name Magon. Markale notes that the Malouine family of Magon (in the ancient diocese of Saint-Mâlo which included Magon de la Balue, a famous cardinal imprisoned by King Louis XI) also lived in this region (Markale 1989:65–66).

102. Markale 1982:117.

103. Markale 1989:231; Weston 1906–1909, 1:254. In the Welsh *Peredur* (Gantz 1976:217–257) the hero also has an encounter with a cup containing a magical salve that is kept by women in a cave. Cf. the Ossetic legend of Sybælc, in which three evil men steal a golden shirt of mail from Uærxtænæg, an aged king, and take it to a cave (Dumézil 1968:141–143).

104. Martin 1872:14, l. 487.

105. This lay was translated into a variety of languages throughout the Middle Ages. The story even survived in the fifteenth-century *Ain Hupsches Vasnachtspill und Sagt von Künig Artus, wie er siben fursten mit iren weyben zuo seinem hoff geladen hert unde wie si durch ain horn geschendet worden gar hupsch zuo hören* (*A Shrovetide Play About King Arthur, How He Invited Seven Kings with Their Wives to His Court and How They Were Embarrassed by a Horn*; Keller 1858:183–215). The story of the test with the magical drinking horn also appears in the fifteenth-century English verse *Romance of Sir Corneus* (also known as *The Cukwold's Daunce*; Hartshorne 1829:206–229) and the sixteenth-century English ballad "The Boy and the Mantle" from the Percy Folio (Child 1884, 1:257–274).

106. Thompson 1931:36–37, 47 ff.

107. For an alternative interpretation of the name Magnon see Hilka (1932:493 ff.). For Amangon see Potvin (1865–1873, 2:14).

108. Dumézil 1941:227; Yoshida 1965:33–34.

109. See, for example, Lagorio 1971.

110. Sulimirski 1970.

111. Sulimirski 1970:106.

112. Colarusso (personal communication) believes that both the Grail and the Nartamongæ are associated with the "moral pinnacle" of the respective war bands, since Batraz's purity, rather than his bravery, is emphasized in the Circassian Nart sagas.

113. The Arthurian adventures, in particular, take place only on major Christian feast days, such as Christmas, Easter, Pentecost, and

Whitsuntide. Although some gatherings of warriors on feast days do take place in a few Celtic legends (e.g., the Knights of the Red Branch in the Ulster tales), the Celtic warriors do not seem to be quite as fanatical about major feasts coinciding with their gatherings (e.g., the gatherings in the *Mabinogi* [Ford 1977]) as are the Knights of the Round Table, who meet almost exclusively on high holy days, and the Narts, who are seldom depicted as doing anything except feasting.

CHAPTER 9

The Alans and the Grail

Given the affinity of the descendants of the Alans for telling stories about cups, the importance of cups in the Alanic religion, and the extent of Alanic influence in the church of Gaul, the chances are good that Robert de Boron may have had an Alanic source for his Grail material as well.[1] In his *Merlin* Robert credits a character named Alain with the transportation of the Grail from Rome to Britain.[2] This odd story makes eminent sense in light of the history of the Alans who settled in southern Gaul. Chrétien seems to have parts of the traditions of both Brittany and southern Gaul available to him. He presents a character called Amagnon, a name that closely resembles that of the Nartamongæ of the Nart sagas (see chap. 8), and his description of the branched candlesticks that accompany a *graal*, or "deep dish,"[3] is suggestive of the treasure from the Temple of Solomon, which was said to include "the lampstand and the lamps, the table, the libation cups and censers, all of solid gold."[4]

The only non-Germanic tribe ever to settle permanently in Gaul,[5] the Alans worshiped a deity who was symbolized by a cup.[6] Lawton and others have proposed that "the subject of *Joseph* is the conversion of pagan royalty."[7] Christianity became widely diffused in the fifth century, at which time Britain became completely Christian.[8] Other pagans, such as the Alans of Gaul, were also Christianized at this time. It is quite possible that the Alans' cup was combined with the Christian cross to form one image,[9] by way of a conversion tactic, at the time of the conversion of the Alans of Gaul, who would qualify both as pagans and as nobility in that region. The geographic distribution of this tribe corresponds almost precisely with that of the Chalice at the Cross motif.[10] Alanic settlements in the areas where the motif appears include Aillainville (Haute-Marne), Alaincourt-aux-Boeufs (Meurthe-et-Moselle), Alaincourt (Aisne), Alaincourt (Ardennes), Alaincourt-la-Côte (Meurthe-et-Moselle), Alains (Eure), Allamont (Meurthe-et-Moselle), Allancourt (Marne), and Sampaigny (Meuse).[11] It is interesting that one of the earliest examples of this motif (975) is in Gerona, a region of heavy Alanic settlement just south of the Pyrenees. Other Alan place-names in Gaul include Alençon-Orne, Alaigne-Aude, "Allain-aux-Boefs" [sic], Allaines, Allainville-en-Drouais, and Allan.[12] Just as the story of the Sword in the Stone may have been influenced by the religion of the Alans of Gaul, who worshiped a god of war by planting swords in the earth,[13] the legends of the Grail may have been influenced by stories of a magic cup. The primary deity associated with the cup in Alanic religion and with this family of Narts is the god of the sun.[14] This cup passes from the Alægatæ, the family of Narts associated with sovereignty, into the care of the Boratæ, the family of Narts associated with cattle.[15] The deities associated with this family are the goddess of the hearth and the god of water, who are represented in the Nart sagas by Satana and Batraz/Don Bettyr.[16] Dumézil notes that although the Æxsærtæghatæ is the Nart family associated with the god of war, that is, the Second Function, this clan is no more warlike than the other families of Narts.[17] The tripartite division in the Nart sagas is based, rather, on the dominant themes of tales set in the homeland of each clan.

The problem boils down to the simple question of whether the similarity between the Grail legends and the Ossetic material is a case of parallel development from a common Indo-European heritage or whether diffusion of the Grail legends from the East to the West actually occurred. Given the absence of such motifs as the Chalice at the Cross (and hence of such legends of the Grail as it was known in the Middle Ages) from Europe prior to the sixth century, a strong case can be made for diffusion if an agent for the transmission can be found. As we have seen, such an agent does exist in the fifth-century Alan invaders of Gaul. The main problem with hypothesizing a direct connection between the prototype of the Nartamongæ as it was known to these Alans and the Grail is that seven hundred years separate the Alanic invasion of Gaul from the recording of the Grail romances. We intend to show that there is an unbroken historical connection between these two events.

From Italy to Gaul: The Alan Invasions

Recall that in Italy the Romans attempted to force the nomadic Alans to remain stationary by settling them on permanent estates. The *Comites Alani*, an elite unit in the Roman army, served in north Italy until ca. 487 and was eventually based in Ravenna. These Alans assimilated rapidly into Roman culture, losing their fighting ability and value as *laeti* within two generations. A few signs of their passing remain. The sixth-century sarcophagus of Archbishop Theodore of Ravenna is decorated with a symbol that Lozachmeur and Sasaki (1984:21) have identified as "the Holy Grail" and which may actually have been a representation of a sacred vessel, such as that which symbolized one of the Alans' primary deities. Although this may not be the full-blown form of the Grail that appears in thirteenth-century Arthurian manuscripts, the conjunction of the image of a vessel with a cross is a precursor to the Grail image in medieval Europe (Malcor 1991:42). Among the royal treasures of King Ratchis of the Lombards was a Scythian-style cup, made from the skull of an enemy of another Lombard king (ca. 568).[18]

Gaul was a different matter altogether. As we have seen, on December 31, 406, a contingent of Alans crossed the Rhine and invaded Gaul.[19] Some of these Alans had contact with the Burgundians who settled temporarily on the left bank of the Rhine.[20] Although some scholars have argued that the Burgundians were not a steppe culture, placing their origin near Denmark, these tribes shared the practice of skull deformation with the Alans.[21] The Alans once again had contact with the Burgundians when they backed the Gallo-Roman usurper Jovinus.[22] At any of these times the stories that would later influence the Burgundian cleric Robert de Boron, who wrote some of the earliest Grail romances, may have passed from the Alans to the Burgundians.

In Italy the part-Vandal Roman general Stilicho was confronting another group of Alans (much farther to the east) who were led by Alaric. In 331 a group of Visigoths invaded Scythia and conquered an Alan tribe that had a strong Hunnish contingent. These Visigoths became Arians in 377, but the Alans and the Huns retained their pagan beliefs. In 382 Alaric was named king of the Goths. In 399 the Goths split in two, with the "Scythian" Radagaisus and Alaric as kings.[23] In 405 Radagaisus raided Italy and was killed, whereupon the tribes of Goths, Alans, and Huns united under Alaric once more. Stilicho had planned for Alaric to take his reunited force to drive Respendial's Alans (as opposed to Goar's Alans, see chap. 1) out of Gaul, using new bases that Alaric was to establish at Mainz and Strasbourg.[24] Alaric was also supposed to depose the usurper Constantine III of Britain (see chap. 1). But Stilicho was executed by Emperor Honorius in 408. In 409 Alaric, with a force that included Radagaisus's troops, entered Italy and sacked Rome in 410 (see map 18). During this raid an incident, which is recounted by Orosius, occurred that made a great impact on the Alans who were later to settle in Gaul:

> While the barbarians were roaming through the City [Rome], one of the Goths, a powerful man and a Christian, chanced to find in a church building a virgin advanced in years who had dedicated herself to God. When he respectfully asked her for gold and silver, she declared with the firmness of her faith that she had a large amount in her possession and that she would bring it forth at once. She did so. Observing that the barbarian was astonished at the size, weight, and beauty of the riches displayed, even though he did not know the nature of the vessels, the virgin of Christ then said to him: "These are the sacred plate of the Apostle Peter. Presume, if you dare! You will have to answer for the deed. As for me, since I cannot protect them, I dare not keep them." The barbarian, stirred to religious awe through the fear of God and by the virgin's faith, sent word of the incident to Alaric. He ordered that all the vessels, just as they were, should be brought back immediately to the basilica of the Apostle, and that the virgin also, together with all Christians who might join the procession, should be conducted thither under escort. The building, it is said, was at a considerable distance from the sacred places, with half the city lying between. Consequently *the gold and silver vessels were*

distributed, each to a different person; they were carried high above the head in plain sight, to the wonder of all beholders. The pious procession was guarded by a double line of drawn swords; Romans and barbarians in concert raised a hymn to God in public. In the sacking of the City the trumpet of salvation sounded far and wide and smote the ears of all with its invitation, even those lying in hiding. From every quarter *the vessels of Christ mingled with the vessels of Peter, and many pagans even joined the Christians in making profession, though not in true faith* (emphasis ours).[25]

There are other aspects of the Grail tradition, in addition to the holy cup, that should be discussed at this point. The Procession of the Grail has received a great deal of attention from scholars over the years (see plate 16). In this procession the Grail is usually floating in the air without a bearer or is carried by a woman dressed in white while other women bear branched candlesticks, a bleeding lance,[26] a severed head on a platter, and/or other objects (all of which are called the "Hallows" of the Grail).[27] Although Grail scholars have traditionally attempted to derive them from Celtic mythology, a number of sources could have supplied these objects. The Grail romancers could have taken the motif of the Lance from art and medieval dramas just as easily as from an ancient Celtic source.[28] Peebles points out that the Lance in the Grail tradition is consistently described as "bleeding" and that no "bleeding" lance exists in Irish or Welsh tradition.[29] Gallais and others have postulated that the Lance was not originally part of the tradition but was added by redactors and interpolators because of the popularity of Longinus in the Crucifixion scene rather than because of any intimate connection between the Lance and the Grail.[30] Robert de Boron does not use the Lance in his *Joseph*.[31]

Others see another, non-Celtic source. Coyajee discusses the parallel between the Grail talismans and the details on Mithraic monuments.[32] He presents Cumont's theories regarding Mithraic symbolism.[33] He sees in this trinity an Iranian origin for the connection of the Grail with water. Ringbom claims that in the legend of Zarathrustra the *Xvarīnah* ("Glory"), the *Fravaši* ("Divine Spirit"), and the *Gohar* ("Innermost Soul") form a trinity of sorts, with the *Fravaši* bearing associations with water.[34] Coyajee also argues for a connection between the

PLATE 16. The Procession of the Grail (MS Paris, Bibliothèque de l'Arsenal 5218, fol. 88). Courtesy of Bibliothèque de l'Arsenal.

The Alans and the Grail

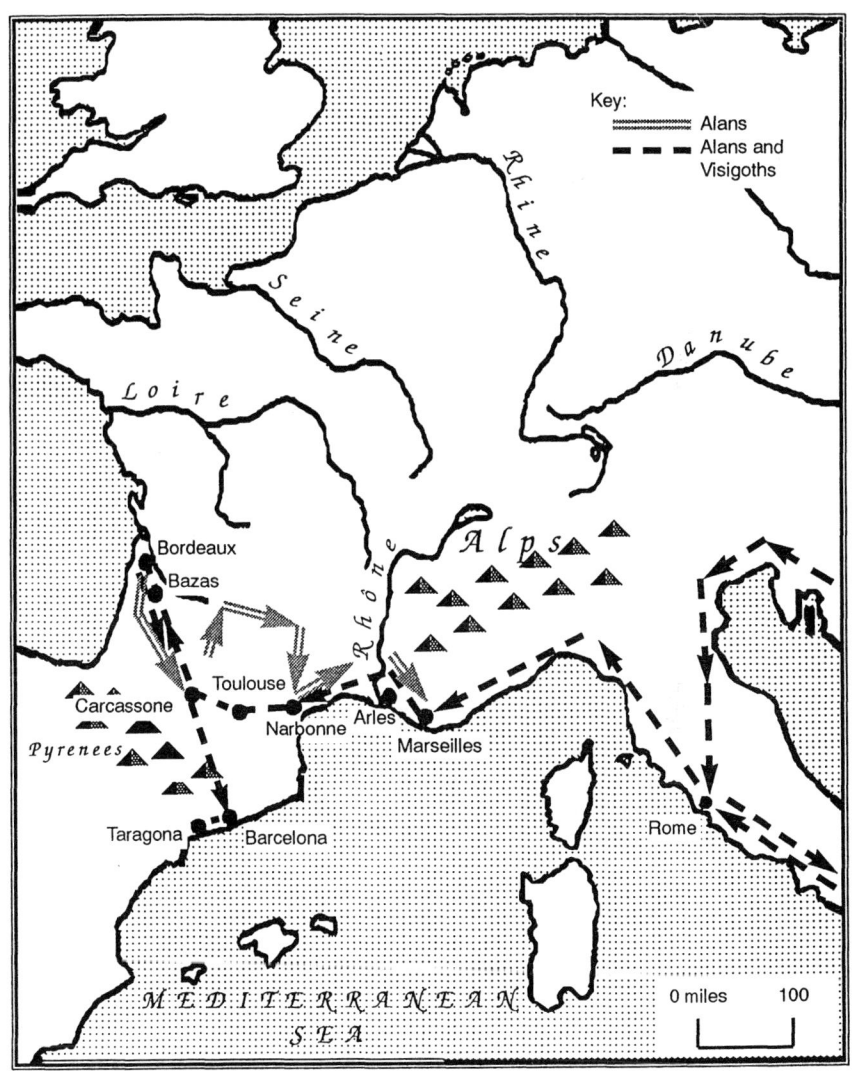

MAP 18. The Sack of Rome and the Invasion of Gaul

Xvarǐnah and the Grail, citing the *Zamyād Yasht* (i.e., the *Zam Yašt*, sections 53–54 and 67–69), which describes the *Xvarǐnah* as

> bringing good pastures and fine horses; *bringing plenty with beauty and weal; powerful and friendly, rich of pastures, prolific and golden.* . . . And there comes with it a horse's strength, there comes with it a camel's strength, there comes with it a man's strength, there comes with it the Kingly Glory; and there is in him, so much of Kingly Glory, *as might extinguish all the non-Aryan nations.* And then (through it) living creatures *(may keep away)* hunger and death.[35]

However, we have just seen a description of a Grail-like procession, led by a virgin carrying a solitary vessel that was already associated with the "vessels of Christ," in the description of the sack of Rome by the Visigoths and the Alans. The building to which the treasure was supposedly returned was the Basilica of St. Peter. Procopius, however, states that among the treasures removed from Rome by Alaric's troops were

> the treasures of Solomon, the king of the Hebrews, a most noteworthy sight. For the most of them were adorned with emeralds; and they had been taken from Jerusalem by the Romans in ancient times.[36]

This treasure, as depicted on the Arch of Titus (see plate 17), contained branched candlesticks (such as those that Chrétien describes in his Grail procession) and possibly containing a cup, which later became associated with Jesus.[37] In spite of Alaric's orders to return the treasure and in spite of the procession a portion of this treasure was missing (along with Honorius's sister, Galla Placidia) when Alaric's troops left Rome.[38]

In all likelihood the pagan barbarians who were "making profession, though not in the true faith" to these cups were the Alans who had joined Alaric in the sack. Some of the Visigoths may have returned for the treasure and then died at sea in the failed attempt to cross to Carthage before Alaric discovered the crime. Or they may have reclaimed the treasure when they returned to Rome after Alaric's death. It is more likely, however, that the non-Christian Alans allied with Alaric took the treasure.

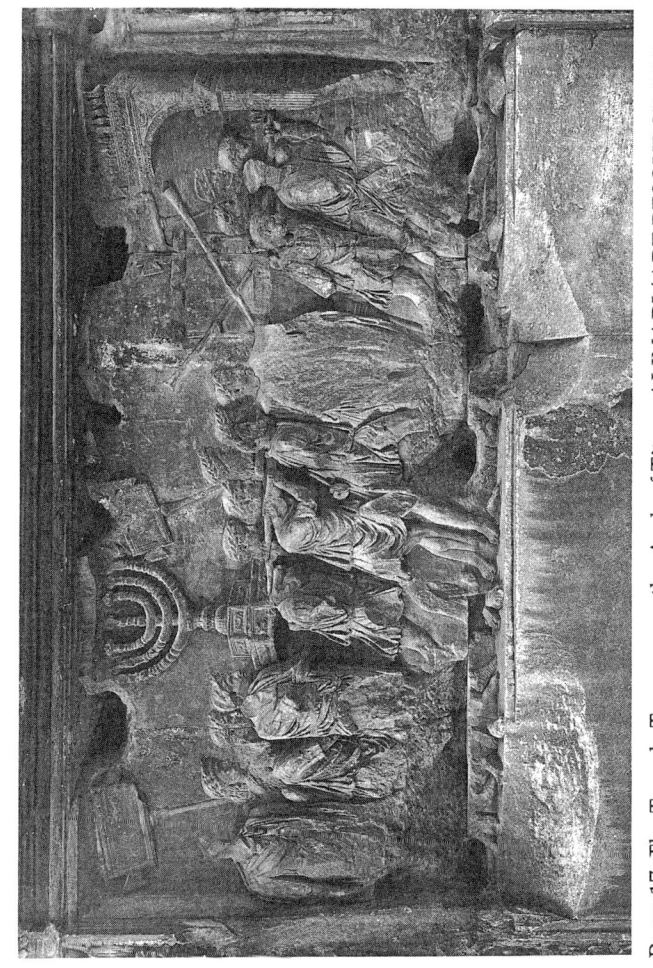

PLATE 17. The Temple Treasure on the Arch of Titus. ALINARI/ART RESOURCE, NY.

Alaric died soon after the sack. According to a German legend, he was buried under a river with the treasure.[39] But, as we shall see in the next chapter, only portions of the treasure probably served as Alaric's grave-goods. The river grave of the type in which Alaric is said to have been buried is Alanic in character.[40] In 410 he was succeeded by his brother-in-law, Athaulf, who had joined him the previous year with "a considerable army of Huns and Goths" from Upper Pannonia.[41] The future Roman general Aëtius took Athaulf's Huns and joined the Huns under Attila who were raiding in the north, while Athaulf aborted the invasion of Carthage and, eventually, marched for Gaul. Athaulf and his troops crossed the Alps and raided toward Marseilles (see map 18), in search of the camp of the usurper Jovinus (who had already been joined by Goar and his Alans from northern Gaul). Athaulf's troops (unsuccessfully) laid siege to Marseilles. In some variants of the Grail tradition Joseph of Arimathea, Lazarus, and others landed at Marseilles and conquered Gaul.[42] Nelli also points out that in the Germanic Grail legends (e.g., *Titurel*) the Grail does not remain in the West but is taken back to the East via Marseilles.[43] In addition one of the fifth-century bishops of Marseilles, in the period when the Alans were settling in that region, was named Joseph, and some scholars have argued that the detail that the Grail came to Europe via Marseilles was added to the story as a memorial to him.[44] In any case this odd variant of the Grail story makes eminent sense in the light of the history of the Alans who settled in southern Gaul.

After the debacle at Marseilles Athaulf led his troops to join Jovinus, but the usurper would not accept Athaulf's help. Meanwhile Honorius had sent Sarus (Alaric's sworn enemy) from Ravenna to meet the menace that Jovinus was posing in the south of Gaul. Athaulf and his forces met Sarus while Jovinus retreated to Narbonne (see map 18). Disillusioned by Jovinus's behavior, Goar and his Alans pulled back to the north of Gaul. Athaulf killed Sarus, then hunted Jovinus to Narbonne. The Narbonnese killed Jovinus before Athaulf reached them, and in his fury Athaulf and his troops sacked the city. While in Narbonne (late January 414) Athaulf wed Galla Placidia in a ceremony that made use of the dishes from treasure stolen during the sack of Rome.[45]

Athaulf's troops then sacked Carcassone, Toulouse, and Bordeaux (see map 18). At Bordeaux, Athaulf encountered for a second time Paulinus Pellaeus, a minor Roman official and the grandson of Ausonius. Paulinus had been made a count by Attalus, the puppet emperor set up by Alaric and Athaulf prior to the sack of 410 who was still with Athaulf at the wedding at Narbonne. Athaulf gave orders that Paulinus and his family were to be allowed to escape from Bordeaux. The Goths in Alaric's forces, who were anti-Roman and who were becoming increasingly unruly as their leader and their Alan allies became increasingly pro-Roman, stripped Paulinus and his retinue of their worldly possessions but allowed them to escape. Paulinus and his family fled to Bazas (see map 18). However, the Goths, who had been rejoined by Athaulf and the Alans, besieged Bazas in 414. Nennius's *Historia Brittonum* (ca. 800) mentions that Arthur's battle of "Bassas" took place on a river, just as these Alans fought their famous battle at the town of Bazas on the Garonne. Paulinus, who had property in the city, had just been confronted by a slave uprising inside Bazas and had recently learned of an assassination attempt on his own person.[46] The unnerved count was relieved to see his old acquaintance Athaulf outside Bazas[47] and went out to meet him. He struck a deal with Athaulf that resulted in the defection of the Alan troops to Paulinus's side and perhaps ultimately in the death of Athaulf himself. This deal, and other details concerning Paulinus, will be discussed in the next chapter.

Shortly thereafter Aëtius, a half-"Scythian" general of Western Rome who had trained with Alaric's Visigoths and Alans as well as with the Huns,[48] began to have a significant impact on Gaul. His father, Gaudentius, is said to have "held a distinguished rank in the province of Scythia" and to have risen "from the station of a military *domestic* to the dignity of master of the cavalry," a description that could easily make him an Alan.[49] As a young boy Aëtius was given to Alaric as a hostage.[50] Aëtius's army numbered 60,000 men in 424, when Galla Placidia named him guardian of her son, Valentinian III. After killing his rival Boniface at Ravenna, Aëtius fled to the Hunnish army in

Pannonia.[51] He used the Huns to reestablish his position as commander of the armies of Western Rome.[52] His son, Carpilio, was raised in Attila's court. Aëtius used barbarians, mainly Alans, to keep the peace in Italy, Spain, Britain, and Gaul for seventeen years (433–450).[53] His troops, first at Orléans, then at Châlons-sur-Marne, defeated Attila in Gaul.[54] Aëtius also used the Alans as a buffer against the Visigoths and the *bacaudae*, or rebellious peasants.

The Alans who were led by Sambida settled around Valence along the Rhône (440), while the Alans led by Goar were settled around Orléans (see chap. 1).[55] The progress of Goar's Alans into Armorica was temporarily halted by the intercession of St. Germanus, who died before a permanent arrangement could be reached.[56] The result was that Goar's Alans conquered Armorica and slotted themselves into the existing society at the level of the nobility. The Gallo-Roman colonists who refused to divide their estates with these Alans found their lands taken by force;[57] however, most of them encouraged the settlement of the Alans and intermarried with them. These Alans were pagan, not Arian, and the policy of settlement in Armorica in large part helped to ensure that the Franks rather than the Goths eventually became the masters of Gaul.[58] When Aëtius lost the support of his Hunnish allies ca. 442, he turned to Goar for help.[59] In return for aid Aëtius allowed Goar to sack and settle in Armorica.[60]

Marx argues that the social setting for the Grail romances is particularly Armorican, considering the monasteries, the bishops with monastic bases, the hermits, the professional harpers and poets, the literature, and the conquests—all of which Marx feels are linked to the environs of Vannes, Rennes, and Nantes.[61] Vannes and Rennes in particular had several rulers named Alan, who were most likely descended from the Alans of Goar's tribe.

The Merovingian kings favored Alanic advisers from Aquitaine while acting openly hostile toward the Alans of what by that time had become Brittany.[62] The Carolingians were also descended from the Alans.[63] It is interesting to note that to this day the dominant families of the region formerly known as

Armorica trace their origins not to Celtic emigrants but to these Gallo-Roman colonists.[64]

The Alans who were settled in both Armorica and southern Gaul became prominent members of the clergy as well. Some of these Alanic clerics may have served as artists in the monasteries and cathedrals where the motif of the Chalice at the Cross appears (see map 19). At the very least they used the motifs from their heritage in their manuscript illuminations. Perhaps the Chalice at the Cross was among them.

Another Alan named Goar, a native of Aquitaine and a namesake of the fifth-century leader of the Alans of Gaul, became a saint.[65] Although his parents had Latin names, they named their son after the greatest Alanic chieftain of the previous century, so it is very likely that St. Goar's parents raised their son with a knowledge of his cultural heritage. According to Bachrach, most of the Alans in Gaul had converted to orthodox Christianity by the "middle of the sixth century."[66] The Alans of Gaul, unlike those of the Eastern Roman Empire whose sacred cup never became associated with the cup of the Last Supper, converted directly to orthodox Christianity, not Arianism, although they most likely celebrated a Gallican form of the mass.[67] In any case St. Goar probably knew about the cup-worshiping religion of the Alans in some detail. While living in Aquitaine, Goar became a parish priest. He traveled from Aquitaine to Trier, where he retired, alone, to a cell at Oberwessel on the Rhine,[68] from which he worked to convert the "pagans" to the Christian religion. St. Goar himself was constantly in conflict with his superiors, notably several bishops of the Rhine region. Bishop Rusticus of Trier charged him with "hypocrisy and sorcery" (i.e., heresy), a charge that probably arose from St. Goar's habit of treating his visitors according to the social customs of the Alans.[69] King Sigebert I of Austrasia acquitted St. Goar of these charges at Metz. The king offered the saint Rusticus's bishopric, but St. Goar died (ca. 575) shortly after his return to his cell to consider the offer.[70] As a result the form of Christianity as it was practiced in the Rhine region was directly influenced by St. Goar and the type of Christianity that he practiced, which like his social habits contained

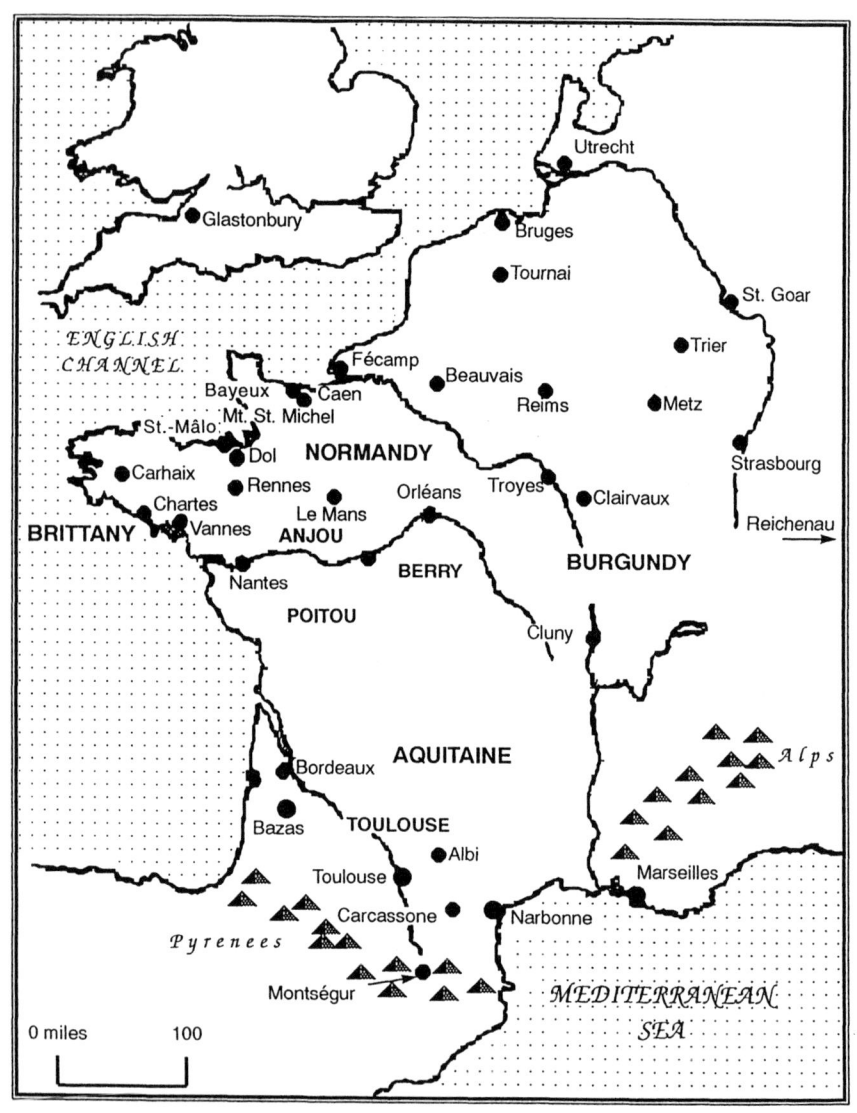

MAP 19. Some Religious Sites in France

Alanic elements. One of the earliest examples of the Chalice at the Cross comes from Trier.

Stories of the Alan god who was symbolized by a cup would have developed into folktales following the conversion of these Alans of Gaul to Christianity. An analogous case in the Caucasus Mountains can be seen in the popular figure of St. George. Abaev pointed out that

> It may be conjectured that the very popular Ossetic Christian "saint" *Wasgergi*—St. George—a knight in a white felt cloak mounted on a white horse, whom the women were forbidden to call by his proper name but referred to as *laegty dzwar*—"god of men"—inherited the features of that Alan god of war[71]

whom the Alans worshiped in the form of a sword.[72]

Other Alans went into the clergy as well. The first Bishop Alanus served the city of Le Mans in the early 500s.[73] A seventh-century Alan from Brittany was venerated as a saint at Bazas.[74] The popular cult of St. Alan arose in Aquitaine in the sixth century. By the early 700s a cult of yet another St. Alanus also developed among the descendants of Goar's tribe in Brittany. A certain St. Alan is said to have built a monastery in Lavaur ca. 700, and at least six churches in the region were dedicated to him. Relics of this saint formed the center for the cult of St. Alanus practiced throughout the Middle Ages.[75] In the late eighth century a St. Alain is recorded near Nantes. Even as late as the 1460s St. Alans were still appearing in Brittany.[76]

Goeric, yet another Alan of Gaul, served as count of Albi in 627.[77] Albi and the surrounding bishoprics, abbeys, and nunneries were ruled by this Alan family from ca. 600 to the mid-1200s. Goeric's niece was the abbess at the nearby convent of Troclar, and Goeric himself took the name of Abbo and became bishop of Metz in 629 or 630.[78] Although not as turbulent a figure as St. Goar, Bishop Abbo would have had some influence on the development of Christianity in his bishopric, considering that a priest could alter the Gallican mass in any manner he desired, as long as he had the approval of his bishop. Here too we note that three of the earliest representations of the Chalice at the Cross come from Metz itself, and many others come from within the lands controlled by Abbo's bishopric. In the tenth century the holdings of this family were attached to the duchy of Toulouse, a region under Alanic influence since the land grant of 415.[79] Two centuries later, with this family still holding Albi and influencing the local bishoprics, the Albigensian heresy surfaced in this region. The Albigensians, also known as Cathars, were rumored to possess a magnificent treasure, possibly the same treasure that the Romans had taken from the Temple of Solomon in 70 C.E. If our scenario is correct, this rumor might well have been true. The Alan presence in the regions that used the Chalice at the Cross motif, as well as in the clergy of those regions, is not overwhelming statistically. The motif itself appears in only a small number of the representations of the Crucifixion that are also found within these regions. The fact that a tribe of cup-worshiping nomads who supplied the church with several saints was present in these regions at all is curious.

The Grail Knights themselves have often been said to be of Celtic origin. Waite argued that the Welsh king Cadwaldar is Galahad, based on the parallels that both heroes removed relics from Britain and died in the Holy Land.[80] Waite also points out that one variant tells that Cadwaldar planned to attack Britain "in a fleet furnished by his kinsman Alain of Brittany, . . . but an angel warned him to desist."[81] Cadwaldar, who was said to be of the lineage of the biblical King David, died in 644. However, we find that he is a kinsman of an "Alan" of Brittany, and, as we have seen, the other Grail Knights (Perceval and Bors) seem to have far more Alanic than Celtic connections.

The Grail legends recorded in Brittany have a great deal in common with Alanic culture. In Biket's *Lai du Cor* (ca. 1150), one of the earliest works in which a Grail-like cup appears, a drinking horn is sent to Arthur by the aforementioned Mangon. The country that the victorious knight wins by drinking from the cup is Esparlot.[82] As mentioned earlier, *Esp-* is cognate to the Scythian word *asp*, or "horse,"[83] and appears as an element in many Alanic names. "Esparlot"[84] may have meant "The Land of Aspar"[85] in a story told by the ancestors of the nobles in Brittany for whom Biket's lay was composed.

Alan families ruled in Gaul well into the 1200s, more than enough time for them to have influenced the Grail tradition of that region. The Alans of southern Gaul may have possessed a tradition of a magic cup that was influenced by their contact with the treasure from the Temple of Solomon. These Alans had a profound influence on the areas where the Grail legends originated. Unbroken family lines control both the nobility and the church from the fifth-century Alanic invasions of Gaul until the twelfth century, when the Grail romances appear in manuscripts. The history of individual Alan families can account for the differences among the Grail traditions of Brittany, southern Gaul, and the church.

Here, then, is a source for stories of vessels traveling from Jerusalem to Western Europe via Marseilles; for cups, branched candlesticks, and dishes carried by virgins; for a Grail Castle located somewhere in the Pyrenees; and, as we shall see in the next chapter, for "kings" who are called Pelles, Pelleas, Pellam, and Pellinore.[86]

NOTES

1. Other stories of a Grail-like vessel appear in Gaul. In *Waltharius* Walter is a knight of Aquitaine (de Vries 1963:36). Here a relic, a gold dish, is taken from Gormant (de Vries 1963:37). In a legend recorded by Geronimo Pujades in his *History of Catalonia* (*Cronica Universal del Principado de Cataluña*, 1607; Pujades 1829–1832) under the date 607 Romans traveled by boat to Spain, where they hid relics in the Pyrenees. Later they could not find the spot. The relics supposedly included the skull and right arm of St. Peter and an ampulla of the blood of Christ.

2. Micha 1979.

3. Littré 1956–1958:186.

4. Josephus in Williamson 1981:47. Although Josephus says that Pompey did not remove the treasure in 63 B.C.E., the Arch of Titus depicts these spoils, and several other ancient authors (e.g., Procopius) also agree that the Temple was sacked and the treasures were taken back to Rome in 70 C.E.

5. Randers-Pehrson 1983:190.

6. Peterson 1986:27–42.

7. Lawton 1983:xli; Van Coolput 1986:34.

8. Waite 1909:448; 1933:355.

9. The idea of a cup in conjunction with the Cross would not have flustered even the most pious cleric of the era, since cups were a familiar Christian symbol by the fifth century (Ferguson 1961:101, 104, 107, 110, 116, 126, 145, 163, 167).

10. Malcor 1991.

11. For a list of references see Bachrach 1973:137–140; see map 9.

12. Sulimirski 1970:175.

13. Littleton 1982:53–67.

14. Abaev 1960:12.

15. Littleton and Thomas 1978:517.

16. Abaev 1960:12–14.

17. Dumézil 1930:19.

18. Randers-Pehrson 1983:218–219.

19. Thompson 1982:17; Bachrach 1973:52 ff.

20. Randers-Pehrson 1983:105.

21. A custom perhaps acquired by both peoples during times when they may have been subject to the Huns; see Randers-Pehrson 1983:190.

22. Randers-Pehrson 1983:116–117.

23. Radagaisus is consistently refered to as a "Scythian" by ancient sources, even though most modern scholars think of him as a Goth. See Randers-Pehrson 1983:109, 116–117.

24. Randers-Pehrson 1983:109, 116–117.

25. Orosius 7.39; Raymond 1936:388–399.

26. While there are bloody spears in Celtic tradition, there are no recorded instances of *bleeding* lances until after the Longinus legend had penetrated Celtic regions (Peebles 1911:passim). The Bleeding Lance in the Arthurian tradition appears to be of continental origin and appears in Celtic regions only as a result of translation from continental texts (Malcor 1991:120–121). The Bleeding Lance of the Grail stories appears to be a device that appealed to the authors because of the Longinus legend, because of the emphasis on the necessity for the ocular proof of miracles by the medieval relic cults, and because of the medieval debates over the doctrine of transubstantiation (Malcor 1991:16, 22–23,

64–66, 198–199, 331–332, 342; cf. 270–272). For an in-depth study of the Bleeding Lance see Peebles (1911:passim). See Pauphilet (1921:94–102) for the importance of ocular proof of the miracle of transubstantiation to the authors of the Arthurian legends. For the confusion between miracles of the *Saint-Sang* cult and the Bleeding Lance see Fisher (1917:76).

27. Markale 1989:235.
28. Peebles 1911:194.
29. Peebles 1911:185. The Bleeding Lance of the Grail legend was connected to Longinus, a traditionally blind Roman soldier at the Crucifixion who pierces Jesus's side with his spear, by writers after Chrétien. In Wauchier's Continuation of Chrétien's *Perceval* a lance bleeds into a silver cup (Peebles 1911:166).
30. Gallais 1972:60.
31. Gallais 1972:60; Nitze and Jenkins 1932–1937, 2:121; Imbs 1956:105.
32. Coyajee 1939:45.
33. E.g., he connects the Mithraic crater with water symbolism; cf. Cumont 1910.
34. Ringbom 1951:485–489.
35. Coyajee 1939:8.
36. Procopius 5.12.41–43; Dewing 1968:129. Dewing's note (1968:129 n. 2) to this passage sets the date of the removal of the treasure from Jerusalem to Rome at 70 C.E. A portion of this treasure was then removed by Alaric in 410, with the remainder disappearing after the sack by Gaiseric in 455.
37. Josephus in Williamson 1959:47.
38. Procopius 5.12.41–43; Isidore 1966:9–11.
39. Ward 1981, 2:13, no. 373. The traditional site is the Busento River, at a spot near Consentia-Cosenza in southern Italy (Wolfram 1988:160). This legend was probably carried to the Rhine region by Alan missionaries from southern Gaul, such as the infamous St. Goar.
40. Sulimirski 1970:194.
41. Zosimus 5.37; Ridley 1982:119. Upper Pannonia was also heavily settled by Alans; Bachrach 1973:60–61.
42. Ussher 1928; Ashe in Lacy et al. 1986:307.
43. Nelli 1951:315.
44. E.g., Ashe in Lacy et al. 1986:307.

45. Olympiodorus, frag. 24; Blockley 1983, 1:187–188; Bury 1889, 1:197.

46. Paulinus ll. 328–341 in White 1921:331; Bachrach 1973:29.

47. The identity of the Alan leader at Bazas has been the subject of much argument. Some scholars (e.g., Levinson 1904:95 ff.) have proposed that this man was actually Goar, who had supported the usurper Jovinus. This argument is troublesome on two counts: Goar and his Alans had already pulled back to their base at Orléans, and the Alan leader at Bazas was a Christian while Goar was still decidedly pagan at this time (Martindale 1980, 2:514–515, 1236). Paulinus says that the leader of the Alans was a former acquaintance, and he would have had a chance to meet both Alaric and Athaulf at Rome (ca. 409, the only place and time he could have met Attalus before the puppet emperor made him a count). Earlier Paulinus names the leader of these troops as Athaulf, and the later reference, which appears to designate an anonymous lieutenant, is probably just an example of the flowery language Paulinus uses throughout his writings. White (1921:331), who edited the Loeb edition of Paulinus's *Eucharisticus*, identified this Alan leader as Athaulf, and we concur with his identification.

48. Herbermann et al. 1907–1912, 1:177.

49. Renatus Profuturus Frigeridus, quoted by Gibbon 1946, 2:1079–1080; Gregory of Tours 2.8 in Thorpe 1974:119.

50. Philostorgius, 12.12; Bidez 1913.

51. Bury 1889, 1:248.

52. Jordanes, sec. 34; Mierow 1915:100–101.

53. Sidonius, *Panegyric on Avitus*, l. 300; Anderson 1963–1965, 1:145–149.

54. Mierow 1915:105; Wenskus in Beck et al. 1881:123; see map 8.

55. Bachrach 1973:62–64; Randers-Pehrson 1983:190; Wenskus in Beck et al. 1881:123.

56. Randers-Pehrson 1983:126–127.

57. Bachrach 1973:62–64; Randers-Pehrson 1983:190.

58. Randers-Pehrson 1983:255.

59. Wolfram 1970:177–178; Levison 1904:95–175; Bachrach 1973:63.

60. Morice 1750–1756:11; Martonne 1885:506–515; Bachrach 1973:63, 115.

61. Marx 1965:10–11.

The Alans and the Grail 253

62. The former were descendants of Athaulf's Alans (e.g., Goeric, aka Bishop Abbo; Bachrach 1973:96) rather than Goar's Alans (e.g., Alan Judual; see chaps. 1 and 4). One example of Merovingian hostility toward the Alans of Brittany can be seen in Alan Judual's imprisonment by Childebert I; Bachrach 1973:84.

63. Through Goeric's relative St. Arnulf; cf. Delaney 1980:260.

64. Markale 1983:53–55.

65. Steine 1981.

66. Bachrach 1978:486.

67. The "Gallican Mass," according to Fortescue (1955:97 ff.), was a term used for any mass that differed from the mass as performed by the Pope in Rome.

68. His name to this day survives in the name of the village St. Goar, which is opposite the Lorelei. For more on St. Goar in the Rhine region see Heyen (1966) and Stiene (1981).

69. E.g., feeding them in the morning before the traditional time a monk should have broken his fast.

70. Delaney 1980:259.

71. Abaev 1960:14. This description of St. George is similar to many descriptions of Sir Gawain.

72. Ammianus Marcellinus 31.2.23; Rolfe 1939:393.

73. Bachrach 1973:79.

74. *Biblioteca Sanctorum* 1961:col. 651; cf. chaps. 8 and 10. According to Augusto Moreschini (*Biblioteca Sanctorum* 1961:col. 652) Alain as the name of a saint in Brittany derives from the Latin name Alanus, which he believes to be from a name of exclusively Scythian origin with respect to ethnicity. Moreschini argues that this name does not appear in church catalogs or medieval Breton ecclesiastical documents, but we are skeptical of this claim, since we know of such instances as the name Alanus appearing on the tomb of Constance. See chaps. 1 and 3.

75. Bachrach 1973:103–106.

76. E.g., the Blessed Alan de la Roche.

77. Goeric's other relatives eventually include such notable figures as Charlemagne and Philippe d'Alsace.

78. Krusch 1888:440, 442–443; Bachrach 1973:96.

79. Friedman 1984:vols. 1 and 2.

80. Waite 1909:442–443.

81. Waite 1909:442–443.

82. Cf. Espor, god of sacrifices from the Ingush variant of the tale of "The Death of Batraz" (Dumézil 1930:72–73).

83. Bachrach 1973:98; cf. Sanskrit *áśva-* (cf. *ashvah*); Buck 1949:167.

84. This name may be derived from the same source as that of Espor, the god of sacrifices (see note 82, above).

85. The name Aspar is prominent in Alanic history. The Alanic military commander of the Eastern Roman Empire during the fifth century bore this name. He not only controlled the Eastern Empire and forged a peace with the Alans and Vandals of North Africa that lasted through his lifetime but also became a prominent official in the Western Roman Empire's government and secured the throne for Valentinian III, the son of Constantius III of Rome and Galla Placidia. For more information see Bachrach (1973:26–73) and Peterson (1985:31–49). The name also appears as an element in the name of P. Aelius Rasparaganus, "Rex Roxolanorum," who is cited in Roman records (Sulimirski 1970:168).

86. Potvin 1865–1873:ll. 3000–3240.

CHAPTER 10

The Grail Keepers

The basic elements of the Grail story as they appear in Malory include the cup shape of the Grail, the connection with Joseph of Arimathea, the Fisher King, the Dolorous Stroke,[1] and the Flowering Wasteland.[2] According to this tradition upon Joseph's death, the cup passes to the Fisher King, who had duplicated Jesus's miracle of feeding a multitude with a fish. This Fisher King guards the Grail until it comes time for him to die, when he passes it on to the next Fisher King. In later Grail tradition a foreign knight, usually Balin, wields the Spear of Longinus against the Fisher King, maiming him.[3] As a result the kingdom of the Fisher King is laid waste until the coming of the Grail Knight, who restores water to the Wasteland, causing the kingdom to bloom once again.

Both the Fisher King and the Maimed King are called by a variety of names, most of which are some variant of the name Pelles. The name Pellinore first appears in the Vulgate Cycle.[4] This name was taken for the name of Perceval's father in the prose *Tristan* and the Huth *Merlin*. From these texts the name was taken for two characters in the *Livre d'Artus*, one of whom is the maimed father of Perceval who sired many sons.[5] The name Pelles itself (or, rarely, Pelle)[6] is used in the Irish translation of the *Queste del Saint Graal* in place of Pellehan or Pellinore as the name of the father of Perceval's sister.[7] The name Peles occurs in the Welsh *Y Seint Greal*.[8] Loomis equates the Celtic Beli with Pelles and Pellehan (with the dubious explanation of "manuscript corruption").[9] In Lovelich's version of the Grail story Pellehan has a son and a daughter, Pelles and Pelle.[10]

The anonymous author of MS P of the *Perlesvaus* was the first author to connect the Royal Hermit of the Grail tradition with Pelles, whom Nitze and Jenkins identify as Pwyll, king of Annwfn.[11] However, Pwyll, aside from having a name that starts with a *P* and that includes a Welsh *ll* (not pronounced anything like the *ll* in Pelles) has little in common with the Grail Keepers, Fisher Kings, or Maimed Kings of the Arthurian legends. A more likely candidate for the source for Pelles, Pellinore, Pellam, and their ilk is the obscure Roman count Paulinus Pellaeus, who, in the last days of the empire, had a close encounter with the Alans who helped Alaric sack Rome in 410, an encounter that Paulinus recorded in 459 after he had become a hermit near Marseilles.

Paulinus Pellaeus

According to the *Eucharisticus* Count Paulinus Pellaeus, during the attack on Bazas in 414, was already acquainted with the leader of the Alan contingent that accompanied Athaulf's Visigoths (see chaps. 1, 3 and 9).[12] This account, brief as it is, has elements that have puzzled historians for centuries, the most important of which is the identity of this Alan leader. The bulk of the evidence indicates that this leader was Athaulf himself. The identity of the woman and the son who were sent into Bazas as part of Athaulf's deal with Paulinus thus becomes possible to deduce. The woman could not have been the emperor Honorius's sister Galla Placidia or Paulinus would certainly have mentioned that fact. In fact Galla Placidia is still with Athaulf in Spain, where she bears their son. Athaulf was also married to Alaric's sister, who had borne him a son. She may have been the woman sent into Bazas, but it does seem odd that Paulinus would have thought that the sister of the infamous Alaric was not worthy of identification. And her son was still with Athaulf in Spain.[13] Some sources state that Athaulf also had a Sarmatian wife by whom he is said to have had as many as four children.[14] Although some scholars attribute this story to a scribal error,[15] Athaulf did come from Upper Pannonia, where it would easily have been possible for him to marry a Sarmatian, or even an Alan, wife.[16] Such a wife would help explain the unusual loyalty of the Alan contingent toward Athaulf even after the Goths started to lose confidence in him, and by the time of the Battle of

Bazas children by such a wife could easily have included a son in at least his twenties who may well have been the commander of the Alan contingent under Athaulf—a worthy hostage indeed! This anonymous Sarmatian or Alan wife and her son, while valuable to Athaulf, would have meant nothing special to Paulinus and would account for his going no farther in their identification.

Paulinus never described in detail the deal that he made with Athaulf. Bachrach speculates that Paulinus promised the Alans land.[17] But the grant that these Alans received from Honorius was precisely the region, Septimania, that they had already conquered (see maps 7 and 9). The Alans, who would have captured Bazas before Constantius of Rome arrived, gained nothing, and Athaulf, who made the deal with Paulinus, was murdered by one of his disgruntled Visigoths within a year. What bargain could Paulinus possibly have struck with Athaulf for which the Alan leader was willing to pay such a terrible price? Consider the following possible scenario.

Paulinus, besieged in Bazas following a slave uprising, recognizes his acquaintance Athaulf as the leader of the Alans and Visigoths besieging the city. Since Athaulf had already helped Paulinus and his family escape from Bordeaux (see chap. 9), the count hopes that the king will offer him similar aid at Bazas. Paulinus, however, misjudges how badly Athaulf has lost control of the Visigoths under his command.[18] Once Paulinus reaches Athaulf's wagons, the leader of the Alans, Athaulf, can see no way to get Paulinus back inside the walls safely—let alone through the hostile enemy camp, along with the sizable retinue that made up Paulinus's household. While Paulinus panics over this turn of events, he notes that Athaulf is wavering between his support of the Visigothic attack and a genuine desire to help the Romans.[19] Athaulf suggests that he could accompany Paulinus inside the city, where Bazas would presumably be turned over to him for his troops to sack. Paulinus offers an alternative: send hostages back with him, then he will send the leaders of the city out to negotiate a deal. Athaulf agrees and sends his Sarmatian wife and his favorite son, who commands the Alans under him, into the city with Paulinus. Because of the son's rank the Visigoths do not suspect anything and do not attack. When the leading citizens of the city come out to meet with Athaulf, the illusion that Athaulf's son is arranging for the surrender of the city is reinforced once more. Athaulf negotiates with the leaders of Bazas for the safety of his family, then orders the Alans to draw their wagons into a circle around Bazas and defend the city. The Alans complete the maneuver at night. In the morning the Visigoths realize that the Alans have joined the Romans—which was probably Athaulf's intention all along, rather than a result of any friendship he might have felt toward Paulinus. The Visigoths are either unwilling or unable to attack their former allies and withdraw toward Narbonne, probably to retrieve Attalus as a puppet emperor, who had already served in this capacity for Alaric and Athaulf (see chap. 9), now that they have lost Athaulf as a leader. At Narbonne the Visigoths learn that the ports are blockaded by the Roman navy and that Constantius is marching south from Arles (see map 18). So they take Attalus and flee into Spain to the relative safety of Barcelona.

Athaulf and the Alans (who numbered about 3,000–4,000) leave Bazas soon after and also head toward Narbonne. We suggest, however, that Athaulf's goal is now Ravenna, where, using Galla Placidia, pregnant with his son, as a bargaining chip, he probably hoped to convince Honorius to name him as co-emperor in much the manner that Constantius of Rome would later use Placidia to achieve the same goal.

The Alans reach Carcassone without incident, but word is waiting for them in the city that Constantius of Rome is marching toward them from Arles and that the Visigoths have taken Attalus and are fleeing toward Barcelona. With a small party, traveling fast, Athaulf figures that he can outrun Constantius and by traveling through a pass in the Pyrenees rejoin the Visigoths at Barcelona (see map 18), somehow hoping to make his peace with this larger portion of his former troops, since the Alans were too small an army to defeat Constantius and to prevent the Roman general from recapturing Galla Placidia.

In order to cross the mountains at a rapid pace Athaulf leaves the bulk of the Alans, as well as most of the treasure from the sack of Rome,[20] under the command of his half-Sarmatian, or half-Alan, son, the one who Paulinus tells us had served as a "hostage" at Bazas. Then Athaulf most likely takes Galla Placidia and his bodyguard through the nearest pass, a road that runs very close to the legendary Grail Castle of the Cathars, Montségur (see map 18).[21] This bodyguard contains several Goths who survived the earlier attack on Sarus, including the brother of Alaric's slain rival. These were probably the messengers from Narbonne who warned Athaulf of Constantius's imminent approach, most likely because they had a blood feud with Athaulf over the death of Sarus and wanted to kill him themselves instead of having him killed by Constantius.[22] Athaulf and his group make the journey to Barcelona safely. There Athaulf once again takes command of the Visigoths, probably by virtue of the legitimate claim he would have on the throne of the empire through the son he has fathered on Galla Placidia and by the fact that, pro-Roman or no, Athaulf was by necessity anti-Constantius, which in the eyes of the Visigoths would make him appear to have reverted to his earlier anti-Roman ways.

Meanwhile Paulinus decides to leave Gaul for his lands in Greece. Burdened with a huge train of women, children, servants, and whatever worldly goods he has left, Paulinus leaves Bazas practically on Athaulf's heels, perhaps hoping that the king will yet again protect him if further danger presents itself. When the count reaches Carcassone, however, his wife is still dead-set against setting sail from Narbonne for Greece, and now a new obstacle presents itself: Constantius and his troops are in the way and chasing Attalus, the former puppet emperor who had made Paulinus a count. Ever mindful of his own skin, Paulinus probably thinks twice about the advisability of a chance meeting with Constantius. He does not have enough money left to support himself and his retinue in Carcassone, and he is equally unwilling to turn back west, where he would be unprotected in the chaos that is reigning in southern Gaul.[23] Instead Paulinus says that he enters the portion of his life where he is "exposed amid barbarous peoples."[24] The odds are that he makes a deal with Athaulf's son.[25] He attaches his household to the son's Alans and pulls north with them past Albi, where Goeric, a descendant of these Alans, would one day rule, and into the county of Lot (see map 18).[26]

According to the *Eucharisticus* Paulinus and his family spent the next ten or so years wandering about the countryside, presumably with these Alans. In 415, after a year most likely spent wandering the countryside around the Lot River, these Alans were given a land grant by Honorius (at the urging of Constantius). The land grant encompassed the region between Toulouse and the Mediterranean (see maps 7 and 9), and the Alans had only to control the coastal roads, making sure that Athaulf and his Visigoths stayed in Spain, so that the Romans would leave them in peace. Perhaps Constantius arranged this grant for this particular group of Alans, in spite of their leader's apparent blood ties to Athaulf, because of the split with Athaulf at Carcassone, which would have made it appear as if the Alans, like the Visigoths at Bazas, had fallen out with the Visigothic king.[27] In any case Paulinus and his family probably continued to travel with these Alans, since Paulinus made it clear that he did not yet return to his own estates.

During this period Paulinus became involved in some form of heresy. This may have occurred at the time that this group of Alans was finally converted to the Christianity. Most Alans converted to the orthodox faith, but, given the Eastern influence on the region in which these Alans were settled, it is quite possible that they converted to a form of Christianity that had been influenced by Manichaeism. The cult of the worship of a mermaidlike goddess, who shows up in medieval legends as Melusine, was also thriving in the region.[28] Romans still tolerated such cults side-by-side with Christianity, and Paulinus may have become an adherent of the religion of this goddess.[29] Alanic gods were openly worshiped at Marseilles.[30] Any of these religions or of the mystery religions or of the eastern-influenced Christianity brought to Marseilles and surrounding regions by missionaries, such as Cassian, may account in part for the peculiarly "eastern" character of the Grail stories from southern Gaul, and the connection of such stories with the legends of Melusine.[31] The presence of Paulinus and the treasure with these Alans could account for the stories of the Fisher King, Pelles, and the tales of the Grail as a vessel from the Holy Land.

Eventually two of Paulinus's sons returned to Bordeaux, one as an adviser to Theodoric I,[32] who succeeded Wallia as king of the Visigoths,[33] and one as a presumably orthodox priest.[34] The rest of Paulinus's family died in a series of illnesses shortly after he returned from some retreat where he had spent six months repenting his "error" and returning to orthodox Christianity. Paulinus contemplated going to Bordeaux to join his sons, but the younger son died of a fever[35] and the eldest had a falling out with Theodoric I, as a result of which the remainder of Paulinus's lands in Bordeaux were confiscated. Paulinus was left with a tiny house inside Marseilles and some rocky land outside the city, presumably near the sea.

To return briefly to our scenario, Paulinus takes the example of the monks of St. Victor's, the monastery that Cassian had established at Marseilles, and builds a house on the crest of a rock on his land outside the city, where he becomes a hermit. He rents the house in the city for income, and he grows what crops he can on the almost worthless soil around his clifftop house.[36] During this time, according to the *Eucharisticus*, Paulinus is also supported by a mysterious source of income.[37] He justifies this source of income by claiming that since what was his belongs to another, so what was another's belongs to him. Whatever this source of income is, Paulinus cannot use it to pay the taxes on his lands, and by the laws of *agri deserti* (see chaps. 1 and 3), the land passes to the control of the local Alans, who were the Roman tax collectors in such instances.

Paulinus's past ties with the Alans in this region would explain why he was allowed to live in the houses in spite of his inability to pay. If the mysterious source of income was by chance from a portion of the Alan treasure, Paulinus could not very well pay the Alans with their own money. Possibly he had been fencing bits and pieces of the treasure for the Alans for the better part of thirty years, maybe not being entirely honest in his accounting to them of the prices he obtained for the less recognizable items. A few of the more sacred vessels, most likely cups, given the Alan proclivity for such vessels, probably survived. These vessels may even have been in the care of Paulinus in his hermitage at Marseilles.

In 454 Valentinian III murdered the general Aëtius.[38] In 455 Gaiseric, king of the Vandals and Alans of Africa (descendants of Respendial's Alans), sacked Rome while two of

Aëtius's retainers murdered Valentinian. When Gaiseric withdrew, the rest of the treasure from the Temple of Solomon was gone.[39] Thus, with this change in the political power of the Western Roman Empire and the disappearance of the rest of the Temple treasure, our hypothetical scenario might have continued with Paulinus deciding to act. In 459 he wrote that he sold his estate at Marseilles to a "Goth" in order to pay his debts. Paulinus, however, hated Goths and would hardly have sold his last estate to one. They were responsible for the loss of his other estates and had held him hostage on more than one occasion. At Bazas, Paulinus proved that he could distinguish Visigoth from Alan; thus it is unlikely that Paulinus made a mistake in the identification of the purchaser. The incident makes far more sense when one realizes that in the 400s "Goth" was synonymous with "Jew" in southern Gaul because of intermarriage between the races.[40] Paulinus probably sold his land to a Jew. In any case Paulinus sold his land, making enough money on the deal for him to live out the rest of his days in his hermitage, and, with this sale, the trail of any treasure Paulinus may have had was lost.

The bulk of the treasure may have stayed with the Alans under the command of Athaulf's son. There is evidence for such an event in the Arthurian legends. As already mentioned, the events at Bazas are reminiscent of the story of King Ban under siege with his wife and son endangered. The Alan who served as a hostage at Bazas, probably Athaulf's own son, and who presumably later led this contingent of Alans to wander over the county of Lot is quite possibly a historical prototype of the figure of the Alan of Lot (see chap. 3). Just as Lancelot recovers his patrimony from an enemy after a long delay, these Alans eventually claimed the land in Septimania that they had conquered upon their initial arrival in Gaul. There may also be a parallel between the historical land grant to these Alans and the legend of the presentation of Joyous Guard to Lancelot after the knight conquered the castle for Arthur with the express understanding that Lancelot would use the strategic position of the castle to keep the "barbarians" in the north of Britain, just as Constantius of Rome arranges the land grant for the Alans in the south of Gaul with the express understanding that these steppe warriors would keep the "barbarian" Goths in Spain. These Alans were also associated with a treasure, just as the families of Lancelot and the Grail Knights were associated with the Grail. And these Alans were in the company of a man named Pellaeus, just as the Grail families spawn such names as Pellam, Pelles, Pelleas, and Pellinore.

The Maimed King

There are two major royal figures in the Grail tradition: the Maimed King and the Fisher King. Eventually these become fused into one character, but in the earliest Grail material they are distinct.

The Maimed King has suffered a wound, usually in the "thigh,"[41] that leaves him impotent.[42] This wound is the result either of a lack of faith with respect to the Grail or of some sin on the part of the injured king. The emphasis in many of the early continental Grail stories, however, is on a sickly rather than wounded king. For example, Lancelot's visions in the *Queste* are of a sickly king. The notion that this sickness is somehow associated with the flesh of the king is also found in the continental material. King Alain, in one manuscript of the *Estoire*, is shown in an illumination using the Grail to heal a leprous king (see plate 18).[43] This king appears for the first time in the works of the Burgundian cleric, Robert de Boron.[44]

In Malory the Maimed King is known as Pellam.[45] He receives his wound at the hands of Balin, who attacks the king with the Spear of Longinus.[46] This spear pierces the king through both thighs, and his kingdom, apparently as a result of this injury, is laid waste. Galahad, the knight who eventually draws Balin's sword from a floating stone, finds this king and heals him during the Grail Quest (cf. Galahad's healing of Mordrains). Some scholars have proposed that this Dolorous Stroke strand of the Grail legend came from the *Mabinogi*, was spread by Breton *conteurs* ("storytellers"),[47] and was then adapted by Geoffrey of Monmouth.[48] According to them, Chrétien combined these Welsh tales with the chronicles (such as those of Geoffrey, Bede, and Nennius), and Wolfram von Eschenbach took his form of the story from Chrétien.[49] The Vulgate version of the tale of the Dolorous Stroke also appears to be based on Chrétien's model. There is a peculiar emphasis on the flesh of the king in this story. When Galahad heals him, Mordrains says, "My flesh which was all dead of oldness is become young again."[50] Curiously Batraz, after winning control of the Nartamongæ, makes his father, Xæmyc, young again.[51] In another variant of the Grail legend Galahad takes blood from the spear that caused the wound to the Maimed King and applies it to the king's injuries. The king then "start[s] upon his feet out of his bed as an whole man."[52] This is a well-established folkloric belief that the cure of an injury is effected by use of the weapon that caused the wound in the first place.[53] There is, however, also an extremely close parallel between this version of the Maimed King story and a saga from the Nart tradition.

One of the earliest Maimed Kings is Evelake (Evelach, Mordrains, Mordrens) of Robert de Boron's *Joseph*. Evelake was supposedly born in Maiux, France, where he lived until he was chosen to serve in the army of Augustus Caesar.[54] Under Tiberius, Evelake went to Syria, where he killed his commander's son in a quarrel.[55] He is baptized under the name Mordrains, and after several years of adventuring with Joseph of Arimathea he is either wounded or contracts an illness because of some sin associated with his treatment of the Grail.

Mordrains, unlike Pellam, has to endure his sickness/injury for several centuries, from the time of Jesus to the time of the Grail Quest. It has been suggested that this waiting parallels the legend of Melchizedek, who served a prototype of the communion service to Abraham, the founder of Israel.[56] According to this legend Melchizedek was doomed to live until the death of Jesus, at which point he ordains Joseph of Arimathea as a priest, who in turn ordains other priests "of the Order of Melchizedek,"[57] a major theological point in the Middle Ages.[58] The story of the ordination of Joseph of Arimathea by Melchizedek is juxtaposed with the legend of Joseph with the Chalice at the Cross and hence figured prominently in the early history of the Grail. Here, then, we have the image of the chalice associated with the legend of an abnormally long-lived king.

ne qui meſtauſ eſtoit ⁊ alaiſ li moſtra
le ſaint graal ⁊ il fu garis

Diſt li contes que quant io-
ſephes fu el trespaſſement del
ſiecle ſi quil ne pot pluſ quil
ne rendi la naturele dete. Il
regarda deuant lui et uit alain q plou

Plate 18. King Alain with the Grail (MS Bonn, Prose *Lancelot* of 1286, Universitätbibliothek 526, fol. 57v). Courtesy of the Universitätbibliothek Bonn.

Nascien (baptized as Seraphe),[59] wounded in his shoulder by an arrow, is another Maimed King.[60] He is eventually blinded because he looks inside the Grail after being instructed not to do so.[61] In the Irish translation of the *Queste* it is Mordrens (Evelake) who is struck blind as a punishment for looking in the Grail.[62] Loomis has suggested that the doom of the blind Mordrens to wait for his healer shows the influence of the Christian tale of the aged (but not blind) Simeon, who was doomed to live until he beheld the baby Jesus.[63]

The figure from the Nart sagas who most closely resembles the Maimed King is the husband of Satana, Uryzmæg. An incredibly old man by the time of the action in most of the sagas, Uryzmæg is usually depicted sitting—ostensibly watching sheep or horses—on a hill near the sea, too aged for normal physical activity, much as the Maimed King in Chrétien's *Conte del Graal* is depicted sitting by the sea, fishing.[64] In one Nart tale the hero Uærxtænæg has grown old,[65] and his son, Sybælc, has married the daughter of the Sun.[66] Uærxtænæg possesses a golden mail shirt that he wears while sitting in the village square waiting for his son's return from a quest.[67] Three sons of an evil sorcerer take the shirt from Uærxtænæg as well as two strips of flesh from his back and return to the mountains, where they hide in a cave. When Sybælc comes home from his adventures, his wife will not let him enter the house until he brings back the shirt and heals his father, who lies, maimed, within. Sybælc, with the aid of his maternal grandfather, Xæmyc, goes in quest of the golden shirt, kills the three sons of the evil magician, and recovers the strips of his father's flesh. He returns to his house, where he restores the flesh to his father's back by striking him with a felt whip, making the flesh like new again, and gives the gold shirt back to his father.[68]

Of particular interest here is the detail that Sybælc undertakes his quest for this golden object with the aid of his maternal grandfather. In several of the Grail legends Perceval's maternal grandfather is the Fisher King, who aids him in the quest for the Grail.

There are several possible historical prototypes for the Maimed King. In 331 the Goths invaded Scythia. During this invasion a tribe of Alans became attached to these Goths. In 369

The Grail Keepers

Athanaric became king of the pagan Goths and drove the Christian Goths into the Roman Empire. In 377 the Goths under Athanaric returned to the Danube, where they split into two groups, a pro-Roman contingent led by Athanaric and an anti-Roman contingent led by Fritigern. The Alans who had become attached to these Goths made up a part of the anti-Roman contingent. The Goths and Alans under Fritigern's command engaged the emperor Valens at the Battle of Adrianople (378; see map 7). Valens was wounded by an arrow. Too injured to continue the fight, the emperor was carried to a house, where he was burned alive by the Goths.[69] Even more Alans joined the victors of this battle, and the combined forces reunited with Athanaric's troops as they marched on Constantinople,[70] where Athanaric made a treaty with Theodosius and then died. At this point Modares, Athaulf's father, deserted to the Roman side and eventually received his own command in the imperial army.[71] Athanaric was eventually succeeded by Alaric, who used this army of Goths and Alans to sack Rome in 410.

Athaulf succeeded Alaric. Just as Evelake and Nascien of the Grail tradition are brothers-in-law, so were Athaulf and Alaric. In 413 Athaulf led the Goths and Alans who had sacked Rome over the Alps and into Gaul. The first major battle he fought with these troops in Gaul took place at Marseilles, where Athaulf was wounded so seriously that he was forced to call off the attack.[72] As we have seen, Constantius of Rome eventually chased these Goths into Spain in 415, after which he arranged a land grant to the Alans who had been at Bazas.[73] Athaulf had probably found the Goths who had been attached to Sarus, the enemy of Alaric whom Athaulf had killed during the uprising of the usurper Jovinus, at Carcassone. These troops accompanied Athaulf into Spain, where one of these Goths murdered Athaulf by stabbing him in the groin,[74] ostensibly because the Visigothic king had joked about the man's diminutive stature.[75] Wolfram, however, argues that the assassin was most likely under the orders of Sarus's brother, Sigeric, who wanted revenge for Athaulf's slaughter of his kin.[76] In any case Athaulf apparently lingered long enough to dictate instructions for his brother, whom he desired to succeed him.[77] Here, then, we have the elements for the legend of the Maimed King, including kin murder and a wound in the groin that is not immediately mortal but that does eventually result in the death of the king.

Constantius pulled the Visigoths out of Spain in 418 and settled them in southern Gaul. These Goths, with their story of Athaulf's death, and the Alans of southern Gaul, with their story of the treasure from Rome, eventually intermarried, providing an opportunity for the legends to join and to sow the seeds of the legends of the Maimed King and of the Grail in southern Gaul.

Goeric, the Alan liaison to these Goths under Alaric II (r. 484–507), was also murdered at Barcelona.[78] Years later Goeric of Albi (ca. 627) entered the clergy as Bishop Abbo (see chap. 9).[79] It is quite possible that a conflation between the stories of these two Goerics with the legend of Athaulf yielded the tale of a Maimed King who became a cleric associated with the Grail.

These stories would also account for the tales of kin murder and maimed kings that are found in Spain. The connection between Alans and these legends could have derived either from Athaulf's earlier connection with the Alans of Bazas, from his marriage to a Sarmatian (or possibly Alanic) wife, or from his contact with the Alans of Spain, who numbered in the tens of thousands by the time of his death.[80]

The Fisher King

The Didot-*Perceval*, which took its Grail story from a developed form of the chronicle version (Lacy et al. 1986:137), tells of the wounded Fisher King. This fusing of the figures of the Maimed King and the Fisher King had begun as early as the thirteenth century and led to some wonderful medieval scholastic explanations of the Fisher King's name: because the king is wounded, all he can do is fish all day, so he is called the Fisher King.[81]

In the earliest manuscripts of the Grail story, however, the Fisher King appears as a figure distinct from the Maimed King. Weston believed that Robert de Boron's explanation was the only "tolerably reasonable account of why the guardian of the Grail bears the title of Fisher King," namely that Bron caught a fish that provided a mystic meal of which sinners could not partake.[82] In the early histories of the Grail a man, usually Alain or Bron, duplicates Jesus's miracle of feeding a multitude with a single fish,[83] thus earning the title "Fisher King." This Grail legend is assigned to Bron by Robert de Boron's *Joseph*, and to Alain, Joseph of Arimathea's nephew, by the Vulgate *Estoire*.[84]

The story of the Fisher King has sparked many discussions of eastern influence on the Grail legends. Markale argued that there were parallels at the hypothetical Indo-European level between Wolfram von Eschenbach's version of the Fisher King and the Indic deity Vishnu.[85] The bulk of the scholarly discussion has centered on the question of the Fisher King's possible Celtic origin. There is a fair amount of evidence to suggest that this enigmatic figure reflects, to a degree, the Celtic god Bran, who was believed to have a castle, Dinas Bran, on the banks of the River Dee—a river noted in ancient times for its abundance of salmon.[86] Some scholars have speculated that the influence of Bron on the story gave rise to the character of the Fisher King, which then became linked with tales of Joseph as the Grail Keeper. These scholars see the story contained in *Sone de Nansai* as a source for Robert de Boron, and they argue that Robert confused Joseph of Arimathea with Bran the Blessed, since Joseph of Arimathea appears as Fisher King in the *Sone de Nansai* (or *Sone de Nausay*).[87] The Joseph strand of the Grail legend appears in Chrétien's *Conte del Graal* and the *Metrical Joseph*. The figure of Joseph of Arimathea, however, may have been replaced by Bran/Bron in other versions of the story. As Bromwich (1969:28 n. 65) notes, "In a Welsh Triad of the 'Three Saintly Lineages of the Isle of Britain,' one of its early editors substituted the name of Bran the Blessed for Joseph of Arimathea." Also, as Nitze (1909:368) has pointed out, there is no strong evidence to support Nutt's hypothesis that either Bron or the fish that fed a multitude was in any way originally connected with Bran of the Celtic tradition.[88] What we could very easily have here is a story that existed outside the Celtic tradition that exhibits Celtic parallels simply because of a Celtic overlay on the original tale. In this case we find the explanation of the origin of the Fisher King's name as deriving from Christian tradition far more satisfying and less of a strain on the imagination than the mental calisthenics needed to derive this Grail figure from the Celtic Bran.

Unlike the early Maimed King, who is simply doomed to live until the Grail Knight appears, the Fisher King always appears as the guardian of the Grail, which is kept in his castle. Gawain's vision of the Grail occurs while he is dining at a table in the bedchamber of the Fisher King.[89] The Continuations of Chrétien's *Perceval* speak of the appearance of the Lance and the Grail in "l'ostel au Roi Pescheor" ("the house of the Fisher King").[90]

Unlike the Maimed King the Fisher King seems to have lived a normal lifespan, then passed his charge on to his successor. The title Fisher King, unlike that of Maimed King, was hereditary, usually transferring from uncle to nephew, since the Fisher King was often chaste (and so childless) in much the same manner that powerful bishoprics were "inherited" within aristocratic families of the Middle Ages.

The Grail of the Fisher King, in spite of his Christian origin, as we have seen, bears a far greater resemblance to the drinking horn in Biket's *Lai du Cor* and to the Ossetic Nartamongæ than to any analogous Celtic cup. Roach noted that although several texts describe the "honor" that Perceval does to the Fisher King, the most reliable text speaks of the "*grant valor*" ("great bravery") of the King himself.[91] Thus we have here a mysterious cup appearing at the table of a "brave" rather than a pure knight.

Instead of the holy or brave king of the French legends, the Germanic stories of the Grail tell of a "Sinner King," who, according to Wolfram von Eschenbach, is maimed when he dons the armor of the Grail in the cause of love rather than in a holy cause. Bergmann has advanced the most intriguing argument concerning Wolfram's "Sinner King."[92] For Bergmann the tale of the Grail Keeper who is maimed because of his sin arises because of a confusion by the mysterious Guyot (Kyot), Wolfram's reputed source, between the words *pêcheur* ("fisher")[93] and *pécheur* ("sinner"), an error that Bergmann rightly points out could be made only in French but that was easy to make in the absence of diacritics. The only point of this argument with which we take issue is that Wolfram, the illiterate German poet, was more likely to have made the error than Guyot, who according to all accounts was a native French speaker.[94]

Ossetic tradition has no surviving clearcut figure who could have developed from a prototype of the Fisher King. The Alægatæ appear as a family associated with a cup, just as Perceval's family is traditionally associated with the Grail. Like the Grail, usually in the famous *Cortêge du graal* ("Procession of the Grail") at the castle of the Fisher King, the Nartamongæ appears at banquets. The woman who leads the Arthurian procession is thought by some scholars to be the daughter of the Fisher King, although she is most probably an allegorical representation known in the Middle Ages as Ecclesia ("Church"; see chap. 8).[95] It is perhaps interesting to note that she is sometimes associated with the Wise Virgins of Christian tradition, and that Satana, the wife of the Nart Uryzmæg, is known in Ossetic tradition both as a Wise Woman and as a virgin.[96] Uryzmæg, however, appears to belong to the Boratæ family (the family paralleled by that of Lancelot in the Arthurian tradition), and the Nart sagas no longer give the name of the patriarch of the Alægatæ (the family paralleled by that of Perceval).

As we have seen, it is indeed possible to detect historical prototypes for the two principal Grail Keepers in Paulinus Pellaeus and Athaulf, who lived just a few decades prior to Riothamus, the historical prototype for the figure of King Arthur. Both Paulinus and Athaulf were contemporaries of Constantine of Britain, the legendary grandfather of King Arthur, and it is interesting to note that the Fisher King of the Grail tradition is sometimes placed in this generation as well.[97]

The role of the Alans in the history of fifth-century Gaul was crucial to the conflation between objectively historical events, figures, and objects, as well as between the resulting treasure legends and the imagery of the Christian and Alanic religions. Historical figures like Riothamus and the Alan leader called out of Lot to settle Septimania[98] were almost certainly caught up in the Batraz-prototype that was carried by the Alans and the Sarmatians.[99] The emphasis on the cup in the Grail legends of Gaul would have developed naturally because of the apparent importance of cups in the religion of the ancient Alans and because of the impact of the story of the treasure from Rome on these Alans. Such an emphasis does not occur in the legends of Arthur, which were probably developed primarily by the Iazyges of Britain, who did not place such an importance on cups and who were not affected by the treasure story.

Thus the dramatic events that occurred at the beginning of the fifth century, the period reflected in the *Nibelungenlied* and the *VUlsunga Saga*, triggered a cycle of folklore that was carried by Alan clerics and clerical families. This folklore, as it developed in Gaul, was transmitted through a partially Gothic, but primarily Alanic, filter. Some of these legends were probably disseminated by the family of the counts of Albi throughout the Pyrenees region, where it eventually fused with the folklore related to the Cathars.[100] Alan missionaries, after their conversion to Christianity, also carried these legends to the Rhine[101] and possibly, just as Joseph of Arimathea supposedly carried the Grail, to Britain. Such missionaries would have been considered "fishers of men,"[102] and the story of a Fisher King (perhaps King of Missionaries?) probably appealed to them. Such tales as the Vulgate *Queste del Saint Graal* were clearly first written in Old French and were later translated to Welsh (*Peredur*) and Irish (*Logaireacht an tSoidigh Naomhtha*). At such times a Celtic overlay could easily have been placed on the legends.[103]

In sum Athaulf, Paulinus Pellaeus, the Alan leader at the siege of Bazas, the sack of Rome in 410, the theft of the vessels from St. Peter's, the curious procession that immediately followed the theft, and Athaulf's murder in 415, are all embedded in this complex corpus of legends, as is the Alans' deep-seated veneration of sacred cups and their caretakers, still attested in the Ossetic legends of the Nartamongæ. Moreover it is noteworthy that contingents of Alans were closely associated with all of the historical persons and events just noted, including the treasure looted from Rome. Indeed, on the basis of the evidence discussed in this chapter, it seems fair to conclude that this peripatetic "Scythian" tribe, which came to have such a major impact on the West in the early fifth century, not only preserved oral accounts of these historical events, but also transformed these accounts into the legends of the Sacred Cup and its Keepers—melding their own veneration of magical cups with half-understood elements of their newly acquired Christian faith.

NOTES

1. This tale relates how Balin took the Spear of Longinus and struck the king of a castle, maiming him and leaving him impotent.

2. This story tells how the injury to the king leaves his kingdom a wasteland. When the Grail Knight, usually Galahad but sometimes Perceval, finds the Chalice and heals the king, the wasteland blooms again (after which Galahad ascends to heaven, and Perceval, in most of the tales, dies trying to return to Camelot). The tale is usually associated with that of Balin and the Dolorous Stroke (cf. Cowen 1969, 1:60–91). Cf. Dumézil 1930:58–59, in which Batraz causes a famine by killing the Angel of the Grains. The presence of Batraz on earth is associated with famine throughout the Nart sagas, and the voluntary death of this cupbearer (i.e., Batraz; cf. Dumézil 1930:171–172) results in the return of fertility to the mares and to the women of the Narts (e.g., Dumézil 1930:72–73; see chap. 3).

3. This Spear is one of the relics of the Passion that often accompanies the Grail.

4. Most scholars see this form of the name as a corruption of Pelles (Bruce 1918:340).

5. Perhaps as a result of influence from the Bron/Alain story; see Bruce 1918:124 nn. 1–2 and Wolfgang 1976:30 for a discussion of this and the other Pellinore. The name Bron most likely derives from the biblical city of Hebron, which was formerly called Cariath-Arbe (*Josue* [*Joshua*] 14:15; 15:13), rather than a mutated form of the Celtic Bran (Ackerman 1952:44; Nitze 1949a:306).

6. Pelle is also given as the name of Lancelot's wife in Lovelich (1974–1905, 2:339).

7. Falconer 1953:xii.

8. Parry 1933:73. This shift in the spelling of "Pelles" to "Peles" could easily occur while translating from French to Welsh with the

single *l* required in the Welsh to preserve the liquid sound of the French *ll*.

9. Loomis 1963a:272.

10. Lovelich 1874–1905, 2:339. This derivation of the daughter's name from the father's is common in the Arthurian legends (e.g., Alphasan/Alphanye in the Vulgate Cycle). The name Elaine, which occurs so frequently in the genealogies, could have derived from the masculine Alain by such a practice, although no such example is explicit in the legends themselves (see discussion of the name Elaine in chap. 3).

11. Nitze and Jenkins 1932–1937, 2:123. Pelles is the ultimate successor of Alain, the original Fisher King. Chrétien, Wauchier, and the Pseudo-Wauchier make no such connection, although this anonymous Grail author probably knew their work.

12. White 1921.

13. The boy and his sister were killed shortly after the murder of Athaulf.

14. E.g., Philostorgius 12.4; Walford 1855:515. Cf. Wolfram 1988:442 n. 302.

15. E.g., Wolfram.

16. Recall the confusion between "Sarmatian" and "Alan" discussed in chapter 1.

17. Bachrach 1973:29.

18. The Visigoths had started to part ways with Athaulf soon after he led them across the Alps into Gaul. While he was trying to join the forces that supported Jovinus, the Visigoths attacked Marseilles in a poorly planned encounter that left Athaulf with a serious wound. Later, at Narbonne, Athaulf began to announce his intentions to support the Roman Empire instead of establishing a Gothic empire, an idea that was presumably unpopular among the anti-Roman Visigoths (although it was supported by the pro-Roman Alans). Further, at Bordeaux, the Visigoths disobeyed Athaulf's orders and attacked Paulinus and his family (in a maneuver not unlike that which the Alans probably used to secure the treasure from Rome that Alaric had ordered returned to St. Peter's).

19. Evidenced at Athaulf's marriage to Galla Placidia at Narbonne, where he announced his intention to reestablish the Roman Empire rather than to establish "Gothia"; Raymond 1936:396.

20. Jordanes says that at least some of the treasure was still with Athaulf in Barcelona (Mierow 1915:96).

The Grail Keepers

21. In 728 Carcassone was occupied by Saracens. In 752 Pepin the Short conquered Carcassone, where the legendary treasure from the sack of Rome was rumored to be (even though it had probably been removed by the Alans). However, no treasure was found. From 819 to 1247 a succession of counts and viscounts ruled Carcassone. The Cathars dominated this city at the beginning of the thirteenth century, and several of the city's counts and viscounts were Cathars. During the last of these reigns the Cathar stronghold of Montségur fell (1244). The Cathars at the Château de Montségur in Ariège are said to have removed the bulk of this legendary treasure from the castle prior to its fall, with the most important artifacts being removed by a handful of Cathar "perfecti," priests of the Cathar religion, at the last minute. No one knows where this treasure was taken, although some scholars have suggested that the destination of these perfecti was Carcassone (this could simply be a conflation with the earlier legend of Athaulf's treasure). In any case Carcassone was legally confiscated from the Cathars in 1247.

22. Athaulf apparently had a few loyal retainers as well, since Sarus's brother and his henchmen, although they could apparently circulate freely in the king's bodyguard, were unable to murder Athaulf until the end of August or early September of 415.

23. A similar collapse can be seen in the Caucasus region, as some of the descendants of the Alans, the southern Ossetians who are in Georgia, struggle for survival in the wake of the disintegration of the Soviet Union.

24. White 1921:337, ll. 406–408.

25. This negotiation is not covered in the *Eucharisticus* because it led to a religious indiscretion about which Paulinus remains vague.

26. Since Athaulf did not take the treasure with him into Spain and since the treasure appears not to have been in Carcassone in 508, when Clovis (partially on the basis of the rumors of the treasure's presence; see Procopius 5.12.41; Dewing 1919:129) tried to sack that city, it is quite likely that the treasure went north with Paulinus and the Alans into the county of Lot. Perhaps the deal that he made with these Alans was to play the front-man in their encounters with towns along their path, fencing pieces of the treasure to help them support themselves, thus enabling them to keep the promise that they had made to the leaders of Bazas that they would support the Romans and keep the peace wherever they went (which meant that they could no longer sack towns to gain the supplies that they needed to live).

27. It is noteworthy that these Alans never engaged Athaulf's troops while the Gothic king was alive.

28. Markale 1983; Walker 1983:631–632.

29. This goddess may have appealed to these Alans as well, since she would have been familiar to them through her parallel figure, the half-serpent goddess of the Scythians; Herodotus 4.9–13; de Sélincourt 1972:273–275.

30. Claudius Marius Victor, *Alethia*, 3.189–194; Schenkl 1888:335–498, 413; Wolfram 1988:238.

31. Markale 1975b:120–121. Some scholars argue that Melusine was a "'Scythian' woman from Central or Eastern Europe, who married Raymond de Lusignan, Count of Poitou" (Markale 1975b:120). This legend is interesting in light of the connection of the very Alanic family of Lancelot and of the Grail legends with Poitou (see chaps. 3 and 4). The idea that Melusine derived from the Scythian Diana is not new. In fact Rabelais seems to have been the first to propose this idea (Markale 1975b:121).

32. This is the Visigothic king, who was succeeded by Euric, who in turn was Riothamus's opponent in Gaul.

33. Constantius settled the Visigoths in Aquitaine in 418.

34. Cf. the clerical Grail Knight Perceval and his warlike brother Lamorak. Lamorak was one of the three "Lions of Britain" (important knights of the Round Table), along with Lancelot and Tristan (cf. the tie between Lancelot, Tristan and Lamorak in Malory 10.24; Cowen 1969, 2:50).

35. Many modern retellings of the Arthurian legends have Galahad and/or Perceval dying of a fever on the way back to Camelot after completing the quest for the Holy Grail.

36. Paulinus (ll. 557–560; White 1921:347) did not see these houses as belonging to him but to someone else who allows him to live in them.

37. ll. 552–553; White 1921:347.

38. It is interesting to note that the Grail Quest supposedly takes place 454 years after the Passion (i.e., ca. 486; Alvar 1980:28–29), according to the *Agravain* (ca. 1230–1240). If the author misidentified the method of reckoning (i.e., if he was actually counting from the birth of Jesus rather than from the Passion), this date corresponds almost exactly to the time when Gaiseric and his Alans (450) absconded with what remained of the treasure of St. Peter's.

39. Procopius 5.12; Dewing 1968:129.

40. Baigent, Leigh, and Lincoln 1982:364.

41. Such words as "knees" and "thigh" are common euphemisms for "genitals" in medieval texts.

42. In some cases he is merely blinded.

43. Loomis and Loomis 1938:96, fig. 218.

44. The legend of the Grail as we have it from medieval Germany and Switzerland does not associate the Grail with the Chalice at the Cross, suggesting that the motif of the Chalice at the Cross did not have its origin in the Grail tradition.

The name Alain will appear frequently in later genealogies of the Grail knights. A King Alain also appears in Wace (ca. 1155, Le Roux de Lincy 1838, 2:291, ll. 15131–15134, 296, ll. 15240–15243).

45. Mordrains also appears in Malory as a Maimed King; however, in this instance, he is blind instead of wounded.

46. This spear was supposedly thrust into Jesus's left side at the Crucifixion.

47. The Welsh storyteller Bleheris served at the court of Poitou (Barber 1961:50).

48. Geoffrey may have taken the tale from Wace.

49. Biket's *Lai du Cor* may also have served as a source for Wolfram.

50. Cowen 1969, 2:361.

51. Dumézil 1930:61.

52. Cowen 1969, 2:366.

53. Leach 1972:474, col. b; cf. Telephus and Achilles's spear, motif D2161.4.10.

54. Lovelich 1874–1905, 1:104, leaf 197 col. 2, ll. 81–84; 1:105.

55. Lovelich 1874–1905, 1:106. Kin murder is repeatedly cited in the Irish material as well as the motivation for the "Scythians" to leave their homeland (e.g., Macalister 1939, 2:23, 39, 45). The victim is usually said to be one Refloir, who apparently held sway over the "princedom" of Scythia (as opposed to the kingdom of Scythia). The death wound is traditionally made by Mil, who plants a javelin in Refloir's thigh (Macalister 1939, 35:67, 107). Most medieval texts give the location of this wound as in the king's "thighs." In addition the traditional wound is caused by a spear or lance, rather than by a sword. This wound is also known in Irish material that does not involve the Scythians. For example, the first king of the Fir Bolg, Eochu, is wounded by a javelin in a similar manner (Macalister 1941, 41:45).

56. E.g., Kolve 1966:70–75.

57. As opposed to Jewish priests, who were descended from the Tribe of Levi; Hebrews 7:17.

58. Medieval theologians wanted to distance themselves from the Jews as far as possible, so they latched onto Melchizedek to avoid having their own priesthood descend from the Levites who were antagonists of Jesus.

59. This is the name that Nascien takes upon being baptized by Joseph of Arimathea. *Seraph* was originally the "Hebrew word for the divine fiery serpent," and only much later came to designate an angel (Walker 1983:905).

60. Lovelich 1874–1905, 1:155.

61. Lovelich 1874–1905, 1:217. In Malory, Galahad successfully looks into the Grail before ascending to heaven (Cowen 1969, 2:370).

62. Falconer 1953:222, ll. 1816 ff.

63. Loomis 1963b:182; St. Luke 2:26; cf. the story of Melchizedek in this chapter.

64. Loomis 1963b:30–31.

65. This is the husband of Xæmyc's daughter, Batraz's half-sister.

66. The goddess of the hearth in Alanic religion, with a close connection to fire and with a father whose symbol was a cup. Dumézil (1968:138–144) uses this tale to demonstrate hypothetical Indo-European parallels between this Ossetic hero and Karṇa of the *Mahābhārata*.

67. Cf. the "Golden Man," frontispiece.

68. The French reads: ". . . les deux bandes adhérèrent de nouveau à la peau, comme elles étaient auparavant." (Dumézil 1968:141–143). Cf. Mordrains's comment to Galahad.

69. Rolfe 1939:479.

70. Ammianus 31.2, 6; 8,4; 12, 1 ff.; 16, 3; Rolfe 1939, 3:383, 437, 463 ff., 501; Bachrach 1973:27.

71. There is a possible conflation between Modares, the betrayer of the Alans and the Goths at Constantinople, and Arvandus, the betrayer of Riothamus in southern Gaul, which eventually yields such forms as Morvandus and ultimately Modred/Mordred.

72. This wound, however, apparently did not leave Athaulf impotent, as he was later able to father a son on Galla Placidia. The traditional point through which Joseph of Arimathea brings the Grail to the same region; cf. Goodrich 1992:34–62.

73. These Goths were most likely the troops who broke off from Athaulf at Bazas.

74. According to Jordanes, sec. 31, this wound was made by a sword (Mierow 1915:96). Although most scholars agree that the murder was committed in a stable while Athaulf was inspecting his horses (e.g., Wolfram 1988:165), the exact location of that stable is not absolutely certain. According to Orosius (Raymond 1936:396) and Isidore of Seville (Donini and Ford 1966:10) it was in Barcelona. Others (e.g., Duckett 1972:112) have located the site of the assassination in Tarraco (modern Tarragona), while Jordanes (Mierow 1915:96) simply states that Athaulf had "entered the interior of Spain" at the time of his murder.

75. Jordanes 31.163; Mierow 1915:96. The diminutive assassin's name is variously recorded as Euerwulf (Mierow 1915:96) and Dubius (Bury 1889, 1:199; Duckett 1972:112; Heather 1991:220).

76. Wolfram 1988:165. Although there is no "smoking sword," if you will, that ties the assassin directly to both Sigeric and the blood feud that resulted from the death of Sarus, the circumstantial evidence is overwhelming (Bury 1889, 1:199). Olympiodorus (frag. 26; Blockley 1983, 2:189) notes: ". . . long ago his [Dubius's] master, a king of the Goths, had been slain by Athaulf, who afterwards took Dubius into his own service. So, in killing his second master Dubius avenged the first."

77. Thompson 1982:47.

78. Thompson 1969:8, 115; Bachrach 1973:94.

79. Krusch 1888:440, 442–443; Bachrach 1973:96.

80. The Alans of Lusitania alone numbered over 30,000 by 411 (Keay 1988:204).

81. Such explanations are found in works such as the *Perlesvaus*; Nitze 1902:54.

82. Weston 1920:116. Sometimes Alain, the youngest of twelve sons of the sister of Joseph of Arimathea, is said to have caught this fish. A duplicate of this meal is later served to the Grail Knights by Josephe, the son of Joseph of Arimathea.

83. St. Matthew 15.34 retells the incident, saying that "a few small fish" were used. "Two fish" were used in the case of Jesus: St. Matthew 14:17; St. Mark 6:38; St. Luke 9:13; St. John 6:9.

84. Sommer 1908–1916, 1:251; Lacy et al. 1986:183. Some sources also cite Josephe as the Fisher King.

85. Markale 1982:156–157.

86. Cf. Jenkins (1975:89). However, Weston (1920:125–136) believes that the Fisher King has ancient roots and that counterparts can be found in a wide variety of traditions from India to Babylon. The fish, she suggests, is essentially a "life symbol," and its presence in the Grail stories is but one manifestation of this well-nigh universal theme.

87. Loomis 1956:244; 1959:278–279.

88. Which is supposedly related to the *Mabinogi* via the Bron=Bran parallel. As mentioned above (n. 5), the biblical name Hebron could easily have served as a source for this name and its variants (Ebron, Hebron, Hebruns, Bron; West 1969:27).

89. Gawain can also see a chapel that is part of this vision.

90. Roach 1949–1983, 4:188 [MS E], ll. 23,951–23,959.

91. Roach 1949–1983, 4:528.

92. Bergmann 1870:26.

93. Falconer (1953:xi) discusses a possible connection between the names Pelles and Pescheor in terms of the figure of the Fisher King, with the two characters probably fusing to render the maimed Fisher King.

94. Jung and von Franz 1970:34.

95. Malcor 1991:138–139. Some go as far as to identify her as Elaine.

96. Her son is born from a rock rather than from her body.

97. E.g., he appears as Perceval's grandfather in MS Berne 113 and the Modena MS; Weston 1920, 1:61, 2:214; cf. Xæmyc, the grandfather of Sybælc in the Nart sagas; Dumézil 1968:141–143.

98. This second figure may even exhibit further conflation with Goar, the famous fifth-century Alan leader who ruled just north of the lands that became the site for the prose *Lancelot*.

99. In the case of the Alan who was held hostage at Bazas his conflation with the Batraz-prototype would have been facilitated by his own association with a holy cup, just as the Nart hero was associated with the magical cup of the Narts.

100. This region produced Bishop Abbo and several other notable clerics.

101. Where the earliest images of the Chalice at the Cross appear.

102. E.g., St. Matthew 4:19; St. Mark 1:17; cf. St. Luke 5:10.

103. As editorial evidence in the Irish translation of the *Queste* shows actually occurred; Falconer 1953:ix–xxxii.

Conclusions

So we come to the end of our journey from Scythia to Camelot. The first Northeast Iranians to make this fateful trek, the Iazyges (ca. 175), managed to preserve their epic traditions more or less intact—albeit most likely colored by the name of their first Roman commander, Lucius Artorius Castus, and by the legends of the indigenous Celtic communities in Britain. But after 469 there was a "real" Arthur in the person of the shadowy figure of Riothamus, whose military adventures in Gaul are attested in contemporary accounts. Therefore, save for a few important aspects (e.g., the death scene), the memory of the Batraz-prototype was submerged beneath this historical overlay.

Meanwhile, in the early years of the fifth century, the Alans, close ethnic cousins of the Iazyges, journeyed westward from Scythia and eventually settled in Gaul and Spain and intermarried heavily with families in Britain. Here too historical figures seem to have conflated with those of the common Northeast Iranian heroic tradition. We can identify a historical King Ban in the Alan leader at Bazas (i.e., Athaulf) and perhaps a historical Lancelot in the person of the Alan man who served as a hostage there (perhaps Athaulf's son by his "Sarmatian" wife). Moreover, in the case of Lancelot, the Alans' legends of the Batraz-prototype continued to develop until they were recorded during the twelfth century. Thus, although the Lancelot–Batraz connection is easier to recognize because of the more immediate kinship between the ancient Alans and the modern Ossetians (the creators of Batraz), both Arthur and Lancelot were derived from the same "Scythian" hero.

There is no single reason why these particular nomads had such a profound impact on the legends of the Middle Ages. That the Romans enlisted Alans as allies, stationed them as "protectors" of the local populace (as were the Sarmatians in Britain), and eventually settled them on estates gave these landowners an aura of legitimate authority that was perhaps missing from contemporary invaders like the Vandals and the Visigoths and from conquerors like the Normans. The descendants of the original nomads certainly did not think of themselves as Alans after a century or two, but they continue to this day to think of themselves as descendants of Roman colonials even before they think of themselves as Celts.[1] These same families survived the Frankish conquests of Gaul under Clovis and the rulers who followed him by becoming trusted advisers and intermarrying high into the ranks of each new invading force, a strategy that they still practiced at the time of William the Conqueror. After the Norman Conquest these same families were the ones who wound up in control of many of the British estates. Many of these nobles, several of whom bore the name Alan, either commissioned or were closely associated with other nobles who commissioned most of the medieval Arthurian romances. In short we do not think that it is sheer chance that these stories reflect folklore and history specific to the Alano-Sarmatian groups who settled in Britain and Gaul.

Whether the descendants of the Iazyges invaded the Continent with Riothamus or fled from the Saxons to settle in Brittany, they almost certainly had contact with the Alans of Gaul. The two groups, telling stories of their greatest heroes, sensed that the characters of these heroes belonged together, and the stories were adapted accordingly. These heroes share the same sword, wife, kingdom, war band—everything except their fate. Arthur, by virtue of Riothamus's exploits, became High King; Lancelot, because of the victories of Clovis, lost his land, went insane, and died (cf. the legends of Batraz).

The Alans of Gaul also had a profound influence on the areas where the Grail legends originated. Unbroken family lines controlled both the nobility and the church from the fifth-century Alanic invasions of Gaul until the twelfth century, when the Grail romances appear in manuscripts. The histories of individual Alan families can account for the differences between the Grail traditions of Brittany, of southern Gaul, and of the church, and there is a high probability that these same Alans were largely responsible for the origin and transmission of the motif of the Chalice at the Cross.

The image of the Sacred Cup, of which the Chalice at the Cross is but one manifestation, is densely layered. It is at once the legendary Chalice of the Last Supper that was supposedly spirited out of Jerusalem by Joseph of Arimathea, one of the vessels stolen from St. Peter's Basilica in 410,[2] and the ancient Alano-Sarmatian prototype of the Nartamongæ, the magical cup that plays such an important role in the Nart sagas. The Keepers of this wondrous cup, the Fisher King and the Maimed King, each has a historical prototype, in the person, respectively, of Paulinus Pellaeus and Athaulf.

Because of the prolonged contact between the Alano-Sarmatian peoples and the Celts in Britain and Gaul, Celtic themes and images overlaid both the steppe-spawned legends and the historical incidents surrounding the Alanic invasions of Gaul. Guinevere herself, whose name firmly links her to the Irish Finnabair, and whose indiscretions with Lancelot play such a prominent part in the later medieval Arthurian romances, is perhaps the best single example of such a Celtic admixture. The same can be said for a number of purely Christian figures and themes. These include Joseph of Arimathea and the association of the Sacred Cup with the Chalice of the Last Supper—to say nothing of the intense moralistic dimension of the fully evolved Holy Grail texts by Chrétien de Troyes, Wolfram von Eschenbach, Robert de Boron, and others.

The weight of the evidence presented in this book does not support the conclusion, so widely held among our fellow scholars, that the medieval legends in question are rooted in Western Europe. Rather any Celtic elements in the tales appear to be later additions to and overlays on material with a very different origin. The evidence clearly suggests that, save for some unique historical events, the core of what later became the Arthurian and Grail literature was born on the steppes of ancient Scythia among a remarkable people whose impact on both the history and folklore of the West is only just beginning to be appreciated.

NOTES

1. The Alan families intermarried with the Celts in the centuries following the initial invasion and preceding the Middle Ages; Markale 1989:90–91; Dunbabin 1985:82; cf. Hollister 1982:33.

2. This, in turn, was probably part of the loot that Titus brought back from Jerusalem after he destroyed the Second Temple.

APPENDIX 1

A Note on Sources

Since the evidence that we have presented in this book comes from a wide variety of sources, a few brief remarks on how these sources relate to each other seemed in order. Although we cover other cultures and periods of history, we have included notes only on the Northeast Iranian tradition and on the historical and medieval manuscript evidence for the tales of King Arthur, the Knights of the Round Table, and the Holy Grail.

The Northeast Iranian Tradition. The oldest literary evidence for Northeast Iranian mythology and folklore is to be found in Book Four of Herodotus's *History* (ca. 450 B.C.E.), which includes a survey of Scythian religious beliefs and practices, among them the origin story (see chap. 1). Herodotus was also the first to mention the "Sauromatae" (most likely the people later called Sarmatians; see chap. 1), although he has little to say about the culture of these eastern neighbors of the Scythians.

Another important source of evidence about the Sarmatians, in this case visual, can be found on Trajan's Column (see plate 1), as well as on several grave steles from Britain and elsewhere (see plate 3).

The *locus classicus* for the history of the Iazyges, the Sarmatian tribe that was defeated by Marcus Aurelius in 165 C.E. and forced to contribute 5,500 *cataphracti* to the Roman garrison in Britain (see chap. 1), is to be found in Dio Cassius's *History of Rome*, which was written ca. 225 C.E. during the reign of the emperor Severus Alexander. The archaeological evidence for the Sarmatians in Britain (that is, at Ribchester, Chester, etc.) is summarized by Sulimirski (1970).

Several Greek, Roman, and medieval historians mention the Alans, such as Ammianus Marcellinus, who gives us a detailed description of these latecomers from the steppes (see chap. 1). Accounts of the movements and leaders of the various Alanic factions and groups can be found in the works of Jordanes, Paulinus Pellaeus, Paulus Orosius, Procopius, and others.

As far as the modern Alans are concerned, the Ossetic Nart sagas began to be collected in the latter part of the last century by such scholars as A. Šifner (Schiffner), Dž. Šanaev, G. Šanaev, and, most importantly, Vs. Miller.[1] Most of these tales are transcribed in the Ossetic vernacular, with Russian translations and glosses, although Hübschmann (1887) published a German-language translation of Miller's 1881 Ossetic texts in the *Zeitschrift der deutschen morgenländischen Gesellschaft*. In 1925 Dirr's *Kaukasiche Märchen* (1922) was translated into English under the title *Caucasian Folk-Tales* by Lucy Menzies.

By far the most extensive corpus of Ossetic texts, however, was compiled by the late Georges Dumézil. Although he was never able to work in Ossetia itself, Dumézil spent the better part of a lifetime working with emigré Ossetians in Turkey (where the French scholar taught from 1928 to 1931) and elsewhere. In the process he became the leading western expert on this heretofore largely overlooked folkloric tradition. Another important contemporary contributor is the Ossetic scholar V.I. Abaev.

As this is written, our colleague John Colarusso (see the Foreword) informs us that a major manuscript of heretofore unpublished Ossetic Nart texts is being prepared for publication in the West. Colarusso is also in the process of translating the Circassian Nart stories, which, when published, will add an important dimension to this growing corpus of Caucasian traditional literature.

The antiquity of the Nart sagas, which, as just indicated, are shared by other North Caucasian peoples, such as the Circassians, the Kabardians, and the Abkhazians, is undoubted; they date from a time when the Alan domain was vastly wider than at present (i.e., modern Ossetia; see map 11). Moreover, although peppered with anachronisms that reflect the changing technological circumstances of the tellers—it is not uncommon for a Nart hero to train a cannon on his enemies—these tales provide a window on the Northeast Iranian past that, when coupled with what Herodotus, Ammianus, and other ancient observers had to say about these peripatetic steppe dwellers, allows us to come to grips with the extent to which their heroic traditions have influenced and, in many cases, engendered the medieval British, French, and German texts.

The Arthurian Tradition. There are three basic types of evidence for information about the Arthurian legends: archaeology, art, and manuscripts.

The archaeological record is haphazard at best. Not only are we searching for information in territories that received a nontrivial, and very physical, pounding in two world wars (not to mention all of the other forms of construction and destruction that have taken place in the fifteen or so centuries since the time of the historical King Arthur), but most archaeological excavations for Arthurian material in particular have been guided by the whims of scholars who perhaps have had more nationalistic than scientific interests at heart. The scholar searching for archaeological evidence during the time period when the Arthurian tradition originated and flourished must be willing to sort through thousands of seemingly unrelated reports of finds in order to glean the few pieces of evidence that even have a chance of relating to the Arthurian tradition. All in all, a search of the archaeological evidence is a time-consuming, frustrating project, but we have tried to point out some areas (e.g., the excavations in southern France and in Brittany) that seem to hold the most promise.

Closely related to the archaeological evidence is the record of Arthurian tradition in art. By "art" we refer to everything from reputed "relics" (e.g., the "graves" of Arthur and Guinevere at Glastonbury) to scenes from the legends that appear on everything from the Archivolt at Modena to the illuminations in the hundreds of surviving texts that mention King Arthur and his knights. Artists produced images from the Arthurian tradition in a variety of media. Formal paintings, stained glass, mosaics, and magnificent sculptures depicting some extant (and several nonextant) tales of the Arthurian world decorate obscure corners of chapels and cathedrals. Tapestries and frescoes with elaborate Arthurian scenes were known from

Britain to Italy. People combed their hair with combs and brushes carved into figures of Tristan and Isolde, examined their reflections in mirrors in the shape of trees that sported the face of the spying King Mark, covered themselves in bed with quilts that were stitched in patterns depicting the legends of Lancelot, Gawain, and other famous knights, stored their jewelry in boxes carved with figures from the Round Table, and asked to be buried in sarcophagi that were detailed with Lancelot, Gawain, and Tristan rather than holy figures from the Bible. Woodcuts and illuminations with Arthurian themes (some of which tell stories that differ from the story as it is told in the manuscript that they decorate) can also be found. These scenes and the stories that they tell are every bit as important to any study of the Arthurian tradition as are the tales recorded in writing.

By far the largest body of evidence comes from manuscripts. These texts include epistles, historiography, ethnography, annals, saints' lives, prose fiction, poetry, romances, sermons, dramas, ballads, and other narrative forms. Epistles include such works as the letters of Sidonius to Riothamus, while histories, pseudohistories, and ethnographies feature such names as Gildas, Bede, Nennius, William of Malmesbury, Giraldus Cambrensis, Ralph Higden, and the ever-popular Anonymous. Annals (records of what supposedly happened when) are found in several countries, although the Annals of Wales are the most popular among Arthurian scholars. Saints' lives often employ an unfavorable portrait of Arthur, with the saint showing the errant king the error of his ways. The lines between prose and poetry, fact and fiction, blur hopelessly in most of the sources. From the Breton lays to Malory's *Morte Darthur* the Arthurian tradition appears in almost every written genre known to the Middle Ages. Abbots preached about Arthur, actors referred to the adventures of the Round Table in their plays, and troubadours sang of the hopeless loves of Lancelot and Tristan. More often than not, the sheer popularity of the Arthurian tradition can lead to scholastic headaches. For example, there are dozens of manuscripts that belong to the Vulgate Cycle (usually in five parts, covering the early history of the Holy Grail, the story of Merlin [and the young King Arthur], the story of Lancelot, the Quest for the Holy Grail, and the death of Arthur). Very few of

A Note on Sources

the manuscripts of each part of this cycle agree for much more than a couple hundred lines at a time. Sometimes the story of Merlin is replaced with a simple listing of his prophecies. Sometimes parts of this cycle are attributed to Walter Map or to Robert de Boron; other times they are not. The Vulgate Cycle of France usually includes the three works that comprise the prose *Lancelot*: *Lancelot*, *La Queste del Saint Graal*, and *La Mort le Roi Artu*. Sometimes two other works are included: *L'Estoire del Saint Graal* by Robert de Boron and the Vulgate *Merlin*. The *Merlin* may be one of two works about Merlin: either the *Merlin* believed to have been composed by Robert de Boron or the *Prophécies de Merlin* attributed to Maistre Richart d'Irlande (which is distinct from the prose *Prophécies de Merlin*), which contains a list of Merlin's prophecies.

As the manuscripts were translated into and out of various languages the confusion multiplied. The prose *Lancelot*, for example, appears in everything from various dialects of Old French to Hebrew. Scribes were not always native speakers of the language of the texts that they were transcribing or redacting, and they were often not proficient in Latin either. Sometimes this resulted in a smorgasbord of languages within single text, as in the case of the Post-Vulgate Grail material that shows up in Gallician-Portuguese (with some Latin and Old Spanish thrown in just for good measure). The reader is referred to the *New Arthurian Encyclopedia*, edited by Norris J. Lacy et al., for summaries of the various bodies of literature on Arthur in everything from English to the Scandinavian languages.

To add to the difficulty of mastering all of this material, there are poetic versions of Robert de Boron's texts, Welsh triads, courtly romances (such as the works of Chrétien de Troyes), a Post-Vulgate cycle (which includes the Spanish and Portuguese *Demandas*), and several other texts that bear titles similar to the title of the Vulgate manuscripts, such as the Alliterative *Morte Arthure*.[2] Some texts, such as Ulrich von Zatzikhoven's *Lanzelet*, defy classification. Dozens of fragmentary texts, such as the Old French *Agravain* and the Spanish *Lançarote*, have been identified as well.

The story of Tristan poses its own problems. Most manuscript versions seem to stem from Thomas of Britain's

Tristan, but the visual arts contain an exceptionally abundant record that does not always match the surviving manuscript narratives. Also, until Malory's *Morte Darthur*, this cycle of Arthurian legends seems to have circulated alongside the Vulgate and Grail traditions rather than as a part of them.

Trying to assign any type of meaningful chronology to these and the other extant Arthurian manuscripts is difficult at best. We have tried to be as consistent as possible in the dating of the texts that we cite in this book. Discrepancies between our dates and those found in the works of other scholars reflect differing schools of thought as well as modifications resulting from the introduction of new evidence for dates on specific texts. For the most part we have used the date of the manuscript for the date of the text and avoided hypothetical dates that place the "creation" of formal narratives sometimes as much as three to five centuries earlier (this is a particular hazard with the Welsh materials). For instance, we date the Vulgate Cycle to 1215–1235, although we know that Eleanor of Aquitaine (d. 1204) had a hand in the compilation of this vast work.[3] Folk narratives are assumed to have been in circulation at periods where there is corroborating evidence from archaeology, art, or non-Arthurian texts, although we have also assumed that these oral narratives were probably not in the same form in which they were finally recorded.

In sum the sources we have consulted for this book are vast and varied. It is impossible in a short note to adequately survey all of this material in any great detail. We intend this section to be simply a guide for readers who are unfamiliar with these sources and not to be in any way a comprehensive discussion of this matter.

NOTES

1. Dumézil 1930:16–18; 1978:15–18.

2. Scholars have muddied the waters even further by referring to the same text by a variety of names. Manuscript and folio numbers provide virtually the only means to determine whether two sources are talking about different or the same texts. (Manuscript numbers alone do not help since several manuscripts contain one or two page fragments inserted amid several folios of another work.)

3. Carman 1973:23–26.

Appendix 2

Genealogies

These genealogies have been compiled from a variety of sources. While the genealogies of historical figures tend to remain somewhat stable, the names and generations on the genealogies of legendary characters vary widely according to the source that is used. For example, in some texts Morgawse of the Orkney clan is called Anna, and in some tales Gawain is Lot's grandson instead of his son. We have tried to present the most common of the names[1] and their relationships in this appendix, but we are fully aware that there are other, equally valid, family trees that can be constructed from these texts.

We have regularized the spelling of the names of the characters to the spelling that we are using in this book. Most of the conventions of standard genealogies (such as the eldest child being presented at the left and the youngest at the right) have been adhered to except where it was necessary to warp the genealogies to fit them on the page. We have tried to indicate where such alterations have been made.

Where additional information of a specialized nature has been included on a chart, we have supplied a key to the symbols we have chosen to use.

We realize that it is possible to construct family trees for most of the historical and legendary figures we have discussed. In the interest of space we have included only those genealogies that are cited elsewhere in this book. These include the House of Athaulf, the House of Albi, the House of Charlemagne, the Historical Houses of Cornwall and Brittany, the Legendary Houses of Cornwall and Brittany (including the Houses of Constantine and Orkney), the House of Joseph of Arimathea, and the House of the Boratæ.

Let us then consider these genealogies, beginning with the families of the Alans of southern Gaul.

General Key to the Genealogies

|	Fairly certain, direct descent
ǂ	Fairly certain descent, several generations may be missing
+	Possibly legendary descent
++	Bastard line
m.	Legitimate line
bold	Historical figure connected with Arthurian legends
CAPS	Name related to an Alanic name

The Alans of Southern Gaul

There are many gaps in the genealogies of the Alans of southern Gaul, mainly because so many records have been destroyed over the years. Here are the truncated genealogies that are referred to in this book.

The House of Athaulf

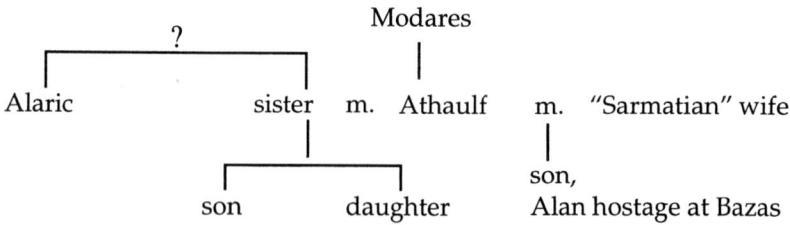

The House of Albi

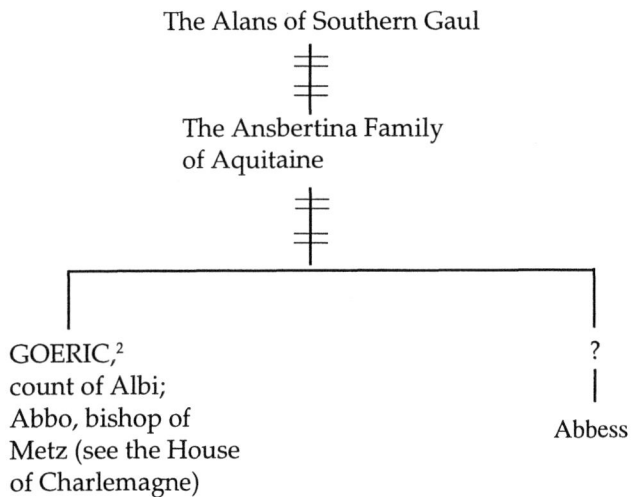

The House of Charlemagne

The genealogy of Charlemagne can be traced from the seventh century and St. Arnulf (who was a relative of Goeric[2] of Albi, an Alan count of southern Gaul; see the House of Albi) to the twelfth century and Philippe d'Alsace, the patron of Chrétien de Troyes. This family was largely responsible for the patronage of manuscripts and other works of art that transmitted the story of the Grail in the form of a Holy Blood relic,[3] more often than not as a Chalice at the Cross.

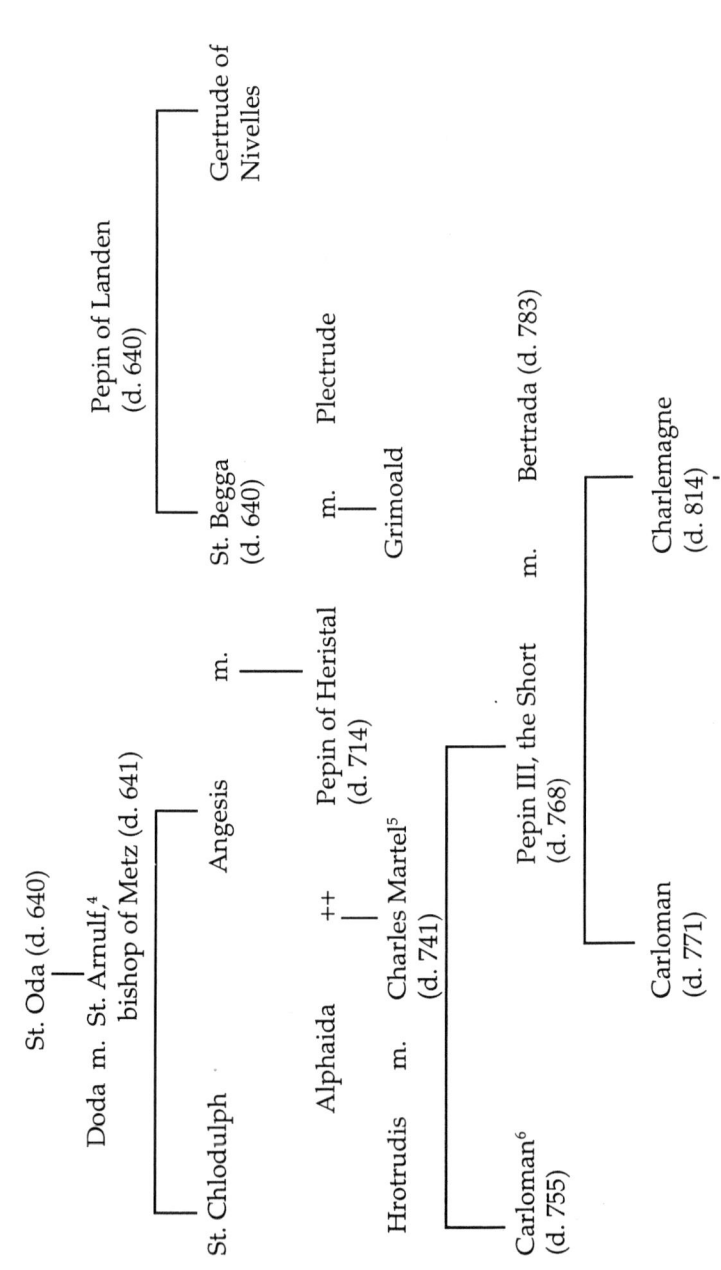

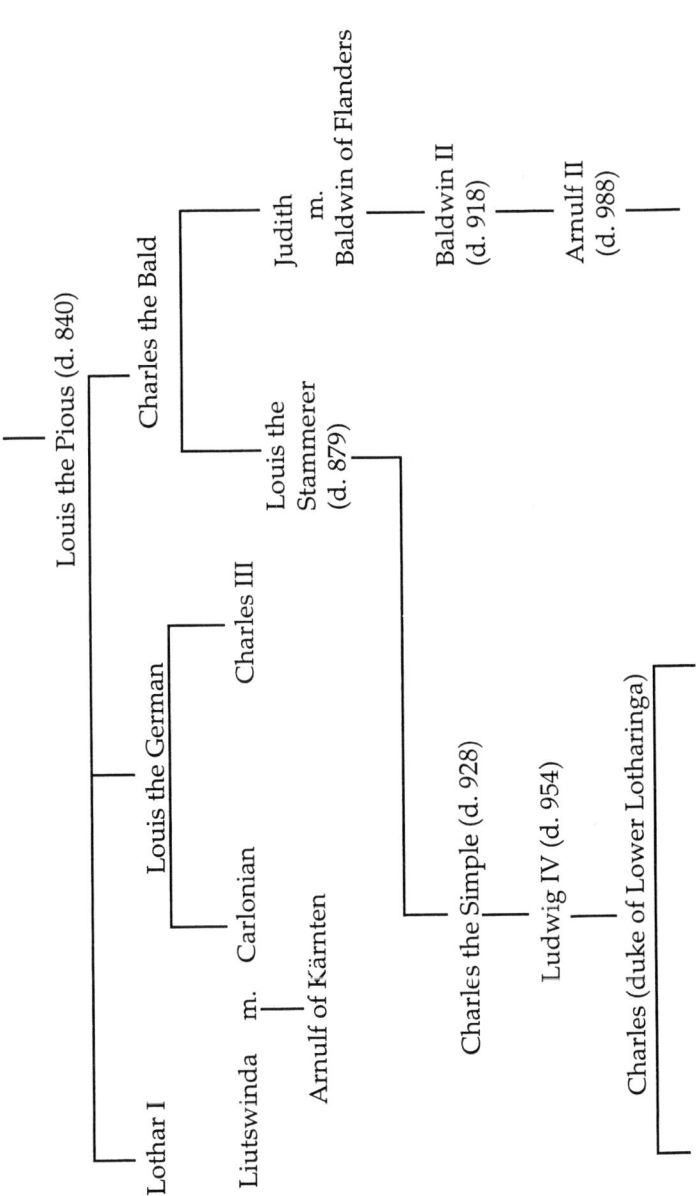

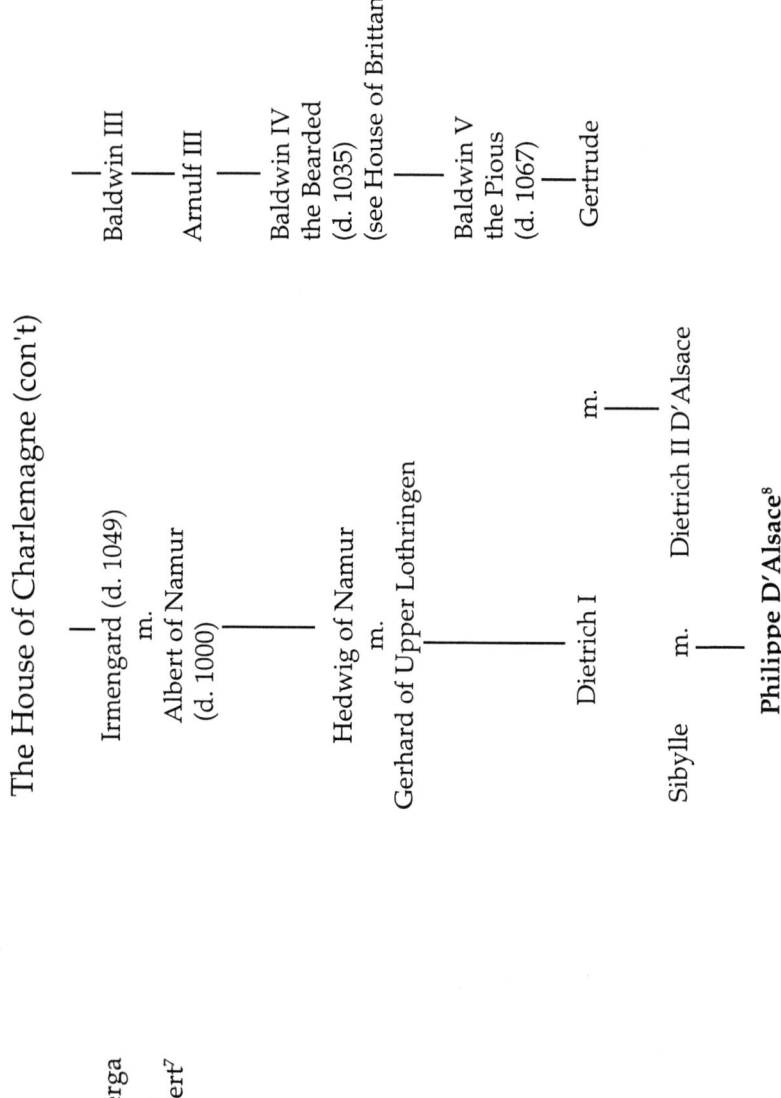

The Historical Houses of Cornwall and Brittany

Cornwall in Great Britain and Cornouaille in Brittany are as confused in the historical genealogies as they are in the Arthurian legends (West 1969:111, 120). The French "Cornouaille" can stand for either the British region or the Breton city. To make matters worse, the Houses of Cornwall and Brittany intermarried at an extremely early date.[9] By the time of Mark Conomor (d. 560) Cornwall and Brittany were united by blood ties that are almost impossible to unravel at this late date. The Dumnonian tribe of Cornwall, in particular, seems to have intermarried with the Alans who were granted the *agri deserti* in Armorica. Some of the lines of descent in these genealogies are still controversial, but we have tried to present the most accepted lineages.

In these genealogies note the number of times the name Alan and its variants appear. Keep in mind that these were the regions that produced the legends of Tristan. Names in capitals indicate Alanic names. Names in bold indicate figures who appear in the Arthurian legends.

The Historical Houses of Cornwall and Brittany

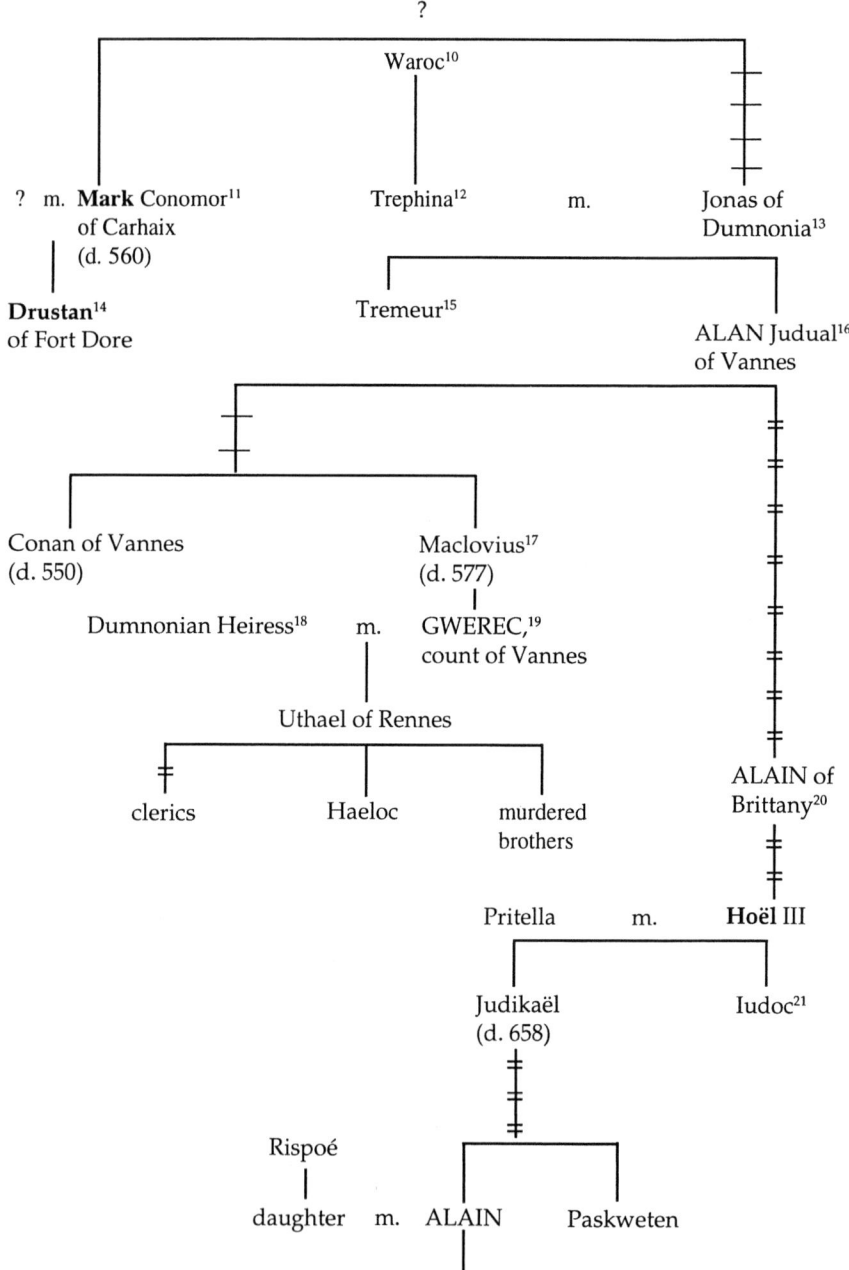

The Historical Houses of Cornwall and Brittany (con't)

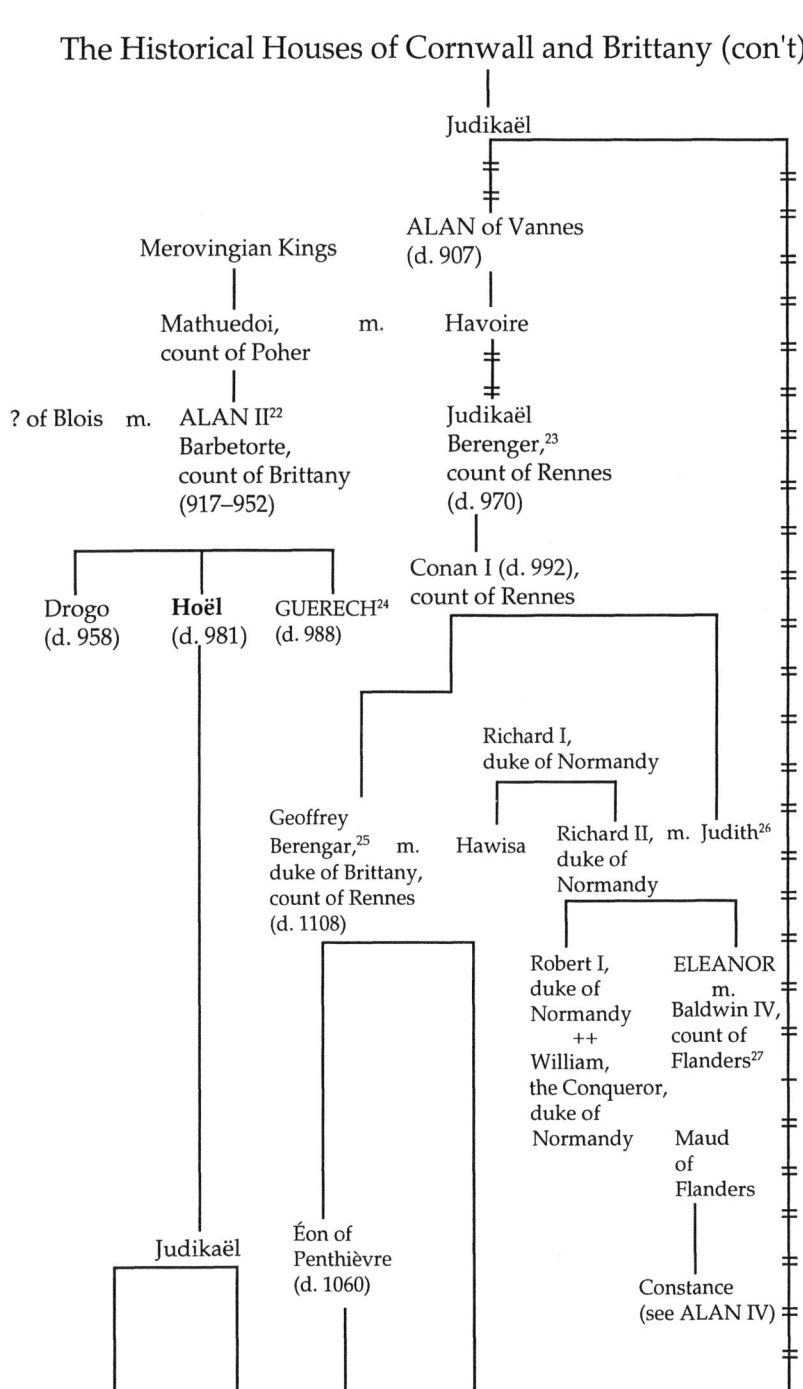

The Historical Houses of Cornwall and Brittany (con't)

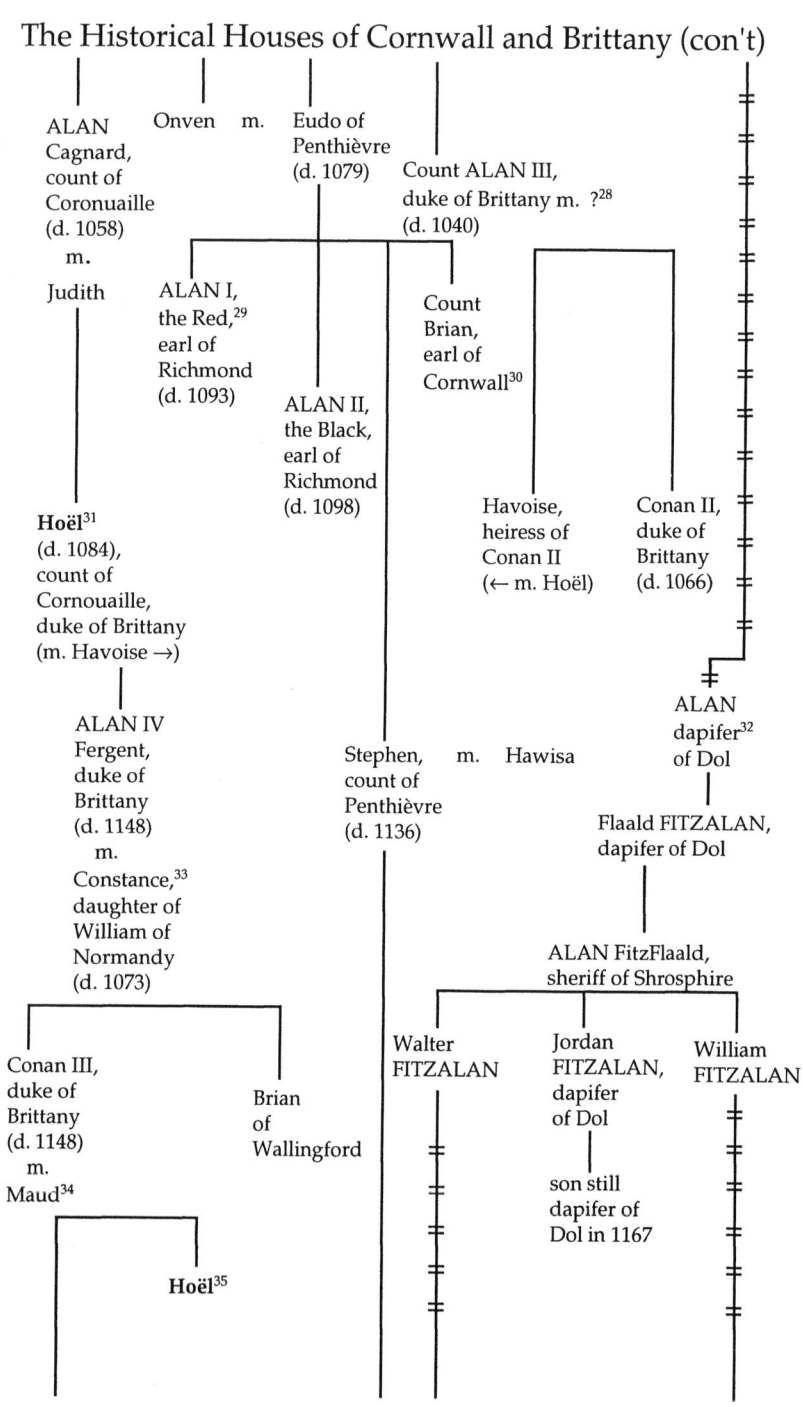

The Historical Houses of Cornwall and Brittany (con't)

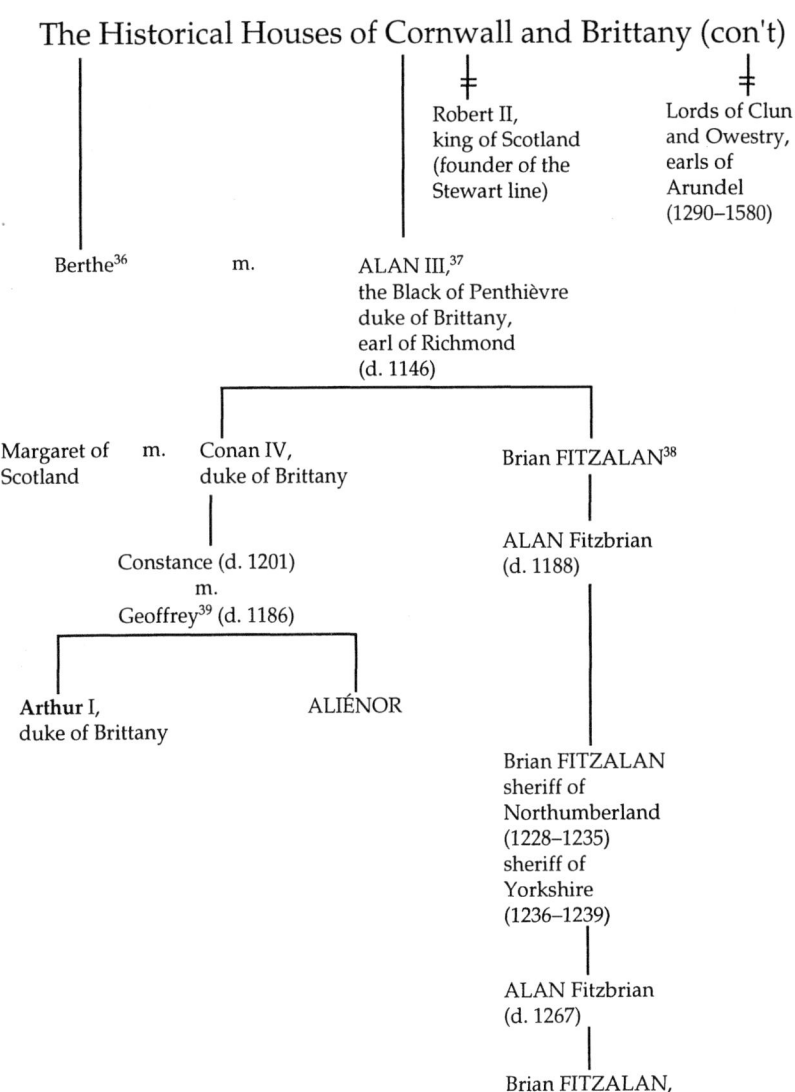

The Legendary Houses of Cornwall and Brittany

The House of Cornwall actually has two separate genealogies in the legends. One includes the family of King Mark of Cornwall (Cornwall I), while the other includes the family of Arthur's mother, Igraine (Cornwall II).[41] In the latter case the House of Cornwall intermarries at an early point in the legends with the Houses of Constantine and Orkney, so we have chosen to group these genealogies together, immediately following the legendary House of Cornwall II. As with the historical House of Cornwall both of the legendary Houses of Cornwall intermarried early with the House of Brittany, so we have chosen to present these genealogies together in this section.

The House of Cornwall I, headed by King Mark, is closely allied to the House of Constantine, whereas the House of Cornwall II (headed by Gorlois, duke of Cornwall and Igraine's husband before Uther Pendragon) provides the primary antagonists for Arthur during the early years of his reign. Note that the historical family that appears to have spawned the tales of King Mark has significant ties to the Alans of Gaul, whereas the legendary family headed by Gorlois boasts no such connections. However, also note the number of times such names as Elaine appear in these family lines.

Many of Arthur's other antagonists come from Cornwall as well, even though they are not all related to either Mark or Gorlois. The eleven kings who stand against Arthur in Malory's *Le Morte Darthur* reign over the kingdoms of Cornwall, Wales, Scotland (the "North"), and Brittany, and the king of Cornwall is based in "Nauntis [Nantes] in Bretayne [Brittany]."[42] As before we find it curious that so many "Celtic" countries are aligned against Arthur in the early days of his reign if Arthur himself was supposed to be this great "Celtic" hero. In contrast we find the historically based, Alanic-influenced family of King Mark as some of Arthur's staunchest supporters—an alliance that argues yet again for the Alano-Sarmatian tradition as the source for the legends of such figures as Arthur and Tristan.

House of Cornwall I

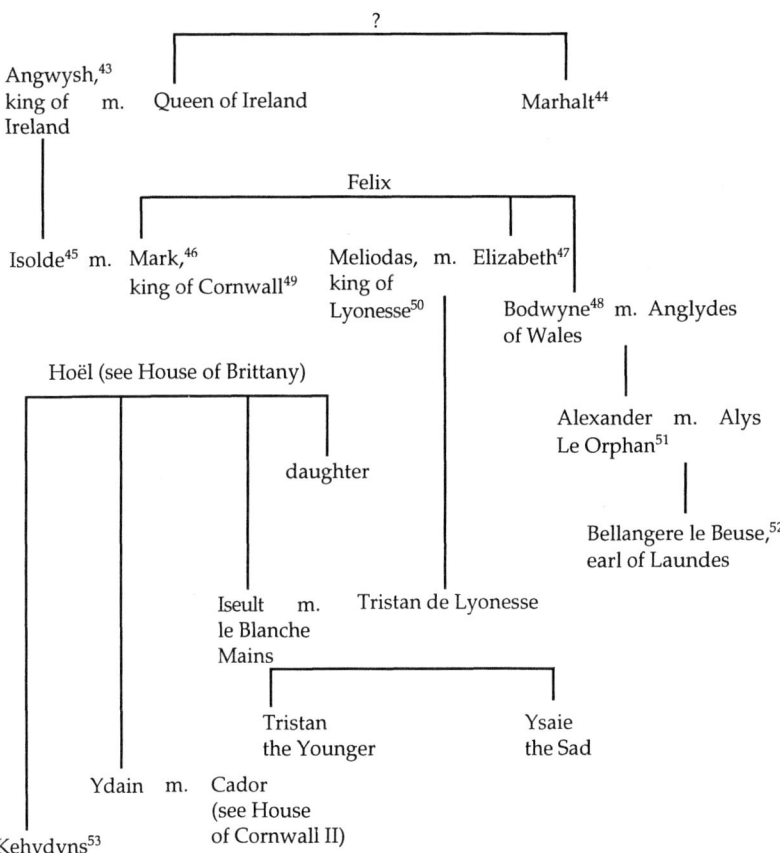

House of Cornwall II

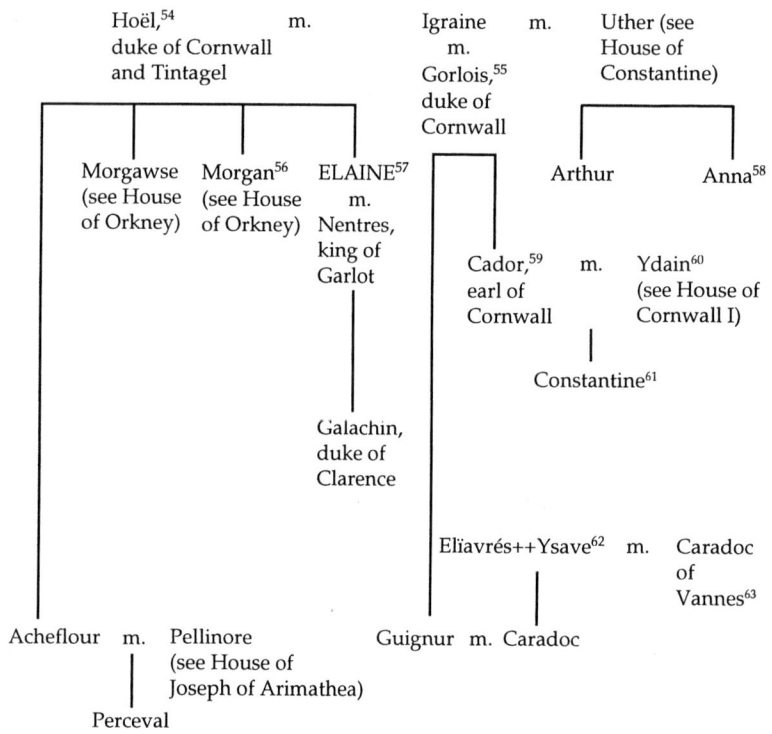

House of Constantine

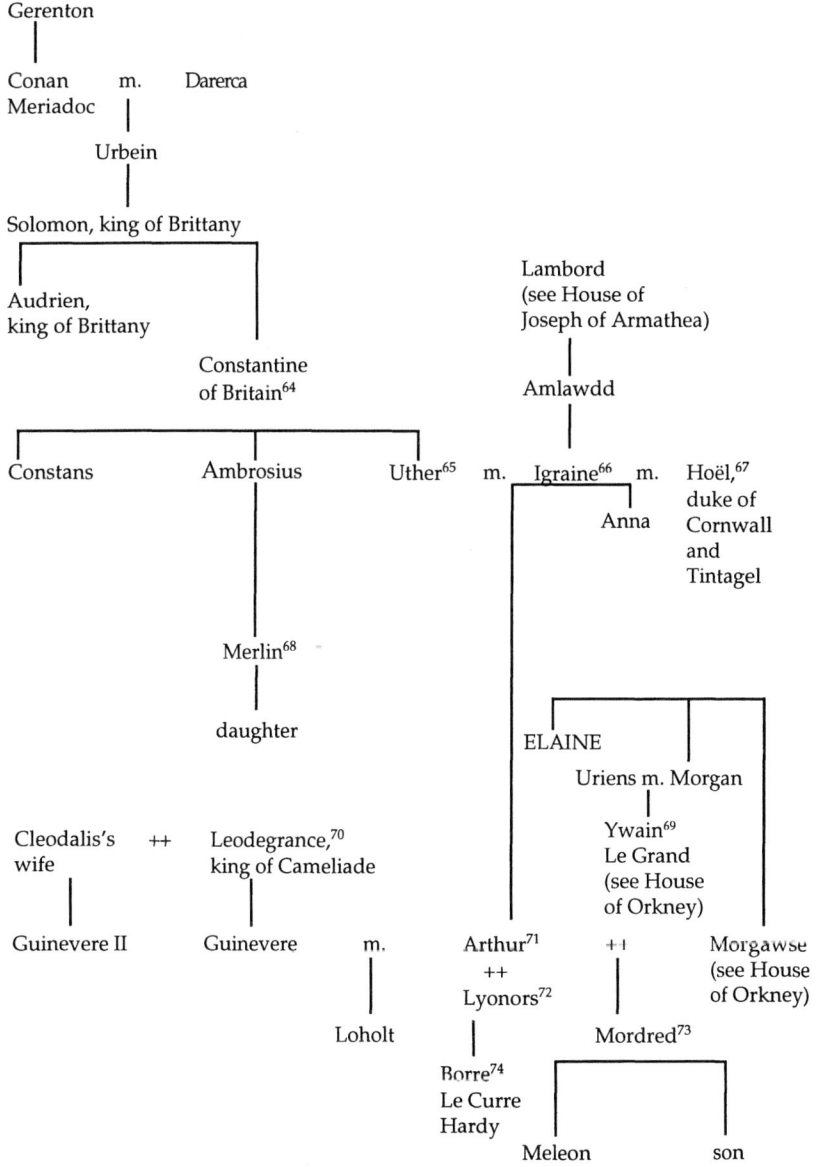

The House of Orkney

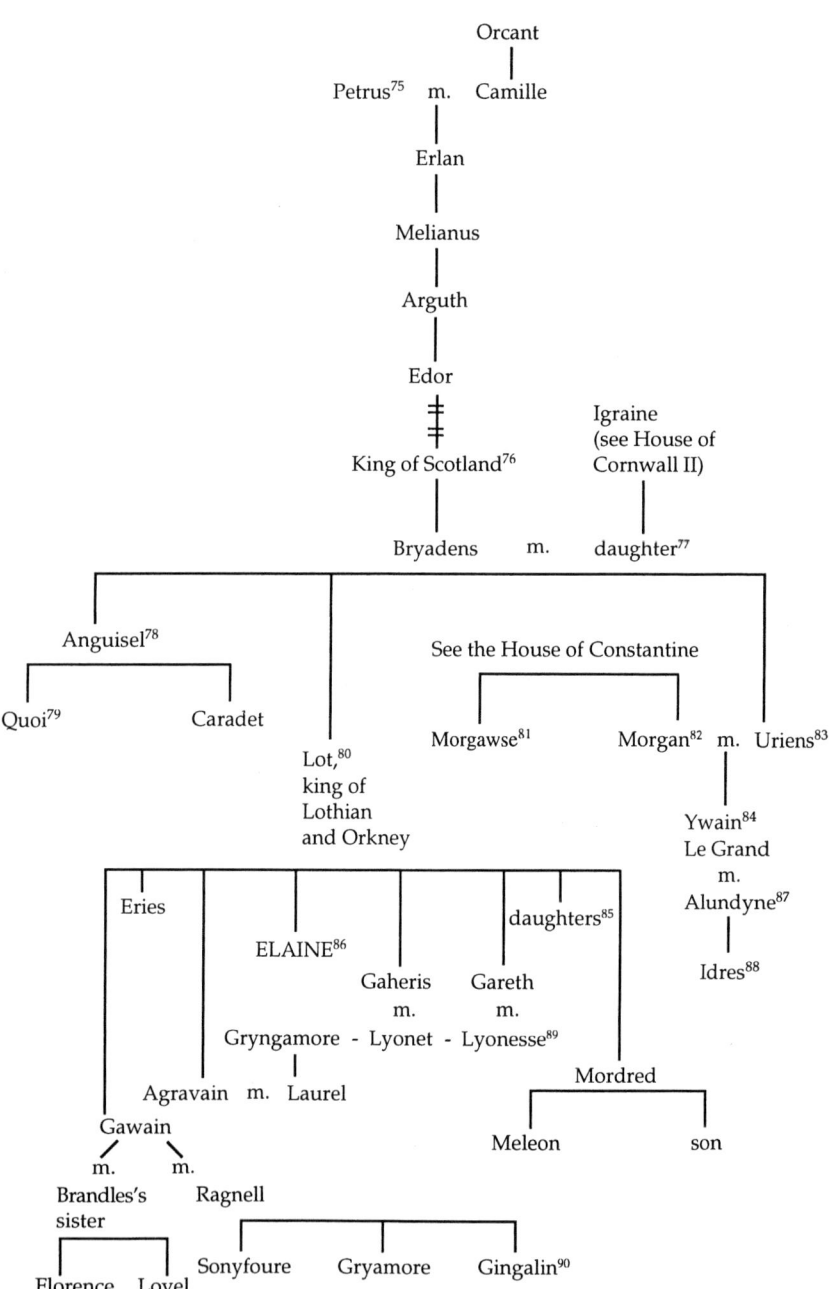

The House of Brittany

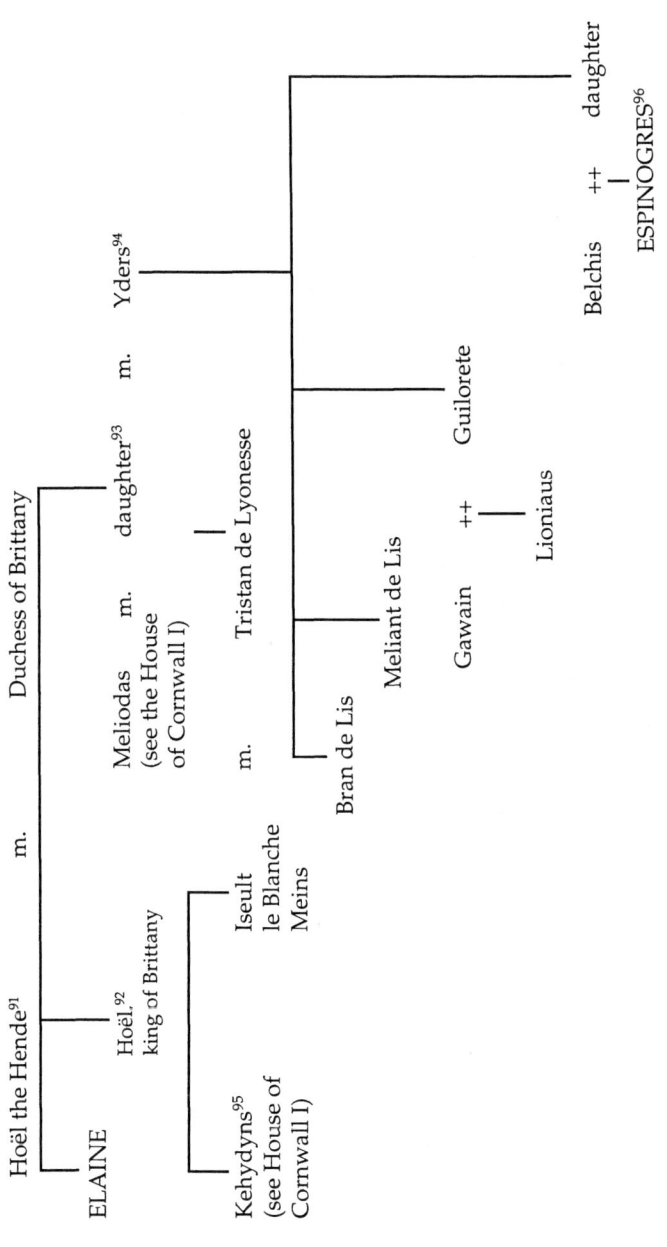

The House of Joseph of Arimathea

The genealogy of the family of Joseph of Arimathea and the history of his adventures in the east appear in the *Estoire del Saint Graal*, *Perlesvaus*, and the *Queste del Saint Graal*.[97] The *Lancelot-Grail*,[98] in particular, is the story of the House of Joseph of Arimathea.[99] This genealogy, then, is intimately connected with the story of the Grail.[100]

We would like to point out the number of times the name Alan and its variants appear in this genealogy, which includes Lancelot and the Grail Knights (Perceval, Galahad, and Bors). According to Nitze and Jenkins, Alain (Alein), the Rich Fisher, was introduced as a descendant of Joseph of Arimathea (through Joseph's sister) in Robert de Boron's *Joseph*,[101] as well as in MS P of the *Perlesvaus*, and in the Didot-*Perceval* (the last of which took its passages about Alain from Robert's *Joseph*).

Also note that this genealogy contains such names as Ban (see chap. 3) and Pelles/Pellinore/Pellam (see chaps. 9 and 10).

Key to the House of Joseph of Arimathea

++	Bastard Line
*	Grail Keeper/Fisher King
**	Maimed King
***	Grail Knight
****	Builder of the Grail Castle
*/**	Fisher King/Maimed King

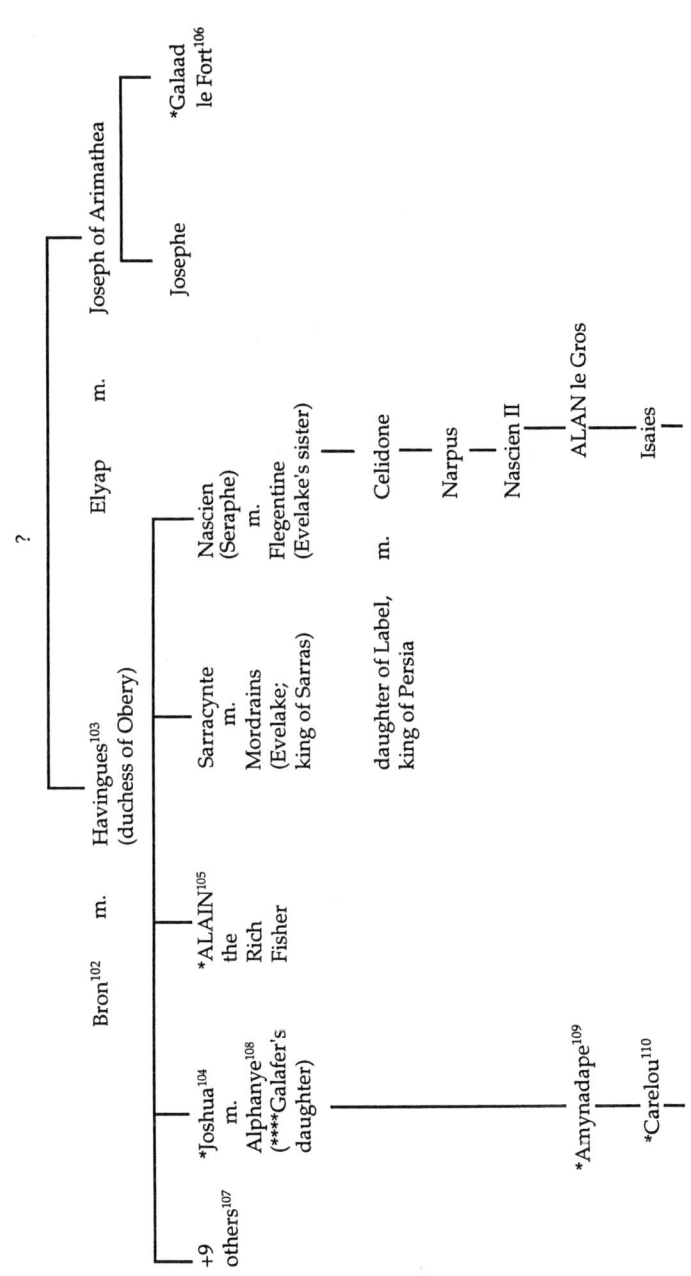

The House of Joseph of Arimathea (con't)

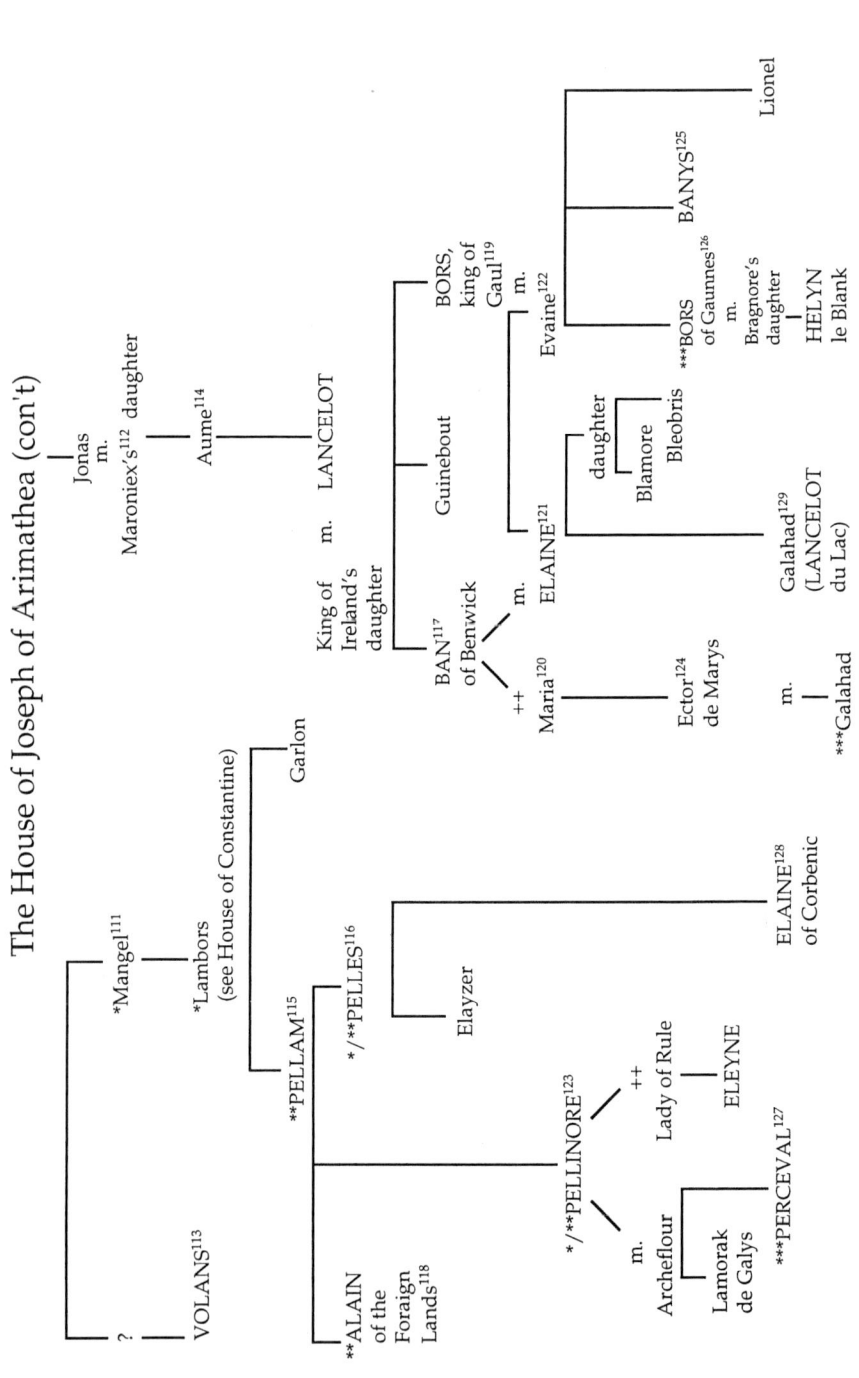

Genealogies of the Narts

Since the majority of the Narts in the tales collected from the Ossetians are from the House of the Boratæ, we have chosen to include only their genealogy of the three families of the Narts.

The House of the Boratæ

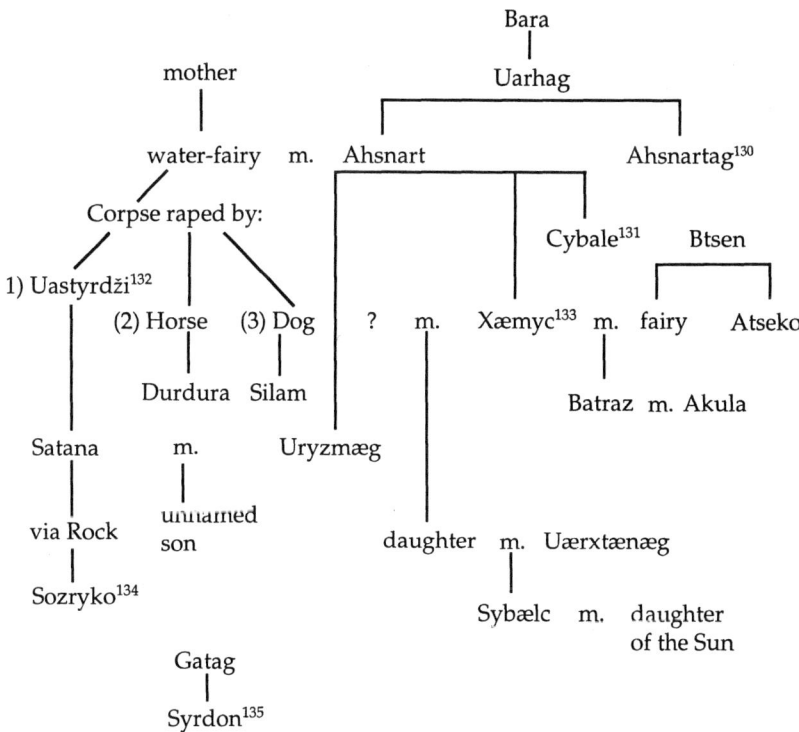

NOTES

1. Some of these alternative names and relationships are presented in many of the notes.

2. Goeric is somehow related to Arnulf, who succeeded him as bishop of Metz. See HOUSE OF CHARLEMAGNE.

3. These are relics that purport to contain the blood of Jesus.

4. This Arnulf was a relative of Goeric, count of Albi, who became Abbo, bishop of Metz, in 629 or 630 (Delaney 1980:260). It is unclear whether the blood ties between these two bishops were on the maternal or paternal side of Arnulf's family; however, the familial relationship seems to have played a role in the selection of Arnulf as Goeric's successor as bishop. Goeric himself was a descendant of the Ansbertina family (see HOUSE OF ALBI). This is the same Arnulf who defeated the Merovingian queen Brunhild.

5. This is an illegitimate line. Charles Martel eventually established his kingdom by right of conquest.

6. Carloman entered a monastery in 747, leaving Pepin as sole heir to Charles Martel's domain.

7. Cf. Lambors in the House of Joseph of Arimathea.

8. Note that this is the patron of Chrétien de Troyes.

9. The material for this section was taken in part from Nitze and Jenkins (1932–1937:4–5); Barrow 1960–1980; Cokayne 1910–1959, 5:391–2; and Round 1901:115 ff.; 129.

10. This figure is identified as the chief of the Venetii, a Gaulish tribe of mariners who were still active in the 500s (Coghlan 1991:216).

11. Mark annexed Dumnonia in 557, the same year Jonas of Dumnonia, the father of Alan Judual, died. It is conceivable that Mark's activities had something to do with Jonas's death and that the antagonism between Mark and Alan Judual stemmed from this period.

12. Sometimes Trephina is said to be a Dumnonian princess instead of a Venetian (Gaulish) princess. In one tale about a miracle of St. Gildas (Coghlan 1991:154), Mark appears as the husband of Trephina, which would place him in a love triangle with Jonas, the father of Alan Judual. This may have inspired the love triangle of Mark, Tristan, and Isolde.

Genealogies

13. There seems to have been some sort of relationship between Mark and Jonas. Perhaps one was a bastard brother to the other. Or perhaps Jonas was Mark's father-in-law.

14. This figure is one of the prototypes for Tristan.

15. Also called Gildas Junior; Coghlan 1991:206.

16. This figure was one of the prototypes for Tristan. His second name is sometimes rendered as Judwal, and he is occasionally called by his brother's name, Tremeur; Coghlan 1991:206.

17. Mark Conomor supposedly made Maclovius king; however, a "King Alain" appointed Maclovius (Maclou, Malo, Machut) as first bishop of Aleth in 578. This "King Alain" could have been Alan Judual, but it is more likely that he is just simply another relative by the same name. Hoël III was Maclovius's antagonist.

18. This may or may not have been the sister of Mark Conomor.

19. Variants of this name include Waroc, Werec, and Guérec.

20. This Alain of Brittany was a kinsman to Cadwaldar (d. 644), a candidate for the historical Galahad, but their relationship is unclear. He was sometimes referred to as Alain Le Grand.

21. This figure goes by a variety of names, including St. Josse, Jodocus, and Judoce.

22. This Alan was descended from an "ancient ruling house" in Brittany (Dunbabin 1985:82), most likely a house that was established in Roman colonial times by a member of Goar's tribe (see chaps. 1 and 9). He is the same as the Alan IV, son of Havoire and Mathuedoi. His exact relationship to Judikaël Berengar is unknown. As with so many Alains of Brittany he is known as both Count and Duke Alain.

23. The family added Rennes to its holdings when Juthael of Rennes abdicated in the 600s.

24. This is yet another form of the Alanic name Goeric.

25. Geoffrey was a direct descendant of Judikaël.

26. Judith may have been older than Geoffrey.

27. This line eventually resulted in Philippe d'Alsace, the patron of Chrétien de Troyes. See HOUSE OF CHARLEMAGNE.

28. Some sources say that Alan III married Constance, daughter of William the Conqueror (see note 34).

29. This is the Alan who led the Breton cavalry at the Battle of Hastings. He was singled out after the battle for his use of the Alanic battle tactic of the feigned retreat. Could these two Alans have inspired the Red and the Black knights of Arthurian tradition?

30. Brian was actually the younger brother of Alan I and the older brother of Alan II. It seems that for a short time after the Battle of Hastings, he was indeed earl of Cornwall in Britain.

31. This could very well be the Hoël of Brittany of Arthurian tradition.

32. "Steward" or "Seneschal."

33. There is some confusion as to whether Constance married Alan III or Alan IV. Most sources point to her as the wife of Alan IV (Douglas 1964:402), although there is the possibility that this Constance was an illegitimate daughter of William of Normandy instead of the legitimate Constance.

34. Illegitimate daughter of Henry I.

35. This son was disowned, so the dukedom passed to the husband of Berthe.

36. Following Alan's death Berthe remarried Eudes III, viscount of Porhoët (d. 1156).

37. Alan III was older than Êon of Penthièvre, thus he, not his brother, succeeded to the dukedom of Brittany. This is the Alan who was cousin to William the Conqueror. He served as regent of Normandy (along with two other of Robert's most trusted friends) and as William's chief tutor (Douglas 1964:29).

38. This could be Brian, son of Scolland, the dapifer of Alan the Black. See Nitze and Jenkins (1932–1937:5).

39. Son of Henry II and Eleanor (Aliénor) of Aquitaine.

40. This is the Brian Fitzalan who owned MS O of the *Perlesvaus*.

41. It is uncertain where Cador, duke of Cornwall, and his son, Constantine (who becomes Arthur's heir), actually fit into these genealogies. Cador may have been a son of Gorlois and Igraine, but other sources indicate that he was simply a commander under Arthur who was given Cornwall when Arthur was fighting to consolidate his kingdom. Because of this confusion we have chosen to leave Cador off the genealogical charts.

42. Vinaver 1967, 1:40.

43. For a discussion on Malory's confusion between the names Angwysh and Marhalt, see Coghlan 1991:152.

44. This villain goes by a variety of names, including Marhaus and Morholt. He is sometimes said to be Isolde's brother, rather than her

uncle, and to have two sons, Amoroldo and Golistant (Coghlan 1991:153).

45. Usually called "La Belle Isolde." Also called Isoud, Iseult, and Yseult, among other names.

46. Somehow Mark succeeds Idres as king of Cornwall, but what their relationship was is unclear.

47. Tristan's mother is also called Blanchfleur and Eliabella in some sources.

48. The character's name also appears as Boudin.

49. West (1969:111, 120) points out that many of the "Cornwall" references in the Arthurian tradition may actually refer to Cornouaille in Brittany. As far as the legend of Tristan is concerned Cornwall seems to be the better reading. In French Arthurian verse Lancïen is the name of Mark's chief residence, which West (1969:99, 111) identifies as Lantyan on the River Fowey in Cornwall (cf. Rickard 1956: 95–98; for similar names of Alanic settlements see chap. 3).

50. Meliodas sometimes appears as the brother of Mark and Pernam/Perhehan. He is also called Rivalin and Rouland in various texts. Meliodas's second wife is the daughter of King Hoël of Brittany.

West (1969:104) identifies Lyonesse as southern Scotland/Northumberland (cf. Tatlock 1950:12; Brugger 1924–1925:159–191); however, the legends suggest that␣Lyonesse is somewhere closer to Cornwall.

51. Elsewhere Alexander the Orphan is the brother of Alys and his wife is Soredamor, a sister of Gawain. In these tales he is the father of Cligés.

52. This is probably Beauce (cf. Allainville-en-Beauce; Bachrach 1973:62; see map 9).

53. Also known as Ganhardin. He was a close friend of Tristan who died because of his own love for Isolde.

54. Hoël is sometimes said to be a cousin of Gawain (West 1969:88), but how he ties into the House of Orkney is unclear in the legends.

55. Several texts also refer to Gorlois as the earl of Cornwall rather than as the duke.

56. Morgan may or may not be identical with Hermesent.

57. This daughter of Hoël and Igraine is also called Blasine.

58. This is the Anna who sometimes marries Lot instead of Morgawse.

59. Cador is somehow related to Guinevere, but the blood tie is never specified. He is also said to be a nephew of Arthur, so perhaps he is the son of an unnamed sibling of Guinevere.

60. This woman is said to be a cousin of Caradoc and a relative of Gawain (West 1969:160), although exactly how this works is unclear.

61. This is the Constantine who succeeded Arthur as king of Britain.

62. This woman, who is also called Ysaine, is said to be Arthur's niece, but by which of his sisters is unclear.

63. See HISTORICAL HOUSES OF BRITTANY AND CORNWALL for the historical genealogy of Caradoc of Vannes.

64. Also known as Biduz.

65. Welsh tradition (Coghlan 1991:29–36) provides this alternative genealogy for Uther:

66. Welsh tradition (Coghlan 1991:29–36) provides these alternative genealogies for Igraine:

Genealogies 319

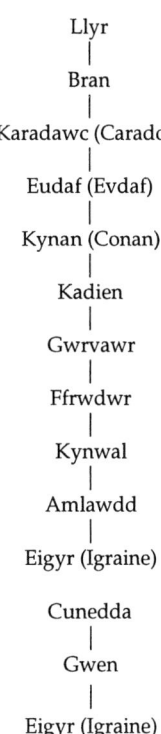

67. Sometimes Igraine's children by Hoël are Blasine, Belisent, and Hermesent. Sometimes Morgan and Morgawse are daughters by Gorlois rather than by Hoël.

68. This is a late tradition that is found in most modern Arthurian works (e.g., Mary Stewart's trilogy: *The Crystal Cave* [1970], *The Hollow Hills* [1973], and *The Last Enchantment* [1979]). In medieval tradition Merlin was the son of an "equibedes" (a type of incubus) and a nun. He was the grandson of either another figure named Merlin or of Conan of Brittany. Welsh tradition (Coghlan 1991:161) supplies the following genealogy:

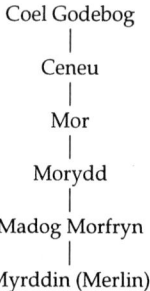

69. Ywain has a sister named Marine, but the legends are unclear regarding the identity of her mother.

70. Also called Leodegan.

71. Marginalia in the chronicle by Robert of Avesbury (at the end of the text) derived Arthur's lineage from Joseph of Arimathea (Fletcher 1906:189). In addition to Loholt, Borre, and Mordred, Arthur's children are said to include Adeluf, Amr, Arthur the Little, ELLEN (daughter), Gwydre, Gyneth (daughter), Ilinot, Llacheu, Melora (daughter), Morgan the Black, Patrick the Red, and Rowland (Coghlan 1991:35).

72. Daughter of the earl of Sanam. Also known as Lysanor.

73. Arthur's bastard son with Morgawse goes by a number of other names, the most common of which are Modred and Medraut.

74. Sometimes called Boarte (cf. Boratæ). Often confused with Loholt.

75. Marginalia in the chronicle by Robert of Avesbury (at the end of the text) derived Lot's lineage from "Petrus, consanguineous Joseph" (Fletcher 1906:189).

76. This king of Scotland is a descendent of Petrus through Brandigan and may or may not be the son of Edor. Lot is sometimes said to be the son of Edor.

77. The legends do not say which of Igraine's husbands was the father of this woman; however, it seems likely that she would have been a daughter of Hoël.

78. In some stories this figure appears as the father of Isolde. He is also called Angwys.

79. This is a variant form of the name Kay, but this figure is not the Sir Kay who was the foster-brother of Arthur.

80. Originally of Norway, later of Orkney. His marriage to a daughter of Hoël and Igraine would be incestuous if his mother was

also a daughter of Hoël and Igraine (see footnote 77). In Robert de Blois's *Beaudous* Lot also has a bastard son named Ermaleü, but the legends are unclear as to who the mother was (Ulrich 1889; West 1969:56). In Welsh tradition Lot is the husband of Anna with Mordred appearing as their eldest son:

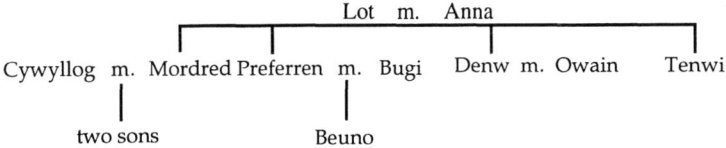

See Coghlan 1991:146.

81. Morgawse is also called Anna and Belisent in many texts.

82. Hermesent, Morgan's sister, is sometimes said to be the wife of Uriens.

83. Uriens has an entire clan of bastards, all of whom are named Ywain.

84. Also known as Yvain, Ivain, Owein, and by a host of related names.

85. The Orkney brothers are also said to have had at least two sisters. The most prominent of these are Soredamor and Clarisant. Soredamor became the mother of Cligés. Clarisant married Guiromelant and became the mother of Guigenor, who married Aalardin du Lac, one of the few figures besides Lancelot to bear the epithet "du Lac."

86. This sister of Gawain appears as Perceval's beloved in the *Didot-Perceval*.

87. This is the Lady of the Fountain, daughter of the Duke of Landuit (see chap. 3 for the loss of the initial A- in Alan names). She is the widow of Salados the Rouse (Esclados li Ros).

88. Also called Ider and Idrus the Young. Not to be confused with Idres, king of Cornwall, who ruled Cornwall during the days when Arthur was trying to consolidate his kingdom.

89. Gryngamore, Lyonet, and Lyonesse are a brother and two sisters.

90. Also called Guinglain.

91. This figure is probably taken from the historical Hoël of Cornwall. In legend Hoël of Brittany is said to be the cousin of King Arthur, although whether he belongs to Uther or Igraine's family is

unclear. There is enough confusion between the characters of Hoël, king of Brittany, and Hoël the Hende, husband of the duchess of Brittany, to suggest that these two characters are really the same person or that one was the son of the other, as we have chosen to show them here. This figure may also be identical with Hoël, duke of Cornwall and Tintagel (see HOUSE OF CORNWALL II).

92. Also called Hoël of Carhaix. This may be the brother of Morgan, Morgawse, and Elaine (see HOUSE OF CORNWALL II).

93. This woman was Tristan's stepmother. She had children by a previous marriage, one of whom died when she tried to poison Tristan.

94. This marriage occurred prior to the marriage to Meliodas, creating Tristan's stepsiblings.

95. Also called Ganhardin, Kaherdin, and Kayadyns, among other names. One particularly interesting variant is Kay Hedyus.

96. One of four knights by this name in the French verse romances (West 1969:59). Cf. chaps. 1 and 3 for discussions of the *esp* element in names. Cf. also Gontier de l'Espine (which is glossed as "Spain") and Espinoble (West 1969:59). Espaigne is the Old French word for Spain; however, we may have some conflation between this name and the *esp* element, which means "horse" in Indo-Iranian dialects, as evidenced by such comments as the one that Spain was famed for its horses (cf. West 1969:59).

97. Marx 1965:68.

98. Formerly known as the *Grand St. Graal*; Hucher 1875–1878; Jung and von Franz 1970:32 n. 71.

99. Birch-Hirschfeld 1877:31.

100. Van Coolput 1986:32. Likewise the genealogies of the Alan families of Gaul are intimately connected with the areas that produced the motif of the Chalice at the Cross.

101. Nitze and Jenkins 1932–37, 2:123. The Vulgate *Estoire* lists Bron in this role. Lovelich combines the two genealogies by making Alain the twelfth son of Bron and the second, rather than the first, Grail Keeper.

102. Bron probably derives from the biblical name Hebron (Nitze 1949:306; see chap. 10).

103. Also called Evgen.

104. In the writings of John of Glastonbury Joshua or Josue is the son of Helaius, Joseph of Arimathea's nephew (Coghlan 1991:119).

105. Other Alans in the legends include Alain, the brother of Davis, and Yonet Alain, whose family ties are as follows:

Genealogies

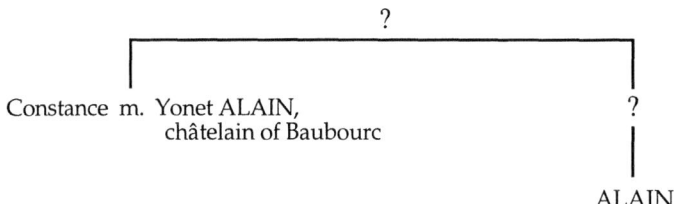

106. Also called Galaas, roi de Gales (see chap. 3 for the discussion of the *Gales/Galles* element in Arthurian names). Marries the daughter of the Roi des Lointaines Iles.

107. One of these is Elinant d'Escavalon, whose son is Alain d'Escavalon.

108. Galafer is called the king of Foraigne (also called Kalafes; Coghlan 1991:134; cf. Alain of the Foraign Lands). He was baptized as Alphasem/Alphasan. His daughter's name derives from this name (see discussion of this practice in chap. 10).

109. Also called Aminbad.

110. Also called Catheloys, Castellon, Carcelois, and Garcelos.

111. Sometimes called Manaal or Manael, hence his confusion with Aume/Manuel of Lancelot's family.

112. Like so many other figures in the Arthurian legends Maroniex is said to be the roi de Gales.

113. Also called Varlans.

114. Yet another roi de Gales. He is sometimes called Manuel.

115. Also called Pellehan.

116. He is sometimes said to be the king of Lystenoyse.

117. Other Bans in the legends include Ban (king of Gomeret), Bangon (king of Avalon; also called Bangos and Bangus), Bangort (a city in Gales and the residence of King Jozefent of Gales, whose son, Durmart, is somehow a cousin to Arthur). Bangort has been identified by some scholars as Bangor in Wales (West 1969:13–14).

118. Also spelled "Foraine" in some manuscripts.

119. Bors is called Aspyol in the *Lanzelet*.

120. Maria is the daughter of Agravadain.

121. Traditionally Elaine is descended from King David, through Solomon. She is often called "sans Pere." This could mean either "without peer" or "without a father." In the last instance compare the

genealogy of Satana in HOUSE OF THE NARTS. In the *Lanzelet* her name is Clarine.

122. The Dame du Lac is an aunt of Evaine's son, Lionel, so she must be a sister of either Ban and Bors or of Evaine and Elaine, but which way the genealogy should be portrayed is unclear.

123. Moorman and Moorman 1978:98. Some texts give the name of Perceval's father as Alain le Gros (who is descended from Nicodemus in some versions rather than from Joseph of Arimathea; e.g., Robert de Boron's *Joseph*) and Bliocadran (e.g., Chrétien's *Conte del Graal*). An alternative genealogy derives Pellinore ultimately from Nicodemus and Acheflour from Joseph of Arimathea (Wolfgang 1976:17, 22). Pellinore had at least three other mistresses as well.

124. Somehow Ector is cousin to Gifflet, who originally threw the sword Excalibur into the lake. Gifflet is the brother of Gawain's squire, Galentivet, and the son of Do de Cardueil, which West (1969:34) glosses as Carlisle in Cumberland.

125. Banys is sometimes said to be the bastard son of Ban of Benoich.

126. Bors de Gaunnes is often confused with his father, Bors, king of Gaul.

127. Wolfram's genealogy for Perceval (Coghlan 1991:182) is markedly different:

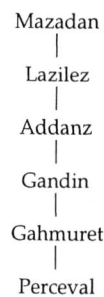

128. This woman is known by various names, including Amite and Pelle (see discussion above). Like Lancelot's mother she is often called "sans Pere."

129. In the *Lanzelet* (Webster 1951) Lancelot marries the daughter of Galagandreiz and Iblis, daughter of Iweret, as well as a winning the right to marry Guinevere and Ade, niece of Linier. He may also marry the Queen of Pluris. In this branch of the tradition Lancelot has three sons and a daughter by Iblis.

130. Twin of Ahsnart.

131. The legends do not specify who was Cybale's father, but he shares the same mother as Uryzmæg and Xæmyc.

132. "St. George."

133. Xæmyc is the twin brother of Uryzmæg. Xæmyc is sometimes said to be the son of Horčesha, whom Batraz marries to the Daughter of the Sun on the same day as Xæmyc marries the Daughter of the Moon and Batraz marries Akula.

134. This hero is sometimes called Soslan as well.

135. Syrdon is said to be a bastard of the Boratæ family.

APPENDIX 3

A Reinterpretation of Nennius's Battle List

Nennius's *Historia Brittonum* lists twelve battles, which Arthur supposedly fought against the Saxons, though other sources, such as Geoffrey of Monmouth, say they were fought against Picts and Scots either in addition to or instead of Saxons. The list probably came from a rhymed poem (Morris 1980:5; cf. Field 1999) and is certainly not in chronological order. The list consists of (1) one battle on the river Glein, (2) four battles on the river Dubglas (Douglas) in the region of Linnuis, (3) one battle on the river Bassas, (4) one battle in the wood of Celidon/Cat Coit Celidon (Coed Celydon), (5) one battle at Castle Guinnion, (6) one battle in the "city of the legion" (more properly, the "city of the legions"; Field 1999), (7) one battle on the river Tribruit, (8) one battle on Mount/Hill/Rock Agned or Breguoin, and (9) one battle at Mount/Hill/Rock Badon (Morris 1980:55).

While some of the sites have been identified linguistically, no corroborating evidence places them in the fifth- or sixth-century. Malcor's recent research has shown, however, that the list does fit the pattern of destruction for the 183-185 C.E. invasion of Britain by the Caledonii, which was most likely repelled by Lucius Artorius Castus and the Sarmatians of Bremetennacum.

In 183 the Roman forts along Dere Street collapsed before the Caledonii (Collingwood and Wright 1965, 1:406-407, 420-424, nos. 1234, 1272, 1277, and 1279-1282; Salway 1993:155, 157). Cassius Dio (73.6; Cary 1927:89) says that in 184 C.E. the invaders breached Hadrian's Wall and attacked Eboracum

(York), where they killed a "general" (i.e., the governor).[1] By the time the replacement governor, Ulpius Marcellus, arrived in 184 C.E., the fighting was no longer south of Hadrian's Wall but in southern Scotland, north of the Forth-Clyde Isthmus (Salway 1993:157). Marcellus ordered the successful commander to pursue a punitive campaign against the invaders (Salway 1993:157).[2] In 185, Castus was promoted to the rank of *dux*, a position conferred on Arthur in association with these battles. These details plus the pattern of destruction from 183 to 185 suggest that Castus was the victorious Roman commander. Consider the following scenario, which overlays Arthur's battle list on the second century battles fought by Lucius Artorius Castus.

After sacking York, the Caledonii continued south along the Roman roads, turned west and crossed the Pennines. The fort Olicana (Ilkey) lies along the most likely road and needed to be restored following the invasion (Collingwood and Wright 1965:214, no. 637). This road led them straight to the hub of roads that was guarded by Bremetennacum (Ribchester), i.e., Breguoin from the battle list.[3] Castus and his Sarmatians won and pursued the Caledonians west along the river Ribble to the tidal estuary, which fits the river Tribruit from the list.[4] Here, Castus defeated the Caledonii again.[5] The Caledonii turned south along the river Douglas. The four battles fought on the river Douglas (Dubglas) would have been within the region controlled by Bremetennacum.[6] Castus chased the Caledonii north to Eboracum (York). Castus won another battle at York, the "city of the legions" (Field 1999), driving the Caledonii north along Dere Street.[7] At Fort Vinovium (Binchester), Castus engaged the Caledonii again, giving rise to the battle at Castle Guinnion.[8] The Caledonii retreated beyond Hadrian's Wall this time, but soon left Dere Street and headed for the river Glen (Glein) in Northumbria,[9] where Castus defeated them and continued the pursuit, possibly now under orders from Marcellus to exterminate the invaders. He and his Sarmatians caught the Caledonii in the Cat Coit Celidon (Coed Celydon) and inflicted yet another defeat on them.[10] The few invaders who survived, fled for home. The next battle was at the river Bassas, possibly somewhere in Scotland (Jackson 1945:48). The last battle was at Dumbarton Rock (Mount Badon) in Strathclyde.[11]

Although Nennius says that Arthur's opponents were Saxons and most later authors copy him, Geoffrey of Monmouth had Arthur fight battles against the invading Picts and Scots at Eboracum (York) twice, on the Duglas (river Douglas), and at Alclud (Dumbarton Rock; Thorpe 1966:218ff.). This is precisely what happened in the second-century, with the Caledonii killing the governor at York, continuing to raid as far as the river Douglas in Lancashire, then being driven back north of the Antonine Wall.[12]

NOTES

1. Nennius (chap. 30; Morris 1980:24) recasts this story as happening to Septimius Severus, who did die at York but of a disease rather than as a result of battle. Whereas Cassius Dio (73.2; Cary 1927:87) says that the barbarians "cut down a general together with his troops" (describing a battle presumably near York during the invasion of 184), Nennius (chap. 23; Morris 1980:24) says that Severus was "killed at York with his generals." The phrasing is close enough to spark speculation that Nennius was working in part from a copy of Dio's *Roman History*.

2. Coins from 184 and 185 commemorate the Roman victories (Salway 1993:157). The scope of the slaughter attributed to Arthur against the Picts and Scots by Geoffrey of Monmouth (Thorpe 1966:219) was definitely consistent with Marcellus's orders to his commander in Scotland (Salway 1993:157; Cassius Dio 73.6; Cary 1927:89).

3. The battle at Bremenium (High Rochester; Jackson 1949-1950:49) possibly took place as Castus pushed the Caledonii north, but Jackson's etymology could just as easily reflect Bremetennacum, which the archaeological record supports (e.g., Collingwood and Wright 1965:196-197, no. 587 shows damage to a building outside fort Bremetennacum.). Jackson dismisses the Mount Agned variant as a corruption.

4. The rivers Dow and Douglas flow into the Ribble's estuary, giving three rivers at an estuary, which some scholars have identified with the Tribruit (Jackson 1945:51). The Ribble also empties into the sea shortly after exiting a limestone landscape and pass that was guarded by Bremetennacum, a place that fits Jackson's "The Strand of the Pierced or Broken 'Place)" (Jackson 1945:52).

5. Geoffrey has the battles on the Douglas occur *after* the battle at the "city of the legions" (York; Thorpe 1966:213). This could mean that the Douglas referred to is the Douglas Waterway south of Glasgow, with the battlefield somewhere southwest of the place where the Douglas joins the Clyde. This alternative scenario would move these battles later in the hypothetical sequence.

6. Jackson (1945:47-48) decided that Lindsey in Lincolnshire was the probable source for "Linnuis." Jackson's etymology, however, would give the "original" as *Linnens and require a shift of a "d" to an "n." Plus, there is still the problem that there is no Douglas river in Lindsey. In Diocletian's time (ca. 314 C.E.), Lindum did control the province of Flavia Caesariensis, which reached from the east coast west to a point just south of the river Douglas. Nennius's vague command of the geography of Roman Britain possibly led him to think the river Douglas lay within the ancient borders of the region controlled by Lindum. The river Douglas actually fell within the boundaries for Britanniae II.

7. Evidence of a Sarmatian presence along Dere Street can be seen in the fact that some bricks (now lost) found at Bainesse near the site of ancient Cataractonium (modern Catterick) bear the stamp "BSAR" (Collingwood and Wright 1992, 2 [Fascicule 4]:207, no. 2479; cf. Jarrett 1994:43).

8. Anscombe (1904:110), Faral (1929:142), Lot (1934:69, 195), Johnstone (1934:381), and Crawford (1935:287) all agree with the identification as Binchester, and Jackson admits that some manuscripts do attest the form Vinnovion, which could possibly render Guinnion in Old Welsh (Jackson 1945:49).

9. Crawford (1935:285) points out that *"in ostium fluminis glein"* could mean a "river- junction." Jackson (1945:46) prefers the Northumberland Glen, though admits the Lincolnshire Glen is a possibility.

10. This would be the Coed Celydon, a wood "within range of Glasgow and Carlisle, perhaps the moorlands round the upper Clyde and Tweed valleys" (Jackson 1945:48).

Attridge, Harold W., and Robert A. Oden, trans. 1976. Lucian of Samosata, *The Syrian Goddess = (De dea Syria)*. Missoula, Montana: Scholars Press for the Society of Biblical Literature.

Bachrach, Bernard S. 1967. "The Alans in Gaul." *Traditio* 23:476–489.

Bachrach, Bernard S. 1969. "Another Look at the Barbarian Settlements in Southern Gaul." *Traditio* 25:354–358.

Bachrach, Bernard S. 1972. *Merovingian Military Organization, 481–751*. Minneapolis: University of Minnesota Press.

Bachrach, Bernard S. 1973. *A History of the Alans in the West*. Minneapolis: University of Minnesota Press.

Baigent, Michael, Richard Leigh, and Henry Lincoln. 1982. *Holy Blood, Holy Grail*. New York: Delacorte.

Baines, Keith, trans. 1962. *Malory's Le Morte d'Arthur*. New York and Scarborough: New American Library.

Barber, E.J.W. 1991. *Prehistoric Textiles*. Princeton: Princeton University Press.

Barber, Richard. 1961. *King Arthur: Hero and Legend*. New York: Dorset.

Barber, Richard. 1972. *The Figure of Arthur*. Totowa: Rowman and Littlefield.

Barrow, G.W.S., ed. 1960–1980. *Regesta Regum Scottorum, 1153–1424*, Vol. 1. Edinburgh: University Press.

Barthélémy, Andre. 1987. *Le Graal au XIIe siècle: sa première révélation*. Ferrières: Poliphile.

Batts, Michael. 1971. *Gottfried von Strassburg*. New York: Twayne.

Baumgartner, Emmanuele. 1981. *L'arbe et le pain: essai sur La queste del Saint Graal*. Paris: Société d'édition d'enseignement supérieur.

Bayer, Hans. 1983. *Gral: die hochmittelalterliche Glaubenskrise im Spiegel der Literatur*. Stuttgart: Hiersemann.

Beck, Heinrich, et al., eds. 1881. *Reallexikon der Germanischen Altertumskunde*. Berlin and New York: De Gruyter.

Bell, A., ed. 1860. Geffrei Gaimar, *L'Estoire des Engleis*. Oxford: Blackwell.

Benecke, G.F., and Karl Lachmann, eds. 1968. Hartmann von Aue, *Iwein: Eine Erzählung*. 7th ed. edited by Ludwig Wolff. Berlin: de Gruyter.

Benveniste, E. 1959. *Études sur la langue ossète*. Paris: Klincksieck.

11. This identification is based in part on Geoffrey on Monmouth's portrayal of Arthur's major battle taking place at Dumbarton Rock rather than at Mount Badon (Thorpe 1966:218).

12. Gildas and other chroniclers corroborate this pattern for Arthur's battles against the Picts and Scots.

References Cited

Aarne, Antti. 1961. *Types of the Folktale*. Enlarged and translated Thompson. *FF Communications* 184. Helsinki: Suom Tiedeakatemia Academia Scientiarum Fennica.

Abaev, V.I. 1949. *Osetinskij jazyk i fol'klor*. Vol. 1. Moscow: N.p.

Abaev, V.I. 1960. *The Pre-Christian Religion of the Alans*. M Oriental Literature.

Abaev, V.I. 1964. *A Grammatical Sketch of Ossetic*. Translated by Ste Hill. Edited by Alison Adams. The Hague: Mouton.

Adams, Alison, ed. 1983. *Yder*. Cambridge: Boydell and Brewer.

Adolf, Helen. 1947. "New Light on Oriental Sources for Wolf *Parzival* and Other Grail Romances." *Publications of the M Language Association* 62:306–324.

Alcock, Leslie. 1971. *Arthur's Britain: History and Archeology, A.D. 634*. Newton Abbot: David and Charles.

Alton, Johann, ed. 1889. *Le Roman de Marques de Rome*. Tübin Litterarische Verein in Stuttgart.

Alvar, Carlos, ed. 1980. *Demanda del Santo Graal/Anonimo*. Mad Editora Nacional.

Anderson, W.B. 1963–1965. Sidonius Apollinaris, *Poems and Let* Cambridge: Harvard University Press. 2 vols.

App, August S. 1929. *Lancelot in English Literature*. Washington: Cath University of America.

Ashe, Geoffrey. 1981. "A Certain Very Ancient Book." *Speculum* 56:3(323.

Ashe, Geoffrey. 1985. *The Discovery of King Arthur*. New Yo Doubleday.

Atchity, Kenneth John. 1978. *Homer's Iliad: The Shield of Memor* Carbondale and Edwardsville: Southern Illinois University Pres

Bergmann, Frederic Guillaume. 1870. *The San Greal: An Inquiry into the Origin and Signification of the Romances of the San Greal*. Edinburgh: Edmonston and Douglas.

Bertoni, Guilio. 1922. *Poeti e poesie del medio evo e del rinascimento*. Modena: Editore Cav. Umberto Orlandini.

Biblioteca Sanctorum. 1961. Rome: Società Grafica Romana.

Bidez, Joseph, ed. 1913. *Kirchengeschichte*. Leipzig: Hinrichs.

Birch-Hirschfeld, Adolf. 1877. *Die Sage vom Gral*. Leipzig: Vogel.

Birks, Walter, and R.A. Gilbert. 1987. *The Treasure of Montségur*. Wellingborough: Aquarian.

Blair, Peter Hunter. 1963. *Roman Britain and Early England: 55 B.C.–A.D. 871*. New York: Norton.

Blockley, R.C. 1983. *The Fragmentary Classicizing Historians of the Later Roman Empire: Eunapius, Olympiodorus, Priscus and Malchus*. Liverpool: Cairns. 2 vols.

Bogdanow, Fanni. 1966. *The Romance of the Grail: A Study of the Structure and Genesis of a Thirteenth-Century Arthurian Prose Romance*. Manchester: Manchester University Press; New York: Barnes & Noble.

Bohigas, Pedro. 1957–1962. *El Baladro del Sabio Merlin, según el texto de la edición de Burgos de 1498*. Barcelona: Selecciones Bibliófilas. 3 vols.

Bolle, Kees. 1970. "In Defense of Euhemerus." In *Myth and Law among the Indo-Europeans*. Edited by Jaan Puhvel. Berkeley, Los Angeles, and London: University of California Press, pp. 19–38.

Borius, R., ed. 1965. *Constance de Lyone: Vie de Saint Germain d'Auxerre*. Paris: Éditions du Cerf.

Branca, Daniela Delcorno. 1971. "I cantari di Tristano." *Lettere italiane* 23:289–305.

Brengle, Richard L., ed. 1964. *Arthur, King of Britain*. Englewood Cliffs: Prentice-Hall.

Brewer, D.S., and A.E. Owen. 1975. *The Thornton Manuscript (Lincoln Cathedral MS. 91)*. London: Scolar. Revised 1977.

Brodtkorb, Lorna Bullwinkle, ed. 1965. *Le Roman de Pelyarmenus*. Ann Arbor: University Microfilms.

Bromwich, Rachel. 1960–1961. "Celtic Dynastic Themes and the Breton Lays." *Études celtiques* 9:439–474.

Bromwich, Rachel. 1961. *Trioedd Ynys Prydein*. Cardiff: University of Wales Press. 2nd ed. 1978.

Bromwich, Rachel. 1969. "*Trioedd Ynys Prydain*" in *Welsh Literature and Scholarship*. Cardiff: University of Wales Press.

Brown, A.C.L. 1900. "The Round Table Before Wace." In *Studies and Notes in Philology and Literature*, Vol. 7:183–205. Boston: Ginn.

Bruce, J. Collingwood. 1978. *Hand-book to the Roman Wall, with the Cumbrian Coast and Outpost Forts*. 13th edition. Edited and enlarged by Charles Daniels. Newcastle-upon-Tyne: H. Hill.

Bruce, James Douglas, ed. 1903. *Le Morte Arthur: A Romance in Stanzas of Eight Lines*. MS Harley 2252. London: Oxford University Press.

Bruce, James Douglas. 1918. "Pelles, Pellinore and Pellean in the Old French Arthurian Romances." *Modern Philology* 16/7:337–350.

Bruce, James Douglas. 1923. *The Evolution of Arthurian Romance from the Beginnings down to the Year 1300*. Göttingen: Vandenhoeck and Ruprecht; Baltimore: Johns Hopkins Press. 2 vols.

Bruce, James Douglas. 1958. *The Evolution of Arthurian Romance from the Beginnings to the Year 1300*. 2nd ed. Gloucester: Peter Smith. 2 vols.

Brugger, Ernst. 1905. "Ein Beitrag zur arthurischen Namenforschung: Alain de Gomeret." In *Aus Romanischen Sprachen und Literaturen: Festschrift Heinrich Morf*. Halle: Niemeyer, pp. 53–96.

Brugger, Ernst. 1924–1925. "Loenois as Tristan's Home." *Modern Philology* 22:159–191.

Brugger, Ernst. 1927. "Eigennamen in den Lais der Marie de France." *Zeitschrift für französische Sprache Litteratur* 49:201–252, 381–484.

Bryant, Nigel. 1978. *The High Book of the Grail—A Translation of the Thirteenth-Century Romance of* Perlesvaus. Ipswich: Brewer; Totowa: Rowman & Littlefield.

Buck, Carl Darling. 1949. *A Dictionary of Selected Synonyms in the Principal Indo-European Languages*. Chicago: University of Chicago Press.

Bumke, Joachim. 1981. *Wolfram von Eschenbach*. 5th ed. Stuttgart: Metzler.

Burnham, Barry., and John Wacher. 1990. *The Small Towns of Roman Britain*. Berkeley and Los Angeles: University of California Press.

Bury, J.B. 1889. *History of the Later Roman Empire: From the Death of Theodosius I to the Death of Justinian*. London and New York: Macmillan. 2 vols.

Buschinger, Danielle. 1972. "La structure du *Tristrant* d'Eilhart von Oberg." *Études germaniques* 27:1–26.

Buschinger, Danielle, ed. and trans. 1976. *Eilhart von Oberge*, Tristrant: *Édition diplomatique des manuscrits et traduction en français moderne avec introduction, notes et index*. Göppingen: Kümmerle.

Bussmann, Hadumod, ed. 1969. Tristrant: *Synoptischer Druck der ergänzten Fragmente mit der gesamten Parallelüberlieferung*. Tübingen: Niemeyer.

Campbell, David E., trans. 1972. *The Tale of Balain, from the Romance of the Grail, a 13th Century French Prose Romance*. Evanston: Northwestern University Press.

Campbell, J.F. 1860–1862. *Popular Tales of the West Highlands*. Edinburgh: Edmonston and Douglas.

Campbell, James, ed. 1982. *The Anglo-Saxons*. Ithaca: Cornell University Press.

Campion, J., and F. Holthausen, eds. 1913. *Sir Perceval of Galles*. Heidelberg: Winter.

Carman, J. Neale. 1973. *A Study of the Pseudo-Map Cycle of Arthurian Romance*. Wichita: University of Kansas Press.

Carter, Henry Hare. 1967. *Liuro de Josep Abaramatia*. Paleographical ed., with introduction, linguistic study, notes, plates and glossary by Henry Hare Carter. Chapel Hill: University of North Carolina Press.

Cary, Earnest, trans. 1927. *Dio's Roman History*, Vol. 9. London: Heinemann; New York: Putnam.

Cavendish, Richard. 1978. *King Arthur and the Grail: The Arthurian Legends and Their Meaning*. London: Weidenfeld and Nicolson.

Chadwick, Nora K. 1962. *The Age of Saints in the Early Celtic Church*. London and New York: Oxford University Press.

Chadwick, Nora K. 1965. "The Colonization of Brittany from Celtic Britain." *Proceedings of the British Academy* 51:235–299.

Chadwick, Nora K. 1969. *Early Brittany*. Cardiff: University of Wales Press.

Chadwick, Nora K. 1970. *The Celts*. Harmondsworth and New York: Penguin.

Chagnon, Napoleon A. 1983. *Yanomanö: The Fierce People*. 3rd edition. New York: Holt, Rinehart and Winston.

Chambers, E.K. 1927. *Arthur of Britain*. London: Sidgwick and Jackson.

Charvet, Louis. 1967. *Des Vaus d'Avalon à la Queste du Graal*. Paris: Corti.

Chavannes, Éd., and P. Pelliot. 1911. "Un traité manichéen retrouvé en Chine." *Journale asiatique* 17:499–617.

Child, Francis James, ed. 1884. *The English and Scottish Popular Ballads*. Boston: Houghton-Mifflin. 5 vols.

Cirlot, J.E. 1983. *A Dictionary of Symbols*. Translated by Jack Sage. 2nd ed. New York: Philosophical Library.

Clark, Grahame, and Stuart Piggott. 1965. *Prehistoric Societies*. New York: Knopf.

Clarke, Basil, trans. 1973. Geoffrey of Monmouth, *Vita Merlini*. Cardiff: University of Wales Press.

Clay, C.T. 1921. "Notes on the Origin of the Fitzalans of Bedale." *Yorkshire Archaeological Journal* 30:281–290.

Coghlan, Ronan. 1991. *The Encyclopedia of Arthurian Legends*. Shaftesbury, Dorset: Element.

Cokayne, George E. 1910–1959. *The Complete Peerage of England, Scotland, Ireland, Britain and the United Kingdom . . .*, Vol. 5. Edited by the Hon. Vicary Gibbs and H.A. Doubleday. London: St. Catherine.

Colafrancesco, Pasqua, and Matteo Massaro. 1986. *Concordanze dei Carmina Latina Epigraphica*. Bari: Edipuglia.

Colarusso, John. 1984. "Parallels Between the Circassian Nart Sagas, the Ṛg Veda and Germanic Mythology." *South Asian Horizons* 1:1–28.

Colarusso, John. 1989. "The Women of the Myths: The Satanya Cycle." *Annual of the Society for the Study of Caucasia* 3:3–11.

Collingwood, R.G., and R.P. Wright. 1965. *The Roman Inscriptions of Britain*. Oxford: Clarendon. 2 vols.

Comrie, Bernard. 1981. *The Languages of the Soviet Union*. New York: Cambridge University Press.

Comrie, Bernard. 1987. *The World's Major Languages*. New York: Oxford University Press.

Cooper-Oakley, Isabel. 1900. *Masonry and Medieval Mysticism: Traces of a Hidden Tradition*. London: Theosophical Publishing House.

Corcoran, John X.W.P. 1968. "Celtic Mythology." In *New Larousse Encyclopedia of Mythology*. London: Prometheus.

Courcelle, Pierre. 1948. *Histoire littéraire des grandes invasions germaniques*. Paris: Hachette.

Cowen, Janet, ed. 1969. Sir Thomas Malory, *Le Morte d'Arthur*. Harmondsworth and New York: Penguin. 2 vols.

Coyajee, Jehangir Cooverjee, Sir. 1939. *Iranian & Indian Analogues of the Legend of the Holy Grail*. Bombay: Taraporevala.

Cumont, F. 1910. *The Mysteries of Mithra*. Chicago: University of Chicago Press.

Cuvier, Georges. 1835. *Discours sur les révolutions du globe*. In *Ossements fossiles*. Paris: Docagne.

Dalton, O.M., trans. 1915. *The Letters of Sidonius*. Oxford: Clarendon. 2 vols.

Dauzat, Albert, and Ch. Rostaing. 1963. *Dictionnaire étymologique des noms de lieux en France*. Paris: Larousse.

Dauzat, Albert, Jean Dubois, and Henri Mitterand. 1964. *Nouveau dictionnaire étymologique et historique*. Paris: Larousse.

Davidson, H.R. Ellis. 1964. *Gods and Myths of Northern Europe*. Harmondsworth and New York: Penguin.

Day, Mildred Leake, ed. and trans. 1984. *The Rise of Gawain, Nephew of Arthur (De Ortu Waluuanii Nepotis Arturi)*. New York and London: Garland.

De Grummond, Nancy Thomson, ed. 1982. *A Guide to Etruscan Mirrors*. Tallahassee, Florida: Archaeological News, Inc.

Deinert, Wilhelm, ed. 1965. *Wolfram von Eschenbach*. 6th ed. Tübingen: Niemeyer.

Delaney, John J. 1980. *Dictionary of Saints*. New York: Doubleday.

Delcourt-Angelique, Janine. 1984. "Le Graal de Chrétien de Troyes: Pour Wolfram von Eschenbach, un 'Objet non Identifié' au Livre V; au Livre IX, une Pierre Baptisée Lapsit Exillîs. Au Terme de Quelle Évolution?" In *Chrétien de Troyes et le Graal: Colloque arthurien belge de Bruges*. Paris: Nizet, pp. 89–105.

Dent, John. 1985. "Three Cart Burials from Wetwang, Yorkshire." *Antiquity* 59/226:85–92.

De Sélincourt, Aubrey, trans. 1972. Herodotus, *The Histories*. Revised by A.R. Burn. Harmondsworth and New York: Penguin.

De Vic, Claude, and J. Vaissete. 1879. *Histoire Générale du Languedoc*, Vol. 7. Toulouse: Privat.

De Vries, Jan. 1942. "Rood, wit, zwart." *Volkskunde* 2:1–10.

De Vries, Jan. 1963. *Heroic Song and Heroic Legend*. London: Oxford University Press.

De Vries, M., and E. Verwijs, eds. 1863. Jacob Van Maerlant, *Spiegel Historiael*. Leiden: Brill. 3 vols.

Dewing, H.B., trans. 1916. Procopius, *History of the Wars, Books III and IV*, Vol. 2. London: Heinemann; New York: Putnam.

Dewing, H.B., trans. 1968. Procopius, *History of the Wars*, Vol. 3. London: Heinemann.

Dirr, Adolf. 1912. *Praktiches Lehrbuch der ostarmenischen Sprache*. Vienna and Leipzig: Hartleben.

Dirr, Adolf. 1925. *Caucasian Folk Tales*. New York: Dutton.

Dixon, Karen R., and Pat Southern. 1992 *The Roman Cavalry: From the First to the Third Century A.D.* London: B. T. Batsford.

Dizionario enciclopedico dei comuni d'Italia. 1950. Milan: Antica Casa Editrice.

Donini, Guido, and Gordon B. Ford, Jr., trans. 1966. *Isidore of Seville's History of the Kings of the Goths, Vandals, and Suevi*. Leiden: Brill.

Dopsch, Alfons. 1937. *The Economic and Social Foundation of European Civilization*. New York: Harcourt, Brace; London: Kegan Paul, Trench, Trübner.

Douglas, David C. 1964. *William the Conqueror*. London: Eyre & Spottiswoode; Berkeley, Los Angeles, and London: University of California Press.

Doutrepont, Georges. 1939. *Les mises en prose des épopées et des romans chevaleresques du XIVe au XVIe siècle*. Brussels: Mémoires de l'Académie Royale de Belgique, Classe de Lettres.

Draak, Maartje, ed. 1979. *Lancelot en het hert met de witte voet*. Culemborg: Tjeenk Willink.

Duckett, Eleanor. 1972. *Medieval Portraits from East and West*. Ann Arbor: University of Michigan Press.

Dumézil, Georges. 1930. *Légendes sur les Nartes*. Paris: Librairie ancienne Honoré Champion.

Dumézil, Georges. 1941. *Jupiter Mars Quirinus*. Paris: Gallimard.

Dumézil, Georges. 1946. "Les 'énarées' scythique et la grossesse du Narte Hamyc." *Latomus* 5:249–255.

Dumézil, Georges. 1958. *L'idéologie tripartie des Indo-Européens*. Brussels: Collection Latomus, Vol. 31.

Dumézil, Georges. 1960. "Les trois 'trésors des ancêtres' dans l'épopée Narte." *Revue de l'histoire des religions* 157:141–154.

Dumézil, Georges. 1963. "Le Puits de Nechtan." *Celtica* 6:50–61.

Dumézil, Georges. 1965. *Le livre des héros*. Paris: Gallimard.

Dumézil, Georges. 1968. *Mythe et épopée*, Vol. 1. Paris: Gallimard.

Dumézil, Georges. 1971. *Mythe et épopée*, Vol. 2. Paris: Gallimard.
Dumézil, Georges. 1978. *Romans de Scythe et d'alentour*. Paris: Payot.
Dumézil, Georges. 1986. *Loki*. New edition. Paris: Flammarion.
Dunbabin, Jean. 1985. *France in the Making: 843–1180*. Oxford: Oxford University Press.
Duval, Paulette. 1979. *La pensée alchimique et le Conte du Graal: recherches sur les structures (Gestalten) de la pensée alchimique, leurs correspondances dans le Conte du Graal de Chrétien de Troyes et l'influence de l'Espagne mozarabe de l'Ebre sur la pensée symbolique de l'oeuvre*. Paris: Champion.
Edwards, B.J.N., and P.V. Webster. 1985–1987. *Ribchester Excavations*. Cardiff: University College. 2 vols.
Eisner, Sigmund. 1969. *The Tristan Legend: A Study in Sources*. Evanston: Northwestern University Press.
Encyclopedia of World Mythology. 1975. London: Octopus.
Entwistle, William J. 1925. *The Arthurian Legend in the Literatures of the Spanish Peninsula*. London: Dent.
Erickson, C.T., ed. 1973. Robert Biket, *The Anglo-Norman Text of Le Lai du Cor*. Oxford: Blackwell.
Evans, J. Gwenogvryn, ed. 1907. *The White Book Mabinogion*. Pwllheli.
Evans, Sebastian. 1898. *In Quest of the Holy Grail: An Introduction to the Study of the Legend*. London: Dent.
Evola, Julius. 1967. *Le Mystère du Graal et l'idée impériale gibéline*. Translated by Yvonne J. Tortat. Paris: Éditions traditionnelles.
Falconer, Sheila, ed. and trans. 1953. *Logaireacht an tSoidigh Naomhtha: An Early Modern Irish Translation of the Quest of the Holy Grail*. Dublin: Dublin Institute for Advanced Studies.
Faral, E., ed. 1929. Geoffrey of Monmouth, *Historia Regum Britanniae*. In *La légende arthurienne*, Vol. 3. Paris: Librairie ancienne Honoré Champion.
Faugère, Annie. 1979. *Les origines orientales du Graal chez Wolfram von Eschenbach: état des recherches*. Göppingen: Kümmerle.
Fawtier, Robert, ed. 1912. *La Vie de Saint Samson*. Paris: Champion.
Ferguson, George. 1961. *Signs and Symbols in Christian Art*. London: Oxford University Press.
Fisher, Lizette Andrews. 1917. *The Mystic Vision in the Grail Legend and in the Divine Comedy*. New York: Columbia University Press.

Fletcher, Robert Huntington. 1906. *The Arthurian Material in the Chronicles, Especially Those of Great Britain and France.* Boston: Ginn.

Fleuriot, J.L. 1959. "Recherches sur les enclaves romanes anciennes en territoire brettonant." *Études celtiques* 8:164–178.

Fleuriot, Léon. 1980. *Les origines de la Bretagne.* Paris: Payot.

Foerster, Wendelin. 1877. *Li Chevaliers as deus espees.* Halle: Niemeyer.

Foerster, Wendelin, ed. 1884. *Chrétien de Troyes, Sämtliche erhaltene Werke nach allen bekannten Handschriften,* Vol. 1: *Cligés.* Halle: Niemeyer.

Foerster, Wendelin, ed. 1887. *Yvain.* Halle: Niemeyer.

Foerster, Wendelin, ed. 1890. *Chrétien de Troyes, Sämtliche erhaltene Werke nach allen bekannten Handschriften,* Vol. 3: *Erec et Enide.* Halle: Niemeyer.

Foerster, Wendelin, ed. 1899. *Christian von Troyes/Der Karrenritter und das Wilhelmsleben.* Halle: Niemeyer.

Foerster, Wendelin, ed. 1908. *Les merveilles de Rigomer.* Dresden: Gedruckt für romanische Literatur, 2 vols.

Ford, Patrick K. 1974. "The Well of Nechtan and 'La Gloire Lumineuse.'" In *Myth in Indo-European Antiquity.* Edited by Gerald James Larson, C. Scott Littleton, and Jaan Puhvel. Berkeley, Los Angeles, and London: University of California Press, pp. 67–74.

Ford, Patrick K. 1976. "The Death of Merlin in the Chronicle of Elis Gruffydd." *Viator* 7:379–390. *Bibliographical Bulletin of the International Arthurian Society.*

Ford, Patrick K., trans. 1977. *The Mabinogi and Other Medieval Welsh Tales.* Berkeley, Los Angeles, and London: University of California Press.

Ford, Patrick K. 1983. "On the Significance of Some Arthurian Names in Welsh." *Bulletin of the Board of Celtic Studies* 30:268–273.

Foreville, Raymonde, ed. 1952. William of Poitiers, *Histoire de Guillaume le Conquérant/Gesta Guillelmi Ducis Normannorum et Regis Anglorum.* Paris: Société d'édition "Les Belles Lettres."

Fortescue, Adrian. 1955. *The Mass: A Study of the Roman Liturgy.* New York: Longmans, Green.

Foster, Herbert Baldwin, trans. 1905. *Dio's Rome.* New York: Pafraets.

Fourquet, J. 1938. *Wolfram d'Eschenbach et* Le Conte del Graal. Paris: Les Belles Lettres.

Fowler, David C. 1975. "*Le Conte du Graal* and *Sir Perceval of Galles.*" *Comparative Literature Studies* 12:5–20.

Frappier, Jean. 1953. *Le Roman Breton*. Paris: Centre de Documentation Universitaire. 4 vols.

Frappier, Jean. 1957. *Chrétien de Troyes*. Paris: Hatier.

Frappier, Jean. 1977. *Autour du Graal*. Geneva: Droz.

Frère, Sheppard S., et al. 1987. *Tabula Imperii Romani: Britannia Septentrionalis*. London: oxford University Press.

Frescoln, Wilson, ed. 1983. Guillaume le Clerc, *The Romance of Fergus*. Philadelphia: Allen.

Friedman, Emanuel, ed. 1984. *Collier's Encyclopedia*, Vols. 1 and 4. New York: Macmillan.

Fuehrer, Mary Rosina, Sister. 1970. *A Study of the Relation of the Dutch* Lancelot *and the Flemish* Perchevael *Fragments to the Manuscripts of Chrétien's* Conte del Graal. New York: AMS.

Furneaux, Rupert. 1966. *Conquest: 1066*. London: Secker & Warburg.

Gallais, Pierre. 1972. *Perceval et l'initiation; essais sur le dernier roman de Chrétien de Troyes, ses correspondances "orientales" et sa signification anthropologique*. Paris: Editions du Sirac.

Gantz, Jeffrey, trans. 1976. *The Mabinogion*. Harmondsworth and New York: Penguin.

Ganz, Peter, ed. 1978. Gottfried von Strassburg, *Tristan*. Originally edited by Reinhold Bechstein. Wiesbaden: Brockhaus.

Gardner, Edmund G. 1930. *The Arthurian Legend in Italian Literature*. London: Dent; New York: Dutton.

Gardner, John, trans. 1971. *The Alliterative Morte Arthure, The Owl and the Nightingale, and Five Other Middle English Poems*. Carbondale: Southern Illinois University Press.

Gerritsen, W.P. 1981. "Jacob van Maerlant and Geoffrey of Monmouth." In *An Arthurian Tapestry: Essays in Memory of Lewis Thorpe*. Edited by Kenneth Varty. Glasgow: French Department of the University, pp. 368–388.

Gianfreda, G. 1965. *Il mosaico pavimentale della Basilica Cattedrale di Otranto*. 2nd ed. Casamari.

Gibbon, Edward. 1946. *The History of the Decline and Fall of the Roman Empire*. Edited by J.B. Bury. New York: Heritage. 3 vols.

Gimbutas, Marija. 1965. *Bronze Age Cultures in Central and Eastern Europe*. The Hague: Mouton.

Glare, D.G.W., ed. 1982. *The Oxford Latin Dictionary*. Oxford: Clarendon.

Glob, P.V. 1969. *The Bog People: Iron-Age Man Preserved*. Translated by Rupert Bruce-Mitford. Ithaca: Cornell University Press.

Glück, Heinrich. 1923. *Die christliche Kunst des Ostens*. Berlin: Cassirer.

Goetnick, Glenys. 1975. *Peredur: A Study of Welsh Tradition in the Grail Legends*. Cardiff: University of Wales Press.

Goffart, Walter. 1980. *Barbarians and Romans: A.D. 418–584*. Princeton: Princeton University Press.

Golther, W. 1925. *Parsifal und der Grâl in der Dichtung des Mittelalters und der Neuzeit*. Stuttgart: Metzler.

Goodrich, Norma Lorre. 1986. *King Arthur*. New York and Toronto: Watts.

Goodrich, Norma Lorre. 1992. *The Holy Grail*. New York: HarperCollins.

Gordon, C.D. 1960. *The Age of Attila*. Ann Arbor: University of Michigan Press.

Grant, Michael. 1985. *The Roman Emperors: A Biographical Guide to the Rulers of Imperial Rome, 31 B.C.–A.D. 476*. New York: Charles Scribners' Sons.

Grenier, A. 1931. *Manuel d'archéologie Gallo-romaine*. Vol. 5. Paris: Picard.

Grisward, Joël. 1969. "Le motif de l'épée jetée au lac: la mort d'Artur et la mort de Batraz." *Romania* 9:289–340.

Grisward, Joël. 1973. "Trois perspectives médiévales." *Nouvelle école* 21–22:80–89.

Hahn, K.A., ed. 1965. *Lanzelet*. Berlin: de Gruyter.

Haidu, Peter. 1968. *Aesthetic Distance in Chrétien de Troyes*. Geneva: Droz.

Hale, William C. 1984. "Morgaine, Morgana, Morgause." *Avalon to Camelot* 1/4:35–36.

Hamel, Mary, ed. 1984. *Morte Arthure: A Critical Edition*. New York and London: Garland.

Hanson, R.P.C. 1968. *St. Patrick: His Origins*. Oxford: Oxford University Press.

Harmatta, John. 1950. *Studies on the History of the Sarmatians*. Budapest: Pázmány Péter Tudományegyetemi Görög Filolóiai Intézet.

Hartshorne, Charles Henry, ed. 1829. *Ancient Metrical Tales*. London: Pickering.

Hatto, A.T., trans. 1967. Gottfried von Strassburg, *Tristan* . . . *with the Surviving Fragments of the Tristan of Thomas*. Baltimore and Harmondsworth: Penguin.

Hatto, A.T., trans. 1980. Wolfram von Eschenbach, *Parzival*. Harmondsworth and New York: Penguin.

Heather, P.J. 1991. *Goths and Romans 332–489*. Oxford: Clarendon.

Helgason, Jón, ed. 1962–1965. *Íslenzk fornkvœ5i*. Copenhagen: Munksgaard. 5 vols.

Herbermann, Charles G., et al. 1907–1912. *The Catholic Encyclopedia*. Vol. 1. New York: Robert Appleton Company.

Heyen, Franz-Josef. 1966. *Zwischen Rhein und Mosel: Der Kreis St. Goar*. Boppard am Rhein: Boldt.

Hilka, Alfons. 1932. *Der Percevalroman (Li Contes del Graal) von Christian von Troyes*. Halle: Niemeyer.

Hill, Joyce. 1977. "The Icelandic Ballad of Tristan." In *The Tristan Legend: Texts from Northern and Eastern Europe in Modern English Translations*. Leeds: University of Leeds, Graduate Centre for Medieval Studies, pp. 29–38.

Hissiger, P.F., ed. 1975. *Le Morte Arthur: A Critical Edition*. The Hague: Mouton.

Hoffman, Donald L. 1984. "The Third British Empire." *Interpretations* (Memphis State University) 15:1–10.

Hogenhout, M., and Jan Hogenhout, eds. 1978. *Jacob Van Maerlant, Torec*. Abcoude, The Netherlands.

Hohl, Ernestus. 1927. *Scriptores Historiae Augustae*. Leipzig: Teubner. 2 vols.

Holder, Alfred. 1891. *Alt-Celtischer Sprachschatz*. Leipzig: Teubner. 3 vols.

Hollister, C. Warren. 1982. *Medieval Europe: A Short History*. 5th ed. New York: Wiley.

Holt, J.C. 1982. *Robin Hood*. London: Thames and Hudson.

Holthausen, Ferdinand. 1948. *Wörterbuch des Altwestnordischen*. Göttingen: Vandenhoeck and Ruprecht.

Hony, H.C. 1957. *A Turkish-English Dictionary*. Oxford: Clarendon.

Howlett, Richard, ed. 1855. William of Newburgh, *Historia Rerum Anglicarum*. In *Chronicles of the Reign of Stephen, Henry II, and Richard I*, Vol. 1. London: Longman, Trübner.

Hubert, Henri. 1974. *Les Celts et l'expansion celtique jusqu'à l'époque de la Tène*. Paris: Albin Michel.

Hübner, Aemelius, ed. 1873. *Corpus Inscriptionum Latinarum*, Vol. 7. Berlin: Georgium Remerum.

Hübschmann, H. 1887. "Sage und Glaube den Osseten." *Zeitschrift der Deutschen Morgenländischen Gesellschaft* 41:523–576.

Hucher, Eugène Frédéric Ferdinand, ed. 1875–1878. *Le Saint-Graal; ou, Le Joseph d'Arimathie; première branche des romans de la Table ronde*. Au Mans: Monnoyer. 3 vols.

Hudson, Alfred E. 1964. *Kazak Social Structure*. New Haven, Connecticut: Human Relations Area Files. Originally published as Yale University Publications in Anthropology No. 20, 1938.

Imbs, M. 1956. *Les romans du graal aux XIIe et XIIIe siècles*. Centre National de la Recherche Scientifique (France). Strasbourg, 29 mars–3 avril 1954. Colloques internationaux du Centre National de la Recherche Scientifique. Sciences humaines, 3. Paris.

Iselin, Ludwig Emil. 1909. *Der morgenländische Ursprung der Graallegende und orientlischen Quellen erschlossen*. Halle: Niemeyer.

Ivy, R.H. 1951. *The Manuscript Relations of Manessier's Continuation of the Old French Perceval*. Philadelphia: University of Pennsylvania, Department of Romance Languages.

Jackson, Kenneth Hurlstone. 1953. *Language and History in Early Britain*. Edinburgh: Edinburgh University Press.

Jackson, Kenneth Hurlstone. 1969. *The Gododdin: The Oldest Scottish Poem*. Edinburgh: Edinburgh University Press.

Jackson, W.T.H. 1971. *The Anatomy of Love: The Tristan of Gottfried von Strassburg*. New York and London: Columbia University Press.

Jaeger, C. Stephen. 1977. *Medieval Humanism in Gottfried von Strassburg's Tristan und Isolde*. Heidelberg: Winter.

Janssens, J.D., ed. and trans. 1985. *Koning Artur in de Nederlanden: Middelnederlandse Artur- en Graalromans*. Utrecht: HES.

Jarman, A.O.H., and Gwilym Rees Hughes. 1976. *A Guide to Welsh Literature*, Vol. 1. Swansea: Davies.

Jenkins, Elizabeth. 1975. *The Mystery of King Arthur*. New York: Coward, McCann and Geohegan.

Jones, Gwyn, and Thomas Jones, trans. 1949. *The Mabinogion*. London: Dent; New York: Dutton.

Jones, Gwyn, and Thomas Jones, trans. 1974. *The Mabinogion*. 2nd ed. London: Dent.

Jones, R.M. 1957. "Y Rhamantau Cymraeg a'u Cysylltiad a'r Rhamantau." *Llên Cymru* 4:208–227.

Jones, R.M. 1960. *Y Tair Rhamant*. Aberystwyth: Cymeithes Lyfrau Ceredigion.

Jones, T. Gwyn. 1926. "Some Arthurian Material in Keltic." *Aberystwyth Studies*, 8:37–93.

Jones, Thomas, ed. and trans. 1967. "The Black Book of Carmarthen 'Stanzas of the Graves.'" *Proceedings of the British Academy*, 53:97–137.

Jones, William Lewis. 1907–1927. *Cambridge History of English Literature*, Vol. 1. Edited by A.W. Ward and A.R. Waller. Cambridge: Cambridge University Press; New York and London: Putnam.

Jónsson, Finnur, ed. 1892–1896. *Hauksbók, udgiven efter de Arnamagnoeanske håndskrifter No. 371, 544 og 675, 4, samt forkellige papirhåndskrifter auf det Kongelige nordiske oldskrift-selskab.* Copenhagen: Thieles bogte.

Jung, Emma, and Marie-Louise von Franz. 1986. *The Grail Legend*. Translated by Andrea Dykes. 2nd ed. Boston: Sigo, 1980.

Junghans, W. 1879. "Histoire Critique des règnes de Childeric et de Chlodovech." Translated and augmented by G. Monod. *Bibliothèque de l'école des hautes études* 37:12–15.

Junk, Victor. 1912. *Gralsage und Graldichtung des Mittelalters*. Vienna: In Kommission bei A. Holder.

Keay, S.J. 1988. *Roman Spain*. Berkeley, Los Angeles, and London: University of California Press.

Keller, Adelbert von, ed. 1836. *Li Romans de Sept Sages*. Tübingen.

Keller, Adelbert von, ed. 1858. "Ain hupsches vasnachtspill und sagt von künig Artus." In *Fastnachtspiele aus dem fünfzehnten Jahrhundert*. Stuttgart: Litterarischer Verein.

Kelly, F. Douglas. 1976. *Chrétien de Troyes: An Analytic Bibliography*. London: Grant and Cutler.

Kelly, Thomas. 1974. *Le Haut Livre du Graal: Perlesvaus*. Geneva: Droz.

Kendrick, T.D. 1950. *British Antiquity*. London: Methuen.

Kennedy, Elspeth. 1986. *Lancelot and the Grail: A Study of the Prose Lancelot*. Oxford: Clarendon; New York: Oxford University Press.

Kilbride-Jones, H.E. 1980. *Celtic Craftsmanship in Bronze*. New York: St. Martin's Press.

Kinsella, Thomas, trans. 1969. *The Táin*. Dublin: Oxford University Press in association with the Dolmen Press.

Kittredge, G.L. 1916. *A Study of Gawain and the Green Knight*. Cambridge: Harvard University Press.

Knopp, Sherron E. 1978. "Artistic Design in the *Stanzaic Morte Arthur*." *Journal of English Literary History* 45:563–582.

Knuvelder, Gerard P.M. 1970–1976. *Handboek tot de geschiedenis der Nederlandse letterkunde*. 5th ed. 's-Hertogen-bosch: Malmberg. 4 vols.

Kölbing, Eugen, ed. 1878. *Tristrams saga ok Ísöndar: Mit einer literaturhistorischen Einleitung*. Heilbronn: Henninger.

Kölbing, Eugen, ed. 1890. *Arthour and Merlin*. Heilbronn: Henniger.

Kolve, V.A. 1966. *The Play Called Corpus Christi*. Stanford: Stanford University Press.

Kouznetsov, Valdimir, and Iaroslav Lebedynsky..1997. *Les Alains: Cavaliers des steppes, seigneurs du Caucase*. Paris: Editions Errance.

Krappe, Alexander Haggerty. 1931. "Le mirage celtique et les sources du 'Chevalier Cifar.'" *Bulletin hispanique* 33:97–103.

Krappe, Alexander Haggerty. 1933. "Le lac enchanté dans le *Chevalier Cifar*." *Bulletin hispanique* 35:107–125.

Krishna, Valerie, ed. 1976. *The Alliterative Morte Arthure: A Critical Edition*. New York: Franklin.

Krohn, Kaarle. 1926. *Die folkloristische Arbeitsmethode*. Oslo.

Krusch, Bruno, ed. 1888. *Liber Historiae Francorum and Vita S. Arnulfi. Monumenta Germaniae Historica: Scriptores Rerum Merovingicarum*, Vol. 2:215–328, 426–446. Hanover: Hahn.

Krusch, Bruno, and Wilhelm Levison, eds. 1920. *Vita Germani: episcopi Autissiodorensis autore Constantio. Monumenta Germaniae Historica: Passiones Vitaeque Sanctorum aevi Merovingici* 7/15:337–428. Hannover and Leipzig: Hahn.

Krusch, Bruno, and Wilhelm Levison, eds. 1951. *Scriptores Rerum Merovinicarum: Gregorii episcopi Turonensis libri historiarum X. Monumenta Germaniae Historica* Vol. 1/1:55. Hanover: Hahn.

Kuhn, Sherman M., and Hans Kurath. 1983. *Middle English Dictionary*. Part P, Vol. 7. Ann Arbor: University of Michigan Press.

Kurth, Godefroid. 1893. *Histoire poètique des Mérovingiens*. Brussels: Société Belge de Librairie; Leipzig: Brockhaus.

Lachmann, Karl, ed. 1833. *Wolfram von Eschenbach.* 6th ed. Berlin: de Gruyter, 1926.

Lacy, Norris J. 1980. *The Craft of Chrétien de Troyes.* Leiden: Brill.

Lacy, Norris J. et al., eds. 1986. *The Arthurian Encyclopedia.* New York and London: Garland.

Lacy, Norris J. et al., eds. 1991. *The New Arthurian Encyclopedia.* New York and London: Garland.

Lair, L. 1898. "Conjectures sur les chapitres XVIII et XIX des livre II de l'Historia Ecclesiastica de Gréoire de Tours." *Annuaire-Bulletin de la Société de l'Histoire de France* 35:3–29.

Lamb, Harold. 1943. *The March of the Barbarians.* New York: Garden City.

Lamberg-Karlovsky, C.C. 1991. "The Search for the Scythians in the U.S.S.R." *Symbols* (Peabody Museum, Harvard University), June, pp. 14–18d.

Lathuillère, Roger. 1966. *Guiron le Courtois: étude de la tradition manuscrite et analyse critique.* Geneva: Droz.

Lawton, David A., ed. 1983. *Joseph of Arimathea: A Critical Edition.* New York and London: Garland.

Leach, Henry Goddard. 1921. *Angevin Britain and Scandinavia.* Cambridge: Harvard University Press.

Leach, Maria, ed. 1972. *Funk and Wagnalls Standard Dictionary of Folklore, Mythology and Legend.* San Francisco: Harper & Row.

Leclercq, Jean. 1968. "Part One: From St. Gregory to St. Bernard: From the Sixth to the Twelfth Century." In *The Spirituality of the Middle Ages.* Translated by the Benedictines of Holme Eden Abbey, Carlisle. New York: Seabury Press.

Leitzmann, Albert, ed. 1902–1906. *Wolfram von Eschenbach* (edition of *Parzival*). Halle: Niemeyer. 5 vols.

Leitzmann, Albert, ed. 1972. Hartmann von Aue, *Erec.* 5th ed. Edited by Ludwig Wolff. Tübingen: Niemeyer.

Lemmon, C.H., et al. 1966. *The Norman Conquest.* London: Eyre and Spottiswoode.

Le Moyne de la Borderie, A., ed. 1883. *Legenda sancti Geoznovii.* In *L'Historia Britonum et l'Historia Britannica avant Geoffroi de Monmouth.* Paris: Champion.

Le Roux de Lincy, M. 1836. *Le livre des légendes.* Paris: Chez Silvestre.

Le Roux de Lincy, M. 1838. *Le Roman de Brut par Wace.* Rouen: É. Frère. 2 vols.

Le Roux de Lincy, M. 1840. *Essai historique et littéraire dur l'Abbaye de Fécamp*. Rouen: É. Frère.

Levison, Wilhelm. 1904. "Bischof Germanus von Auxerre und die Quellen zu seiner Geschichte." *Neues Archiv* 29:95 ff.

Levison, Wilhelm, ed. 1920. *Vita Germani: episcopi Parisiaii. Monumenta Germaniae Historica: Passiones Vitaeque Sanctorum aevi Merovingici* 7/15:225–283. Hannover and Leipzig: Hahn.

Levy, Reuben 1967. *The Epic of the Kings, Shāh-nāmah*. Chicago: University of Chicago Press.

Lewis, Charlton T., and Charles Short, eds. 1907. *A New Latin Dictionary, Founded on the Translation of Freund's Latin-German Lexicon*. New York: American Book.

Lewis, Henry, and Holger Pedersen. 1961. *A Concise Comparative Celtic Grammar*. Göttingen: Vandenhoech and Ruprecht.

Lewis, J. Saunders. 1957. *Braslun o Canol*. Cardiff.

Lindsay, Jack. 1958. *Arthur and His Times*. London: Muller.

Littleton, C. Scott. 1979. "The Holy Grail, the Cauldron of Annwn, and the Nartyamonga: A Further Note on the Sarmatian Connection." *Journal of American Folklore* 92:326–333.

Littleton, C. Scott. 1981. "Susa-nö-wo versus Yamata nö Woröti: An Indo-European Theme in Japanese Mythology." *History of Religions* 20:269–280.

Littleton, C. Scott. 1982a. *The New Comparative Mythology: An Anthropological Assessment of the Theories of Georges Dumézil*. 3rd ed. Berkeley, Los Angeles, and London: University of California Press.

Littleton, C. Scott. 1982b. "From Swords in the Earth to the Sword in the Stone: A PossibleReflection of an Alano-Sarmatian Rite of Passage in the Arthurian Tradition." In *Homage to Georges Dumézil*. Edited by Edgar C. Polomé. Washington, DC: The Journal of Indo-European Studies Monograph Number 3, pp. 53-67.

Littleton, C. Scott. 1983. "Some Possible Arthurian Themes in Japanese Mythology and Folklore." *Journal of Folklore Research* 20:67–82.

Littleton, C. Scott. 1991. "The Tripartite Division of Labor (Priests, Warriors, Cultivators) in Ancient Indo-European Mythology." In *Ancient Economy in Mythology: East and West*. Edited by Morris Silver. Savage: Rowman and Littlefield, pp. 73–106.

Littleton, C. Scott. 1995. "Yamato-takeru: An 'Arthurian' Hero in Japanese Tradition." *Asian Folklore Studies* 54:259-274.

Littleton, C. Scott, and Linda A. Malcor. "Did the Alans Reach Ireland? A Reassessment of the 'Scythian' References in the *Lebor G_bala _renn*." In *Homage to Jaan Puhvel, Part II*. Edited by Edgar C. Polomé. Washington, DC: The Journal of Indo-European Studies Monographs Number 21, pp. 161-182.

Littleton, C. Scott, and Linda A. Peterson. (unpublished MS) "Did the Alans Reach Ireland?: A Study of the Scythian References in the *Lébor Gabála Érenn*." Presented at the American Folklore Society Annual Meeting in Cincinnati, Ohio, October, 1985.

Littleton, C. Scott, and Ann C. Thomas. 1978. "The Sarmatian Connection: New Light on the Origin of the Arthurian and Holy Grail Legends." *Journal of American Folklore* 91:512–527.

Littré, Émile. 1956–1958. *Dictionnaire de la langue française*. Éd. intégrale. Paris: Pauvert.

Loenertz, P.R. 1932. "Les missions dominicaines en Orient au XIVe siècle et la Société des Frères Pérégrinants pour le Christ." *Archivum Fratrum Praedicatorum* 2:1–83.

Longnon, A. 1920. *Les noms de lieu de la France*, no. 612. Paris: Champion.

Loomis, Roger Sherman. 1927. *Celtic Myth and Arthurian Romance*. New York: Columbia University Press.

Loomis, Roger Sherman. 1941. "The Spoils of Annwn." *Publications of the Modern Language Association* 56:884–936.

Loomis, Roger Sherman. 1949. *Arthurian Tradition and Chrétien de Troyes*. New York: Columbia University Press.

Loomis, Roger Sherman. 1956. "Les légendes hagiographiques et la légende du Graal." In *Les romans du Graal aux XIIe et XIIIe siècles*. Centre National de la Recherche Scientifique (France). Strasbourg, 29 mars–3 avril 1954. Colloques internationaux du Centre National de la Recherche Scientifique. Sciences humaines, 3. Paris.

Loomis, Roger Sherman, ed. 1959. *Arthurian Literature in the Middle Ages, A Collaborative History*. Oxford: Clarendon.

Loomis, Roger Sherman. 1963a. *The Development of Arthurian Romance*. London: Hutchinson.

Loomis, Roger Sherman. 1963b. *The Grail: From Celtic Myth to Christian Symbol*. Cardiff: University of Wales Press; New York: Columbia University Press.

Loomis, Roger Sherman, and Laura Hibbard Loomis. 1938. *Arthurian Legends in Medieval Art*. London: Oxford University Press; New York: Modern Language Association of America.

Lot, Ferdinand. 1899. "Carados et Saint Patern." *Romania* 28:568–578.

Lot, Ferdinand. 1918. *Étude sur le Lancelot en prose*. Paris: Champion.

Lot-Borodine, Myrrah. 1919. *Trois essais sur le roman de Lancelot du Lac et la quête du Saint Graal*. Paris: Champion.

Loth, Joseph, ed. and trans. 1913. *Les Mabinogion du Livre Rouge de Hergest avec les variantes du Livre blanc de Rhydderch, traduits du gallois avec une introduction, un commentaire explicatif et des notes critiques par J. Loth*. rev. ed. Paris: Fontemoing. 2 vols.

Loubo-Lesnitchenko, E. 1973. "Imported Mirrors in the Minusinsk Basin." *Artibus Asiae* 35:28–29.

Lovelich, Herry. 1874–1905. *The History of the Holy Grail, Englisht, ab. 1450 A.D., by Herry Lovelich, Skynner, from the French Prose (ab. 1180–1200 A.D.) of Sires Robiers de Borron. Re-edited from the Unique Paper Ms. in Corpus Christi College, Cambridge*. Edited by Frederick J. Furnivall. London: Kegan Paul, Trench, Trübner for the Early English Text Society. 2 vols. (bound as 1).

Lovelich, Herry. 1904–1932. *Merlin*. MS Corpus Christi (Cambridge) 80. Edited by Ernst A. Kock. London: Kegan Paul, Trench, Trübner for the Early English Text Society.

Lozachmeur, Jean-Claude, and Shigemi Sasaki. 1984. "Part II, Researches on the Mystery of the Grail: Modern Critical Hypotheses." *Avalon to Camelot* 1/4:20–23.

Macalister, R.A.S., ed. and trans. 1939a. *Lébor Gabála Érenn*, Part 1. Dublin: Educational Company of Ireland.

Macalister, R.A.S., ed. and trans. 1939b. *Lébor Gabála Érenn*, Part 2. Dublin: Educational Company of Ireland. Reprint of 1935 edition.

Macalister, R.A.S., ed. and trans. 1940. *Lébor Gabála Érenn*, Part 3. Dublin: Educational Company of Ireland.

Macalister, R.A.S., ed. and trans. 1941. *Lébor Gabála Érenn*, Part 4. Dublin: Educational Company of Ireland.

Macalister, R.A.S., trans. and ed. 1956. *Lébor Gabála Érenn*. Part 5. Dublin: Educational Company of Ireland. Reprint of 1942 edition.

MacCana, Proinsias. 1970. *Celtic Mythology*. London: Hamlyn. MacCana, Proinsias. 1977. *The Mabinogi*. Cardiff: University of Wales Press.

MacCulloch, John Arnott. 1918. *Celtic Mythology. Mythology of All Races*, Vol. 3. Boston: Marshall John.

Maenchen-Helfen, Otto. 1973. *The World of the Huns.* Edited by Max Knight. Berkeley, Los Angeles, and London: University of California Press.

Magne, Augusto, ed. 1953. *Dicionairo etimológico da língua latina.* Rio de Janeiro: Ministério da Educação e Cultura.

Malcor, Linda A. 1991. *The Chalice at the Cross: A Study of the Grail Motif in Medieval Europe.* Ph.D. diss., University of California, Los Angeles; Ann Arbor: University Microfilms.

Malcor, Linda A. (unpublished MS) "First Bath: The Washing of the Child Motif in Medieval Christian Art." Presented at the California Folklore Society Annual Conference at the University of California, Los Angeles, May 1991.

Malcor, Linda A. 1999. "Lucius Artorius Castus, Part 1: An Officer and an Equestrian."*The Heroic Age,* http://members.aol.com/heroicage1/homepage.html

Malcor, Linda A. n.d. "Lucius Artorius Castus, Part II: The Historical King Arthur." *The Heroic Age,* http://members.aol.com/heroicage1/homepage.html

Mallory, J.P. 1989. *In Search of the Indo-Europeans: Language, Archaeology and Myth.* London: Thames and Hudson.

Malone, Kemp. 1924. "The Historicity of Arthur." *Journal of English and Germanic Philology* 23:463–491.

Malone, Kemp. 1925. "Artorius." *Modern Philology* 22:367–377.

Markale, Jean. 1971. *L'épopée celtique en Bretagne.* 3rd ed. Paris: Payot.

Markale, Jean. 1975a. *La tradition celtique en Bretagne amoricaine.* Paris: Payot.

Markale, Jean. 1975b. *Women of the Celts.* Translated by A. Mygind, C. Hauch, and P. Henry. London: Gordon and Cremonesi.

Markale, Jean. 1977. *Arthur: King of Kings.* Translated by Christine Hauch. London: Gordon and Cremonesi.

Markale, Jean. 1982. *Le Graal.* Paris: Retz.

Markale, Jean. 1983a. *Le christianisme celtique et ses survivances populaires.* Paris: Imago.

Markale, Jean. 1983b. *Melusine ou l'androgyne.* Paris: Retz.

Markale, Jean. 1985. *Lancelot et la chevalerie arthurienne.* Paris: Imago.

Markale, Jean. 1986. *Montségur et l'énigme cathare.* Paris: Pygmalion, Gérard Watelet.

Markale, Jean. 1989. *Broceliande et l'énigme du Graal*. Paris: Pygmalion, Gérard Watelet.

Martin, Ernst, ed. 1872. *Fergus, Roman von Guillaume le Clerc*. Halle: Waisenhaus.

Martindale, John Robert. 1980. *Prosopography of the Later Roman Empire: 395–527*, Vol. 2. Cambridge: Cambridge University Press.

Martonne, A. de. 1885. "Deux nouveaux évèques du Mans." *Revue historique de l'ouest* 1:506–515.

Marx, Jean. 1952. *La Légende arthurienne et le Graal*. Paris: Presses Universitaires de France.

Marx, Jean. 1960. "Le cortège du Château des Merveilles dans le roman gallois de Peredur." *Études celtique* 9:92–105.

Marx, Jean. 1965. *Nouvelles recherches sur la littérature arthurienne*. Paris: Klincksieck.

Matarasso, P.M., trans. 1969. *The Quest of the Holy Grail*. Harmondsworth and New York: Penguin.

Matthews, John, ed. 1984. *At the Table of the Grail: Magic and the Use of the Imagination*. London and Boston: Routledge and Kegan Paul.

Matthews, John, and Bob Stewart. 1987. *Warriors of Arthur*. London: Blandford.

Matthews, William. 1960. *The Tragedy of Arthur: A Study of the Alliterative "Morte Arthure."* Berkeley, Los Angeles, and London: University of California Press.

Mattingly, H., trans. 1970. Tacitus, *The Agricola and the Germania*. Revised by S.A. Handford. Harmondsworth and New York: Penguin.

McMunn, Meradith Tilbury, ed. 1978. *Le Roman de Kanor*. Ann Arbor: University Microfilms. 2 vols.

Megaw, Ruth and Vincent Megaw. 1986. *Celtic Art: From its Beginnings to the Book of Kells*. New York: Thames and Hudson.

Meliadus de Leonnoys. 1528. Paris: Galliot du Pré.

Mellinkoff, Ruth. 1970. *The Horned Moses in Medieval Art and Thought*. Berkeley, Los Angeles, and London: University of California Press.

Mendelssohn, L., ed. 1887. Zosimus, *Historia Nova*. Leipzig: Tübner.

Meyer, Rudolf. 1956. *Der Gral und seine Hüter*. Stuttgart: Urachhaus.

Meyrat, J., ed. 1959. *Dictionnaire national des communes de France*. 17th ed. Paris: Michel.

Micha, Alexandre. 1948. "L'épreuve de l'épée." *Romania* o.s. 70:36–50.

Micha, Alexandre, trans. 1957. Chrétien de Troyes, *Cligés*. Paris: Champion.

Micha, Alexandre, ed. 1980. *Merlin, roman du XIIIe siècle*. Geneva: Droz.

Micha, Alexandre. 1987. *Essais sur le cycle du Lancelot-Graal*. Geneva: Droz.

Mierow, Charles Christopher, trans. 1915. *The Gothic History of Jordanes*. Princeton: Princeton University Press.

Migne, J.P., ed. 1855. *Chronicon Montis Sancti Michaelis in Periculo Maris*. In *Patrologia Latina*, Vol. 202, col. 1323. Paris: Migne.

Miller, Dean A. 1989. "The Twinning of Arthur and Cei: An Arthurian Tessera." *Journal of Indo-European Studies* 17:47–76.

Miller, Vsev. F. 1881. "SkazanijaoNartah." *Ossetische Studien* 1. Moscow.

Mommsen, Theodor, ed. 1873. *Corpus Inscriptionum Latinarum: Inscriptiones Asiae Provinciarum Europae Graecarum Illyrici Latinae*. Vol. 3, Part 1 and Supplement. Berlin: Reimer.

Mommsen, Theodor, ed. 1892. *Chronica Minora (Saec. IV.V.VI.VII), Prosperi Tironis epitoma Chronicon, Chronica Gallica a. CCCCLII et DXI*. Berlin: Weidmann.

Moorman, Charles, and Ruth Moorman. 1978. *An Arthurian Dictionary*. Jackson: University Press of Mississippi.

Morice, Hyacinthe. 1750–1756. *Histoire ecclésiastique et civile de Bretagne*. Revised ed. Paris: De Delaguette. 2 vols.

Morris, John, ed. and trans. 1980. Nennius, *British History and the Welsh Annals*. In *History from the Sources*, Vol. 8. Chichester: Phillimore.

Müllenhoff, K., and W. Scherer. 1964. *Denkmäler: Deutscher Poesie und Prosa aus dem VIII–XII Jahrhundert*. Berlin and Zurich: Weidmann. 2 vols.

Muret, Ernest, ed. 1962. Béroul, *Le Roman de Tristan*. Paris: Champion.

Nelli, René. 1951. *Lumière du Graal. études et textes présentés sous la direction de René Nelli*. Paris: Cahiers du Sud.

Neubuhr, Elfreide. 1977. *Bibliographie zu Hartmann von Aue*. Berlin: Schmidt.

Newark, Tim. 1989. *Women Warlords*. London: Blandford.

Newstead, Helaine H. 1939. *Bran the Blessed in Arthurian Romance*. New York: Columbia University Press.

Newstead, Helaine H. 1945. "Perceval's Father and Welsh Tradition." *Romanic Review* 36:3–31.

Newstead, Helaine H. 1967. "Arthurian Legends." In *A Manual of the Writings in Middle English 1050–1500*, Vol. 3. Edited by J. Burke Severs. New Haven: Connecticut Academy of Arts and Sciences.

Nickel, Helmut. 1973. "Tamgas and Runes, Magic Numbers and Magic Symbols." *Metropolitan Museum Journal* 8:165–173.

Nickel, Helmut. 1975a. "Wer waren König Artus' Ritter? Über die geschichtliche Grundlage der Artussagen." *Zeitschrift der historischen Waffen- und Kostümkunde* 1:1–18.

Nickel, Helmut. 1975b. "The Dawn of Chivalry." *Metropolitan Museum of Art Bulletin* 32:150–152.

Nickel, Helmut. 1983. "About Arms and Armor in the Age of Arthur." *Avalon to Camelot* 1/1:19–21

Nickel, Helmut. n.d. "The Last Days of Rome in Britain and the Origin of the Arthurian Legends." Unpublished manuscript.

Niedzielski, Henri, ed. 1966. *Le Roman de Helcanus*. Geneva: Droz.

Nitze, William A. 1902. *The Old French Grail Romance* Perlesvaus. Baltimore: Murphy.

Nitze, William A. 1909. "The Fisher King in the Grail Romances." *Publications of the Modern Language Association* 24:365–418.

Nitze, William A., ed. 1927. *Le roman de L'Estoire dou Graal*. Paris: Champion.

Nitze, William A. 1949a. *Perceval and the Holy Grail: An Essay on the Romance of Chrétien de Troyes*. Berkeley, Los Angeles, and London: University of California Press.

Nitze, William A. 1949b. "Arthurian Names." *Publications of the Modern Language Association* 64:585–596.

Nitze, William A. 1953. "Messire Robert de Boron: Enquiry and Summary." *Speculum* 28:279–296.

Nitze, William A., and T. Atkinson Jenkins, eds. 1932–1937. *Le haut livre du graal:* Perlesvaus. Chicago: University of Chicago Press. 2 vols.

Norroena: Embracing the History and Romance of Northern Europe, Vol. 6. 1907. London and New York: Norroena Society. c. 1905.

Nutt, Alfred. 1881. "The Aryan Expulsion-and-Return Formula in Folk- and Hero-Tales of the Celts." *Folklore Record* 4:1–44.

Obayashi, Taryo, and Atsuhiko Yoshida. 1975. *Tsurugi no Kami, Tsurugi no Eiyu: Takemikazuchi no Shinwa no Hikaku Kenkyu*. Tokyo: Hosei Daigaku Shuppankyoku.

Offord, M.Y., ed. 1959. *The Parlement of the Thre Ages*. London: Oxford University Press.

O'Gorman, Richard. 1969. "Ecclesiastical Tradition and the Holy Grail." *Australian Journal of French Studies* 6: 3–8.

O'Gorman, Richard. 1970. "The Prose Version of Robert de Boron's *Joseph d'Arimathie*." *Romance Philology* 23:449–461.

O'Gorman, Richard. 1971. "La tradition manuscrite du *Joseph d'Arimathie* en prose de Robert de Boron." *Revue d'histoire des textes* 1:145–181.

Ólason, Vésteinn. 1982. *The Traditional Ballads of Iceland: Historical Studies*. Reykjavik: Stofnun Árna Magnússonar.

Olcott, Martha Brill. 1987. *The Kazakhs*. Stanford: Stanford University Press.

Oman, Charles. 1910. *England Before the Norman Conquest, Being a History of the Celtic, Roman, and Anglo-Saxon Periods down to the Year A.D. 1066*. London: Methuen.

O'Rahilly, Thomas F. 1946. *Early Irish History and Mythology*. Dublin: Dublin Institute for Advanced Studies.

Országh, László. 1953. *Magyar-angol Szotar*. Budapest: Akademiai Kiado.

Owen, D.D.R. 1968. *The Evolution of the Grail Legend*. Edinburgh and London: Oliver and Boyd.

Owen, Lewis. *Chivalric Friendship and Its Survival in the Sixteenth Century English Versions of Medieval Chivalric Romance*. D.Litt. diss., University of London.

Palermo, Joseph, ed. 1963–1964. *Le Roman de Cassiodorus*. Paris: Picard. 2 vols.

Paris, Gaston. 1899. "Carados et le Serpent." *Romania* 28:213–231.

Paris, Gaston, and Jacob Ulrich, eds. 1886. *Merlin*. Paris: Didot.

Parry, J.J., ed. and trans. 1925. Geoffrey of Monmouth, *Vita Merlini*. Urbana: University of Illinois Press.

Parry, Thomas. 1933. *Saint Greal; y chwedl wedi ei hailadrodd gun Tom Parry*. Aberystwyth.

Paton, Lucy Allen. 1903. *Studies in the Fairy Mythology of Arthurian Romance*. Boston: Ginn.

Paton, Lucy Allen, ed. 1926. *Les Prophécies de Merlin*. New York: Heath. 2 vols.

Paton, Lucy Allen, trans. 1929. *Sir Lancelot of the Lake*. New York: Harcourt, Brace.

Pauphilet, Albert. 1921. *Études sur* La Queste del Saint Graal *attribuée à Gautier Map* . . . . Paris: Champion.

Pauphilet, Albert, trans. 1923. *La Queste del Saint Graal.* Paris: Champion.

Payen, Jean Charles, ed. 1983. *La légende arthurienne et la Normandie, Hommage à René Bausard.* Condé-sur-Noireau: Corlet.

Payen, Jean Charles. 1984. *Le Moyen Âge: littérature française.* Paris: Arthaud.

Peebles, Rose Jeffries. 1911. *The Legend of Longinus in Ecclesiastical Tradition and in English Literature, and Its Connection with the Grail.* Baltimore: Furst.

Pekkanen, Tuomo. 1973. "On the Oldest Relationship Between Hungarians and Sarmatians: From Spali to Asphali." *Ural-Altaische Jahrbücher* 45:1–64.

Pentikäinen, Juha. 1968. *The Nordic Dead-Child Tradition.* Translated by Antony Landon. Helsinki: Suomalainen Tiedeakatemia.

Perry, George, ed. 1865. *Morte Arthure.* London: Kegan Paul, Trench, Trübner. Revised by Edmund Brock, 1871.

Peterson, Linda A. 1985. "The Alan of Lot: A New Interpretation of the Legends of Lancelot." *Folklore and Mythology Studies* 9: 31–49.

Peterson, Linda A. 1986. "The Alans and the Grail: The Theft, the Swindle, and the Legend." *Folklore and Mythology Studies* 10:25–41.

Pflaum, H.-G.. 1960. *Les carrières procuratoriennes questres sous le Haut-Empire romain.* Paris: Librairie Orientaliste Paul Guenther. 3 vols.

Phillips, E.D. 1965. *The Royal Hordes: Nomad Peoples of the Steppes.* New York: McGraw-Hill.

Pickford, C.E., ed. 1977a. *Lancelot du Lac.* Facsimile reproduction of the Rouen and Paris 1488 printings of the prose *Lancelot.* London: Scolar.

Pickford, Cedric E., ed. 1977b. *Gyron le Courtoys.* Facsimile reproduction of the Paris ca. 1501 printing by Antoine Verard of *Gyron le Courtoys.* London: Scolar.

Pietsch, Karl, ed. 1924–1925. *Spanish Grail Fragments: El libro de Josep Abarimatia, La estoria de Merlin, Lançarote.* Chicago: University of Chicago Press. 2 vols.

Piggott, Stuart. 1941. "The Sources of Geoffrey of Monmouth." *Antiquity* 15:305–319.

Piggott, Stuart. 1983. *The Earliest Wheeled Transport: From the Atlantic Coast to the Caspian Sea*. London: Thames and Hudson; Ithaca: Cornell University Press.

Poag, James F. 1972. *Wolfram von Eschenbach*. New York: Twayne.

Pokorny, Julius. 1959. *Indogermanisches Etymologisches Wörterbuch*. 2 vols. Bern and Stuttgart: Francke Verlag.

Ponsoye, Pierre. 1957. *L'Islam et le Graal: étude sur l'ésoterisme du Parzival de Wolfram von Eschenbach*. Paris: Denoel.

Potvin, Charles, ed. 1865–1873. Chrétien de Troyes, *Perceval le Gallois: ou, Le conte du Graal*. Mons: Dequesne-Masquillier.

Puhvel, Jaan. 1987. *Comparative Mythology*. Baltimore and London: Johns Hopkins University Press.

Pujades, Geronimo. 1829–1832. *Cronica Universal del Principado de Cataluña*. Barcelona: Torner. 8 vols.

Raglan, FitzRoy Richard Somerset, Baron. 1936. *The Hero*. London: Methuen.

Rahn, Otto. 1933. *Kreuzzug gagen den Gral*. Freiburg: Urban-Verlag.

Randers-Pehrson, Justine Davis. 1983. *Barbarians and Romans: The Birth Struggle of Europe, A.D. 400–700*. Norman: University of Oklahoma Press.

Ranking, D.F. de l'Hoste. 1908. "The Tarot." *Journal of the Gipsy-Lore Society* n.s. 2:14–36.

Raymond, Irving Woodworth, trans. 1936. Paulus Orosius, *The Seven Books of History Against the Pagans*. New York: Columbia University Press.

Rees, Alwyn, and Brinley Rees. 1961. *Celtic Heritage*. New York: Thames and Hudson.

Rhys, Ernest, ed. and trans. 1928. *Arthurian Chronicles Represented by Wace and Layamon*. Introduction by Lucy Allen Paton. London: Dent, 1912.

Rhŷs, John. 1891. *Studies in the Arthurian Legend*. Oxford: Oxford University Press.

Rhŷs, John. 1901. *Celtic Folklore*. Oxford: Oxford University Press; London: Wildwood House. 2 vols.

Richmond, I.A. 1945. "The Sarmatae, Bremetennacum veteranorum, and the Regio bremetennacensis." *Journal of Roman Studies* 35:15–29.

Rickard, P. 1956. *Britain in Medieval French Literature 1100–1500*. Cambridge: Cambridge University Press.

Ridley, Ronald T. 1982. *Zosimus, New History: A Translation with Commentary.* Sydney: Australian Association for Byzantine Studies.

Ringbom, Lars Ivar. 1951. *Graltempel und Paradies; Beziehungen zwischen Iran und Europa im Mittelalter.* Stockholm: Walhlström and Widstrand, i kommission.

Rivoallan, Ana. 1957. *Présence des Celtes.* Paris: Nouvelle Librairie Celtique.

Roach, William, ed. 1941. *The Didot-Perceval.* Philadelphia: University of Pennsylvania Press.

Roach, William, ed. 1949–1983. *The Continuations of the Old French Perceval of Chrétien de Troyes.* Philadelphia: University of Pennsylvania Press. 4 vols.

Roach, William, ed. 1956. Chrétien de Troyes, *Le roman de Perceval; ou Le conte du Graal.* Geneva: Droz.

Robinson, Henry Leon. 1935. *The Language of the Scribes of the Oxford Manuscript Hatton 82 (Perlesvaus): A Part of a Dissertation Submitted to the Faculty of the Division of the Humanities in Candidacy for the Degree of Doctor of Philosophy, Department of Romance Languages and Literatures, 1933.* Chicago: Private edition, distributed by the University of Chicago Libraries.

Rodriguez, Marcia. 1976. Sir Perceval of Gales: A Critical Edition. Ph.D. diss., University of Toronto.

Rogers, Deborah Weston, trans. 1984. Chrétien de Troyes, *Lancelot: The Knight of the Cart.* New York: Columbia University Press.

Rolfe, J.C., trans. 1939. *Ammianus Marcellinus.* Cambridge: Harvard University Press.

Rolle, Renate. 1980. *The World of the Scythians.* Berkeley, Los Angeles, and London: University of California Press.

Rombatus, E., N. de Paepe, and M.J.M. de Haan, eds. 1976. *Guillaume le Clerc, Ferguut.* Culemborg: Tjeenk Willink.

Roques, Mario. 1910. "Fragments d'un MS. du Roman de Renart." *Romania* 39:3–43.

Roques, Mario, ed. 1952. *Les Romans de Chrétien de Troyes:* Erec et Enide, Le Chevalier de la charrette *and* Le Chevalier au lion (Yvain). Paris: Champion.

Rose, H.J. 1959. *A Handbook of Greek Mythology.* New York: Dutton.

Ross, Anne. 1967. *Pagan Celtic Britain.* London: Routledge and Kegan Paul; New York: Columbia University Press.

Rostovtzeff, M. 1922. *Iranians and Greeks in South Russia*. Oxford: Oxford University Press.

Rostovtzeff, M. 1929. *Le centre l'asie, la russie, la chine, et le style animal*. Translated by S. Murat. Prague: Seminarium Kondakovianum.

Rothstein, Andrew. 1954. *A People Reborn: The Story of North Ossetia*. London: Lawrence and Wishart.

Round, John Horace. 1901. "The Origin of the Stewarts." In *Studies in Peerage and Family History*. Edited by John Horace Round. Westminster: Constable, pp. 115–146.

Round, John Horace. 1910. *Peerage and Pedigree; Studies in Peerage Law and Family History*. London: Nisbet. 2 vols.

Runte, Hans, J. Keith Wikeley, and Anthony J. Farrell. 1984. *The Seven Sages of Rome and the Book of Sinbad: An Analytical Bibliography*. New York and London: Garland.

Sabarthés, A. 1907. "Étude sur la toponomastique de l'Aude." *Bulletin de la Commission Archéologique de Narbonne* 9:288–316.

Sabarthés, A. 1912. *Dictionnaire topographique du department de l'Aude*. Paris.

Saintsbury, George, trans. 1922. *The Heptameron of the Tales of Margaret, Queen of Navarre, Translated into English from the Authentic Text of M. Le Roux de Lincy with an Essay upon the Heptameron*. London: Privately printed for the Navarre Society Limited. 5 vols.

Salway, Peter. 1965. *The Frontier People of Roman Britain*. Cambridge: Cambridge University Press.

Schach, Paul. 1964. "Tristan and Isolde in Scandinavian Ballad and Folktale." *Scandinavian Studies* 36:281–297.

Schach, Paul. 1965. "The Style and Structure of Tristrams saga." In *Scandinavian Studies: Essays Presented to Dr. Henry Goddard Leach on the Occasion of His Eighty-fifth Birthday*. Edited by Carl F. Bayerschmidt and Erik J. Friis. Seattle: University of Washington Press for the American-Scandinavian Foundation, pp. 63–86.

Schach, Paul, trans. 1973. *The Saga of Tristram and Ísönd*. Lincoln: University of Nebraska Press.

Schenkl, C., ed. 1888. "Claudii Marii Victoris oratoris Massiliensis Alethia." *Corpus Scriptorum Ecclesiasticorum Latinorum* 16:335–498.

Schiller, Gertrud. 1972. *Iconography of Christian Art*, Vol. 2. Translated by Janet Seligman. London: Lund Humphries.

Schmidt, A.V.C., and Nicolas Jacobs, eds. 1980. *Medieval English Romances, Part Two*. London: Hodder and Stoughton.

Schofield, William Henry. 1895. *Studies on the Libeaus Desconnus*. Boston.

Schröder, Werner, ed. 1978. Wolfram von Eschenbach, *Willehalm*. Berlin and New York: de Gruyter.

Schroeder, L. von. 1910. *Die Wurzel der Saga von heiligen Graal*. Vienna.

Seeck, Otto, ed. 1876. *Notitia Dignitatum*. Frankfurt am Main: Unveränderter Nachdruck.

Segal, Robert A. 1993. "Foreword" to Jessie L. Weston, *From Ritual to Romance*. New Jersey: Princeton University Press.

Sharrer, Harvey, L. 1977. *A Critical Bibliography of Hispanic Arthurian Material*, Vol. 1. *Texts: The Prose Romance Cycle*. London: Grant and Cutler.

Simpson, J.A., and E.S.C. Weiner, eds. 1989. *The Oxford English Dictionary*. 2nd ed. Oxford: Clarendon.

Sodmann, Timothy, ed. 1980. Jacob Van Maerlant, *Historie van den Grale und Boek van Merline*. Cologne: Böhlau.

Sommer, Oskar, ed. 1908–1916. *The Vulgate Version of the Arthurian Romances*. Washington: Carnegie Corporation. 8 vols.

Soudek, Ernst. 1972. *Studies in the Lancelot Legend*. Rice University Studies. Houston, Texas: William Marsh Rice University Press.

Staerk, Willy. 1903. *Über den Ursprung der Grallegende: ein Beitrag zur christlichen Mythologie*. Tübingen and Leipzig: Mohr.

Stein, Ernst. 1949–1959. *Histoire du bas-empire*. 2 vols. Paris: Desclée de Brouwer.

Stein, Walter Johannes. 1988. *The Ninth Century and the Holy Grail*. Translated by Irene Groves. London: Temple Lodge.

Steine, Heinz Erich. 1981. *Wandalbert von Prum: Vita et Miracula sancti Goaris*. Frankfurt am Main and Bern: Lang.

Stewart, Mary. 1970. *The Crystal Cave*. London: Hodder and Stoughton.

Stewart, Mary. 1973. *The Hollow Hills*. London: Hodder and Stoughton.

Stewart, Mary. 1979. *The Last Enchantment*. London: Hodder and Stoughton.

Stokes, Whitley. 1892. "The Bodleian Dinnshenchas." *Folk-Lore* 3:467–516.

Stubbs, William, ed. 1887–1889. William of Malmesbury, *Gesta Regum Anglorum*. In *Willelm Malmesbiriensis Monachi de Gestes Regum Anglorum Libri Quique*. London: Eyre and Spottiswoode. 2 vols.

Sulimirski, Tadeusz. 1970. *The Sarmatians*. New York: McGraw-Hill.

Tatlock, J.S.P. 1950. *The Legendary History of Britain*. Berkeley, Los Angeles, and London: University of California Press.

Teichmann, Frank. 1986. *Der gral im Osten: Motive aus der Geistesgeschichte Armeniens und Georgiens*. Stuttgart: Freies Geistesleben.

Thomas, J.W., trans. 1978. *Eilhart von Oberge's* Tristrant. Lincoln: University of Nebraska Press.

Thomas, J.W., trans. 1982. Hartmann von Aue, *Erec*. Lincoln: University of Nebraska Press.

Thompson, Albert Wilder. 1931. *The Elucidation, a Prologue to the* Conte del graal. New York: Institute of French Studies.

Thompson, E.A. 1969. *The Goths in Spain*. Oxford: Clarendon.

Thompson, E.A. 1982. *Romans and Barbarians: The Decline of the Western Empire*. Madison: University of Wisconsin Press.

Thompson, E.A. 1985. *Who Was Saint Patrick?* Woodbridge: Boydell.

Thompson, Stith. 1955–1958. *Motif Index of Folk-Literature*. Bloomington: Indiana University Press. 6 vols.

Thorpe, Lewis, ed. 1950. *Le Roman de Laurin*. Cambridge: Bowes and Bowes.

Thorpe, Lewis, trans. 1966. Geoffrey of Monmouth, *History of the Kings of Britain (Historia Regum Britanniae)*. Harmondsworth and New York: Penguin.

Thorpe, Lewis, trans. 1974. Gregory of Tours, *History of the Franks*. Harmondsworth and New York: Penguin.

Thurneysen, R. 1912. "Mittelkymr. *UCH PEN*." *Zeitschrift für celtische Philologie* 8:347–349.

Tobin, Prudence Mary O'Hara, ed. 1976. *Les lais anonymes bretons*. Geneva: Droz.

Topsfield, L.T. 1981. *Chrétien de Troyes: A Study of the Arthurian Romances*. Cambridge: Cambridge University Press.

Turnbull, W.D. 1838. *Arthour and Merlin: A Metrical Romance*. Edinburgh: Abbotsford Club.

Ulrich, Jacob, ed. 1889. Robert de Blois, *Beaudous*. In *Robert von Blois: Sammtliche Werke*, Vol. 1. Berlin: Mayer and Müller.

Ussher, James. 1928. *Glastonbury Traditions Concerning Joseph of Arimathea*. Translated by H. Kendra Baker. London: Covenant.

Van Coolput, Colette-Anne. 1986. *Aventures querant et le sens du monde: aspects de la réception productive des premiers romans du Graal* cycliques dans le Tristan en prose. Leuven [Louvain]: Leuven University Press.

Vendryes, Joseph. 1950. "Les éléments celtiques de la légende du Graal." *Études celtiques* 5:1–50.

Vernadsky, George. 1943. *Ancient Russia*. New Haven: Yale University Press.

Vernadsky, George. 1963. "The Eurasian Nomads and Their Impact on Medieval Europe." *Studi Medievali* 4:401–434.

Veselovski, A.N., ed. 1888. *Trischan i Izhotta: Igtorii Romana i Povesti*. Petrograd.

Vinaver, Eugene. 1958. "King Arthur's Sword." *Bulletin of the John Rylands Library* 60:511–520.

Vinaver, Eugene, ed. 1967. *The Works of Sir Thomas Malory*. 2nd ed. Oxford: Clarendon. 3 vols.

Wacher, John. 1978. *Roman Britain*. London: Dent.

Waite, Arthur Edward. 1909. *The Hidden Church of the Holy Grail, Its Legends and Symbolism Considered in Their Affinity with Certain Mysteries of Initiation and Other Traces of a Secret Tradition in Christian Times*. London: Rebman.

Waite, Arthur Edward. 1933. *The Holy Grail, Its Legends and Symbolism: An Explanatory Survey of Their Embodiment in Romance Literature and a Critical Study of the Interpretatio Placed Thereon*. London: Rider.

Walford, Edward, trans. 1855. *The Ecclesiastical History of Philostorgius, As Epitomized by Photius, Patriarch of Constantinople*. London: Bohn.

Walker, Barbara G. 1983. *The Woman's Encyclopedia of Myths and Secrets*. San Francisco: Harper and Row.

Wallace-Hadrill, J.M. 1962. *The Long-Haired Kings*. London: Methuen.

Wapnewski, Peter. 1962. *Hartmann von Aue*. Stuttgart: Metzler; 7th ed. 1979.

Ward, Donald J. 1968. *The Divine Twins*. Berkeley, Los Angeles, and London: University of California Press.

Ward, Donald J., ed. and trans. 1981. *The German Legends of the Brothers Grimm*. Philadelphia: Institute for the Study of Human Issues. 2 vols.

Warren, W.L. 1973. *Henry II*. Berkeley, Los Angeles, and London: University of California Press.

Webster, Kenneth G.T. 1934. "Ulrich von Zatzikhoven's 'Welsches Bouch.'" *Harvard Studies and Notes in Philology and Literature* 16:203–214.

Webster, Kenneth G.T., ed. and trans. 1951. Ulrich von Zatzikhoven, *Lanzelet*. Revised by R.S. Loomis. New York: Columbia University Press.

Werner, Joachim. 1956. *Beiträge zur Archäologie des Attila-Reiches*. Munich: Verlag der Bayerischen Akademie der Wissenschaften.

Wertime, Richard A. 1972. "The Theme and Structure of the Stanzaic *Morte Arthur*." *Publications of the Modern Language Association* 87:1075–1082.

Wesselofsky, A.N. 1901. "Zur Frage über die Heimath der Legende von heiligen Gral." *Archiv für slavische Philologie* 23:321–385.

West, G.D. 1969. *An Index of Proper Names in French Arthurian Verse Romances 1150–1300*. Toronto: University of Toronto Press.

Weston, Jessie L. 1901a. *The Legend of Sir Lancelot*. London: Nutt.

Weston, Jessie L. 1901b. *The Romance Cycle of Charlemagne and his Peers*. London: Nutt.

Weston, Jessie L., trans. 1903. *Sir Gawain at the Grail Castle*. London: Nutt.

Weston, Jessie L. 1906–1909. *The Legend of Sir Perceval: Studies Upon Its Origin, Development, and Position in the Arthurian Cycle*. London: Nutt. 2 vols.

Weston, Jessie L. 1910a. *Chief Middle English Poets*. Boston: Houghton-Mifflin.

Weston, Jessie L. 1910b. "A Hitherto Unconsidered Aspect of the Round Table." *Mélanges de philologie romane offerts à M. Wilmotte*. Paris; Geneva: Slatkine, pp. 883–894.

Weston, Jessie L. 1913. *The Quest of the Holy Grail*. London: Cass, by arrangement with Bell.

Weston, Jessie L. 1920. *From Ritual to Romance*. Cambridge: Cambridge University Press.

Wheatley, Henry B., ed. 1865–1899. *Merlin, or the Early History of King Arthur: A Prose Romance*. London: Kegan Paul, Trench, Trübner for the Early English Text Society. 4 vols.

White, Hugh G. Evelyn, trans. 1921. Paulinus Pellaeus, *The Eucharisticus*. In *Ausonius*, Vol. 2. New York: Putnam, pp. 293–351.

White, T.H. 1938. *The Sword in the Stone*. London: Collins.

Wikander, Stig. 1941. Review of Carl-Martin Edsman, *Le baptême de feu*. *Svensk teologisk Kvartalskrift* 17:228–233.

Wilhelm, James J., and Laila Zamuelis Gross, eds. 1984. *The Romance of Arthur*. New York and London: Garland.

Williams, Mary Rhionnan. 1909. *Essai sur la composition du Roman Gallois de Peredur*. Paris: Champion.

Williams, Mary Rhionnan, ed. 1922–1925. Gerbert de Montreuil, *Le continuation de Perceval*. Paris: Champion. 3 vols.

Williams, Robert, Rev. 1865. *Lexicon Cornu-Britannicum: A Dictionary of the Ancient Celtic Language of Cornwall, in Which the Words Are Elucidated by Copius Examples from the Cornish Works Now Remaining; with Translations in English. The Synonyms Are Also Given in the Cognate Dialects of Welsh, Armorican, Irish, Gaelic and Manx*. Llandovery: Roderic; London: Trübner.

Williamson, G.A., trans. 1959. Josephus, *The Jewish War*. New York: Dorset.

Wilson, John C., ed. 1961. Sir Thomas Malory, *Le Morte Darthur*. New York: University Books.

Wilson, Robert A. 1967. "Malory and Caxton." In *A Manual of the Writings in Middle English 1050–1500*, Vol. 3. Edited by J. Burke Severs. New Haven: Connecticut Academy of Arts and Sciences.

Wind, Bertina H., ed. 1960. Thomas, *Les fragments du Roman de Tristan, poème du XIIe siècle*. Geneva: Droz.

Windisch, E. 1912. *Das keltische Britannien bis zu Kaiser Arthur*. Leipzig.

Winterbottom, Michael, ed. and trans. 1978. Gildas, *The Ruin of Britain*. In *History from the Sources*, Vol. 7. Chichester: Phillimore.

Withycombe, E.G. 1947. *The Oxford Dictionary of English Christian Names*. New York and London: Oxford University Press.

Withycombe, E.G. 1950. *The Oxford Dictionary of English*. Oxford: Oxford University Press.

Wixman, Ronald. 1984. *The Peoples of the USSR: An Ethnographic Handbook*. Armonk: Sharpe.

Wolfgang, Leonora D. 1976. *Bliocadran: A Prologue to the* Perceval *of Chrétien de Troyes*. Tübingen: Niemeyer.

Wolfram, Herwig. 1988. *History of the Goths*. Translated by Thomas J. Dunlap. Berkeley, Los Angeles, and London: University of California Press.

Woods, Barbara Allen. 1955. *The Devil in Dog Form: A Study of the Literary and Folkloristic Background of the Poodle Motif in Goethe's Faust*. Ph.D. diss., University of California, Los Angeles.

Woods, Barbara Allen. 1959. *The Devil in Dog Form: A Partial Type-Index of Devil Legends*. Berkeley, Los Angeles, and London: University of California Press.

Woods-Marsden, Joanna. 1988. *The Gonzaga of Mantua and Pisanello's Arthurian Frescoes*. Princeton: Princeton University Press.

Wright, Peter Poyntz. 1986. *The Battle of Hastings*. Salisbury: Russell.

Yoshida, Atsuhiko. 1965. "Sur quelques coupes de la fable greque." *Revue des études anciennes* 67:31–36.

Yoshida, Mizuho. 1994. "A Study of the Grail Quest in Malory." *Seikeigakuin Journal of Literature* (Tokyo), No. 2 (March), pp. 1-24.

Zenker, Rudolf. 1923. "Zu Perceval-Peredur." *Germanisch-Romanische Monatsschrift* 11:240–256.

Zenker, Rudolf. 1926. "Weiteres zur Mabinogionfrage." *Zeitschrift für französische Sprache und Literatur* 48:402–410.

Zimmer, Heinrich. 1890. Review of Alfred Nutt, *Studies on the Legend of the Holy Grail, with Special Reference to the Hypothesis of Its Celtic Origin*. *Göttingischen Gelehrten Anzeigen* 12:488–528; June:516–517.

Zimmer, Heinrich. 1946. *Myth and Symbols in Indian Art and Civilization*. Edited by Joseph Campbell. New York: Pantheon.

Zirra, Vlad. 1976. "The Eastern Celts of Romania." *Journal of Indo-European Studies* 4:1–42.

Index

Aalardin du Lac, 125
Abaev, V. I., 247
Aballach, king, 162
Abazas, xix
Abbo, Bishop. *See* Goeric
Abduction, of Guinevere, 85, 94
Abegg, Emil, 213
Abkhaz, xix
Abkhazians, 286
Abraham, 264
Acheflour, 306, 312
Achilles, xiii, 168
Adder. *See* Serpent and dragon image
Adoption, 63
Adrianople, battle of, 267
Aegidius, 33
Aëtius, 28, 32, 33, 38, 94, 131, 242, 243–244, 261–262
Afghanistan, 5, 215
Agamemnon, xiii
Agned, Mount, 23, 327
Agravain, 90
Agravain of Orkeny, 308
Agri deserti, 32, 107, 261
Agrimontin Mountains, 213

Ahsnart, 313
Ahsnartag, 313
Ailan, 25
Aillainville (Haute-Marne), 234
Airvault, 83
Akula, 313
Alægatæ, 222, 234, 271
Alagna, 31
Alagna Lomelina, 31
Alaign, 31
Alaigne-Aude, 234
Alain, king, 263
Alain, name, 25, 98–99
Alain, St., 25, 99, 247
Alain, son of Judikaël, 34
Alain Barbetorte, 36
Alaincourt (Aisne), 234
Alaincourt (Ardennes), 234
Alaincourt-aux-Boeufs (Meurthe-et-Moselle), 234
Alaincourt-la-Côte (Meurthe-et-Moselle), 234
Alain de Gomeret, 132
Alain Fergant. *See* Alan IV
Alain le Grand, 34
Alain le Gros de la Vales, 98, 132

Alain IX de Rohan. *See* Rohan, Alain IX de
Alain of Brittany, 248
Alains (Eure), 234
Alain the Black. *See* Alan II
Alain the Great. *See* Alain le Grand
Alain the Red. *See* Alan I
Alain the Rich Fisher, 132, 233, 263, 265, 269, 310–311
Alan, as a surname, 16, 25
Alan, St., 247
Alan I (the Red), 34, 36
Alan IV (Fergant), 25, 36
Alancelot, 95
Alania, xviii, 40, 41
Alanic, 27
Alan Judual, 36, 141
Alan of Gallowy, 25
Alan of Vannes, 138, 141
Alans
  ageism and, 34
  animals of, 36–37
  background of, xv, xvii–xix, xxvi, xxviii–xxx
  as bishops, 38–39
  Christian, 27, 34, 245, 247
  confused with Sarmatians, 13, 16, 25
  death and, 34
  description of, 26–39
  in the East, 39–40
  Holy Grail and, 233–249
  Lancelot and evidence of Alanic culture, 107–108
  marriage and, 26, 27
  military/weapon tactics, 36–37
  northern contingent, 28–37
  religion and, 27, 91–92, 185, 186
  Romans, relations with, 26–27, 28, 37
  settlements, 27–28, 32–34
  southern contingent, 37–39
  sword worship, 185, 186
  women, 162
Alanus (name), xxviii–xxix, xxx, 96
Alanus, St., 247
Alanus ab Insulis, 132
Alaric I, 38, 236, 240, 242, 267
Alaric II, 268
Albacin, Spain, 108
Albanians, xv
Albericus Trium Fontium, 61
Albi, count of, 247, 248
Albigensians, 132, 248
  See also Cathars
Albrecht, 215
Alclud. *See* Dumbarton Rock, battle of
Alcock, Leslie, 19
Alein (name), 25, 99
Alençon, 96, 234
Alenzon, 96
Alethia, 185
Alexandria, 219
Aleyn (surname), 16
Allain-aux-Boefs, 234
Allaines, 234
Allainville-en-Drouais, 234
Allan, 234
Allancourt (Marne), 234
Allamont (Meurthe-et-Moselle), 234
Alps, 239, 242, 246, 267
Altai Mountains, 3
Amaethon, 223
Amagnon, 223, 233
Amangon, 23
Amazons, 8, 161
Ambrosius Aurelius, 64

Index

Amfortas, 223
Amiens, 28
Ammianus Marcellinus, 26, 184, 186
Anāhitā, 165, 221
Aneirin, 23
Angers, earl of, 125
Animals
    See also Serpent and dragon image
    Alans and, 36–37
    dogs, 199
    horsemanship, 107–108, 132–133
    Scythian use of, 8
    white, 102–103
Anjou, house of, 215
Annales Cambriae (Welsh Annals), 23, 61, 62, 70
Annwfn, cauldron of, 217–221
Anthemius, 64
Antonine Wall, 329
Aorsi, 13
Aphrodite, 185
Api, 185
Apollo, 164, 185, 200
Apollo Maponus, 19
Aquitaine, 33, 244, 247
Arabs, influence of, 215
Aral Sea, 5
Aranrhod, 168
Arch of Titus, 240
Ares, 185
Argimpasa, 185
Arians, 236
Armenia, xv, 43
Armor, heavy body, with scales, 8
Armorica/Armoricans, 28, 32, 33, 34, 35, 244, 245
Arnulf, St., 33
Arpoxaïs, 11

Arras, 28
Art/artifacts
    Grail tapestries, 128
    Sarmatian, 19
    Scythian, 11
    serpent and dragon images, 195–196
Artemis, 164, 199
Arthour and Merlin, 189
Arthur, King
    dates used for, 62
    death of, 62, 66–71
    historical, 62–66, 105
    massacres and, 104
    origins of, xiv, xxix
    Sarmatian Connection and, 61–71
    sword of, 104
Arthur (name), 62–63
Arthurian sites, 23, 24
Arthurian tales
    influence of, xiii
    origins of, xxv–xxxi
Arthyr, 62
Artorius, 62, 104–105
Arvandus, 64
Aryan influence, 216
Asding Vandals, 28
Ashe, Geoffrey, 33, 66, 218
Aspar, 39–40, 64
Aspianis, 25
Athanaric, 267
Athaulf, 38, 242–243, 256–260, 267, 294–295
Athene, 157, 199
Attalus, 243, 258
Attila, 32, 131, 242, 244
Aube, Department of, 108
Augustine, St., 27
Augustus Caesar, 264

Aukhatai. *See* Scythians, Warrior
Ausonius, 243
Avallach, 162
Avallana, 70
Avallon, 66
Avalon, 66, 70, 160, 162
Avesta, 213
Azerbaijan, 43

Bacaudae, 28, 32, 244
Bachrach, Bernard S., xv, 25, 35, 95, 99, 185, 187, 245, 257
Badon, Mount, 23, 327, 329
Badon Hill, battle of, xxiii, 23, 61, 327, 329
Baeios, 126
Bainesse, 330
Balin, 181, 255, 263
Balkars, xix
Ban, king, 81, 85, 90, 168
    name of, 99–101
Ban, term of, 99–101
Banadaspes, 100
Ban de Benoich. *See* Ban, king
Bandemagus/Bandemagu/Bandemagús/Baudemagus/Bandimagus, 101
Bani, 100–101
Bannum, 100
Bannum benvoîcum/banvoïcum, 100
Banvou/Banvo, 100
Barber, R., 218
Barcelona, 268
Barzu-Name, 213
Bassas River, 23, 327, 328–329
Batraz, xxvi, xxix, 43, 168, 264
    Gawain and, 135
    King Arthur and, 68, 70
    Lancelot and, 92, 103–106

    massacres and, 104
    Nartamongæ, xxvii, xxx, 104, 221–225
    Perceval and, 133
    sword of, xxvi, 68, 104, 183–184
    water and, 104, 221
Bayeux, 126
Bazas, 38, 81, 243, 247, 256–257
Beauce, 125
Bedale, Brian FitzAlan de, 25–26
Bede, 62, 263
Bedevere the Frenchman of Beauce, 125
Bedievere of Neustria, 125
Bedivere, 125–126, 128
Bedwyr. *See* Bedivere
Befort, 159
Beheading, 92
Beheading game, 107, 134, 137
Belarus, xvii
Beli, 155
Benoich/Benwick, 81, 99, 100
Beowulf, xiii
Bergmann, F. G., 270
Béroul, 138
Berry, 64, 101, 106
Bethlehem, 201
Biket, 223, 248, 270
Binchester, 328
Bishops, Alans as, 38–39
Black Chapel, 165
Black Serpent, 201
Bliocadran, 132
Bogdanow, F., 99
Bohort (name), 101
Boniface, 243
Book of Caradoc, 133–134, 199
Boort (name), 101, 103
Bora, house of, 313

Index

Boratæ, 101, 103, 222, 234, 271
Bordeaux, 243
Bors/Boortz/Boerte, 98, 100–101, 104, 158, 168
Bort (name), 101
Bort (town), 101
Bourges, 64
Braithwaite, Thomas, 19
Bran, 221, 269
Branwen, 218
Brèche d'Allanz, 96
Breguoin, 327, 328
Bremenium, battle of, 329
Bremetennacum Veteranorum, xxvii, 18–19, 23, 63, 197, 328
Bretons, 34
Britain, Sarmatians in, 18–26
Brittany, 32, 33, 34, 37, 188, 244, 248
  dukes of, 141, 299–303, 309
Bron, 268–269
Bromwich, R., 138, 269
Brown, A.C.L., 133
Bruce, J. D., 183
Buddha, 201
Buka, 100
Burgundians, 28, 32, 131, 235
Burgundy, duke of, 128

Cadwaldar, 248
Caen, 125
Cai. *See* Kay
Caledonians, xxiii, 18, 62
Caledonii, 327, 328
Caliburnus, 69, 184
Camboglanna, 70
Camelot, xiii, 61
Camlann, battle of, 61, 66, 70
Campbell, J. F., 40
Camp des Rouets, 34

Canaan, 91, 183
Caradoc of Nantes, 134
Caradoc of Vannes, 133–134, 199
Carcassone, 243, 258
Carman, J. N., 106
Carolingians, 33, 201, 244
Carpilio, 244
Carthage, 108, 242
Carts, riding in, 108
Cassian, 27, 260, 261
Cassius Dio, 327
Castle Corbenic, 217
Castle Death, 158
Castle Dodone, 159
Castle Dore, 139
Castle Guinnion, 23, 327, 328
Castle of the Cathars, 259
Castus, Lucius Artorius, 327, 328
  career of, xxiii, xxvii, 62–63
Cataphracti, xxv, xxvi
Cataractonium, 23
Cat Coit Celidon, 23
  battle of, 327, 328
Cathars, 214, 215, 220, 248, 272
Catterick. *See* Cataractonium
Caucasus Mountains and people, xvii–xix, 40, 201, 213, 247
Cauldron of Annwfn, 217–221
Cavalry
  cataphracti, xxv, xxvi
  Scythian, 5, 8
Cavendish, R., 210
Cei. *See* Kay
Celidon. *See* Cat Coit Celidon
Celts/celtic influence, 25, 34, 35, 36, 40
  cauldron of Annwfn, 217–221
Cevennes Mountains, 107
Chalice at the Cross, 130, 131, 201, 233–234, 245, 247, 248

Chalice of the Last Supper, 209–210, 213
Châlons, battle of, 37
Châlons-sur-Marne, 244
Chanaan. *See* Canaan
Chapel Nigramous, 165, 183
Chapel Perilous, 102
Charlemagne, house of, 296–298
Charles VI, 128
Chastity, 164
Châteauroux, 64
Charvet, Louis, 25
Che. *See* Kay
Chechens, xviii, xix
Chester, 23, 197
Childebert I, 141
Childeric, 33
China, 43
Chinon, 125
Chlothar I, 141
Chrétien de Troyes, 32, 37, 61, 88–89, 91, 102, 210, 223, 233, 263–264
    Conte de la charrette (Knight of the Cart), 71, 82, 86, 88, 90, 108, 154
    Conte del Graal, 96, 132, 133, 216, 269
    Erec et Enide, 137
Christian communion ceremony, 210, 213
Christianizing of tales, 133, 210, 213
Christians, Alans as, 27, 34, 245, 247
Chronicle of Elis Gruffydd, 69–70, 197
Chronicle of Mont-Saint-Michel, 62
Chronicles of Anjou, 64
Churches
    at Vannes, 35–36
    of St. Victor, 27
Circassians, xviii, xix, 40, 134, 187

Cîteaux, 132
Clarent and Claris (sword), 184
Claudas, 81, 90, 106, 158
Claudas de la Deserte, 159
Claudius Marius Victor, 185
Clodwig, 90
Closs, Hannah, xxx, 215
Clovis, 33, 90–91
Clovis I, 90–91
Coed Celydon. *See* Cat Coit Celidon, battle of
Colarusso, John, 70, 165, 187, 225
Comites Alani, 235
Conan IV, 36
Conan Meriadoc, 35, 36, 63
Constance, 36
Constans, 126
Constantine, house of, 307
Constantine Cadorson, 126
Constantine of Britain, 126
Constantine III, 28, 38, 236
Constantinople, 267
Constantius, 38, 81–82, 94, 258, 260, 267, 268
Conte de la charrette (Knight of the Cart), 71, 82, 86, 88, 90, 108, 154
Conte de la Perle, 214
Conte del Graal, 96, 132, 133, 216, 221, 269
Cooper-Oakley, I., 213
Corbenic, 210
Cornwall, 138, 139, 141
Cornwall, earl of, 126, 299–306
Cotini, 40, 43
Coyajee, J. C., 128, 130, 135, 165, 216, 237
Creiddylad, 219
Cross
    Chalice at the, 130, 131, 201,

Index

233–234, 245, 247, 248
crucifixion, 201, 209, 237, 248
Crudel, 219
Crusades, influence of, xxx, 214, 215
Cūchulainn, 135, 169, 220
Culhwch and Olwen, 126, 181, 218–219
Cumont, F., 237
Cunomorus. *See* Mark Cunomorus
Cup(s)
    Alanic, 201, 233, 234
    Holy Grail as, 210
    Jamshid, 216
    Kai Khosraw, 216
    magical, 133, 220–225
    Nartamongæ, xxvii, xxx, 104, 221–225
    Sarmatian, 13
    Scythian, 11, 235
Cynan, 63

Dacia, 16
Dacian Wars, 16
Dagda, 220
Daghestanis, xviii, xix
Dame du Lac/Lady of the Lake, xxvii, 81, 84
    absence of, in some legends, 166–168
    categories of stories, 159
    early versions of, 154, 156–157
    female sword bestower, 168–169
    foreknowledge of, 157
    lake/home of, 164–166
    as Lancelot's guardian, 159–160
    magic used by, 157–158
    as Merlin's lover, 163–164
    nature of, 154, 156
    as opponent of Morgan Le Fay, 160–163
    other names for, 154
    snakes and, 199
    white and, 156
Danube, 40
Dead
    Egyptian cult of the, 201
    Isle of the, 218
Dea Syria, 221
Death
    of Alaric, 242
    Dame du Lac and, 158, 164
    of King Arthur, 62, 66–71
Dee, River, 269
Demanada Mort Artu, 139
Déols, 64
Dere Street, 327, 328
Desert, in Lancelot, 106
Devil, 130
Dialogue with Glewlwyd, 162
Diana, 164
Diane, 164
Didot-*Perceval*, 132, 268
Dinas Bran, 269
Dio Cassius, xxvi, 18
Dirr, Adolf, 68
Dobruja, 27
Dodone, 106, 159
Dogs, 199
Dol, 141
Dolorous Stroke, 255, 263, 264
Dominicans, 43
Don, 223
Don Bettyr, 11, 221, 234
Don River, 11, 16
Dordogne, 106
Dorin, 158
Draco Normannicus, 37
Dragons. *See* Serpent and dragon image

Dream of Rhonabwy, The, 184
Drest, 139
Drostan, 139
Drustan, 126
Drustanus, 139, 141
Dubglas/Douglas River, 23, 327, 328, 329
Dumbarton Rock, battle of, 329
Dumézil, Georges, xv, 68, 221, 224, 234
Dumnonii, 34, 35, 138
Durdura, 168
Dux bellorum, 63
Dzaujikau, xix

Earht, 185
Eboracum, 19, 327, 328, 329
Ecclesia tradition, 217, 271
Ector, 28, 91, 137
Egyptian cult of the dead, 201
Eilhart von Oberge, 139
Eisner, Sigmund, xxxi
Elaine (name), 98–99
Elaine of Benoich, 81, 99, 164, 168
Elaine of Corbenic, 85, 217
Elainus, 25
Eleanor (Aliénor) of Aquitaine, 37
Elen, 63, 64
Elïavrés, 134
Elis Gruffydd, 96–97, 197
Ellaini, 25
Elucidation, 221, 223
Enide, 138
Eothar, 28
Erec, 86
Erec (knight), 94, 137–138
Erec (name), 138
Erec et Enide, 137, 138
Ernée/Ernier, 100
Esparlot, 248

Estoire del Saint Graal, 139, 167, 183, 197, 269
Étienne de Rouen, 37
Etna, Mount, 161
Eucharisticus, 256, 260, 261
Euric, king, 28, 64, 66
Evaine, 168
Evans, S., 132
Eve, 202
Evelake/Evelach, 209, 264
Excalibur, 68–69, 128, 158, 160, 184
Æxsætæghatæ, 222, 234

Fairies, 154, 155
Faugère, A., 214, 216
Female sword bestower, 168–169
Fergus (Guillaume le Clerc), 96
Fergus et Galienne, 25, 223
Finnabair, 153
Firdausi, 128
Fire in the water, 216
Fisher King, 217, 223, 255, 268–273
FitzAlan, as a surname, 16, 25–26
FitzAlan, Brian, 25
FitzAlan de Bedale, Brian, 25–26
FitzBryans, Alan, 25
Flavia Caesariensis, province of, 330
Fleuriot, 64
Flore and Blanscheflur, xxx
Flowering Wasteland, 255
Ford, Patrick K., 79–80, 218
Forest
    Fair Forest Befort, 159
    in Lancelot, 106
Fowey, 139
France. *See name of city/region*
Franks, 28, 32, 33
Frava_i, 237
Freibergs, Gunar, 96

Index

Fritigern, 267
Fylde, 19

Gaevani, 135
Gahmuret, 215
Gaiseric, 38, 261–262
Galahad, 85, 95, 98, 104, 159–160, 181, 186–187, 213, 248, 263, 264
Galahaut, 107
Galahaut de Haut Desert, 107
Gales li Caus, 132
Gallais, P., 165, 216, 221, 237
Galla Placidia, 32, 38, 240, 242, 243, 256, 258, 259
Gallo-Franks, 36
  See also Franks
Gallois, 131–132
Gallo-Romans, 35, 244–245
  See also Roman Empire
Galvagin, 135
Ganges, 213
Garden of Eden, 202
Gareth, 137
Garonne River, 107, 243
Gaudentius, 243
Gaul, 27–28, 38–39
  Alan invasions from Italy to, 235–249
Gaul, church of, 27
Gaunnes, 101
Gauvain, 135
Gawain (knight), xxvii, 85, 94, 134–137
Gawain (name), 135
Gayomart, 213
Geoffrey of Monmouth, 35, 61–62, 64, 101, 135, 181, 263, 329
Georgia, Republic of, xviii
Georgians, xix, 40, 43
Gereint and Enid, 138

German-Iranian influence, 214–215
Germanus, Bishop of Auxerre, 32, 244
Gerona, 234
Gervais of Tilbury, 70
Gevān, 135
Gharmet, 213
Gicquel, 34
Gifflet, 128
Gildas, 23, 33, 62, 219
Gimbutas, Marija, 5
Giw, 135
Glastonbury, 224
Glasgow
Glein River, 23, 327, 328
Gnosticism, 219–220
Goar (Alan leader), 27, 28, 32, 131, 242, 244
Goar (name), 27–28, 131
Goar, St., 245, 247
Gododdin, 23
Goeric, 28, 33, 138, 247, 268
Goetnick, G., 217
Goffart, Walter, 27, 32
Gohar, 216, 237
Gordian, 19
Gospel of Nicodemus, 215
Goths, 27, 39, 236, 243, 262, 268
Grail. *See* Holy Grail
Grand Saint Graal, 200
Graves
  Galahad stories and, 159–160
  hearths on, 91, 92, 160
  mirrors in, 108
  river, 242
Great Fâl, 210
Green knight, 107, 137, 160
Gregory of Tours, 64
Grisward, Joël, xxv, xxvi, 69
Guellans Guenelaus, 132

Guérec, 138
Guigemar, 102
Guillaume le Clerc, 96, 223
Guimier, 134, 199
Guinevere, 38, 81, 153
    abduction of, 85, 94
    meaning of name, xiv
Guingamor, 102
Guinnion Castle, 23, 327, 328
Guyot. *See* Kyot
Gwalchmai, 135
Gwerec, 138
Gwyn, 219

Hadrian, 16
Hadrian's Wall, 18, 23, 135, 199, 327, 328
Hallows, 224, 237
Hartmann von Aue, 37, 86, 137
Hastings, battle of, 34, 36, 37, 210
Hecate, 164
Helaine (name), 99
Helen (name), 99
Henry of Huntingdon, 62
Henwen, 103
Hephaistos, 157, 199
Herakles, 185, 197, 199
Heraldic device, 8
Herodotus, 3, 5, 8, 11, 13, 184, 185, 195, 285
Hesperides, 166
Hestia, 11, 185
Historia Anglorum, 62
Historia Brittonum, 243
History of the Kings of Britain, 61–62, 181
Hollister, C. W., 139
Holy Grail
    Alans and, 233–249
    Bearer, 217
    Castle, 166, 210, 213–214, 222
    cauldron of Annwfn, influence of, 217–221
    as Chalice of the Last Supper, 209–210, 213
    as cup versus stone, 210
    Hallows, 224, 237
    Keepers, 161, 255–273
    Knight, 186, 209, 215, 248
    light of, 215–216
    maidens of, 166, 216, 217
    origins/influences on, 213–217
    procession of, 237, 240, 271
    relic, 137
    serpent images, 200
    water and, 221
Holy Grail, quest for
    Alan connection, xxix–xxx
    compared to Nart sagas, xxvii
Holy Grail Quest tapestry, 128
Honorius, emperor, 28, 32, 81, 236, 242, 257
Horsemanship, 107–108, 132–133
Hundred Years War, 35
Hungary, Iazyges in, 16
Huns, xvi, 99, 103, 185–186, 236, 242, 244
Hunt for the white stag, 102–103
Huntress-goddess, 164
Huth *Merlin,* 96, 99, 200, 255
    See also Merlin (Robert de Boron)

Iazyges/Jazyges
    Castus and, 63
    description of, xxiii, xxvi–xvii, xxviii, 13, 16, 18, 25

Gawain and, 135
influence on the legends of
Lancelot, 104–105
Iblis, 158
Igraine, 160
Iliad, xiii
India, 43, 215, 216
Indo-Aryans, xv
Indo-European influence, xv–xvi, 215, 216, 220–221
Indo-Oriental hypothesis, 213
Ingushetia, xix
Iran/Iranians
influence of, 213–214
origins of steppe, xv–xvii
Ireland, influence of, 216, 218–220
Isabelle of Bavaria, 128
Iselin, L. E., 213
Isle of Man, 162
Isle of the Dead, 218
Isolde, 138, 139
Italy, 125
Alan invasions from, to Gaul, 235–249
Iweret, 159

Jacob van Maerlant, 105
Jacques de Guise, 61
Jamshid, 216
Javelin, 8
Jazyges. *See* Iazyges
Jenkins, T. A., 103, 256
Jesus, 209, 269
Jews, 262
Jézéquel, 34
Jinn, 218
Johannine Rite, 219
Jonas, 141
Jordanes, 64

Joseph (Robert de Boron), 90, 130, 132, 167, 209, 233, 237, 264, 269
Joseph of Arimathea, 27, 91, 132, 209, 210, 242, 264, 310–312
Josselin, 35
Jovinus, 235, 242
Judikaël, 34

Kabardians, 40
Kai, 126
Kai Khosraw, 128, 216
Kain, 125
Kamper, F., 213
Karachays, xix
Katiaroi. *See* Scythians, Agricultural
Kay (knight), xxvii, 125–126, 128
Kay (name), 126
Kazakhs, 5
Kerch Peninsula, 100
Khazar Empire, xviii
Knight of the Cart. See Conte de la charrette
Knights
Bedivere, 125–126, 128
Erec, 94, 137–138
Gawain, xxvii, 85, 94, 134–137
genealogies for, 98–99
Holy Grail, 186, 209, 215, 248
Kay, 125–126, 128
Perceval, 99, 104, 128, 130–134
Templar, 214
Kolaxaïs, 11, 225
Kurgan, xvi
Kynvawr, 141
Kyot, 215, 270–271

Lac, king, 137
Lady of the Lake. *See* Dame du Lac

Laeti, 26, 235
Lai du Cor, 223, 248, 270
Lake
   Dame du Lac and, 164–166
   Diane, 164
   in Lancelot, 106, 107
   People of the, 165, 166
Lançarote, 95
Lance, 237
Lancelot
   Batraz and, 92, 103–106
   Dame du Lac as guardian to, 159–160
   death of, 70–71
   etymology, 94–101
   evidence of Alanic culture, 107–108
   first written references to, 32
   Gawain and, 135, 137
   generosity of, 92
   geography, 106–107
   grandfather of, 92, 94
   legends of, 81–84
   Lug and, 84–94
   massacres and, 104
   meaning/origin of name, 82, 84–85, 88, 94–96, 98
   origins of, xiv, xxviii–xxix, 79–81
   place-names, 95–96, 98
   sword of, 104
   water and, 103, 104, 106–107
   water fairies and, 86
   Welsh geography, knowledge of, 86, 88
   white animal, 102–103
Lancelot, 82, 84, 88–89, 90, 91, 103–104, 154, 158, 163, 166, 167
Lancelot and the Deer with the White Foot, 102

Land of Maidens, 165
Land of Women, 165, 166
Lanzelet (Ulrich), 32, 38, 82, 86, 88, 89–90, 94, 102, 106, 153, 154, 158, 168, 197, 199
Lavaur, Abbey of, 25, 99, 247
Lawnslot, 96
Lawton, D. A., 233
Layamon, xiv, 126, 181
Lazarus, 209, 242
Lebor Gabála Érenn, 197
Legend of St. Goeznovius, 62, 63
Legion, city of, 23
Le Mans, 247
Le Morte Darthur, xxv–xxvi, 69, 102, 105, 128, 166
Leo I, 39, 62, 64
Leontius, 39
Lindum, 330
Linnuis, 23, 327, 330
Lionel, 158
Lipoxaïs, 11
Li Roumans du bons chevalier Tristan, 213
Littleton, C. Scott, xxv, xxvi–xxviii, 79, 168
Liuro de Josep Abaramatia, 92
Livre d'Artus, 255
Lizard People, 13, 195
Lleu, 85–86
Lleu Llaw Gyffes, 168
Lludd, 219
LLwch Llawynnawc, 88, 94–95
Lombards, 235
Longinus, 237
   spear of, 263
Loomis, R. S., 84–85, 88, 94–95, 102, 130, 135, 161, 210, 255, 266
Lorengel, 131

Index

Lot
  in Old French, 95
  region of, xxix, 98, 107, 259–260
Lot, Ferdinand, 101, 199
Lot of Orkney, 85
Lot River, 98
Lovelich, H., 92, 200, 255
Lozachmeur, J.-C., 235
Lucius of Rome, 85
Lug, xxviii, 84–94
Lugh, 85, 86

Mabinogi, 63, 102, 126, 162, 218, 263
Mabuz, 158
MacCulloch, J. A., 165
Macha, 156
Maechen-Helfen, O., 108
Magnon, 223
Maimed King of the Vulgate Cycle, 132, 166, 255, 263–268
Mainz, 236
Maiux, 264
Malcor, Linda A., xxviii–xxx
Malduc, 94
Mallory, J. P., xxv
Malory, Thomas, xiii, 107, 154, 160, 164, 183, 263
  Le Morte Darthur, xxv–xxvi, 69, 102, 105, 166
Manannán, 162, 221
Manessier, 210, 223
Mangon, 223
Manichaeism, 214, 215, 260
Map, Walter, 82, 88
Marcellus, Ulpius, 328
Märchen, 130
Marcomanni, 18
Marcomannian War, xxvi
Marcus Aurelius, 18, 285

Margaret of Flanders, 128
Margon, 223
Markale, Jean, 27, 34, 35, 36, 95, 135, 153, 169, 200–201, 210, 214, 215, 223, 269
Mark Conomar, king. *See* Mark Cunomorus
Mark Cunomorus, 105, 141
Mark, king, 138, 139
Marriage
  Alans and, 26, 27
  Scythian, 11
Marseilles, 242, 260, 261, 267
Martinus Polonus, 61
Marx, J., 131, 138, 210, 220, 244
Mary Magdalene, 209
Massagetae, 5
Maximinus the Thracian, 39
Maximus, 63–64
Medb, 153
Melchizedek, 264
Meleagant, 85
Meliades, 163, 164
Melusine, 260
Mériadeuc, 132
Meriadoc, Conan, 35, 36, 63
Merlin, Dame du Lac as lover of, 163–164
Merlin. See Prophécies de Merlin
Merlin (Robert de Boron), 90, 96, 186, 233
Merovingians, 33, 244–245
Metrical Joseph, 269
Metz, bishop of, 247
Micha, A., 100, 101
Mi5gar5 serpent, 201
Miller, V., 68, 126
Mime, 188
Mirrors, 108

Mithraic Chronos, 201
Mithraic influence, 220, 237
Modares, 267
Modena Cathedral, 125
Modron, 162
Monks
    Christianizing of tales, 133
    Scythian, 39
Monsalvatsch/Montsalvat, 213–214
Montségur, 259
Moraine, 223
Mordrains/Mordrens, 209–210, 219, 263, 264, 266
Mordred, 64, 69–70, 85
Morgan, 85
Morgana, 161
Morgan Le Fay, 160–163
Morgawse of Orkney, 85
Morrīgan, 157, 161
Morte le roi Artu, 70, 158, 166, 167
Morvandus, 64
Morville, Hugh de, 88, 89, 91
Mountains, in Lancelot, 106

Nantes, 34, 134, 244
Narbonne, 242
Nart sagas, xix, xxvi–xxvii, 40
Nartamongæ, xxvii, xxx, 104, 221–225
Nascien, 200, 209, 219, 266
Nelli, R., 99, 242
Nennius, 23, 62, 243, 263, 327–329
Nerthus, 221
Neustria, 125
Newstead, H. H., 221
Nibelungenlied, 187, 272
Nickel, Helmut, xv, xxviii, 8, 70, 101, 126
Nicodemus, 132
Nimué, 154, 164

Niniane, 154, 157, 163–164
Nitze, W. A., 103, 256, 269
Noricum, 38
Normandy, 101, 126
Normans, 34
Northumbria, 328
Nudd, 219
Nutt, A., 130, 156, 269

Oberwessel, 245
Odin, 183, 201
Odyssey, xiii
Oetosyrus, 185
"Ogre's Daughter, The," 218–219
Olicana (Ilkey), fort, 328
Optila, 38
Orcamp, 64
Orkney, house of, 308
Orléans, 28, 32, 33, 131, 188, 244
Orosius, 236
Orpheus, 200
Ossetes/Ossetians
    Batraz, xxvi, xxix, 43, 68, 70
    description of, xviii–xix, xxv–xxvi, 3, 40–43
Otranto, Cathedral of, 43
Owen, D.D.R., 215

Paimpont, Abbey of, 34
Palamedes, 137, 139
Pannier, Karl, xxx
Pannonia, xxv, 16, 18, 28, 242, 244
Pannonian War, 100
Pant, 99
Pantdragon, 99, 101
Panticapaeum, 100
Papaeus, 185
Paralatai. *See* Scythians, Royal
Paris, Gaston, 199

Parzival, 130, 213, 214, 215
Parzival, 213
Parzival (name), 131
Paskweten, 34
Paton, L. A., 61, 154, 156, 184
Paulars, 139
Paulinus of Pella, 81
Paulinus Pellaeus, 38, 162, 243, 256–263
Pauphilet, A., 201
Peebles, R. J., 237
Peles, 255
Pellam, 263
Pelleas, 164
Pellehan, 255
Pelles/Pelle, 132, 161, 255–256
Pellinore, 132, 255
Perceval, 132, 156
Perceval (name), 99, 131
Perceval (knight), 99, 104, 128, 130–134, 200
Perchevaux, 131
Peredur, 88, 199
Peredur, 201, 217
Perilous Cemetery, 91, 183
Perle, 131, 216
Perlesvaus, 25–26, 84, 90–91, 103, 104, 107, 132, 166, 167, 183, 255–256
Perlesvaux, 131
Peronnik the Fool, 130
Persian, influence, 213–215
Peterson, L. A., 104
Philippe d'Alsace, 128
Philippe de Vigneulles, 61
Philip the Bold, 128
Philip the Good, 128
Phillips, E. D., 213
Picts, 18, 62, 141, 329

Plague, 33
Poitou, 131
Poland, xvii
Pontic steppes, 5
Poseidon, 185
Post-Vulgate Cycle, 137
Preiddeu Annwn, 218
Preves/prive, 70, 197
Prigorodny, xix
Procopius, 240
Prophécies de Merlin, 154, 156, 157, 162, 199
Pwyll, 256
Pythian Apollo, 200
Pythian Artemis, 199

Quadi, 18, 40
Queste del Saint Graal, 92, 139, 160, 167, 183, 200–201, 272
Quest for the Glory, 135

Radagaisus, 37, 236
Raetia, 38
Randers-Pehrson, J. D., 39
Ratchis, king, 235
Ravenna, 235
Ravenna Cosmography, 19
Reichenau, 137
Reims, 28
Religion
    Alanic, 27, 91–92, 185
    Scythian, 11, 184–185
    sword worship, 184–186
Rennes, 34, 244
Respendial, 28, 38, 100
Rg Veda, xiii, xv
Rhine region, 131, 210, 235, 245
Rhône River, 28, 244
Rhŷs, J., 223

Ribble River, 18, 328
Ribchester, xxiii, xxvii, 18, 19, 25, 188, 328
Richmond, I. A., 19
Ringbom, L. I., 131, 216, 237
Riothamus, 61, 64, 66
Rispoé, king, 34
River Dee, 269
Roach, W., 270
Robert de Boron, 90, 130, 132, 166, 167, 186, 209, 215, 233, 235, 237, 263, 264, 268, 269
Robert of Torigni, 135
Rohan, Alain IX de, 35
Rohans, 35
Rollon à Saint-Clair, 101
Roman Empire, xvi
    Alans, relations with, 26–27, 28, 37
    Iazyges and, 16, 18
    sack of, 94, 236, 240
Roman History (Dio Cassius), xxvi
Romanians, 43
Roman Moesia, 16
Rostovtzeff, M., 197
Round Table, knights of. *See* Knights
Roxolani, 13, 16
Royal Hermit, 255
Russia, xvii, xix
Rusticus of Trier, 245

Safa, 168
St. George, 92, 166, 247
St. Germanus, 244
St. Goar, 245, 247
St. Michael's dragon, 200–201
St. Peter, Basilica of, 240
St. Victor, 261
Sajnæg Ældar, 168
Saka, 5

Sal-wadsche, 214
Salzburg Annals, 61
Sambida, 28, 244
Sampaigny (Meuse), 234
Sangiban, 32–33, 100
Saône Valley, 108
Sapaudia, 28
Saraide, 158, 161, 164, 165
Sarmatians, xv, xxvi, xxviii, 33, 40
    ancestors of, 5, 13
    in Britain, 18–26
    confused with Alans, 13, 16, 25
    description of, 13–18, 195
    Iazyges/Jazyges, xxiii, xxvi–xvii, xxviii, 13, 16, 18, 25
    mirrors and, 108
    women, 161, 225
Sarmatian Connection, King Arthur and, 61–71
Sarmatians, The (Sulimirski), xxv
Sarmaticus, 18
Sarus, 37, 242
Sasaki, S., 235
Satana, xxvii, 92, 134, 153, 156, 157, 162, 165, 168–169, 199, 271
Saumur, 101
Sauromatae, 5, 11, 13, 195, 285
Savoy, 28, 131
Saxons, 23
Schroeder, L. von, 213
Scotland/Scots, 25, 199, 329
Scythia, xxv, 3, 4, 236
Scythian Ares, 185, 186
Scythia Minor, 27
Scythians, xv
    Agricultural, 5, 11
    Ares, 11
    cups, 11, 235
    description of, 3–13

Index

proto, 5
religion, 11, 184–185
Royal, 5, 11, 185
Warrior, 5, 11
white animal, 102–103
women, 8, 11, 161
Sea fairy, 154
Sea gods, 221
Septimania, 257, 262
Septimius Severus, 329
Seraphe, 266
Serpent and dragon image
   on artifacts, 195–196
   as a barrier around castles, 200
   Black, 201
   connection between snakes, women and royalty, 197–200
   at the Cross, 201
   Eve and, 202
   flying, 197
   in Grail tales, 200
   kissing a snake which than turns into a women, 197, 199
   Lizard People, 13, 195
   Mi5gar5 serpent, 201
   St. Michael's dragon, 200–201
   snake images, 195, 197
   trees killed by, 200
   white, 154, 199
Seraphe, 209
Shield, magic, 158
Sidonius, 64
Siege Perilous, 213
Siegfried (Sigurd), xiii, 187–188
Siegmund, 183
Sigebert I, 245
Sigeric, 267
Siling Vandals, 28
Sinner King, 270–271

Sir Gawain and the Green Knight, 107, 137
Sir Gawain at the Grail Castle, 210
Sir Perceval of Galles, 130, 133
Skull deformation, 235
Slavs, 43
Snakes, 195, 197–198
   See also Serpent and dragon image
Soissons, 33
Solomon, treasures of, 240
Sone de Nansai/Nausay, 269
Soslan/Sozryko, xxvii, 135, 222
Sovereignty principle, 210, 217
Sozryko, 70, 104, 133, 156, 199, 222
Spain, 128
   See also under name of city/region
Spaudia, 131
Spear of Lug, 95
Spoils of Annwn, The, 181, 218
Stanzas of the Graves, 125
Stein, Walter Johannes, xxx
Stilicho, 37–38, 235, 236
Stone
   Holy Grail as, 210
   precious, in Holy Grail, 216
Strasbourg, 108, 236
Strathclyde, 329
Studies in the Fairy Mythology of Arthurian Romance (Paton), 154
Suevi, 28
Suhtschek, Friedrich von, 128, 130, 213, 215
Suite du Merlin, 84, 99
Sulimirski, Tadeusz, xxv, 16, 23, 108, 184, 224
Svans, xix
Switzerland, 32

Sword(s)
    Arthur's, 104
    Batraz's, xxvi, 68, 104, 183–184
    Caliburnus, thrown into the sea, 69
    Clarent and Claris, 184
    in the earth, xxvii
    embedded, 91, 187–188
    Excalibur, 68–69, 128, 158, 160, 184
    female sword bestower, 168–169
    forging of, 188
    Lancelot's, 104
    long slashing, use of, 8
    in the Stone episode, xxvii, 181–189
    thrown into the sea, xxvi, 68, 69
    War and Peace, 184
    worship, 184–186
Sword in the Stone, The (White), 181
Syagrius, 33, 66
Sybælc, 266
Syrdon, xxvii, 126, 134

Tabiti, 11, 185
Táin Bó Cuailgne, 153
Taliesin, 218, 219
Tamgas, 8, 195
Tanais, 11
Targitaos, 11, 225
Teichmann, F., 201
Templars, 214
Temple of Solomon, 214, 233, 248, 262
Thagimasadas, 185
Theodore of Ravenna, 235
Theodoric I, 100, 260–261
Theodosius, 39, 267
Theseus, 183
Thetis, 168
Thomas, Anne C., xxvii, 79

Thomas d'Angleterre, 138
Thompson, S., 181, 223
Thraustila, 38
Thyssagetae, 5
Tiberius, 264
Timber-Grave Culture, 5
Tintagel, 139
Titurel, 215, 242
Tlepsh, anvil of, 187
Toulouse, 243, 248
Tournai, 33
Trajan, 16
Trajan's Column, 8, 101
Transylvania, 16
Traspies. *See* Scythians, Agricultural
Treasures of Solomon, 214, 233, 240, 248, 262
Tree(s)
    killed by snakes, 200
    of Knowledge of Good and Evil, 202
    of the Life and the Cross, 201
    World, 201
Trente, battle of, 35
Tribalibot, 213
Tribruit River, 23, 327, 328
Trier, 28, 245
Tristan, 105, 138–141
Tristan (name), 139, 141
Tristan, 132, 138, 255
Troclar, 247
Troyes, 108, 131
Turkestan, 43
Turks, xvi
Tydorel, 156
Tyolet, 102

Uæxtænæg, 266

Index

Ubykhs, xix
Ulpius Marcellus, 328
Ulrich von Zatzikhoven, 32, 82, 86, 88–89, 91, 102, 153, 154
Ural Mountains, 5
Uriens, 158
Uryzmæg, 102, 157, 221–222, 266, 271
Uther Pendragon, xxvii, 158, 199
    hunt for the white stag and, 102
    meaning of name, xiv, 101

Valence/Valencia, 28, 244
Valens, 39, 267
Valentinian III, 32, 38, 39, 94, 243, 261, 262
Valerin, 38, 94
Vandals, xxviii, 28, 38, 94
Vannes, 35–36, 130, 133–134, 199, 244
Vannes, count of, 138, 141
Vannius, 16
Vinovium, Fort, 328
Vishnu, 269
Visigoths, xxviii, xxix–xxx, 28, 33, 37, 38, 81, 100, 219, 236, 240, 261, 268
Vitalian, 39
Viviane, 154, 156, 163–164
Vladikavkaz, xix
Vulgate Cycle, 32
    Dolorous Stroke, 264
    Estoire del Saint Graal, 139, 167, 183, 197, 269
    Gawain and, 137
    Maimed King of the, 132, 166, 255, 263–268
    Merlin, 154, 156, 167, 197
    Queste del Saint Graal, 92, 139, 160, 167, 183, 200–201, 272
VULsunga Saga, 181, 183, 272

Wace, xiv, 61, 125, 126, 181
Waite, A. E., 200, 215, 219, 248
Wales, 106, 219
Wallia, 260
Walter, Archdeacon, 62
War and Peace (sword), 184
War/weaponry technology
    Alans, used by, 37
    feigned retreat, 36, 37
    Sarmatian, 8
    training of warriors by women, 161
Warrior-priestesses, 161
Water
    See also Dame du Lac
    Batraz and, 104, 221
    fairies, 156
    fire in, 216
    Holy Grail and, 221
    Lancelot and, 103, 104, 106–107
    life force, 165
Water fairies, 86
Weapons. *See* War/weaponry technology
Webster, K. G. T., 88–90
Welsh Annals (Annales Cambriae), 23, 61, 62, 70
Welsh origin hypothesis, 79, 84–94, 131–132, 217–221
Werec, 138
Weston, J. L., 25, 80, 88, 199, 215, 217, 220, 268
White
    Dame du Lac and, 156
    otherworld and, 166
    People of the Lake and, 166
    serpent, 154, 199
    stag, 102–103

White, T. H., 181
William of Normandy, 36, 210
William the Conqueror, 134
Wolfgang, L. D., 132
Wolfram von Eschenbach, 130, 213, 214–215, 263–264, 269, 270–271
Women
    See also Dame du Lac
    Amazons, 8, 161
    connection between snakes, royalty and, 197–200
    Land of, 165, 166
    maidens of the Grail, 166, 216, 217
    Morgan Le Fay, 160–163
    omitted from some versions, 167–168
    Sarmatian, 161, 225
    Satana, xxvii, 92, 134, 153, 156, 157, 162, 165, 168–169, 271
    Scythian, 8, 11, 161
    training of warriors by, 161
    as warriors, 161–162
World Tree, 201

Xæmyc, xxvii, 101, 102–103, 134, 168, 199, 223, 264, 266
Xvarlnah, 185, 165, 216, 237, 240

Yama, 216
Yima, 216
York, 19, 23, 328, 329
Yorkshire, 23, 25
Yoshida, A., 224
Ysave, 134
Y Seint Greal, 126, 255

Zamyād Yasht (Zam Yast), 240
Zanticus, 18, 100

Zarathrustra, 237
Zeus, 185
Zimmer, H., 201